From Jesus Christ
to Christianity

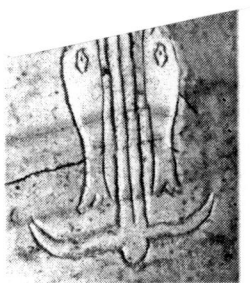

EARLY CHRISTIAN LITERATURE IN CONTEXT

Edited by Gerhard van den Heever and
Eben Scheffler

University of South Africa, Pretoria

© 2001 University of South Africa
First edition, second impression
First edition, third impression 2008

ISBN 9 78186888 196 3

Published by Unisa Press
University of South Africa
P O Box 392, UNISA, 0003, REPUBLIC OF SOUTH AFRICA

Electronic origination by Compleat Typesetters
Printed by Lesedi Printers

Editor: Diana Coetzee
Cover design and Layout: Elsabé Viljoen

© All rights reserved. No part of this publication may be reproduced in
any form or by any means - mechanical or electronic, including
recordings or tape recording and photocopying - without the prior
permission of the publisher, excluding fair quotations for purposes of reseach or review.

CONTENTS

Foreword   x

Acknowledgements   xiii

INTRODUCTION: READING EARLY CHRISTIAN LITERATURE IN CONTEXT   1
Gerhard van den Heever

    Christianity, religion and identity   1
    The need for this book   3
    Three different contexts   4
    A critical and 'consensus' approach   4
    A bridge to the reader's context   5
    Taking the human aspect seriously   6

PART 1: THE GRAECO-ROMAN WORLD: CONTEXT FOR EARLY CHRISTIANITY   9

1. The emergence of the Graeco-Roman world
Gerhard van den Heever   11
1.1   The Graeco-Roman world in overview   11
1.2   The Graeco-Roman religious world   17

2   The arrival of the Roman Empire
Pieter Botha   32
2.1   Introduction   32
2.2   From city to world power   32

3   Judaism in the Graeco-Roman world
Pieter Botha   42
3.1   The politics and socio-economics of Palestine   42
3.2   After Herod: kingdoms, provinces and war   46
3.3   The road to war   49
3.4   Judaea 70 to post-135 CE   53
3.5   Religion   55
3.6   The temple and temple ideology   57
3.7   The Pharisees   62
3.8   The Sadducees   63

3.9	Messiahs, prophets and teachers	64
3.10	Essenes	67
	Excursus: Qumran	68
3.11	Radicals	77
3.12	Eschatology	78
3.13	Rabbinic Judaism	80
3.14	Diaspora Judaism	83
4	**Conclusion**	**85**

PART TWO: THE TEACHING OF THE HISTORCIAL JESUS (27–30 CE) — 89
Maretha Jacobs

5	**Historical context (65 BCE–30 CE)**	**91**
6	**Jesus as a historical figure**	**92**
6.1	Sources on Jesus	92
6.2	Quests for the historical Jesus	94
6.3	Examples of historical images of Jesus	96
7	**The life of Jesus**	**101**
8	**The teachings of Jesus**	**107**
8.1	Jesus's teaching about the kingdom of God	107
	Excursus: The contents of Jesus's teaching	109
8.2	Jesus's subversive wisdom or reversal of values	112
8.3	Jesus's ethical teaching	115
8.4	Criteria for authenticating sayings and deeds of Jesus	115
9	**The death of Jesus**	**116**
10	**Conclusion**	**119**
	Excursus: Jesus and Christianity	
	Gerhard van den Heever	120

PART THREE: THE EARLIEST CHRISTIAN LITERATURE (30–70 CE) — 127

11	**Historical context**	
	Maretha Jacobs	129
12	**The formation of Jesus traditions**	**131**
12.1	The *Sayings Gospel Q*	131
	Excursus: The Two-Source Hypothesis	131
12.2	The *Gospel of Thomas*	137

13	**Pauline literature**	
	Emil Pretorius	139
13.1	Historical context of Paul and his letters	
	Emil Pretorius and Gerhard van den Heever	139
13.2	Paul's Letter to the Galatians	149
13.3	The First Letter to the Thessalonians	152
13.4	The First Letter to the Corinthians	153
13.5	The Second Letter to the Corinthians	158
13.6	Paul's Letter to the Romans	159
13.7	Paul's Letter to the Phillippians	163
13.8	Paul's Letter to Philemon	166
14	**Conclusion**	167

PART FOUR: THE CHRISTIAN LITERATURE OF THE LATE FIRST CENTURY (70–100 CE) 171

15	**Historical context**	
	Maretha Jacobs	173
16	**The aftermath of the Jewish War**	
	Maretha Jacobs	175
16.1	The Gospel of Mark as the first Jesus story	175
17	**Echoes of Paul: the deuteropauline literature**	
	Emil Pretorius and Gerhard van den Heever	179
17.1	The Letter to the Colossians	179
17.2	The Letter to the Ephesians	181
17.3	The Second Letter to the Thessalonians	185
17.4	The First Letter to Timothy	186
17.5	The Second Letter to Timothy	188
17.6	The Letter to Titus	189
18	**General letters**	
	Emil Pretorius, Gerhard van den Heever and Maretha Jacobs	190
18.1	The First Letter of Peter	190
18.2	The Letter of Jude	194
18.3	Second Letter of Peter	197
18.4	The Letter of James	200
18.5	The First Letter of John	203
18.6	The Second Letter of John	205
18.7	The Third Letter of John	206
19	**The Letter to the Hebrews**	
	Emil Pretorius	207

20	**Manifold Jesuses: gospel images of Jesus**	
	Maretha Jacobs	210
20.1	The Gospel of Matthew	210
20.2	The Gospel of Luke and the Acts of the Apostles	214
20.3	The Gospel of John	220
21	**Intimations of the end-time: the Revelation of John**	
	Maretha Jacobs	227
21.1	The book of Revelation	227
	Excursus: Revelation as apocalypse	
	Maretha Jacobs	227
	Excursus: Apocalyptic, apocalypticism and apocalypses	
	Gerhard van den Heever	234
22	**Conclusion**	**239**

PART FIVE: BEYOND THE NEW TESTAMENT: THE MAKING OF CHRISTIANITY AND ITS EMERGENCE INTO THE WORLD 241
Gerhard van den Heever

23	**Creating Christianity**	243
24	**Christianity in the second century**	247
	Excursus: Christianity as cultic society	
25	**Jewish–Christian gospels**	254
25.1	The *Gospel of the Hebrews*	255
25.2	The *Gospel of the Nazarenes*	256
25.3	The *Gospel of the Ebionites*	256
26	**Apocalyptic literature**	257
26.1	The *Sibylline Oracles*	257
26.2	The *Apocalypse of Peter*	258
26.3	Other apocalyptic works	259
27	**The Apostolic Fathers**	261
27.1	The *Didache*	262
27.2	The *Letter of Barnabas*	265
27.3	The *First Letter of Clement*	265
27.4	The *Second Letter of Clement*	267
27.5	The *Letters of Ignatius*	268
27.6	The *Letter of Polycarp*	270
27.7	The *Shepherd of Hermas*	270
28	**Christian Apologetics**	271
28.1	Justin Martyr	272
28.2	Apologies and writings addressed to a pagan or Gentile readership	273

28.3	Other apologetic works	274
29	**On the way to defining 'mainstream' and popular Christianity**	**276**
29.1	The *Protevangelium of James*	276
29.2	The *Gospel of Thomas*	278
29.3	Apocryphal Acts of the Apostles	278
29.4	Tatian and his harmony of the four Gospels	283
29.5	Theophilus of Antioch	284
29.6	The *Sentences of Sextus*	285
29.7	The *Odes of Solomon*	285
30	**Narratives about the Christian martyrs**	**286**
30.1	The *Martyrdom of Polycarp*	287
31	**Heterodox Christian writings**	**289**
	Gnosticism	290
31.1	*Apocryphon of John*	295
31.2	The *Gospel of Philip*	296
31.3	The *Gospel of Truth*	298
31.4	Marcion and his theology	298
32	**The emergence of the Christian canon**	**300**
32.1	The term *canon*	300
32.2	Early Christian Apocrypha	301
32.3	The emerging authority of Scripture	302
32.4	Witnesses to the formation of an authoritative collection of Christian writings	303
32.5	Factors in the formation of the New Testament canon	307
33	**Conclusion**	**311**
Index		315

FOREWORD

Desiring to fill a gap, the authors of this book interpret the New Testament as 'human verbalisation of religious insights and inspiration' during a time in the past which bears remarkable similarities to our own day. In the words of these authors, Alexander the Great and his successors had 'shrunk the world' during 333 to 30 BCE by gathering multiple ethnic, geographical, racial, religious, and political groups together under one large political domain. By the first century CE, the Roman Empire had overtaken this domain and created the Hellenistic–Roman world in which Christianity emerged. The emergence of new cities with immigrant populations throughout this world made virtually everyone a foreigner. In other words, not only were the large numbers of immigrant people foreigners, but the local people became foreigners in their own homeland in the context of the immigrant populations.

For the authors of this book, it is important to keep a sharp eye on this 'shrunken world' as one reads and interprets the writings in the New Testament. To replace the loss of kinsfolk networks that resulted from the intensive mixing of society, people formed social clubs and associations with cultic and religious rites and practices. Modes of 'religiosity' emerged that interwove dimensions of national, political, ethnic, and institutional forms of religious practice and thought in new ways. Religious traditions and practices that had spread both East and West throughout this large domain began to find new locations in households, marketplaces, village streets and buildings in cities constructed and financed through tribute fees, duties, and political and religious taxation. In this context, significant numbers of people began to participate in religious movements and groups sponsored by patronage from bureaucratic officials, rich landowners and wealthy merchants, rather than simply in religions sponsored by hierarchies of client-kingdoms and temple-kingdoms.

The Roman Empire in which Christianity emerged, the authors point out, was an agrarian society. Thus two main social groups, small ruling elite in the cities and a mass of labouring agriculturists in the villages, populated the world under the highest levels of imperial elite. Since Jesus's hometown Nazareth was in Galilee, rather than Judaea to the south, his way of life was orientated toward agrarian, village and city life in the regions around the Sea of Galilee.

After the death of Jesus, however, the Jesus movement spread quickly beyond the villages and cities to which Jesus had travelled. Through the leadership of an energetic Jew named Paul, the Jesus movement moved decisively into major cities in Asia Minor, Macedonia, Greece and Rome, and it welcomed Gentiles into its membership without requiring males to undergo the ordeal of circumcision.

Letters that Paul sent to Christians in major cities represent the earliest Christian writings in the New Testament (*c.* 48–62 CE). In these letters, Paul uses the skills of Bible interpretation associated with Jews known as Pharisees to guide Christians in a responsible way of life both in their communities and in the world. This use of Scripture set a standard for later Christian literature. All of the New Testament Gospels (written *c.* 70–100 CE) contain extensive interpretation and application of the Torah, the Prophets and the Writings in the Old Testament. Thus, the 'inner texture' of most New Testament writings contains references to people in the Old Testament and phrases that are 'biblical', that is, a reader can find them in the Old Testament. In addition, some New Testament writings contain extended and substantive Old Testament 'intertexture', that is, they recite extended passages from the Old Testament and use major story lines concerning Adam, Abraham, Noah, Moses, David, Solomon, Elijah, Elisha and Jeremiah in the formation of the epic story line that continues in Christianity. But beyond this, as the writers of this introduction to the New Testament show, early Christian writings show extensive 'social, cultural and ideological texture'.

In other words, New Testament writings exhibit how early Christians participated vigorously in multiple social and cultural environments of the Roman Empire. In addition, the writings reveal that certain early Christians developed ideological alliances with one another to advance their understanding of Jesus Christ (like people who showed special allegiance to the views of Paul rather than the views of James or Jude, who were brothers of Jesus). By maintaining a focus on historical, social, cultural and ideological phenomena in the Mediterranean world in which Christianity emerged, the authors of this volume exhibit the substantive 'incarnational' (enfleshed) nature of the 'religious insights and inspiration' communicated by the New Testament writings. In summary, the authors of this volume not only show how every writing in the New Testament has its own distinctive inner texture and sacred texture, but they also show how these writings have distinctive social, cultural and ideological textures as a result of the participation of early Christians in multiple contexts of the Hellenistic–Roman world during the first and second centuries.

The content of this volume encourages every reader of the New Testament to correlate and integrate literary, rhetorical, social, cultural, ideological and religious phenomena in the New Testament writings in a manner appropriate and instructive for the twenty-first century. This book prepares one not only to read the New Testament and other early Christian writings. It prepares a person to read Jewish, Greek and Roman writings outside the Bible, and it also invites one to read the Qur'an and other Muslim writings with interest. As a matter of fact, it encourages a person to read with care and interest the writings of any religious group or tradition, including the major world religions of Hinduism and Buddhism. One can only hope that many will use this volume as a springboard for understanding all kinds of religious groups and traditions that have become part of the inner fabric of the global world that has 'shrunken' around humans as they begin the twenty-first century, according to a calendar established through the heritage of Christianity in the Western world.

Vernon K Robbins
(Winship Distinguished Research Professor of New Testament and Comparative Sacred Texts in the Humanities, Emory University, Atlanta, United States of America. Visiting Professor, University of Stellenbosch, South Africa.)

ACKNOWLEDGEMENTS

From Jesus Christ to Christianity: Early Christian Literature in Context was born at a time of tumultuous changes in South African society. We have been engaged in rethinking our responsibility to society as well as to our students for a number of years now. In the process we have not remained untouched by what is happening around us, how our society changed, or how our student profile changed. These are questions that in some way or another determine how we envisage the content of a book on the New Testament, as well as how we should address the relevant issues arising both from the context and from the scholarly community. We should, therefore, like to thank all the students and colleagues (both local and foreign) who have through their questions and critical remarks, helped shape our own thinking and, through that, contributed to the making of this book. In a sense, this book thus represents not just the voices of the authors but also a multitude of other voices speaking through us.

A number of people need to be specially singled out to thank. Graydon Snyder kindly offered us his photographic material originally used in his book *Ante Pacem. Archaeological Evidence for Church Life before Constantine* (2nd rev. ed. Mercer University Press). Our colleagues from the Department of Classics, Richard Evans and Sira Dambe, contributed with advice and photographic material (Sira's husband, Peter Dambe, kindly made photographs available for use). The Biblical Archaeology Group at the University of South Africa supplied graphic material and photographs. We thank Chris le Roux, Coenie Scheepers and Eben Scheffler for their assistance. Fred P Miller kindly supplied an image of the Isaiah Scroll from Qumran.

Our copy editor, Diana Coetzee, started her career at the university with this manuscript and slaved many hours on the manuscript to get it into shape for publication, and for that deserves our utmost gratitude. The design artist, Elsabé Viljoen, performed small miracles on graphic material in order to make this the aesthetically pleasing book it has turned out to be. Our sincere thanks go to her too. Finally, we sincerely wish to thank the publisher, Ms Phoebe van der Walt, for her patience and willingness to accommodate this book in the publication programme of Unisa Press.

Unless otherwise specified, all translations are the authors' own.

ACKNOWLEDGEMENTS

The following persons graciously provided the following graphic material used in this book:

Graydon F Snyder: Fig 23.1; 23.3; 23.4; 23.5; 23.6; 23.7; 24.3; 27.1; 30.1

Richard J Evans: Fig 21.7; 21.8; 24.1; 28.2; 32.1

Peter Dambe: Fig 13.1; 13.3; 13.4; 13.6; 18.1; as well as the cover photograph

Chris le Roux: Fig 17.2; 20.1

Coenie L van W Scheepers: Fig 1.2; 1.3; 3.1; 3.2; 3.4; 3.5; 3.8; 3.9; 3.10; 3.11; 3.13; 3.14; 7.1; 7.2; 7.3; 7.4; 7.5; 7.6; 7.7; 7.8; 7.9; 8.1; 8.2; 8.3; 8.4; 8.5; 9.1; 9.2; 9.3; 9.4; 13.7; 13.8; 17.1; 17.3; 19.1; 20.2; 21.1; 21.2; 21.3; 21.4; 21.5; 21.6

Eben Scheffler: Fig 3.15; 17.2

Gerhard van den Heever: Fig 1.1; 1.4; 1.5; 2.1; 2.2; 2.3; 2.4; 2.5; 2.6; 2.7; 2.8; 2.9; 2.10; 3.3; 3.6; 3.7; 3.12; 5.1; 13.2; 13.5; 13.9; 13.10; 13.11; 15.1; 15.2; 18.2; 23.2; 24.2; 28.1; 30.2; 32.2

Fred P Miller: Fig 3.16

Cover: Eleventh-century mosaic of Emperor Constantine IX Monomachos, flanked by Christ and the Empress Zoe. (Photograph: Peter Dambe.)

The authors

Introduction

READING EARLY CHRISTIAN LITERATURE IN CONTEXT

Christianity, religion and identity

Religion is not on the wane as was predicted 40 or 50 years ago. Instead, there is a global resurgence in religious sentiment. This is a phenomenon that affects all religious traditions, from Hinduism in India, Islam in the Middle East, Buddhism in the Far East, Eastern Orthodoxy in Russia, to African traditional religion, to name but a few instances. In a world united by a global economy and global culture there is a renewed emphasis on the intimate connection between religion on the one hand, and nationalism and group identity, on the other. More and more people are searching for roots, and find the foundations for their sense of self and group identity in religious traditions.

Christians too are experiencing a revitalised interest in what Christianity is about and this is accompanied by a burgeoning interest in the Bible. The 'growth industry' of Bible schools and Bible study groups in South Africa and elsewhere attest to this phenomenon. The reason for renewal is, arguably, the tremendous changes that swept across South African society in the last decade or so. Not only has the visible face of society changed irrevocably, but South Africans have also had to reinvent themselves as a nation. In conjunction with this, the many serious challenges to morality and a vast array of ethical issues have forced the South African public into vigorous debates about values, worldview and ethical praxis in their effort to overcome the legacy of a racist and traumatic past. How to use the Bible as a resource in these debates or in reconceptualising identity is a vital issue in the quest for a healed and meaningful future.

For Christians, the Bible functions as a foundation for Christian identity, group identity, life orientation and worldview. Christianity is constantly recreated and sustained by taking recourse to its foundational document; its 'constitution'. However, the Bible is not only the Christian 'constitution' but also the Christian's 'court of appeal'. It provides the shared or common terms of reference for a wide spectrum of moral debates, political questions and issues of social re-engineering. A study of the ways in which the Bible is used will reveal how it forms the middle ground through which the various operations by which social formations and symbolic universes are created become apparent. The singer Paul Simon called a recent series of concerts 'Born at the Right Time'. By analogy, we can call what is offered here in this book 'Questioned at the Right Time', for this is not only a time of global upheaval but also, and especially in the South African context, a time of recreation and creativity. However, the Bible did not suddenly become this foundational myth for Christians. As one scholar put it: 'It was not a revelation faxed from heaven.'

Historically speaking, it is not the 27 books of the New Testament or the 66 books of the combined Old and New Testaments that formed the 'constitution' or foundation for early Christianity. It is, rather, from the crucible of a vast literary production that far exceeded the later biblical canon that early Christianity was conceived or 'put together'. For this reason, more than just the New Testament texts were included in this overview. A historical overview of the literary matrix of early Christianity must also include such diverse (and early) texts as the Pseudepigrapha, Apocrypha, Apostolic Fathers, Jewish–Christian writings, Apologists, martyrologies, Christian apocalypticism and heterodox writings. The Bible itself and early Christian literature in general are cultural products created in the course of more than five centuries. In the process, epic traditions, images, transmitted teachings, borrowings from contemporary (other) religious traditions and so on were utilised in order to 'manufacture' Christianity and Christian culture. This entails that people negotiate their social location in the world ('social formation') by means of a constructed, all-encompassing World, with a view to certain desired ends ('social interests'), which may range from understanding the world and providing directions for desired action to organising community and structuring relationships. The way in which this is accomplished is through a process of mythmaking. Mythmaking, as Ron Cameron puts it,

> describes the way in which people make the world work, place themselves in relation to their historical past and social present, negotiate structures of purity and power, produce conviction and schemes of meaning, define the boundaries of shared codes and conventions, and meditate on the differences between symbolic and social worlds.
>
> (Ron Cameron, 'Mythmaking and Intertextuality in Early Christianity', in *Reimagining Christian Origins*, Elizabeth A Castelli and Hal Taussig (eds). Valley Forge, PA: Trinity Press International, 1996, 38.)

Thus defined as a human discourse, religion is a human 'way of speaking'; a way of presenting reality as this or that; an imagination of how things are ('the order of things') and of how they should or could be; a fictional-factual account of what matters. Above all, it is about carving a meaningful, coherent whole out of the chaotic stream that is social reality.

This book is about the origins and creation of early Christianity and the way early Christian literature presented a new vision of the world in dialogue with the context in which it originated. But it is more than that. By focusing on this aspect of Christianity and Christian literature, the reader is led to engage in a similar process of using early Christian literature as a resource to define his or her Christian identity, worldview and practice or agenda for Christian action and ethics. This should be done thoughtfully and critically. By this is meant that one should take one's moral responsibility for establishing Christian identity and agenda for action seriously.

The need for this book

From Jesus Christ to Christianity: Early Christian Literature in Context (as was the case with its companion volume *Ancient Israelite Literature in Context* – cf Boshoff *et al* 2000) was conceived, and purposely written, as a bridge and a gap-filler. In many other countries the public, church-going and even the more irreligious are well served by an abundance of publications in the field of religious and biblical studies which inform in a popularising way about current research, stimulate debate on critical issues and which raise the level of intelligent discourse about matters religious. Having lectured Biblical Studies for quite a number of years, the authors are convinced that a gap exists in the local market of religious publications for books aimed at raising the level of knowledge about the Bible and the world in which it originated. It remains a strange fact that knowledge of the Bible is not commensurate with the predominance and influence of Christianity in South African society, even after many years of biblical and religious education in South African schools. Not even the recent growth in the number of Bible schools (within the context of the churches) has completely remedied the situation, since, in the authors' experience, an underemphasis of the historical (and thus *human*) aspect of Christian Scripture continues to characterise approaches to the Bible. This book was written for the large number of envisaged readers who would not have been exposed to the history of the ancient world in their school years and, consequently, would not have any reasonable competence to read the Bible in the first place as the collection of ancient literature which it, in essence, is.

Three different contexts

The purpose of the book is to provide the reader with information about biblical books, their contents, message and context of origin. Extra-biblical literature such as the Apocrypha of the New Testament have been included as the authors believe that any reconstruction of the history of the religion of early Christianity should include all the religious writings that Christians produced in the formation of their religious outlooks, even if such writings did not in the end become part of the established, 'official' scriptural canon. This is placed within the framework of the history in which these works took shape, and the cultural context in which these biblical and extra-biblical books made sense is traced.

Most of the biblical texts that exist today did not experience a singular birth, but grew through many life phases of adding on, changing parts, shedding 'text weight', reinterpretation, recontextualisation and reappropriation. Taking this into account, this book operates on the principle of a juxtaposition of three distinct facets or contexts, namely (1) the wider context of ancient history, (2) the narrower context of the cultural world in which each document communicated and (3) the composition history, context of situation, contents and message of each individual biblical and extra-biblical book, in its final form as well as its pre-final redactional phases. The authors believe that this combination and the interplay of these three facets make this work unique and singular as introduction to the New Testament and its world. The authors know of no other book that combines such different sets of information into one concise and accessible New Testament study source book.

A critical and 'consensus' approach

Although this book is not a critical scholarly work in the sense that it takes issue with various theories, and debates the pros and cons of each position, it was not conceived without prior critical scholarly study. While the authors endeavoured to keep references to an absolute minimum and the discussions concise, they strove to expose the reader to the current critical scholarly consensus in a popular and easily accessible format. The authors had to make up their own minds about the critical issues beforehand and then to set out the themes accordingly. The book thus comes with a bit of attitude. Although what is presented represents unashamedly the authors' selection of relevant information and viewpoints, and unavoidably their interpretation of the issues involved, it is their firm belief that what the reader has before him or her represents a fair construction of the state of scholarly consensus.

The reader will realise soon enough that this book was not meant to address every issue or present all the minute details of each theme discussed. Given the limits set by the number of pages available, the authors had to settle for a less-detailed and therefore more general introduction to the New Testament and its world. Their aim was to provide just enough information to enable an initial informed reading of the New Testament and to stimulate the reader's imagination to enter into the New Testament world as a first step, but also to kindle interest in further study of the Bible. Where, moreover, slight unevenness exists in the treatment of different sections, that too was due to a deliberate decision not to prevent the personalities of the different contributing authors from shining through in their treatment of the chapters for which they were responsible.

A bridge to the reader's context

This book was, furthermore, designed to function as a bridge. Although it is an introduction to early Christian literature, a short history of the ancient world and a concise cultural history of the New Testament all in one, and therefore eminently usable for students of the Bible, it is also aimed at a wider public. It is with this goal in mind that the authors present scholarly thinking about the Bible and its world in an accessible format. The Bible has always been an important book in many contexts, given the influence and predominance of Christianity in many countries.

With this book the authors hope to stimulate further reflection on the Bible and its message, and hope that Bible readers will become better equipped to enter into debates about biblical, religious and ethical issues, and thus to contribute to a more credible use and function of the Bible in society. It is their contention that they should share what happens in the lofty halls of scholarly biblical studies with the reading public. This is, in their view, the public responsibility of the scholar of religion who is funded by government subsidies and other public funds.

Critical scholarly study of the Bible is often denigrated as sceptical or, at worst, irreligious. The authors have heard concerns raised by students and members of the public alike that what they do diminishes the meaning and value of the Bible for the spirituality of ordinary believers. The authors prefer to look at it differently. We live in a world regularly rocked by spectacular and violent ends to religious movements and quasi-Christian cults deriving their (eventually) catastrophic worldviews from a dangerously literal and one-sided understanding of the Bible. One need only think of such high-profile cases as the People's Temple of Jim Jones in Guyana, the Branch Davidians of David

Koresh in Waco, Heaven's Gate in Los Angeles and the recent massacre of followers of the Movement for the Restoration of the Ten Commandments of God in Uganda – not to mention the many wars fought with the Bible in hand. Thus, it is of paramount importance that the Bible-reading public be empowered to resist downright dangerous and exploitative readings of the Bible. For this, one needs to be equipped with the intellectual tools to read the Bible critically, but also to evaluate all manner of biblical interpretations bandied about in the public domain, especially when clothed in definitive claims to authority. This book then is meant to enable readers to make up their own minds as to the biblical message. In short, the authors aim to 'democratise' insight into the meaning of Christian Scripture.

Taking the human aspect seriously

However, critical Bible reading is not merely motivated by a concern about the pathological. If there is any truth in the belief that the Bible represents God's word in human language, then the 'human' aspect needs to be taken seriously. Critical biblical scholarship helps one to focus on the human dimension of the formation of Christian Scripture, how the human verbalisation of religious insights and inspiration is embedded in, and is a response to, historical events and cultural frameworks. This does not mean that the reader is not addressed from a transcendent realm whenever he or she reads the religious writings of ancient Israel and early Christianity, and it is not the authors' aim to deny the reality of the intertwining of divine presence and human history. It does mean that the reader can only hear this transcendent voice through the filters of human conceptualisation and experiences of human history. The authors sincerely believe that an approach such as the one taken here will serve to 'bring the Bible home' to readers wishing to grow in their spirituality.

It also needs to be pointed out that critical study of the Bible never takes place in a vacuum. The questions dealt with in critical study arise from one's experiences of history (and the reader will find many examples of the 'history-relatedness' of the critical reconstructions throughout the book). One's questions always, in some way or another, respond to the way one perceives oneself, one's world and one's history. Thus, critical study is an indispensable way of religiously understanding oneself and the world in which one lives. In short, it furnishes people with the intellectual tools to make sense of the context and to cope with a rapidly changing world. In this way, a critical look at the Bible serves as reflection on Christian spirituality and religious life, and in itself becomes an enriching experience.

Suggested reading

Braun, Willi & McCutcheon, Russell T (eds)
2000   *Guide to the Study of Religion.* London/New York: Cassell.

Krüger, Jacobus S
1997   *Along Edges. Religion in South Africa. Bushman, Christian, Buddhist.* Pretoria: University of South Africa. (Hiddingh-Currie 5)

Maluleke, Tinyiko Sam
2001   'Identity and Integrity in African Theology: A Critical Analysis.' *R&T*8/1 - 2:26-41.

McCutcheon, Russell T
1998   'Redescribing Religion as Social Formation: Toward a Social Theory of Religion.' In *What is Religion? Origins, Definitions, and Explanations*, Thomas A Idinopulos and Brian C Wilson (eds), 51-72. Leiden: Brill.

Taylor, Mark C (ed)
1998   *Critical Terms for Religious Studies.* Chicago: University of Chicago Press.

Van den Heever, Gerhard
2001   'On How to Be or Not to Be. Theoretical Reflection on Religion and Identity in Africa.' *Religion and Theology* 8/1 and 2:1-25.

Part one

The Graeco-Roman world: context for early Christianity

1 THE EMERGENCE OF THE GRAECO-ROMAN WORLD

1.1 The Graeco-Roman world in overview

The conquests of Alexander (from 333 BCE to 323 BCE) and the establishment of the successor kingdoms changed the face of the known world. The world had known large political empires before: the Hittites, the Assyrians, the Babylonians and the Medo-Persians, but none on such a grand scale and covering as vast a territory and including as many different peoples as the Graeco-Macedonian empires. At their height, the Graeco-Macedonian empires stretched from Greece and Macedonia on the northern shores of the Mediterranean Sea and Cyrenaica and Egypt on the southern shores, right across Asia Minor, the Middle East and Persia into northern India (*see* Figure 1.1).

The world had shrunk and it is this shrinking that is of concern. What effects did it have on the people inhabiting that world? What was it like living in such a world? These are pertinent questions, since this very complex and diverse world formed the living context in which Jewish, and eventually Christian, communities found themselves. Living in the Graeco-Roman world shaped their responses to the world and events around them, their manifold identities and their outlook on the divine as much as it had changed that of the adherents of other religious traditions.

So what was new about the Graeco-Roman world?

> ### HELLENISM AND THE GRAECO-ROMAN PERIOD
>
> The term *Hellenism* has been used since the nineteenth century in scholarly literature to denote the spread of Greek (= Hellenic, from *Hellas* 'Greece') culture in the ancient world in the wake of Alexander the Great's conquests. The term also implied a break with classical Greek culture in that Hellenism was understood to signify the mixture of oriental and Greek cultures. As a quasi-political term, Hellenism was thought to give way to the period of the Roman Empire after the battle of Actium in 31 BCE which saw Octavian (the later Augustus) defeat Mark Antony and his consort – the last Hellenistic ruler – Cleopatra VII of Egypt. Historical periods, however, do not allow such easy demarcations. From epigraphic evidence it is clear that Greek culture had penetrated the Near East from Asia Minor to far beyond, well before Alexander's conquests. Similarly, the predominance of Greek culture did not suddenly end after 31 BCE. Indeed, while Rome exercised political

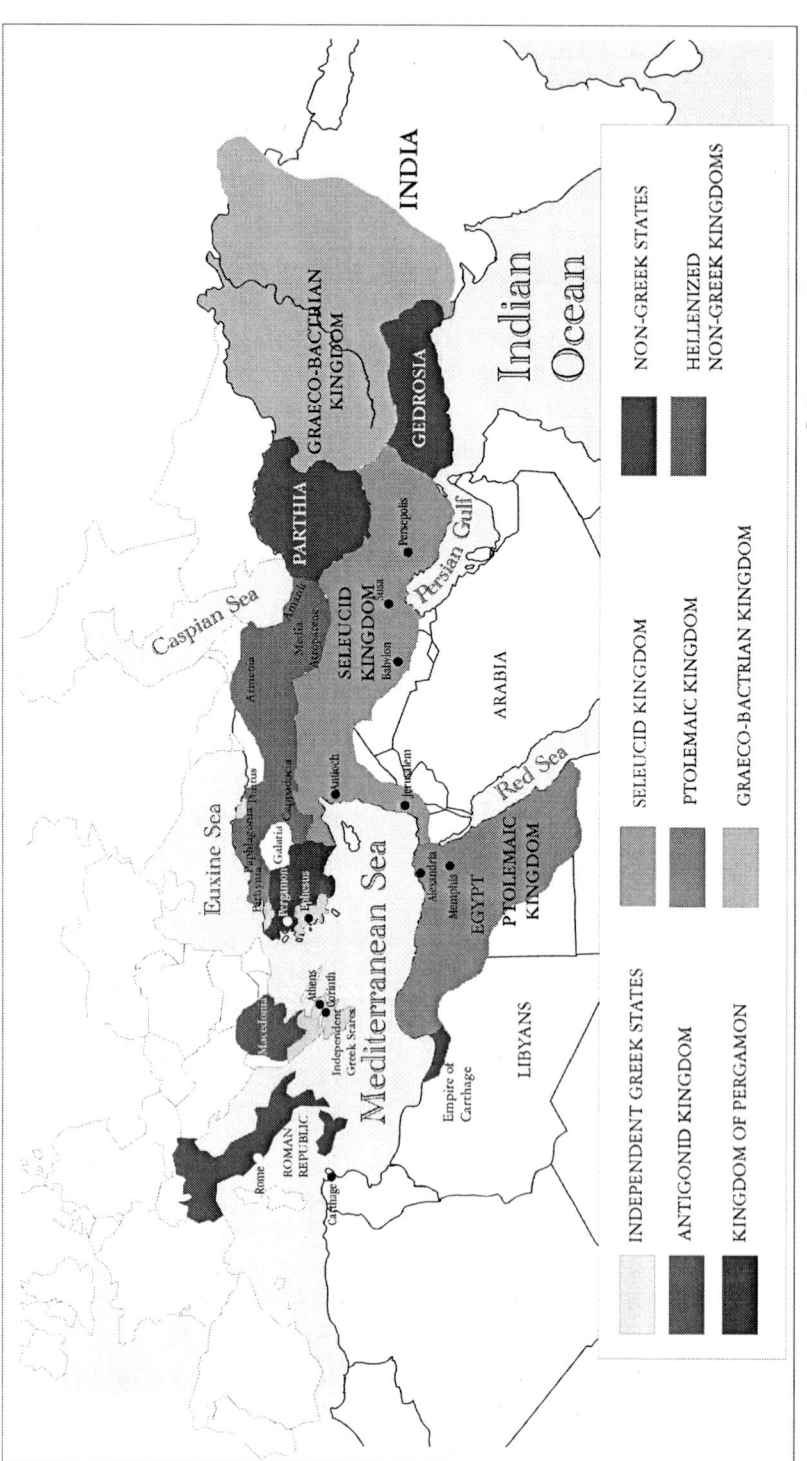

Figure 1.1　The Hellenistic world around 185 BCE: the successor kingdoms between the death of Alexander and the emergence of the Roman Empire

> hegemony across the Mediterranean world, Greek culture, thought and language remained dominant throughout the Roman Empire. Greek culture provided the continuity with the later Eastern Roman Empire or Byzantium, which endured through the Middle Ages until its final conquest by the Turkish Muslims in 1453 CE. Various solutions have been offered to solve the difficulties inherent in the use of the term *Hellenism* (among others, the use of *early Hellenism* as opposed to *late Hellenism*). In this book, *Hellenism* and *Graeco-Roman* are used interchangeably. The term *Graeco-Roman* has the advantage of suggesting the continuity of Greek culture in the period under consideration; from the period of Graeco-Macedonian domination through the first centuries of the Common Era (CE) under the Roman Empire. *Graeco-Roman period* therefore (loosely) denotes a particular cultural set-up as well as a historical period without implying any sharp boundaries or specific demarcations.

In the successor kingdoms of the Ptolemies and the Seleucids the face of the world changed, literally. It was a world of mostly new cities. Apart from Egypt, which remained less urbanised than the other kingdoms, many new cities were founded throughout Asia Minor, Syria, Palestine, Mesopotamia and into the furthest reaches of the Greek world – Bactria, Sogdiana and Gandhara (the present Afghanistan, Tadzikistan and Kashmir/northern India).

Many older, existing cities were refounded with new, Greek names. The typical Hellenistic city reflected the same social organisation as the classical Greek city, but was populated by a motley crowd of former war veterans of Greek and Macedonian stock, military settlers and mercenaries in royal service, philosophers, musicians, poets, tradesmen, artists and craftsmen, who all set out for the newly opened colonies in search of employment and a better life, and, of course, there were slaves and local people from the indigenous populations. The mixed populations of the cities meant that, on the one hand, the cities represented Greek presence and cultural influence in the Hellenistic world, but also, on the other hand, served as the crucible for a syncretic culture born out of the interchange between Greek and oriental cultures.

In the classical period, Greek cities were independent city–states loosely connected in federal states or leagues. On the Greek mainland, some of these leagues remained, but now most Hellenistic cities had lost this independence (and the newly founded Hellenistic cities never enjoyed it to start with). The cities were still governed by their councils as if they were independent, but in reality, real power lay with the king represented by the local governor. That was where the important decisions were made. The loss of independence was indicated by the duty to pay taxes and tribute to the sovereign, except where

Figure 1.2
Intrusions of Hellenistic culture: Jerash in Jordania, the site of the city of Gerasa of biblical times, was founded by Alexander the Great for his army veterans on the site of long-standing earlier settlements from the Stone, Bronze and Iron ages. During the time of the Roman occupation, Gerasa was included in the Decapolis as a city–state. Pictured here is the elliptically shaped forum, from which the main street, the Cardo Maximus, runs

this was expressly remitted. Often Hellenistic kings would present themselves as 'saviours and benefactors' who restored the 'freedom, autonomy and immunity' of cities, but this had a hollow ring to it and never really approached the freedom they had enjoyed in a previous age. It did mean that the king could be approached to finance public building projects, or the restoration of a city after a natural disaster such as an earthquake, or the distribution of free corn in times of famine.

The upshot of this was that the character of public life changed. Individuals who clamoured for public pre-eminence often volunteered to undertake embassies on behalf of the city to other cities or royal courts, often at great expense to themselves, in order to secure privileges or aid for the city. Hellenistic society was characterised by a sharp difference in social status between the upper echelons of society consisting of the rich and landowners, on the one hand, and the freedmen and entrepreneurs and the lowest on the social

Figure 1.3
Gerasa suffered destruction during the first Jewish War, but was rebuilt in grand style under the Flavian emperors and their successors. It housed a theatre, various temples and a hippodrome, and reached its zenith in the second century. Second-century colonnades along the Cardo Maximus are pictured here. Although Gerasa is named in Luke 8:26ff and Mark 5:1 as the place where Jesus healed the demoniac, the event certainly did not take place here, as it is located about 59 km south-east of the Sea of Galilee without any steep cliffs dropping to the lake shore as presupposed by the story

scale, the outcasts, misfits and slaves, on the other. A network of personal relationships called *patronage* and *clientship* ensured the distribution of benefits and privileges among those on different rungs of the social ladder. To be successful in life meant being successful at social posturing. The top rungs of the social ladder were occupied by Greeks who formed an exclusive Greek club, jealously guarding their traditions and Greekness. Outsiders, locals or natives, were mostly excluded from real positions of power. At most, they could aspire to positions of petty officialdom, on whom Hellenistic governments had to rely in order to deal with the local population. Still, obtaining a Greek education and learning to speak Greek remained a sought-after goal for anyone aspiring to employment or climbing the social ladder. While, on the whole, there was probably not much cultural interaction between the upper levels of society and local indigenous culture, evidence does suggest that lower down on the social ladder mixed marriages accompanied by a mixture of culture were not uncommon.

The phenomena of migration and resettlement, so pervasive a social fact in urbanised Hellenistic society, deprived individuals of that ancient cornerstone of socialisation, namely kinsfolk; of being absorbed into a uniform group with uniform traditions. As a result, a dominant feature of Hellenistic society was the growth of societies or clubs. In ancient Greece, congregating in societies was frowned upon as politically subversive, although societies or clubs were tolerated as the meeting places for foreigners (since they were excluded from citizenship). In Hellenistic society, however – where in a sense everyone was a foreigner – *eranoi*, or *thiasoi* as they were called, functioned as burial societies and social clubs. Membership was open to anyone who fulfilled the conditions of entry and membership (and indeed non-Greeks also found a social home here). While these clubs usually reflected the same hierarchical status structure of society, membership was open to Greeks and non-Greeks, men and women, slaves as well as freedmen. What was also new about Hellenistic clubs was the fact that apart from the obvious social function – be it as burial society or club for socialisation – they were also cultic or religious by nature, being organised around the veneration of some patron deity. Since the art of living was an important concern for inhabitants of the Hellenistic world ('The reason for discovering philosophy,' Xenocrates had said, 'is to allay that which causes disturbance in life.' All philosophy, and religion, one might add, had an ethical bias), these societies and clubs provided members with an alternative society in which to be at home.

On the economic front, conditions were very harsh and most people, apart from the rich and powerful, barely eked out a living. The Hellenistic kings treated their dominions as 'spear-won territory' and thus, as personal property. Most of the land was regarded as crown land which could be allotted to freedmen as tenant farmers to farm on behalf of the crown, or one could find imperial estates farmed by slaves. The flow of income headed upwards from the land to the king's treasury. This was ensured through heavy taxation, import and export duties, and the paying of tributes by cities. This was needed to finance the wars in which each dynasty was continually embroiled, as well as the public generosity expected of the position. This heavy burden had the effect that most people barely survived at subsistence level. There was no lack of reaction to such harsh conditions. Peasant and slave revolts are known from Sicily to Egypt to Palestine. These movements were aimed at creating an alternative society where present conditions were turned upside down; where slaves were kings and kings slaves, and nature was bountiful and toil unnecessary for daily living. Desperate people dreamt up fantastic utopias. When one did not revolt, one could also choose just to abscond from the land or the workplace. When the yoke of taxation pressed too hard or when the income and tax targets could not be met, one could become a wandering displaced person, or take refuge in a temple.

Reigning the dominion was tantamount to running the kingdom as a business enterprise, and the aim was to make and spend money. Hellenistic economy did not dictate that fiscal resources be reinvested in the economy. That is why the Hellenistic kings not only owned the land, but also directly intervened in the economy. Central planning determined what could and should be produced, where, when and how much (because the desired income depended on this). The scales of competition in business were even further tipped in favour of the king: royal monopoly existed on the production and sale of a number of goods. A burgeoning bureaucracy was needed to oversee the 'farming of money', to ensure the flow of money to the treasury and to make sure nobody cheated. Posts proliferated: ministers of finance, managers of imperial estates, local governors, secretaries, inspectors and tax farmers abounded. In the end, the Hellenistic world collapsed under the weight of this burden.

1.2 The Graeco-Roman religious world

The Graeco-Roman world was a time of both continuity and great changes. This held true for religions too. Greek religion (or 'religions', for Greek religion is actually a collective for a number of different cults expressing different facets of Greekness) was transported throughout the Hellenistic world to all newly opened territories and newly founded cities, to become the basis of city or *polis* religion there. Traditional Greek religion showed a remarkable vitality in the Graeco-Roman period.

The pervasive ostentation characteristic of the Hellenistic age also affected religion. Extensive building works expanding cult centres and temples into large complexes are attested to in this period, especially where these were popular places of pilgrimage, like Epidauros. Festivals (which were always religious; there was no secular space alongside religion – religion was everywhere) were held on a lavish scale.

A RELIGIOUS PROCESSION

City or public religion 'took place' in the open and normally involved quite a large crowd. On feast days, cult adherents would snake through the city in colourful and noisy procession. The following excerpt from Apuleius's novel *The Golden Ass* (or *Metamorphoses*, second century CE) describes such a procession of the Isis cult in Corinth:

Then the head of the grand procession came into view. It was composed of a number of people who dressed in all manner of fancy dress. There is a man with a soldier's sword belt; another dressed as a hunter, a thick cloak round his waist with hunting knife and spear; another with golden sandals, wig, silk dress and expensive jewellery who pretended to be a woman. Then a man with heavy boots, shield, helmet and sword looking as if he had walked right out of the gladiator's school ... and behind them came the procession proper.

At the head walked women crowned with flowers, who continued to pull flowers from the folds of their beautiful white dresses and scattered them along the road, openly displaying their joy in the Saviouress [=Isis]. Then came women with polished mirrors tied to the back of their heads, which gave all who followed the illusion of coming to meet the goddess instead of walking in front of her. Next came a group of women with ivory combs who pantomimed the combing of the goddess's royal hair and another group with bottles of perfume sprinkling the road with balsam and other precious perfumes. They were followed by a mixed group of women and men who addressed the goddess as "Daughter of the Stars" and who pacified her by carrying every kind of light, lamps, torches, wax candles and so on.

Next came musicians with pipes and flutes followed by a group of specially selected choirboys singing a hymn in which the origin of the procession had been explained by the poet who had composed it. The temple brass band of the great god Serapis was there too, playing their religious anthem on brass trumpets with slanted mouthpieces and curved tubes; also a number of attendants and smoke wavers crying: "Make way there, make way for the goddess!" After them followed the great crowd of the initiates of the goddess, men and women of all classes and all ages, with brightly shining white linen clothes. The women had their hair tied up in shiny coils under gauze head-dresses, while the men had their hair completely shaven, representing the bright earthly stars of the goddess. They carried brass, silver and some, gold rattles which continued to jangle shrilly and never-endingly.

The leading priests, also clothed in white linen, drawn tight across their breasts and hanging down to their feet, carried the emblems of the deity. The high priest held a bright lamp, which did not resemble the lamps used at nocturnal banquets at all. It was in the shape of a golden boat with a tall flame rising from a hole in the centre. The second priest held an *auxiliaria*, or sacrificial pot, in each hand, called this because the name recalls the goddess's providence in helping her devotees. The third priest carried a miniature palm tree with gold leaves as well as the serpent wand of Mercury . . .

Next in the procession followed all those deities that were purported to walk on human feet. Here was the frightening messenger of the gods of heaven, and of the gods of the dead, namely Anubis, whose face was black on one side and gold on the other, walking upright with his herald's wand in one hand, and in the other a green palm

> branch. Following him came a man who danced while carrying a statue of a cow on his shoulders representing the goddess as the fruitful Mother of us all. After him came a priest carrying a box containing the secret implements of her wonderful cult. Another fortunate priest had an ancient symbol of her godhead hidden in his robe: not made in animal shape at all, not birdlike nor humanlike, the exquisite beauty of its craftsmanship as well as the originality of its design elicited admiration and awe. It was a symbol of the sublime and ineffable mysteries of the goddess which are never to be revealed: it was a small vessel of highly polished gold, crammed with Egyptian hieroglyphics, with a round bottom and long spout, and a curving handle around which curled an asp, raising its head and displaying its scaly, wrinkled, puffed throat.
>
> (Lucius Apuleius: *The Golden Ass*, Book XI)

Not only was Greek religion transported throughout the Graeco-Roman world, oriental and Near Eastern cults were also distributed wherever their adherents migrated and settled throughout. Oriental cults were already present in classical Greece, and on the islands of the Mediterranean and Aegean Seas among foreigners at trading posts. However, now, throughout this period, because of the mixed populations of the Hellenistic cities, different cults and religions of very different origins existed side by side in the same cities and sometimes within the same 'suburbs' or quarters. Migration of religions meant that all religions existed both in their original homelands in the traditional forms, as well as in centres of the diaspora in the rest of the world to which they had been transplanted. In these centres religions took on a different form, all being hellenised in some form or another, and mutually influencing one another. The Greeks had long been accustomed to identifying their gods with other oriental and Near Eastern gods. This process gained momentum and led to what is called *syncretism*: the fusion of gods and cults.

Religion was everywhere. Its myths, its folklore, its traditions and its iconography pervaded everything from art, literature and poetry, business contracts, social relations and customs to cultural events, such as seasonal festivals. *Polis* religion was played out in public. Next to the public nature of religion, there was a growth in the 'private side' of religion – the phenomenon of religious associations. These burial societies or social clubs or crafts guilds were organised around the veneration of a specific deity. Sometimes the social lives of the members were also regulated by such religious acts as an entry oath, a pledge to be honest with the other members, not to harm them, live a pure and (sexually) undefiled life, and not to participate in magic, murder or infanticide.

CULT GROUPS

Religion in ancient society was mostly practised in public, and religious activities usually involved the whole community. Social identity was constituted by the common religious tradition and practices. It was, however, also possible to belong to cult groups with special membership and devoted to specific deities. These cults did not replace civic or public religion, but existed alongside it as a vehicle for socialisation amidst an increasingly diversified society. Under the title of 'cult group' would count societies such as philosophical schools, burial societies, trade guilds, clubs or voluntary associations, the main activity of which consisted of regular banquets and mutual assistance. In contrast to the public, civic religion to which one 'belonged' by virtue of being born into, or becoming part of, the community worshipping the particular deity or deities, membership of a cult group was voluntary. It was a case of select membership for which one applied, often the result of being called by the deity itself. Many religious societies were not founded primarily to worship a specific deity or deities, but all had some patron deity whose worship was promoted in their meetings. Membership was subject to the meeting of strict criteria, and the social control facilitated by the strict rules of conduct made these institutions ideal for the moral upliftment of society. When Christianity (just as Judaism before it) emerged into the Graeco-Roman world, it was in the form of such private societies meeting in a host's house.

A Hellenistic cult group

The following inscription provides the 'constitution' of a cult group which met in Dionysus's house. It dates from the first century BCE and was found at Philadelphia in Asia Minor. The text describes the reconstitution of the cult by introducing new gods into the worship of the society, thereby displaying something of the dynamism inherent in the religious life of Graeco-Roman society.

> To Good Fortune
>
> For the health and common salvation and best reputation the ordinances given to Dionysus in his sleep were written up, giving access to his house to men and women, free and household slaves.

For in this place have been erected altars to Zeus Eumenes and Hestia his associate, and the other saviour gods, and Eudaimonia [= Happiness], and Plutus, and Arete [= Virtue] and Hygieia [= Health] and Agathe Tyche [= Good Fortune], Agathos Daemon [= Good Guiding Spirit], Mneme [= Remembrance] and Charitae [= the Graces] and Nike [=Victory]. Zeus gave to this man ordinances for the purifications and the expiatory rites as well as the mysteries to be performed according to the ancestral customs, and as has now been written.

When going into this house, men and women, free and slave, shall be made to swear by all the gods that they have no knowledge of or administered any deception of any man or woman, nor harmful poison to men, or harmful spells; and that they have not administered themselves nor recommended it or plotted with someone else to administer love potion, seducing drug, contraceptive nor any other abortion-inducing drug. They are also not to refrain from good intentions towards this house. And whosoever does these things or plots them, they must neither permit them nor stay silent about them, but shall expose them and defend themselves.

Apart from his own wife, a man must not have sexual relations with another woman whether free or slave, neither is he to seduce boy or young girl, nor advise it to anyone else. But if he connives at it with someone, whether man or woman, it shall not be concealed nor be kept silent. Woman and man, whoever does what has been written above, must not enter this house. Because the gods who have been set up in this house are great and they keep watch over these things, and they will not tolerate those who transgressed the ordinances.

A free woman must be pure and not know the marriage bed of, or have sexual intercourse with, another man apart from her own. If she has such knowledge, such a woman is not pure but she is defiled and completely polluted, and not worthy to worship this god of whom these holy things have been set up, nor is she to be present at the sacrifices or may she interrupt [strike against?] the purification and the expiatory rites nor watch the performance of the mysteries. If she does any of these things from the time they heard these ordinances inscribed, she shall have evil curses from the gods because she disregarded these ordinances. For the god neither wishes these things to take place at all, nor does he want it, but to be obeyed. The gods will be merciful to those who are obedient and always give them all good things, whatever gods give to people whom they love. But if some transgress, they will hate those and inflict severe punishments on them.

These ordinances have been placed next to Agdistis, the most holy guardian and mistress of this house. May she produce good thoughts in men and women, free and slave, so that they will obey what was written here. And at the monthly and annual sacrifices let them who have confidence in themselves, men and women, lay their hands on this inscription on which the ordinances of the god are written so that those who are obedient to the ordinances may become manifest as well as those who are disobedient.

Saviour Zeus, mercifully and kindly accept the touch of Dionysus, and be well disposed towards him and his family. Give him good rewards, health, salvation, peace and security on land and at sea.

A few salient points need to be noted which will help one understand the significance of this cult group for an understanding of early Christianity as a social entity. First, the cult meets regularly in the private house of its patron/founder, Dionysus. It can be surmised that the house must have been large enough to accommodate a sizeable group, and thus that Dionysus was probably financially well off. This inscription was put up in order to advertise to outsiders what the cult was about as well as to provide the members with private discipline as constitution of the cult group. When one looks at the various factions in the Christian churches in Corinth (cf 1 Cor 3:4–9] as well as the presence of discord in the same community due, probably, to class differences among the members (1 Cor 11:17–34), one can see the social results of such a type of organisation. Second, the initiative for the refounding of the cult group comes from the god [Zeus] who appeared in a dream to Dionysus and communicated to him his vision for the group. The formation of the group was therefore literally the result of obedience to divine revelation. Compare this, for example, with the Letter to the Ephesians where the first three chapters provide such a divinely revealed vision and foundation for the organisation and moral quality of the community. Third, in accordance with the international scope of the group (the combination of Greek gods with the traditional Phrygian deity Agdistis, which reflects the new cosmopolitan composition of the group) membership is open to all classes of people. Men, women, free as well as slaves, are eligible for membership. The same concern for transcending class, race and gender boundaries is found in early Christian groups and is reflected in such places as Galatians 3:28 ('There is no such thing as Jew and Greek, slave and freeman, male and female, for your are all one person in Christ.' *See also* Col 3:11). Fourth, the moral injunctions focusing on interpersonal relations, especially concerning relations between men and women, are similar to the injunctions ruling group relations and behaviour in the so-called *Haustafel* of Ephesians 5:1 to 6:9 or Colossians 3:18 to 4:1. In general, the morality promoted by this cult group represents the typical moral concerns of people of the Graeco-Roman world. Apart from the obvious lists in the letters of the New Testament, one needs to consider similar lists of vices in early Christian literature (cf e g *Didache* 2.2ff '. . . you shall not commit adultery; you shall not commit sodomy; you shall not commit fornication; . . . you shall not use magic; you shall not use philtres; you shall not procure abortion, nor commit infanticide . . . you shall not commit perjury . . . you shall not bear malice') to understand how much Christian house societies were 'morally at home' in the Graeco-Roman world.

A Samaritan association

The above-mentioned type of cultic association was not limited to Graeco-Roman cults. Evidence for the same type of organisation has been found for Jewish groups too, of which the organisation, at least on the surface, looked similar to that of other voluntary associations and cult groups. The following inscription (one of two found on the island of Delos) gives evidence of an association of schismatic Jews, Samaritans, on the island. Note the same evidence of a patron paying for the establishment of a cult centre:

> The Israelites of Delos who
> contribute to sacred Mount Gerizim
> crown with a golden
> crown Sarapion, son of Jason,
> from Knossos because of his benefaction
> towards them.
>
> (Llewelyn, S R 1998. 'New Documents Illustrating Early Christianity'. Vol 8. *A Review of the Greek Inscriptions and Papyri Published 1984–1985.* Grand Rapids: Eerdmans, 148.)

Next to participation in the official *polis* religion (which increasingly took on the character of civic religion), experience of union with the divine was sought in initiation and participation in mystery religions. Ancient Greece had known this in the well-known cult of Demeter at Eleusis in which only Greeks could participate. In the Hellenistic period people had themselves initiated *en masse* in the mysteries, often into more than one mystery cult. There were the various cult groups of Dionysus, the mysteries of the Cabiri at Samothrace and the various oriental gods, most notably Isis. Through participation in the dramatic rituals, a happy life here and now was ensured.

Another new feature of Hellenistic religion was the development of ruler cults. The origins of this lay in the hero cults in ancient Greece; the cultic veneration of legendary founders of cities or persons who had performed remarkable feats, and in the Near Eastern ideology of the king as related to the god (such as was found in Babylonia and Assyria). Alexander himself stepped into this role by having himself venerated as divine, but not as a god. It was only later under the successor kings that a cult in honour of kings who were already dead and later on of kings who were still alive was promoted. They set themselves up as 'temple-sharing deities' and placed their images in existing temples next to the locally venerated gods. The Seleucids traced their descent from Apollo and the Ptolemies from Dionysus. The purpose was to legitimise royal dynasties who had no natural claim to legitimacy, since they were not national kings who

Figure 1.4
Marble plaque showing the emperor Augustus performing sacrifices as pontifex maximus, from the altar in front of the Temple of Vespasian in Pompeii

reigned by the grace and appointment of their people. The Hellenistic rulers were never gods in the same sense that Zeus was god. Calling them 'saviours', 'gods' or 'saviour gods' did express something of the experiences evoked by these titles – here were people who could deliver what was normally expected of the gods: benefactions, help in times of need and control over the changes brought about by fate.

IMPERIAL CULT

The process of commemorating superhuman achievements with awards of divine honours had already started under the Greeks. Successful generals and kings were especially honoured in this way. The first Roman general-cum-dictator to be honoured as a god was

Figure 1.5
Bust of Augustus, depicting him wearing the head-dress of pontifex maximus – chief priest of the state religion – a position to which he succeeded after the death of Lepidus in 12 BCE

Julius Caesar, when after his death and cremation his soul was seen flying up to heaven in the form of an eagle – a sign of his divinisation. Octavian (the later Augustus), his adoptive son, then became 'son of the god, Caesar'. While the early emperors only achieved divine status after their death, increasing use of honorific language and divine titles in the course of the first century CE led to the living emperors being put in a class of their own, as gods. From 'god' and 'son of god' the divine honours developed and increased through a multiplication of titles such as 'saviour,' 'saviour of the world', 'benefactor', to 'lord' and 'lord and god' (*dominus et deus* at the time of Domitian). The imperial cult derived its form from that of other public and civic cults and often, in the early stages, the image of the emperor shared a temple with other deities. Cities competed for the right to erect and dedicate a temple to the emperor and his cult (much like cities compete for the right to host the Olympic Games today – and for the same reason: a special relationship with the emperor meant an inflow of capital investment, and financial and other benefactions). The following inscription deals with the authority granted by emperor Tiberius to the city of Gytheon in Greece to organise a cult to his predecessor, Augustus, some time after Augustus's death in 14 CE:

> Tiberius Caesar Augustus, son of the god Augustus, Pontifex Maximus, tribune for the sixteenth time, to the magistrates and city of Gytheon, greetings. The ambassador Decimus Tyrannius Nicanor whom you sent to me and my mother delivered your letter to me, in which the regulations were enclosed that you established for due worship of my father and the honoring of myself. In reply, I approve of your actions, for I consider it appropriate both to all men in common and to your city in particular to keep exceptional those honours suitable to the gods for the magnitude of the benefactions of my father toward the whole world. I myself, however, am satisfied with honours more modest and mortal . . . The priest should place an image of the god Augustus Caesar

the father on the first pedestal [?], one of Julia Augusta on the second from the right, and one of Tiberius Caesar Augustus on the third, the images having been provided him by the city. He must set a table [for sacrifices] in the middle of the theatre as well as an incense burner, and the representatives and all magistrates must offer sacrifice – but not until the musical performances enter – on behalf of our rulers' salvation. He must conduct the festival on the first day in honour of the god Augustus the Saviour and Liberator, son of the god Caesar; the second, of the emperor Tiberius Caesar Augustus, father of the fatherland; the third, of Julia Augusta, Good Fortune of our province and city; the fourth, of [her grandson] Germanicus Caesar, who shares a temple with Victory; the fifth, of [her grandson] Drusus Caesar, who shares a temple with Aphrodite; the sixth, of Titus Quinctius Flamininus [Roman conqueror of Macedonia in 197 BCE]; and he must see to the good order of competitors. After the competition, in the first Assembly, he must supply the city with the accounts for all the costs of the musical performances and administration of the sacred monies . . . After the celebration of the days for the gods and rulers, the market supervisor must introduce the musical sections of the theatrical competition, which must run for two days, one in memory of Gaius Julius Eurycles, [ruler and] benefactor of the nation and of our city in many matters; the other day, in honour of Gaius Julius Laco [son and successor to Eurycles, c. 14 BCE], patron of the watchfulness and safety of our nation and city. He must stage the competitions beginning with the day of the goddess, on those days on which he may be able to do so; but when he leaves office, he must turn over to his successor supervisor, by written public record, all the sacrificial victims for the competitions, and the city must get a receipt from the recipient. When the supervisor is staging the theatrical competitions, he should direct the parade to proceed from the temple of Asclepius and Hygieia [Health] with the youths and all the young men and other citizens participating in the parade wearing laurel wreaths and clad in white. The priestesses, maidens, and wives must move in procession with them in their sacred garments. When the procession reaches the imperial cult temple, the magistrates must sacrifice a bull for the well-being of the rulers and gods, and the eternal continuation of their rule; and, when they have sacrificed, they must require the Table Companies and the officials to offer incense in the public square . . . In the presidency of Chairon and his priesthood of the god Augustus [14–19 CE], the magistrates under Terentius Viada must present three painted portraits of the god Augustus, Julia Augusta, and Tiberius Caesar Augustus, and the stage for the chorus in the theatre and four actors' entrances and stools for the orchestra. They are to set up a stone column, engraving on it the cult regulations, and deposit a copy of the cult regulations also in the municipal archives, so that the regulations, in a public place and in the open and visible to all, may make continually manifest to all men the gratitude of the Gythean people toward the rulers.

As the Hellenistic age progressed, there was, to a large extent, a tendency to experience the gods as being withdrawn and distant. Thus the divine were described in abstract terms: not as the gods, but 'the divine'. Personified abstract forces such as Fate, Fortune, Health and Peace were also venerated. It was the figure of Fortune (Tyche) which came to dominate the religious consciousness of the age. It was in this figure that the experience of being exposed to the random changes of history was concentrated.

The flowering and growth of astrology, magic and oracles represented an attempt to pierce the mystery and unfathomability of the driving forces behind experiences of daily life and historical events. It was an attempt to unravel the secrets of how the world worked and how history would play out.

MAGIC

In a world increasingly experienced as unintelligible and unpredictable, people resorted to all sorts of remedies to influence the outcome of events. Magic, or ritual power, is such an attempt to steer the course of events, to change one's fortunes, or to gain insight into the future, or even to make the gods appear. Typical requests dealt with healing from illness, success with business ventures, success in love, protection against magic, curses and spells.

Magic and healing

The following inscription comes from the healing shrines at Epidauros in Greece. Epidauros was a very well-known centre of pilgrimage in antiquity for those seeking healing from illness. There were various temples, the most important of which was that of Asclepius, the god of healing. Apart from the temples, there were also rooms (to stay in), banqueting halls, and perhaps the most well-known and certainly best-preserved theatre from antiquity. Those seeking healing usually slept in the temple at night (called *incubation*). During this period, the god appeared in the form of a snake and touched the body of the sleeper, or the part afflicted by the illness. Those who had received healing were expected to make an offering. The attitudes displayed by these magical texts show something of the helplessness experienced by the vast majority of the people of the time in the face of inexplicable suffering. This overwhelming feeling of helplessness explains why people were willing to seek out healers – medicine men, miracle-workers or philosophers who had a reputation for miraculous cures. The following inscription presents such an offering made by a healed woman named Klio:

> God and Good Fortune
> Remedies of Apollo and Asclepius
>
> Klio was pregnant for five years. After she had already been pregnant for five years, she came to the god as a supplicant and slept inside the temple. As soon as she got out

and left the temple precinct, she gave birth to a boy who immediately washed himself at the fountain and walked around with his mother. After obtaining these favours she wrote on her offering: "It is not the big size of the tablet that should be admired, but the divinity, as Klio carried the heavy burden of pregnancy in her womb for five years until she slept in the temple and he healed her."

(IG IV.121)

A love charm

The following is a typical charm, written on a triangular-shaped lead tablet and rolled up. The mixture or permutations of vowels denotes and invokes the divinity addressed:

Sit koum
aieouo ieae
ieo uo ieo
aieou eu iae ia
o aeuia ioa ieo
ea iao oai I beseech and
request your power
and authority
k iaeou asor askatanthiri
setonekoii bring Termoutis whom
Sophia gave birth to, to Zoel whom
Droser gave birth to, with crazed, unceasing
and everlasting love. Now quickly!

An amulet against epilepsy and seizure

Amulets are little texts containing magical formulae, rolled up and inserted in a small container or phylactery, which is worn on the body or round the neck. They are used as magical charms to ward off illness or ill fortune. Magical and astrological texts comprise the vast majority of texts preserved from antiquity. This example dates from the third century CE. The strange letters and names of the deity (a mixture of mostly Jewish divine names or adaptations of them, including names of spirit beings or angels, as well as Graeco-Egyptian and native god names) function as magical formulae.

The god of Abraham, the god of Isaac, the god of Jacob,
and our god, save
Aurelia
from every
evil
spirit and from every epileptic fit
and seizure.
I beseech you Lord Iao
Sabaoth, Eloaion, Uriel,
Misichuel, Raphael, Gabriel,
Sarael, Rasochel,
Ablanathanalba, Abrasax,
xxxxxxnnnnnna
oaaiiiiiiiiiixouuuuu
uuaaoooooooono
[chi Rho symbol] Sensengen-
barpharanges, protect,
Epphin Io Erbeth
... [11 characters]
... [10 characters]
... [9 characters]
... [2 characters], protect
Aurelia from every seizure,
from every seizure,
Iao, Ieou, Ieo,
Lammo, Iao, Charakoopou,
Sesengenbarpharanges,
Iao, aieiouai, Ieou, Iao
Sabaoth, Adonaie, Eleleth,
Iako

Written to the left of the text and at right angles to it: protect ...

In the same way, Hellenistic philosophical schools attempted to give guidelines on how to live a happy and undisturbed life of peace in the midst of great social upheaval and disturbance. Various philosophical schools made their presence felt in the Hellenistic world, the most important being Stoicism (eventually the most enduring of the philosophical schools), Epicureanism, Cynicism and Neopythagoreanism. In different ways they were all reactions to, and interpretations of, the Hellenistic history. Although philosophical criticism of religion was not new in the Hellenistic world, these philosophies represented a confluence of religion and philosophy to such a degree that the two became virtually indistinguishable, and various philosophical groups indeed functioned as cultic associations.

Ancient Greek religion was built on the assumed fundamental difference between humans and gods. The boundary between divine and human was increasingly crossed in the Hellenistic era. Evidence suggests an increased experience of epiphanies (sudden appearances of the gods) and dream appearances of the gods. Epiphanies could take the form of a visible appearance of the god, a sudden awareness of divine presence, or a god could be experienced as being present in a human being. From here it was only a short step to the appearance of divine men in the Hellenistic world. The category of divine men encompassed a variety of personalities – miracle-workers, philosophers, healers, sages and visionaries. The immediacy of divine presence was what made them exceptional. In this way these men were the 'ligaments' connecting the divine and human world. They mediated between the world of the divine and the world of humans. In this sense, taken together, they were 'the mediators'.

> ### A HOLY MAN
>
> Officially, contact with divine powers was mediated by temple institutions, temple traditions, temple personnel (priests, etc) and rituals, as was the case with civic or public religion, the religion of the country, city or community. But alongside this arose the phenomenon of 'religious entrepreneurs', mendicant holy men who either claimed or were said to embody divinity and through their example, actions and words gave access to divinity. Some were 'divine' philosophers, like Plotinus or Apollonius of Tyana; some were miracle-workers or healers, like the Jewish Honi the rainmaker and Hanina ben Dos;, still others ascetics like the early Christian saints, to name but a few. The following example is an excerpt from Philostratus's *Life of Apollonius*. Apollonius of Tyana, whose life is recounted in a five-volume work, was roughly a contemporary of the Apostle Paul in the first century, and lived well into the second century. He was widely travelled and famous as philosopher, holy man, healer, miracle-worker and cult restorer/reformer. Even in

antiquity, parallels were drawn between Apollonius and Jesus Christ (e g in the work of the philosopher Hierocles):

> While he was discoursing on the issue of libations, a rich young man happened to be present in the audience who had such a bad reputation for licentiousness that his conduct had been the subject of coarse street corner songs. His homeland was Corcyra, and he traced his lineage to Alcinous the Phaeacian who played host to Odysseus. So, Apollonius was talking about the libations and was urging them not to drink from a particular cup, but to reserve its use for the gods, and never to touch it or drink from it. But when he also urged them to attach handles to the cup and to pour the libation over the handle, because that is the part of the cup at which men will least likely drink, the young man burst out into a loud guffaw, drowning Apollonius's voice. He looked at him and said: 'It is not you that uttered this insult, but the demon that drives you without your knowing it.' In fact, a demon *had* come into the young man, for he would laugh at things no-one else laughed at and then he would suddenly turn to weeping for no reason at all, and he would talk and sing to himself. Most considered it youthful boisterousness that had carried him to such extremes, but he was really speaking on behalf of the demon although it looked like drunken frolics that he was performing on that occasion. When Apollonius looked at him, the ghost uttered screams of fear and rage such as there are when people are branded or racked, swearing never to return or take possession of human beings again. He addressed [the demon] with anger as a master would a cunning, unscrupulous and shameless slave and so on, and ordered him to leave the young man with visible proof [of his leaving]. 'I will throw down,' the demon said, 'that statue over there,' pointing to one of the images in the royal portico, where all this took place. But when the statue first gently moved and then fell down, the uproar over this and the way they clapped their hands over the miracle, can anyone ever describe it? The young man rubbed his eyes as if he had just woken up and he looked towards the rays of the sun, and he won the respect of all who turned to him. He showed himself not to be licentious any longer, nor did he stare madly about, but he had returned to his own true self as if he had been treated with drugs. He gave up his dainty dress and light clothes and the other luxuries and fell in love with the austerity [of the philosopher's lifestyle] and their cloak and he modelled his life on that of Apollonius.
>
> (Philostratus: *Life of Apollonius* 4.20)

Note: Apollonius was a Neopythagorean philosopher, and while the narrative about him recounts his philosophical expositions and exploits as travelling sage, he is also portrayed as a holy man, cult reformer and miracle-worker. It is the combination of philosopher and healer-cum-miracle worker that is of interest here. In the emerging early Christian tradition Jesus is cast in similar terms, namely as a teacher who is simultaneously a miracle-worker and healer. When one moves into the world of second and third-century Christian literature,

> especially the apocryphal acts of the apostles, one finds the literature brimming with pictures of the apostles as miracle-working holy men.

All the aforementioned factors were thus in place when the table was set for the emergence of Christianity in the late Hellenistic world.

2 THE ARRIVAL OF THE ROMAN EMPIRE

2.1 Introduction

The term *Roman Empire* refers to the complex of cultural, military, social and political forces which controlled the Mediterranean world and Western Europe from 30 BCE to the fifth century CE. Christianity emerged within the Roman Empire and developed its main characteristics as a phenomenon of the empire. In the fourth century, Christianity was recognised as the religion of the state.

Although the Roman Empire included an incredibly vast area and a historical process spread over many centuries, in this discussion the focus will be on the eastern part of the Roman Empire during the first century (from Augustus to Trajan). How did it come about that Rome dominated the Mediterranean world during the first century?

2.2 From city to world power

The Roman Empire grew from small beginnings. It started as a small city–state in central Italy in the eighth century BCE and grew through wars of acquisition. Through trade it exerted a strong economic influence and political domination in areas surrounding the Mediterranean Sea, and areas as far afield as North Africa, Spain, Gaul, Greece and Asia Minor. The seeds for the later imperial power were sown already as early as the sixth century BCE, when Rome became a republic under the governance of two magistrates (known as the time of 'the Republic'). Wealthy and powerful families vied for power and dominance over the republican Senate, with the last century of the Republic

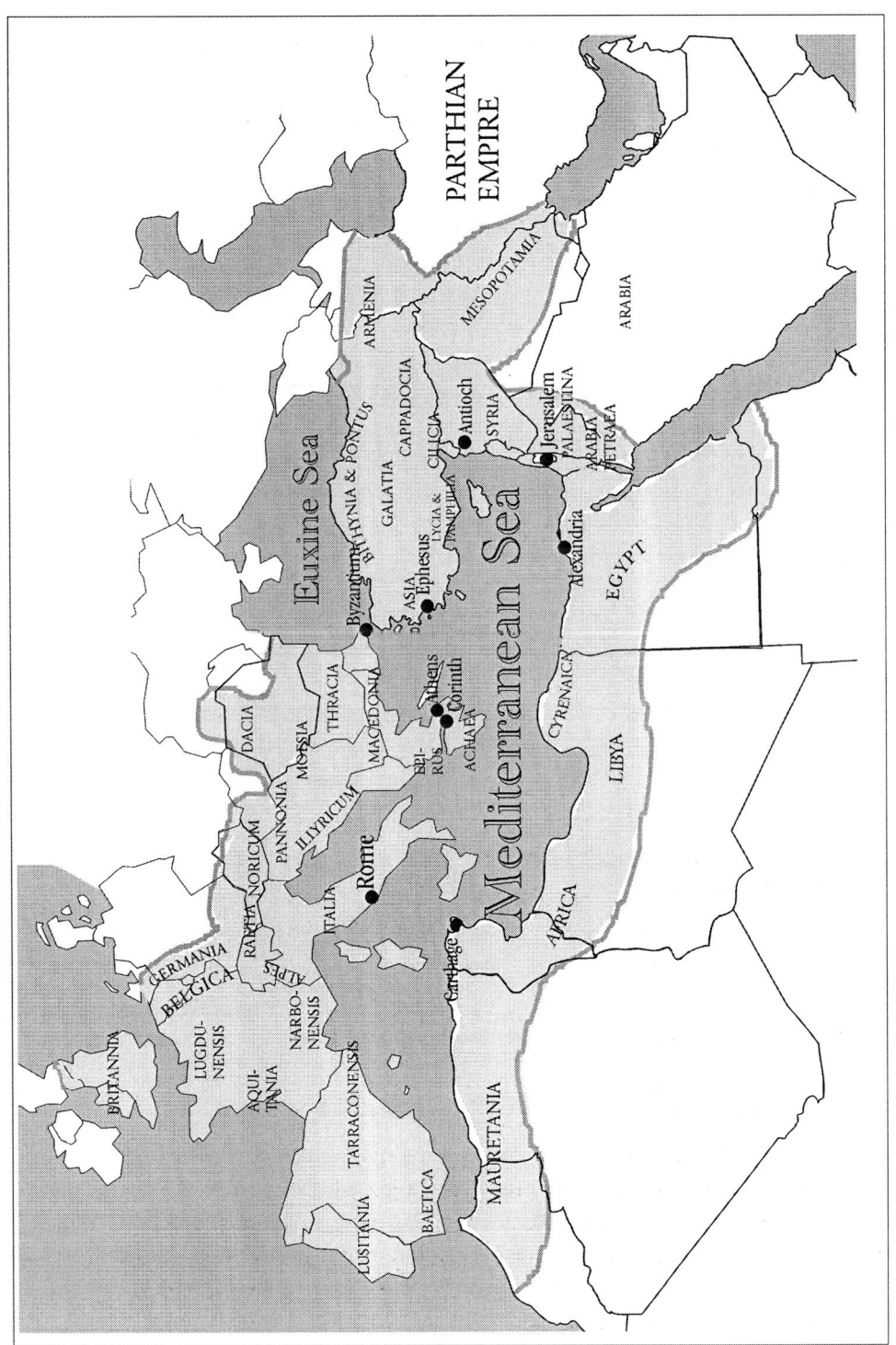

Figure 2.1 The extent of the Roman Empire at the beginning of the third century CE

(±140–50 BCE) especially characterised by intense conflicts and social troubles, compounded by strife between the commoners (the *plebeians*) and the Senate, as well as slave revolts.

These problems were exacerbated by the rise in piracy along the eastern Mediterranean coast which threatened the grain supply to Rome, as well as by the actions of the Parthian (or Persian) king, Mithridates. He saw in the unrest and conflicts in Rome an opportunity to expand the already vast dominions he held in the east further into the west. Although a Roman army under a general Sulla had driven Mithridates from Asia Minor, in 67 BCE to 66 BCE, the Senate voted 'special powers' to another Roman general, Pompey, to do what was necessary to deal with the pirate problem and the Parthian threat. After a successful campaign, the Parthians were driven back from Asia Minor and the pirate forces were destroyed. Rome also acquired new territories such as Armenia (as client kingdom), and Syria (64 BCE) and Palestine (63 BCE) as provinces.

Upon Pompey's return to Rome – now fabulously wealthy through war booty and famous as a victorious general with the loyal support of his troops – the political crisis in Rome came to a head. As a result of general dissatisfaction with the republican system of government, a dictatorship was established, led by the famous 'triumvirate' (literally 'band of three men') of Pompey, Crassus (a multimillionaire estate owner) and Julius Caesar.

The triumvirate soon fell apart, resulting in a devastating civil war from which Julius Caesar emerged as victor. Julius Caesar then appropriated ultimate power and autocratic authority into his own position. Resistance to his dictatorship as well as a desire for his position led to his assassination in 44 BCE. His designated heir, his nephew Octavian (Augustus), took control of the armies and rooted out all opposition during another round of devastating civil wars, which ended with the defeat and death of former ally and co-ruler Mark Antony at the battle of Actium in 31 BCE. Octavian assumed extraordinary constitutional powers and control of the important provinces. Rome was now an empire with an emperor (27 BCE).

Unlike his uncle, Octavian was careful to veil his tyrannical power. After the battle of Actium, Octavian prudently restored the outward forms of the republic. He took the title *princeps*, meaning 'first citizen', and the name *Augustus*, which carries solemn and religious overtones (it means 'holy', 'majestic', 'dignified'). It is because of the title *princeps* that the Roman Empire is often called the *principate*. In a very real sense, Augustus created the Roman Empire over which he was to rule for 43 years. Almost a century of peace, relative security and prosperity (for the elite groups) ensued, hence the famous description of the Roman Empire as the *pax romana*, or 'the Roman peace'.

The resulting empire encompassed a large part of the then-known inhabited world and included, it is generally agreed, almost 50 million people within its borders during the first century CE. The city of Rome, itself the largest city of the empire, counted about half-a-million inhabitants. Other major cities such as Alexandria, Carthage and Antioch had populations of about a hundred thousand inhabitants each. Cities were mostly extremely crowded and very densely populated. Apart from the few very large cities, more common were large towns of between ten and fifteen thousand people. By far the majority of inhabitants of the empire lived in little towns, villages or hamlets of at most a few hundred inhabitants. These towns were scattered thoughout the countryside and were connected to the large towns and cities in networks of economic exchange as sources of income and produce. The cities and large towns functioned as centres of land control, political and tax systems and religious activities.

The population of the Roman Empire was sharply divided between the propertied classes (the *honestiores*) and the rest, mostly poor people (*humiliores*). Possession of land was the basis of wealth and most rich men derived their income from their estates. So, the safest investment to be made, whether it be by the rich, would-be rich, freeborn or ex-slave, lay in the acquisition of land. According to the mentality of the time, people were not equal. Birth, wealth and citizenship determined one's position in society. Wealth, sometimes vast amounts of it, bought access to government office; from membership of the most insignificant municipal council to the senate itself. The rich did not sully their hands with labour. They 'earned' their income indirectly through financing loans or through trade and agriculture for which they employed freedmen or slaves. Some slaves performed what would today be called 'professional work', for which they were better paid and thus better off than poor freedmen. On the whole, however, apart from the landed classes, the rest – whether freeborn, tradesman or slave – were barely eking out a

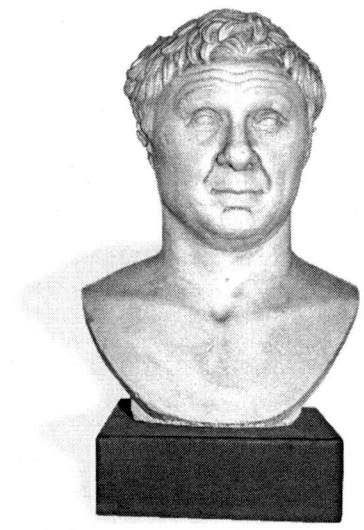

Figure 2.2
Bust of Pompey

Figure 2.3
Statue of Julius Caesar, member of the first triumvirate with Pompey and Crassus; Roman consul and dictator 59 to 44 BCE

Figure 2.4
Statue of Augustus, Roman emperor 29 BCE to 14 CE. The adoptive son of Julius Caesar, Octavian avenged Caesar's death in 44 BCE and after a protracted civil war, consolidated dictatorial power upon himself. Careful not to offend Roman political sensibilities, he disguised his *de facto* dictatorship with titles such as *princeps* (first citizen . . . among equals). In 27 BCE he received the title *Augustus*, a title that conveyed the meaning of being elevated above all other human beings. Jesus Christ was born during the long reign of Augustus

living. Some freedmen were, however, known to be rich.

The economy of the Roman Empire was heavily burdened by taxation. Customs duties, as well as a general sales tax of one per cent were levied at various transit points. There was a five per cent tax on all emancipation of slaves and inheritances of Roman citizens. Other sources of revenue included bequests, fines, booty acquired in war, the proceeds from the state-owned mines and the yield from imperial estates.

Outside Italy, a direct tax called *tributum* was levied on land and personal property. The rights to collect provincial taxes, including a ten per cent tax on agricultural produce were sold to *publicani* (from which the well-known 'publicans' of the New Testament were derived). These publicans were supervised by the provincial governors, but abuses were fairly common. A few emperors, such as Tiberius and Domitian, were very harsh on culprits in this regard.

All the monies collected went to the treasury of the senate, but for all practical purposes it came under the control of the emperor. In times of natural crises, such as earthquakes or floods, the emperor often contributed vast sums for relief. In Augustus's day the annual income of the treasury was apparently around 100 million denarii. By the time of Vespasian, imperial revenues approached 650 million denarii. (Vespasian, one should add, was faced with the daunting task of making the empire solvent after the civil wars of 69 BCE).

The harsh reality of living in any of the cities of the Graeco-Roman world was one of extreme filth, poor water supply, and inefficient or non-existent sewage disposal and sanitation. The resulting stench could be smelt miles away, whilst the cities were smothered in flies, mosquitoes and other insects. The upshot of these circumstances was that the

Figure 2.5

Ara Pacis: Altar to the Augustan peace in Rome. After the devastating civil wars that ensued after the murder of Julius Caesar when powerful generals scrambled to attain power, Octavian (the later Augustus) consolidated his own position and achieved supreme power, inaugurating half a century of stability and relative peace. He himself portrayed it as the inauguration of a new era; the return of the mythical Golden Age

Figure 2.6

Pax Augusti Sacrum: Altar to the Augustan peace

Figure 2.7
A model of an *insula* or apartment block in Rome. The original stood at the foot of the Capitoline Hill. Shops and workshops occupied the ground floor and the shopkeeper and his family used the mezzanine as their home. The higher floors housed increasingly smaller apartments, and it was common practice to sublet rooms in these apartments. High occupation density; no sanitation or water supplies (everything had to be carried up and down); the constant threat of fire (food was cooked over open fires in bronze braziers); excessive heat in the summer months due to lack of ventilation, and bad construction with the attendant threat of collapse (developers also tried to save on construction costs in ancient times!) made life for ordinary people very difficult

Graeco-Roman world was frequently struck by deadly epidemics and plagues on a large scale which lasted for years and killed thirty to fifty per cent of the population each time.

Obviously, disease and high death rates were not evenly spread across all elements of the population, but the health of most people who did make it to adulthood, would have been atrocious. Parasites were very common in everyday life. For example, half of the hair combs found at Qumran, Masada and Murabbat (Jewish communities of the first century) were infested with lice and lice eggs, probably reflecting conditions elsewhere. Approximately five per cent of the population was killed by infected teeth.

Given that the Graeco-Roman city was a pest hole of infectious diseases, one realises that the high figures of migration to cities do not indicate upward social mobility. The landless people migrated to urban areas because of the immense need of new labour forces; created not by economic opportunity, but by the high mortality rate due to the dreadful health conditions among the urban non-elite.

Infant mortality rates averaged thirty per cent, and life expectancies were extremely short by current, Western standards. Children, in general, suffered from disease and malnutrition, and many never made it to adulthood before their parents either became ill or died. About sixty per cent of those who survived their first year of life were dead by the age of 16 and in few families both parents would still be alive by the time the youngest child reached

Figure 2.8
Model of Rome as it was in the fourth century showing the 'heart of the empire': the Capitoline Hill and the forum: (1) The Capitoline Hill with the Temple of Jupiter Optimus Maximus ('Jupiter the Highest and the Best') (2) Basilica Julia (3) House of the Vestal Virgins (4) Temple of Castor (5) Temple of the Divine Julius (6) Temple of Saturn (7) Basilica Paulii (8) Temple of Divus Antoninus and Diva Faustina (9) Basilica of Maxentius (10) Temple of Roma and Venus (11) Meta Sudans (large monumental fountain erected by Domitian) (12) Arch of Constantine (13) Colosseum (14) Forum of Augustus with the Temple of Mars Ultor (15) Forum of Nerva (16) Forum of Caesar (17) Curia or Senate House (18) Temple of Peace (19) Domitian's Hall (20) Temples of Victory and the Great Mother (21) Temple of Apollo (22) Domitian's palace (23) Theatre of Marcellus (24) Temple of Portunus (25) Round temple and Forum Boarium ('livestock market') (26) Circus Maximus (27) Temple of the deified Claudius (28) Baths of Trajan, built on top of Nero's palace, the Golden House.

puberty. A child born among the lower classes during the first century had a life expectancy of little more than 20 years.

In summary, poor housing, non-existent sanitation, unscientific medical care and bad diet – as much as one-fourth of a male Palestinian peasant's calorie intake came from alcohol – all added up to make common people's experience of everyday life stressful, even frightening. Life was brief, terrible and often incomprehensible. Given the belief in the activities of evil spiritual powers and the widespread physical suffering prevalent within the context of ancient cosmology, one can understand the ubiquitous fear and anxiety characterising the period. The pervasive presence of violence must also be added – apart from the many and extensive wars one must remember the Roman way of maintaining order, which can be described as 'institutionalised terror'. Given these stressful conditions, it is understandable that psychosomatic illness prevailed.

The Roman Empire was an 'agrarian society'. This means the society was basically stratified into essentially two social groups: a small ruling elite in the cities and a mass of toiling agriculturalists in the villages. Village life centred

Figure 2.9
Bar in Pompeii. This typical fast-food outlet was open to the street (in the foreground) and had amphorae (clay pots) built into the counter from which the drinks were served

Figure 2.10
The forum in Pompeii. The large building in the background is the basilica or lawcourts. Public spaces such as these were an important facet of ancient society, providing the opportunity for social and political interaction

round agricultural activities where families worked together to produce some specialised product. Surplus village labour was absorbed by the labour needs of the large estates owned by the elite. Such workers were paid wages by the day. Peasant villagers of the first century can be described as general labourers, that is, they were proficient in a variety of agricultural and domestic tasks. A peasant family normally produced and consumed most of what it needed in-house. Agriculture did not keep villagers occupied year round, so there was opportunity for them to adopt other economic pursuits. Many villages tended to specialise in certain crafts, notably those related to clothing, building, special foods, fishing, medicine, metalwork and tool making. Most of the products produced by craftsmen were, however, for all practical purposes only available to the elite. In the villages the predominant activity at all times remained agriculture.

Visits paid by relatives, travelling teachers and merchants, and religious festivals provided the major social events and entertainment in village life. The seasonal visits of tax and rent collectors, and armies passing nearby caused stressful periods.

The ruling groups, local elite and temples dominated life in the towns and cities of the Roman Empire. The urban non-elite were mostly illiterate groups who provided the goods and services the elite required. At the outer limits of the city lived the poorest inhabitants, frequently in walled-off sections of the city. Usually, occupational and ethnic groups lived and worked together in city blocks. Outside the city walls lived beggars, prostitutes, persons in undesirable occupations (such as tanners) and sometimes even wealthy freedmen, such as traders. Landless peasants who came to the city in search of labour opportunities often found a place to live outside the city walls. All these people required access to the city during the day, but were locked out at night. Gates inside the city could also be closed at night to prevent non-elite persons from accessing elite areas.

It is under these circumstances that the Christian message of salvation and resurrection, practices such as healing and social care, and open-table fellowship created a new society providing a safe haven from, and alleviation of, the stresses of everyday life under extremely harsh conditions.

3 JUDAISM IN THE GRAECO-ROMAN WORLD

3.1 The politics and socio-economics of Palestine

After Pompey's conquest of Palestine, Judaea (as the province was called) retained some form of self-government. The high priest, Hyrcanus, was allowed some civil authority, but his territory was much reduced. However, the politics of Judaea was influenced by power struggles between four groups. There were the supporters of two brothers of the Hasmonean dynasty, Aristobulus II and Hyrcanus II, both of whom competed against each other and against Rome for power over Judaea. Then there were religious leaders seeking the abolition of Judaean kingship and rather government by the temple institution. Finally, there was the family of Antipater, an influential family with Arabian connections.

To quell the turmoil, the province was divided into five administrative councils whose membership was made up of aristocratic families (of priestly or of Hasmonean origins). This created the impression of self-rule. However Antipater recognised that the Romans were interested in alliances – forms of self-rule that would recognise Roman superiority. The family of Antipater, especially his son Herod, actively sought Roman support for some form of acceptable independence. As a result of this, these family members came into prominence: Herod appointed king (technically) of Judaea in 41 BCE, and after he had repelled a Parthian invasion and defeated Aristobulus II and his supporters, he became king in reality in 37 BCE. Herod ruled until his death in 4 BCE and his family continued to play an important role in the political world of the Roman Empire until the end of the first century.

Herod ruled Judaea as a client king (or friendly king) of Rome. Client kings were not uncommon during the early part of the Roman Empire. Client kingship was useful to the Romans because the client kingdom served as a buffer to the areas not under Roman control and could be called upon to render military aid when needed. This was particularly convenient with regard to Palestine, as the Persian Empire was Rome's major rival in the eastern parts at the time (Rome and Persia being the two 'world powers' of the period).

Client kingship was, furthermore, useful, as Rome did not have to expend valuable resources in administration and the posting of legions on a permanent basis, because the client kingdom took care of its own administration and defence of its borders under normal circumstances.

Herod began his reign with the much-reduced state of Judaea, as it was left after Pompey's redistribution of territory. By the end of his reign, Herod controlled a state reaching from southern Lebanon to the Negev, and from the Mediterranean to Transjordan. It was an area as large as that ruled by Alexander Janneus and larger than anything Solomon had governed.

IMPERIAL EDICT ON THE RIGHTS OF JEWS IN ASIA

The position of Jews in Graeco-Roman society was always a contentious issue for a number of reasons. Their food laws prevented them from taking part in public sacrifices and feasts. Their adherence to one god prevented them from sacrificing to, or worshipping the civic gods or the emperor. Keeping the Sabbath also precluded military service (for fighting might take place on the Sabbath). Added to that, the organisation of Jewish society as a separate entity in the various cities earned them the reputation of being misanthropists, and often made them the scapegoats in turbulent times of social unrest or natural disasters. It appears from the evidence that Jews often suffered local opposition to their rights and privileges. In such cases they often had to appeal to Roman authorities who always ruled in their favour. Thus, from time to time, after local disturbances, their rights had to be reaffirmed. In 12 BCE Augustus issued the following edict (set up in a temple dedicated to Augustus by the Commonwealth of Asia) regarding the rights of Jews in Asia (west coast of modern-day Turkey):

> Caesar Augustus Pontifex Maximus with tribunician power decrees: Since the Jewish nation has been found to be well disposed to the Roman people, not only in the present but also in the past, and especially to my father, the emperor Caesar, as also their high priest, Hyrcanus, it has been decided by my council and me with an oath, with the consent of the Roman people: that the Jews may follow their own customs according to their ancestral law, just as they did under Hyrcanus, high priest of the Most High God; that the sacred money be inviolable and be sent to Jerusalem to be given to the treasurers in Jerusalem; and that they need not give surety [i e to appear in court] on the Sabbath or on the day of preparation before the Sabbath from the ninth hour. If someone is found stealing their sacred books or the sacred money either from the house in which the Sabbath service is held or from the banqueting hall, he shall be regarded as sacrilegious and his property will be confiscated to the Roman public treasury. The resolution offered me by them concerning my piety towards all men and concerning Gaius Marcius Censorinus together with this decree, I order to be put up in the most conspicuous place consecrated to me by the Commonwealth of Asia in Ancyra. If anyone transgresses any of the above-mentioned decrees, he shall receive severe punishment.
>
> (Josephus: *Jewish Antiquities* 16.162–165.)

This was inscribed on a pillar in the temple of Caesar.

Herod the Great played a major part in securing the rights of Jews in Asia Minor when he toured the eastern Roman provinces with Agrippa, the son-in-law of Augustus. He was instrumental in having the Jewish philosopher and orator, Nicolaus of Damascus, plead the case of the Jews before Agrippa. This edict was one of a series of similar edicts; the result of submissions made during that tour.

As a client king, Herod maintained good relations with the emperor, the rest of the imperial family and the imperial administration. Herod was a good administrator and a successful businessman who amassed great wealth. He governed his country with rigour, eliminating marauding robber bands (a perennial problem in the provinces of the Roman Empire), fortifying the borders, supporting trade ventures (opening up the coastal cities for trade and bringing them under Judaean control) and setting up wide-ranging 'diplomatic' relationships with neighbouring countries.

Herod's rule was not unwelcome from an economic point of view. He ended the long period of fighting for power between factions of the Hasmonean dynasty and ushered in an extended period of peace. Very importantly, as client king he got the Romans out of the province. Because of his friendship with Augustus and his sound political policies, Herod eliminated the heavy financial burden of war indemnities as well as the Roman tribute levied by Pompey, and later governors, to finance the Roman civil war, as well as military campaigns against the Parthians. Herod was thus able to reduce the tax burden (which included local and religious taxes) to realistic levels. He, furthermore, lavishly spent on agricultural and building projects. He followed a policy of developing some of the sparsely populated areas by bringing in settlers, opening up the land to cultivation and launching irrigation projects.

Figure 3.1
The fortress Antonia (in the middle of the photograph) adjoining the porticoes of the Jerusalem temple (on the right). The fortress was built by Herod the Great between 37 and 35 BCE and named after his patron, Mark Antony. A military garrison was stationed there both to protect the temple and to exercise control over activities in the temple grounds (as evidenced by the arrest of Paul after the disturbance in the temple courts (Acts 21:27–23:35)). In popular piety this is the place where Jesus was condemned and flagellated, but these events from the gospel narrative (cf John 18:28–19:16) took place at the citadel, the Herodian palace that was used as the official residence of the Roman procurators in Jerusalem

Herod's enormous building programme (which included the new temple in Jerusalem) provided work for many thousands of workers.

Opposition to Herod was fuelled by his undermining of the power of the traditional aristocracy through his way of levying tax (which left them out of the process, much in the manner of Rome) and his curtailing of the Sanhedrin's influence; the council of aristocrats which usually directed government. Herod was therefore slandered for his Edumaean (Arabian) background, although according to evidence, he was an earnest Jew with a pious concern for the Torah. Apparently, few accepted the defamation (except for the Hasmoneans) and Herod was actually widely accepted also in his own country.

It can be argued with good reason that the Jews were better off economically at the end of Herod's reign than at the beginning.

3.2 After Herod: kingdoms, provinces and war

When Herod died in 4 BC, his son Archelaus became the principal successor. However, a number of disturbances broke out and several groups organised rebellions, all seeking the opportunity to gain a kingdom. The Syrian governor, Varus, launched a war in Judaea, rounded up as many of the rebels as he could find (about 2 000 were crucified) and sent off a number of leaders to Rome for trial before Augustus.

Different factions of Herod's family also took the opportunity to present the emperor with conflicting claims on the rule of Judaea. There was even a delegation asking for *direct* Roman rule of Judaea. In the presentations before Augustus, wide-ranging accusations and issues were raised; the emperor's final decision was to split Herod's realm, giving Judaea, Idumaea and Samaria to Archelaus, with the title *ethnarch* (part king). Herod's other son, Antipas, received Perea and Galilee. Batanea, Trachonitis and Auranitis went to Philip. Philip's mother, who was Herod's Egyptian wife, was called Cleopatra (not the famous one). Archelaus and Antipas's mother was Malthace.

The rule of Archelaus soon came to an end. His subjects complained to Augustus that Archelaus was an inefficient and cruel ruler. The emperor paid heed to their voices, deposed Archelaus and exiled him to Gaul. In 6 CE Judaea, once again, became a full Roman province.

Philip ruled from 4 to 34 BCE over the territories that can broadly be described as northern Transjordan. Like his father, he preferred balanced policies, and furthered trade and peace. Josephus praises his regime for its liberality and tranquility. Also, like his father, Philip engaged in building projects. After Philip's death in 34 CE his tetrarchy was incorporated into the province of Syria until 37, when it was joined by the then emperor Gaius Caligula to the Judaean kingdom of Agrippa I, whose son Agrippa II was to rule over Philip's tetrarchy from 50 to 94 CE.

Figure 3.2
Herodian bath at Masada. This particular bath is part of a complex of baths, ranging from cold through tepid to hot baths. Note the painted wall with its simulated marble finish

Antipas ruled over Galilee and Perea as a client king of the Romans from 4 BCE until 39 CE, when he was removed from office under suspicion of sedition. He was king during Jesus's lifetime. The gospel authors confusingly call him 'Herod' (Mark 6). Antipas maintained personal and political relations with the emperors and their court, and was a typical native ruler, adapting to Roman customs and practices outside his own country but, when at home, for the most part fulfilling his obligations toward Judaism. Like his father, Antipas attempted to promote all the various cultural sensibilities in the kingdom. His support of Hellenistically inclined people angered some Jews, while his tolerance towards Jewish sensibilities provoked suspicion among others.

He engaged in large building projects and cultivated patrons in Rome. Initially, Antipas married a Nabatean princess, but divorced her in favour of his sister-in-law, Herodias, with the ease of an upper-class Roman. As the ruler responsible for keeping the peace, he was apprehensive about the growing reputation of Jesus, as he had been about John the Baptist whom he had executed for criticising his biblically forbidden marriage (Mark 6.14, Luke 13:31; cf also Luke 23:7–12). That marriage turned out to be a cause of considerable effect. Not only did this draw John the Baptist's criticism (which resulted in the prophet's death), but the Nabatean king, Aretas IV, was insulted by these events (his daughter was returned to him without due reason). Antipas, not quite the military man his father was, could not deal with the Nabatean invasion. The Syrian armies had to intervene; and the resulting instability led to Antipas being banished to Gaul by the emperor Gaius Caligula.

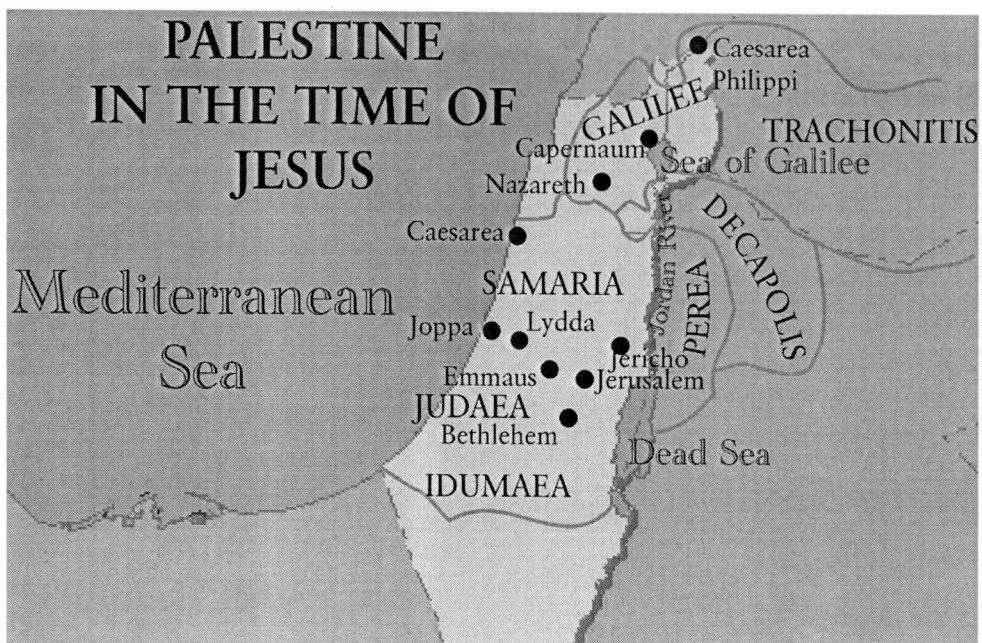

Figure 3.3
Palestine during the time of Herod and his successors

The Herodians mentioned in the Gospels (Mark 3:6; 12:13) were the officials and upper-class supporters of Herod the Great, but also of the Herodian families. In New Testament times, people functioned within the context of a family; the Herodians represent the families involved with the ruling Herods and their courts. They, one can imagine, sought to blunt the influence of movements whom they saw as dangerous new political forces and threats to their control – as, for instance, the growing Jesus movement.

Something must be said about Agrippa I, a grandson of Herod the Great. His full name was Marcus Julius Agrippa and he ruled (as king) over Judaea for a brief period (41–44 CE). Why Luke refers to Agrippa as 'Herod' is unclear (Acts 12:1). 'Herod' is not part of Agrippa's name; Luke was either confused (thinking of Agrippa's brother Herod Chalcis) or ignorant.

The greater part of Agrippa's life was spent in Rome, where he squandered his fortune and acquired the reputation of being an extravagant and licentious young man. He did, however, have the good sense to cultivate the friendship and patronage of Caligula. When Caligula became emperor, Agrippa was given the territories of Philip (37 CE) and two years later the land of Antipas (who was exiled) was assigned to him. In 41 CE he was also appointed as ruler over Judaea, Samaria and Idumaea. Thus, for a brief period, his grandfather's entire kingdom was, once again, united. Agrippa played a decisive role during the conflict between the Jews and Caligula when the emperor attempted to have a statue of him installed in the temple. Caligula, fortunately, cancelled his plans on Agrippa's advice. This was actually a very important event in Jewish history, with all sorts of repercussions. Agrippa died in 44 CE.

3.3 The road to war

After Archelaus's exile (6 CE) Judaea became a Roman province once more. The reorganisation of the kingdom began under the direction of the Syrian governor Quirinius and the newly appointed Judaean governor Coponius. Whereas the tetrarchies of Philip and Antipas flourished for several decades, and continued to do so under Agrippa I and Agrippa II, the story of Judaea in the first century CE is a tragic one. Events during this time would affect the history of the world up to today. Out of the disastrous conflict between Judaeans and Romans two major religious traditions developed (Judaism and Christianity) and the roots of a third (Islam) were formed. When Herod the Great died, a group of Judaeans appealed to Augustus for direct Roman rule, a wish that soon came true. The consequences were meaningful.

As a Roman province, Judaea now became liable for its share of the Roman tax burden, some of which was collected directly by the Romans. Quirinius and Coponius immediately set up a census of the people and property. For the Judaeans, the tax assessment was difficult: they 'were at first shocked to hear of the registration of property' (Josephus, *Jewish Antiquities* 18.1.1). Most were persuaded by the arguments of the high priest that there was little option, but two leaders, Judas the Galilean and Zadok the Pharisee, led some sort of rebellion. Their view was that only God was their master and to accept the assessment was to submit to slavery (and a Jew, so the conviction was, could only be slave to another Jew).

Furthermore, insensitivity towards the Jewish sentiments and provocation on the part of the Roman governors elicited many disturbances, which yet again led to brutal repression. Some of the most notable examples of these occurred under Pontius Pilate. Growing polarisation in Jewish society between the aristocracy and the poor and landless, the repressive regime of the Roman authorities and severe economic hardships combined to make the collapse of Jewish society imminent. There had been rebellions and unruly elements at various times since Pompey, but under the procurators these forces escalated: various bandit groups, sporadic appearances of prophets and the rise of terrorist gangs all contributed. A series of natural and social disasters compounded the situation: more and more people became disaffected and

Figure 3.4
View across the mountain of Masada with the Dead Sea in the background. The ramp built by the Romans to attack the fortress is visible in the middle

Figure 3.5
Part of the Herodian winter palace of Masada with a view across the valley to the Dead Sea. In view are the middle and bottom parts of the palace on the north-western face of the mountain

took to brigandage as an easier means of livelihood in difficult circumstances. There were dozens of smaller revolts against Rome and its representatives in various provinces, all of which were forcibly suppressed. Luke 13:1 mentions one such lesser conflict. There were three revolts in Palestine: in 4 BCE, in 66 CE (which led to full-scale war, ending only when the Romans destroyed Jerusalem and the temple in 70) and in 132 to 135 CE (when Jewish military power was completely broken by the Romans).

The very nature of Roman rule, namely brutal military conquest, often left little option than to resort to extreme violence – and this was particularly true in the province of Judaea. The Romans treated the inhabitants ruthlessly in order to achieve submission and maintain obedience. Repeatedly, the Roman armies burnt and sometimes completely destroyed towns and either slaughtered, crucified or enslaved the male populations.

The governor during whose term of office the war with Rome began, was Gessius Florus (64–66 CE). The war with Rome had a variety of causes; it did not suddenly begin with a single event.

The response from Rome was to appoint a seasoned general, Flavius Vespasianus, to deal with the rebellion. Vespasian arrived in the spring of 67 CE and launched a systematic campaign to subdue the affected territories. The battles were bloody – particularly on the Jewish side – and one-sided. In June 69 CE Jerusalem was isolated and surrounded.

By autumn, a number of important events took place. As Vespasian moved to Egypt (to secure the grain supply to Rome), he was acclaimed emperor. He embarked for Rome and sent Titus, his son, to finish the task of taking Jerusalem. The full siege started in the spring of 70 CE. The noncombatants, particularly the wo-

Figure 3.6
Bust of Vespasian, Roman emperor 69 to 79 CE. Vespasian was the general dispatched by Nero to quell the uprising in Palestine in 66 CE. Having subdued most of the country, he left command of the operation to his son Titus upon being hailed emperor by his army after the death of Nero and the subsequent instability in Rome. He marched off to Rome to take imperial power but first stopped over in Egypt to secure grain supplies

Figure 3.7
Looting of temple treasures. Carved relief showing the triumphal procession carrying looted treasure from the temple in Jerusalem in celebration of Titus's victory in the Jewish War of 66 to 73 CE. The relief depicts the table of the shew bread, the seven-branched candelabrum and the trumpets used for summoning the people carried away. The original is on the inside of the triumphal arch of Titus in the forum in Rome

men and children, suffered tremendously from famine and horrific atrocities perpetrated by both military sides. The temple was destroyed sometime in August 70 CE and the city was finally taken completely during September. Most of the survivors were sold as slaves, but Titus kept a large number to throw to the beasts in shows at Caesarea–Philippi and Berytus (Beirut). Some were also taken back to Rome to be exhibited in Titus's triumphal procession (a Roman way of honouring a successful military leader).

The war finally ended in 73 CE when Flavius Silva with the Tenth Legion took the only remaining fortress in rebel hands, namely Masada.

Despite the long and bloody conflict, Judaism remained a permitted religion, and there is no indication that Jewish worship was in any way infringed. However, one change came about: the former annual donation of all Jews to the Jerusalem temple, was now converted into a Jewish tax of two drachmas.

3.4 Judaea 70 to post-135 CE

The 66 to 70 CE war had several consequences. Vast tracts of Jewish land were expropriated and some were given to Roman war veterans as settlement so that Jews became tenants on the land which they had previously owned. Thousands of Jews died in the war and many more sold into slavery. The countryside was devastated.

However, Galilee and areas far removed from Jerusalem did not suffer that extensively and society recovered fairly quickly. As a whole, the country reverted to a subsistence economy which consisted chiefly of tenant farmers, hired labourers, crafts workers and small businesses.

From a religious perspective, however, there was definitely a major crisis. The Jerusalem temple, until this time the centre of Judaism, was in ruins. This led to deep soul-searching as to why God had allowed it to happen as well as to apocalyptic expectations that God would intervene to destroy the Romans and exalt the faithful Jews in the near future.

The destruction of the temple also had other consequences. Groups involved in the running of the temple worship, such as the priests and Sadducees, lost their position in society. The Jewish groups that survived and flourished were those who had assumed perspectives that allowed them to conceive and develop substitutes for the temple and its cult. These groups were Pharisees and the Christians. Christians had long substituted Christ for the temple and its sacrificial system.

Although Luke pictures the Jewish members of the Jesus movement as continuing to observe temple and ritual practice after the resurrection of Jesus (Acts 2:1; 21:17–26), he also preserves a tradition that rejects the temple completely (Acts 7:44–50).

The Pharisees too had a religious system capable of functioning without a physical temple. The first-century Pharisees can be described as a table fellowship movement, in which the home represented the temple; the hearth represented the altar, and the householder (the 'Pharisee' himself), the priest. A Pharisaic layman in his home was able to re-enact the temple cult symbolically. It is therefore hardly surprising that the Pharisees were an important factor in the post-70 CE reconstruction of Jewish society. Also, the situation placed the Pharisees and other groups in a favourable position in that the war had removed many rivals from the scene.

Parallel with the developing attitudes of acceptance and transformation, some Jews rejected the new situation. Jews participated in various revolts against the Romans, there were uprisings in Cyrene, Egypt and Cyprus, and unrest in Judaea. Apocalyptic and messianic fervour continued to boil among the Jews, and this led to one more attempt at establishing a messianic kingdom. The Jews of Palestine rose up, once again, in 132 to 135 BCE .

Figure 3.8
The ruins of the 'synagogue' at Gamla. Situated in the mountainous area north-east of the Sea of Galilee, Gamla was a Jewish fortress town taken by the Romans only after very fierce resistance during the Jewish War of 66 to 73 CE. As at Masada, many Jews preferred suicide by jumping off the steep cliffs rather than surrender. The identification of the building as a synagogue is by no means certain. Although the layout and floor plan resemble that of other synagogues, the absence of specific Jewish features in design or decoration warns against easy identification

This Second Revolt was dominated by one leader: Simon son of Kosiva who was given the title Bar Kokhba ('Son of the Star'). Bar Kokhba operated mainly in the area to the south of Jerusalem and west of the Dead Sea in what was a guerrilla war rather than pitched battles with the Romans. His men tunnelled hide-outs in mountainous and inaccessible places. These denlike dwellings dug into the rock, formed bases of operation and allowed the Jewish fighters to hide undetected, and to emerge when the opportunity presented itself for a swift blow at the enemy, and then to disappear once more.

The Roman reaction was severe. Bar Kokhba and his men made their last stand in the hilltop fortress of Betar, 10 km south-west of Jerusalem in 135 BCE. During the three years of the revolt, many thousands of Jews died in the fighting. Even more perished from famine and disease, and those who had escaped death were mostly enslaved. The

Second Revolt took an extreme toll on Jewish lives. After the defeat, the glut of slaves was so great that the price dropped drastically in the Eastern markets for almost a year. Roman casualties, too, were high. This was the last revolt: Jerusalem was made off-limits to Jews, and the official name of the province became 'Syria Palestina' instead of 'Judaea'. Aelia Capitolina became a reality, and for a long time Jews were officially excluded, even from entering the city. Only in the fourth century were Jews again formally allowed access to the temple site, and then only once a year on the ninth of Ab, the traditional date of its destruction.

3.5 Religion

Jews believed that they had a special relationship with God. This was confirmed by the circumcision of Jewish males. Certain practices also distinguished them from their neighbours: the refusal to eat particular foods, the observance of the Sabbath or other festivals and, perhaps, purity regulations.

In Palestine, worship and religion in the Land of Israel was dominated by the annual festival calendar and the pilgrimage to the temple in Jerusalem. That is, the central institution was the cult, which also represented a spiritual centre for Jews in the Diaspora.

The ideals important to practically every Jew (i e Jewish identity) were usually bound up with specific items: belief in one God, the concept of being part of the 'chosen people', the rejection of images in worship, the Torah (i e those traditions and interpretations of the Old Testament seen as important for religious identity and observance) and circumcision. Most of these characteristics are straightforward; they seem to have occured in almost all groups claiming to be Jewish, as far as can be determined; and Graeco-Roman writers often remark on them.

Though often seen as the most prominent identity marker, the Torah is, in fact, a problematic item, because evidence exists that different Jews had different ideas about what should be included in the concept (canon), about the interpretation of that which was included (exegesis) and about the relative importance of the accepted traditions (authority).

According to the Torah, each male Israelite was to 'appear before the Lord' three times during the year (Deut 16:16), that is, at Passover; Pentecost (Shavuot); and the festivals of the month of Tishri, namely the festival of Trumpets, the Day of Atonement (Am ha-Kippurim) and, especially, the Feast of Tabernacles (Sukkot). This was a time when vows would be made, sin and thanksgiving offerings would be brought to the altar, the regular sacrifices solemnly observed, and other ceremonies associated with the festival celebrated. This was not an optional extra or a side issue to being a Jew. For most Jews, this was the primary form of worship. There were additional aspects to being a Jew, including ethical and moral conduct, private devotions, and theological speculation, but participation in the temple cult was the *sine qua non* of service to God. This was how sins were forgiven and how one renewed one's relationship with God. This is what it meant to be a temple-centred religion. Yet, many Jews did not abide by the command to come to Jerusalem to worship three times a year (cf John 7:29) because of the interruption of work and loss of income it implied, the security risks involved and the expense of the visit. This fact did not preclude other aspects of worship and practice, such as private prayer, the public observance of the Sabbath and annual festivals in the local area.

Education, ideally, lay with the family and especially with the father. It was centred on family history and religious aspects. There was undoubtedly some instruction in the temple during the festivals because the cult would otherwise have been meaningless. The scribes – in rural areas the 'scribe' refers to the village clerk – may have been official communicants on religious law.

Even though most people were not members of a religious sect, a religious outlook was frequently influenced by teachers and groups who may not have had a large number of actual followers. People who were ill or 'had a demon' would seek out those whom they thought could help them, whether it was the priest in the temple, or a place reputed to have healing powers (cf John 5:2–7, text variant), or the travelling healer-cum-exorcist. There is evidence for the popularity of astrology among the Jews. The peripatetic preacher (one who travels around) – whether Pharisee, Essene, ascetic or mystic – could always draw a crowd. It was a diversion and one of the few forms of entertainment available. There were always a few curious persons in these crowds who would then experience enlightenment. These people might continue to follow the preacher when he moved on, perhaps abandoning their home and livelihood. Such periods of involvement were probably brief for all but the hard-core believers. However, usually a few individuals in any village would, nevertheless, become engaged in such discipleship, even if for a short time.

Thus the various teachers, preachers and sectarians made their mark on society, even though only a few had permanent followers or devotees. Jesus was only one of many; the difference was that his movement survived and grew. Popular religion in the form of veneration of holy sites, including the tombs of holy men, with pilgrimages made to them, was probably widespread in Palestine.

The average Jew was probably what the later rabbis referred to as an *am haaretz* (a 'countryman'). That is, they were men and women who were pious in their own way but whose main focus of attention was eking out an existence on the land. They could not afford the luxury of devoting a great portion of their time and energy to the insignificant details of religious observance which others of different persuasion and more strenuous commitment may have regarded as essential.

For some, poverty and intense devotion went hand in hand, and judging from the preserved literature, many Jews entertained an apocalyptic worldview with an expectation of a sudden appearance of a divine deliverer, punishment of the wicked, rewarding of the righteous, and a restoration of a new heaven and a new earth.

In Palestine many Jews had enough to contend with in their daily struggle to make a living, so that any involvement in apocalypticism was not their first concern, although it may have served as a diversion from a life of misery for some people. Outside Palestine there were Jews who saw their future life not in apocalyptic terms, but in personal salvation of the soul.

3.6 The temple and temple ideology

Jerusalem is a very old city which gained fame in the Roman Empire as a result of the 'development programme' of Herod the Great. As far as the population of Jerusalem is concerned, it would appear that about 30 000 people lived there. Jerusalem was really a temple city. The development, economy, importance and eventual destruction of ancient Jerusalem was closely allied to the city's religious role and, more specifically, to the temple that stood on the city's eastern hill.

The temple was the most impressive building in Jerusalem – in fact, the most impressive in all of Palestine. It stood on an enormous platform, the foundations of which were almost 2 km in circumference. The entire complex could accommodate 70 000 people during festivals. The massive platform, or temple square, was decorated with impressive colonnades.

One entered the temple area through the eastern entrance. The general rule was to keep to the right, therefore everybody moved in more or less the same direction and left the complex by the western gate. In this way, people who left the temple purified, did not have to bump into the still impure ones coming in. By walking up the steps, one arrived at the Court of the Gentiles. Here, and also between the colonnades, a number of activities took place. Profane money had to be exchanged for temple currency (at a price); financial transactions

Figure 3.9

The Western Wall ('Wailing Wall') of the temple in Jerusalem. The massive building works needed for the raised platform on which the temple was built can be seen clearly in the photograph. The golden dome of the Dome of the Rock is projecting just above the wall in the middle

were concluded (in the ancient world, temples also served as banks), and lectures and debates were presented. The Royal Porch (or colonnade) was about 20 m wide and 30 m high. The other porches were smaller. The temple proper – called the 'Holy' or 'Holy of Holies' – was a massive construction in its own right, about 45 m high (16 storeys!) and was decorated with gold and special wood carvings. In fact, according to Josephus, so much gold was used, that when the Romans destroyed the temple and sold the gold they had looted from it, the bullion market was overtraded for months and gold prices reached record lows.

However, the impact of the building was due to more than its imposing architecture. In Jewish mythology, the temple is a reflection of, but also the point of contact with, the supernatural world (Ezek; *I Enoch* 6–36; *Testament of Levi*; *Apocalypse of Abraham*). Worshipping inside the temple was seen as a duplicate of heavenly liturgy, and the architecture tries to copy the structure of heaven.

Figure 3.10
Model of the temple in Jerusalem showing the dividing wall (in front) with the cube-like structure of the Holy and the Holy of Holies rising at the back

Figure 3.11
Another view of the model of the temple in Jerusalem with the Antonia fortress in the middle immediately behind the temple. Colonnaded porches surround the temple

The acts performed by the priests represented the acts and attitudes of God himself. Because of this supposed link with the supernatural, the design of the temple, the liturgy and the priestly offices all contributed to creating sanctity (i e divinity).

The temple, being the most crucial Jewish institution in the period before 70 CE, could be said to be determinative of time and space for the Jews. The Temple Mount, Zion, was seen as the centre of the earth (*Jubilees* 8:19); the spot where creation began and where heaven and earth touched each other. Like ripples on a pond when a stone is cast in it, so does the world emanate from the Holy of Holies in the temple, according to the reasoning of ancient Jews.

> There are ten degrees of holiness. The land of Israel is holier than any other land ... The walled cities (of the land of Israel) are still more holy ... Within the wall (of Jerusalem) it is still more holy, for there only they may eat the lesser holy things ... The temple mount is still more holy ... The Rampart [the inner courts of the temple complex] is still more holy, for no Gentiles and none that have contracted uncleanness from a corpse may enter therein. The Court of the Women is still more holy ... The Court of the Israelites is still more holy, for none whose atonement is yet incomplete may enter therein ... The Court of the Priests is still more holy ... Between the Porch and the Altar is still more holy, for none that has a blemish or whose hair is unloosened may enter there. The sanctuary is still more holy, for none may enter therein with hands and feet unwashed. The Holy of Holies is still more holy, for none may enter therein save only the high priest on the Day of Atonement.
>
> (Mishnah, Kelim 1.6–9.)

In ancient Jewish times, the worth of all places was determined by the relationships they had with the temple. Holy places were regarded as special because in one way or another they had some connection to the temple; all places that did not have a link to the temple were unclean, unholy and profane. This logic was extended even to the cosmic order. Josephus writes that the temple furniture and even the high priest's apparel had to reflect and represent the universe (*Jewish Antiquities* 3.180–184).

The rules and regulations of the priests constituted an integral part of the functions of the temples, and thus contributed to the maintenance of the sacred as opposed to the profane. The priests and their activities distinguished and set apart that which was clean from that which was unclean; they held apart and indicated the life-giving powers and the forces of death. Those who lived in God's presence, and who honoured his laws and his institutions lived in sacred space. Those beyond this space were unclean and lived in areas that were crawling with demons.

The temple did not only determine the Jewish experience of geography, but also their view of status. The social implications of this can be seen from the temple architecture (*see* Figure 3.12). Non-Jews were limited to the outer Court of the Gentiles, the furthest away from the Altar. Inscriptions on a wall threatened Gentiles with execution if they were to transgress. Jewish women were allowed a little closer to the centre than Gentiles, but they were excluded from the Court of the Israelites. Ordinary Jewish men could not move across the Court of the Priests, which only the priests could cross; and only the high priest was allowed to enter the Holy of Holies, and even then only once a year. The sick, the deformed and the mutilated had to stay outside altogether; the mentally and physically handicapped too were ostracised. These limitations reveal the self-image and values of ancient Judaism.

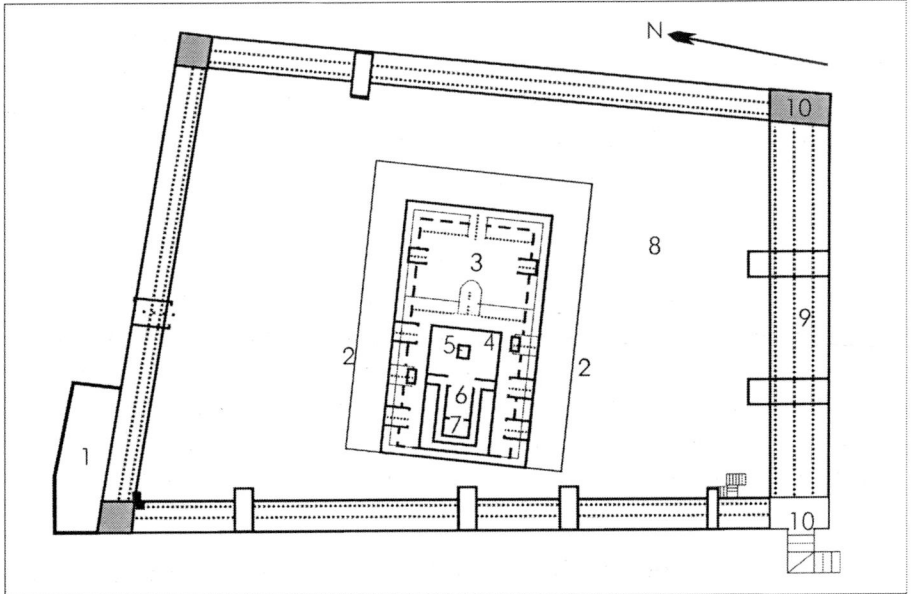

Figure 3.12
Reconstruction of the Jerusalem temple built by Herod the Great. (1) The Antonia fortress (2) The dividing wall separating the Court of Gentiles from the Court of the Women (3) Court of the Women (4) Court of the Priests (5) Altar (6) Holy (7) Holy of Holies (8) Court of the Gentiles (9) Royal portico (10) Stairs to the lower city

3.7 The Pharisees

In one's quest for historical understanding it is important to avoid anachronistic conceptions when it comes to the Pharisees. They were not a political leadership group (and *not* a political party), nor a learned scholarly group, nor a lay movement in competition with the priests.

The 'Pharisees' were a number of families who were loyal to one another and, in line with the social values of the time, sought to promote the influence of *their* families within Jewish society through politics and involvement in society. At times their membership was large, with many families claiming loyalty and joining the tradition; at other times only a few major families stuck together. Among the Pharisees were priests, artisans and poor workers. Sometimes even the high priest would be a Pharisee – if, owing to a number of factors, things went their way. Generally speaking, they rarely had direct power during the 150 years or so since the time of the Syrian overlordship. On the whole, only a few were or became members of the governing class.

It is extremely difficult to reconstruct the history and teachings of the Pharisees. Basically, four sets of evidence exist: (1) Josephus, (2) the New Testament writings, (3) rabbinic literature and (4) the Qumran documents. However, these writings depict the Pharisees not only differently, but often in conflicting terms. None of the available sources are interested in a neutral or impartial presentation; they all use the Pharisee traditions to further their own ends. Furthermore, because the Pharisees, Sadducees and scribes are depicted in the New Testament as the opponents of Jesus, the importance and roles of these groups in Jewish society are often vastly overemphasised by Christian scholars.

Furthermore, the 'teachings' of the Pharisees changed according to developments. The social, political and economic standing of Palestinian Jews underwent a number of upheavals in the Graeco-Roman period, which demanded adaptation of Jewish customs and a reinterpretation of the Jewish identity fashioned by the biblical tradition. Like most other groups in the Jewish world, the Pharisees strove to do this.

According to Josephus, the Pharisees affirmed the influence of divine activity on human life, the interrelatedness of human freedom and fate, and reward and punishment in the afterlife. The New Testament depicts the Pharisees as having unique interpretations on tithing, purity and the Sabbath. A clear picture emerges of how the Pharisees sought to promote their way of observance and defend their validity against the challenge of other groups, such as the priests, the Essenes and the Jesus movement. The purity rules, which seem mysterious to modern Westerners, regularised life, and separated the persons and objects making up the world into 'normal' and 'life-giving' parts, and 'abnormal' and ambiguous, hence 'life-threatening' parts. In contrast to humanists and evolutionists who believe that the order of the cosmos is a natural phenomenon, the underlying idea of a purity religion such as that of the Pharisees is that select humans have received a 'key' to enforce order onto the natural world.

Paul is the only first-century author claiming to be a Pharisee whose writings exist (cf Phil 3:5), that is, besides Josephus. However his claim of allegiance to Pharisaism is highly problematic. Paul's description of his way of life as a Pharisee is very brief. Like Josephus, Paul says that the Pharisees had a distinct interpretation of the Torah, though neither says what it is. Although both Paul and Josephus say that they were once Pharisees, they never again refer to Pharisaism as part of their identities.

After the war, a number of Pharisees became very prominent in the rebuilding of Judaism. These Pharisees became rabbis (teachers) to the Jews seeking understanding after the disasters of the wars. These teachers with a Pharisaic background, though probably originally only a handful, reinterpreted, adapted, changed and developed their traditions for a new situation in a highly successful manner. Eventually, a century later, this adapted and developed form of living the Jewish life, namely rabbinic Judaism, would be dominant. The rabbis of the late second and third centuries sought to show how the first-century Pharisees were their spiritual forebears.

The Gospels were written during the last couple of decades of the first century. Interestingly, their depictions of the Pharisees differ from one another. In the main, it could be said that the construction of the Pharisees in the Gospels reflects the conflicts and polemics of the Jewish and Christian communities of the late first century CE. The Pharisees are mostly portrayed as a single group of opponents to the Jesus movement and as leaders of the opposition to Jesus. Luke's picture is a bit more complex, since he portrays Pharisaism and the teachings of Jesus as being compatible.

3.8 The Sadducees

The Sadducees were a group of families who shared similarities and owed one another primary loyalty. They were, however, politically speaking, rather more successful than the Pharisees during pre-70 CE times.

The earliest references to the Sadducees in Josephus show them in rivalry with the Pharisees at the court of John Hyrcanus, the Hasmonean king (135–

104 BCE). Initially, the king accepted Pharisaic counsel, but after some impudent criticism by a Pharisee named Eleazar, Hyrcanus became patron to the Sadducees. Although probably a smaller group than the Pharisees, they remained very influential in Judaean politics.

Sources tend to characterise the Sadducees in terms of particular religious positions, but these presentations are made up rather miscellaneously and also disagree with one another. Sources do not offer proper data to build up a coherent set of beliefs held by the Sadducees. What seems fairly certain, however, is some sort of connection between the Sadducees and the priestly establishment.

Their religious convictions tended to be conservative, even rejecting the afterlife as 'it is unworthy that God should be worshipped under the promise of a reward' (cf *Pseudo-Clementine Recognitions* 1.54).

The Sadducees were politically very active. Often the high priest came from among one of the families supporting the Sadducean way of being Jewish. From Josephus (and Acts 5) one can deduce that the Sadducees were among the upper socio-economic class – something that is compatible with an association with the priestly establishment and membership of the Sanhedrin – but not all Sadducees were priests or even wealthy, and not all priests or upper-class individuals were Sadducees.

Sadducees shared the essential points of 'common' Jewish theology, namely that God had chosen Israel and Israelites were to obey the law. They were expected to love God, thank him for his blessings and treat other people decently, as the law required. Generally, like most Pharisees, they were simply good Jews.

Most scholars believe that, after the first war with the Romans and the destruction of the temple, the influence of the Sadducees declined sharply (most of them were probably killed during the war).

3.9 Messiahs, prophets and teachers

There were many different teachers, 'sects,' movements and tendencies within Jewish society. Some sought a public means of propagating their message and attracting followers. Others withdrew and lived apart from general society. Still others lived within society, but primarily in enclaves, thus maintaining separateness while not withdrawing altogether. Some teachers remained primarily lone individuals, whereas others built a following which eventually formed a sect or movement. Like the rest of the Graeco-Roman world,

Palestine was in a constant state of flux: teachers rose up and disappeared; sects began, flourished, withered and died; small beginnings led to large followings, or to nothing. Single men and entire groups came and went without leaving a mark in history.

Numerous prophets or teachers started a movement or 'school'. Some movements were peaceful, others revolutionary, still others potentially revolutionary. Those that caught the attention of the Romans were scrutinised with suspicion. The slightest hint of sedition could lead to a severe crackdown. The advantage of forming a school was that it gave autonomy. A school could regulate its own affairs according to its regulations: matters of internal regulation, *halakah*, initiation and excommunication were the hallmarks of a sectarian movement. If Essenes wanted to accept members only after a three-year initiation period or expel members for apparently small infractions, then that was their business. A Pharisee could pronounce anathema on ex-Pharisees, but it would mean something only to other Pharisees and perhaps not even to all of them. An example of an alleged religious attempt to suppress dissidents required the authority of the high priest (and, by implication, the Sanhedrin), not Pharisees or other sectarians (Acts 9:1–2). Even this attempt is suspect because the high priest of Jerusalem would have no powers to authorise the arrest of citizens of Damascus, which was not even under Judaean jurisdiction. The one New Testament account of excommunication from the synagogues is equally unlikely (John 9).

The Pharisees were probably the largest single group and were evidently influential, when their size is taken into account. Yet there were only six thousand of them at the time of Herod, hardly an overwhelming percentage of the population. Then again, how does one measure influence?

Rabbinic literature puts special emphasis on the influence of two rabbis, namely Hillel and Shammai and their disciples (called the *Houses of Hillel* or *Shammai* in rabbinic literature), during the period before 70 CE. Most Pharisees must have belonged to one or the other. There is also an indication that a considerable portion of the Houses of Hillel and Shammai could all meet in one reasonably sized room; suggesting that they numbered in the dozens, not in the hundreds or thousands.

Therefore, it is historically sound to assume the existence of a variety of Pharisaic teachers, each with his own band of disciples, rather than a tightly knit organisation or authoritarian hierarchy. In fact, in all probability, Hillel and Shammai were not very important in their own time. They dominated the tradition only because their houses happened to have become dominant at Yavneh, with the House of Hillel eventually winning out.

A more influential group of teachers were itinerant philosophers, individual teachers, miracle-workers and prophets.

Several prophets succeeded in acquiring a large following for a short time, but because large followings equalled sedition to the Roman armed forces, generally the larger the following the shorter its lifespan. The Romans did not conduct precise inquiries into whether or not some of the prophets known today were genuinely attempting to start a revolt. They quickly executed the shepherd and scattered the flock in most cases. Theudas, an alleged miracle-worker, gathered a group which he promised to take across the Jordan River dry-shod; his miraculous powers were never tested (or perhaps they were) because Fadus's soldiers intervened (Acts 5:36; cf Josephus, *Jewish Antiquities*. 20.5.1). Sources refer to a number of other prophets and popular leaders for the last decade or so before the revolt, such as an Egyptian Jew who evidently intended to take direct action against the Romans, again without success (Josephus, *Jewish War* 2.13.4–6; *Jewish Antiquities* 20.8.6; Acts 21:38).

Josephus mentions individual teachers a number of times. For example, there was an Onias noted for his ability to make rain at the time that the Romans extended their hegemony over Palestine. Another, named Judas, was known as a prophet during the reign of Aristobulus I. Judas was an Essene, and other individual Essenes were known for their ability to predict the future, such as Manaemus and Simon. The two individuals, Judas and Matthias, who showed their zeal for God by removing the eagle that Herod had erected, apparently had some disciples, although one is not told precisely how many, but the figure '40' in the narrative may indicate dozens, even if it is only a round figure.

Although the data is skimpy, there are tantalising hints of the existence of other spiritual trends and groups. John the Baptist was not an isolated individual, as the Gospels might imply, but only one of a number of baptismal movements that connected physical washing of one sort or another to spiritual purity and salvation. There is some evidence that the Jordan Valley, with its readily available supply of running water, was the home of several such groups, and one of these is thought by many still to exist in the small sect of the Mandaeans. The issue of origin and history is a complicated one, as are others concerning Jewish Gnosticism and mysticism. Mystical trends are found early in apocalyptic writings, with their speculations on the mysteries of the heavens and God's universal plan for the earth. It is only a matter of emphasis. Some apocalypses focus on the culmination of world history and the events of the end-time, but others, similar to later Merkavah mysticism, seem to concentrate more on the geography of the heavens and the vision of God's throne. For one who can gain direct access to the divine vision, issues of eschatology might seem somewhat unimportant.

Gnosticism is usually interpreted as being anti-Old Testament and, consequently, anti-Jewish. This assessment may be correct of Gnosticism in its developed form, but still does not answer the question of whether Gnosticism may have had a home in Judaism. The tendency of 'two powers in heaven' is strong in the wisdom tradition, with its speculation about Wisdom (*Sophia*) and Word (*Logos*). Philo, the Wisdom of Solomon, and even such earlier writings such as Proverbs 8 can be used to argue that particular developed features of Gnosticism were known in incipient form in Judaism. There is almost universal agreement that a number of features of the gnostic mythology have come from Judaism by some path or other, even though there was never anything which could be labelled *Jewish Gnosticism*. Nevertheless, a number of scholars have long argued that Gnosticism grew out of 'heterodox' Judaism.

3.10 Essenes

The Essenes were not much smaller in number than the Pharisees, numbering four thousand at the time of Herod, according to Josephus and Philo. If one accepts the consensus that Qumran was an Essene community, one might think it likely that the site also served as the organisational and spiritual centre of the movement. It is also possible, however, to see Qumran as a split from, or breakaway movement within, Essenism. Qumran could by no means accommodate several thousand adherents as permanent residents. Rather, the bulk of the Essenes lived all over Palestine in local towns and villages, according to both Josephus and Philo.

The Essenes were evidently one of the groups that lived in society for the most part, but were not of it. Even in the local communities they apparently had their own enclaves or communes, organised along community-orientated lines. They would work in the community but put their earnings in the common fund. There may have been periodic pilgrimages to Qumran for festivals, but the relationship of the Qumran community with the rest of the Essene movement is by no means established. Although, from extant knowledge, the beliefs and organisation of the order appear to be fairly rigid. One cannot talk of absolute unity, but should consider some differences within the movement and perhaps even subsects. It is possible that the group described and named by Philo as the Therapeutae represent a local Essene group in Egypt. There were also Essenes who were apparently known to the public, such as Judas, who had a reputation for prophesying, and John, who was one of the military leaders in the war against Rome. Therefore, the

Essenes, despite an exclusivistic approach to religion, were apparently well known to the wider community and were not an unknown fringe group as they are sometimes pictured.

QUMRAN

Qumran is the Judaean wilderness site associated with the discovery of the Dead Sea Scrolls. The site is located on the north-western shores of the Dead Sea and is south of Jericho. A very small settlement existed there since the monarchical period. The main occupation at Qumran began sometime during the reigns of the Hasmonean kings Jonathan Maccabaeus (152–142 BCE) and Simeon Maccabaeus (142–134 BCE). The new occupants reused an older cistern and dug two more nearby.

During the reign of John Hyrcanus I (134–104 BCE), Qumran assumed the complete form familiar to tourists today. The buildings were greatly enlarged and a massive main building with a tower was constructed, and a central courtyard, a meeting room and a dining hall with connected pantry were built. On the west side a potter's shop housing two kilns, and areas for preparing clay and manufacturing pots was constructed. To the west, a second courtyard building was constructed with storage rooms around it. Cisterns and workshops stood between the west building and the main building. North-west of the tower was a large courtyard with a pool in its north-western corner (some scholars maintain that this pool was a ritual bath). Among the ruins, archaeologists recovered caches of uneaten meals of sheep, goat, calf, or cow in the form of bones, as well as broken dishes. No provision was made for living inside the buildings. An elaborate water system brought water in from the Wadi Qumran, which lies to the west of the buildings, in an aqueduct resting directly upon the ground. The aqueduct fed the complex of eight cisterns and ritual baths for which Qumran is famous.

This era of occupation (called phase 1) ended with an earthquake in 31 BCE. The earthquake damaged the tower and brought down the ceiling of the pantry onto the assembled dishes, smashing them. The western cistern collapsed, and damaged the corner of the second building. An associated conflagration burnt extensively and left thick layers of ash and burnt soil in open areas near the buildings. Consequently, the ruin was left abandoned for a period.

With the accession of Herod Archaelaus as tetrarch of Judaea in 4 BCE, the site was reoccupied (the so-called phase 2). The walls were strengthened where they had been damaged, and the tower was reinforced with a buttress around its lower story. A few rooms went out of use, but on the whole, the occupation continued along the lines of earlier usage. The potter continued manufacturing pottery at the site. There was a kitchen with five ovens, a flourmill and a baker's establishment. In the remains from the upper storey of one of the rooms of this phase, archaeologists found a long table with very low

Figure 3.13
View of the Qumran caves. Note their inaccessible location high up on the cliff faces

Figure 3.14
Close-up of the famous Cave 4 at Qumran

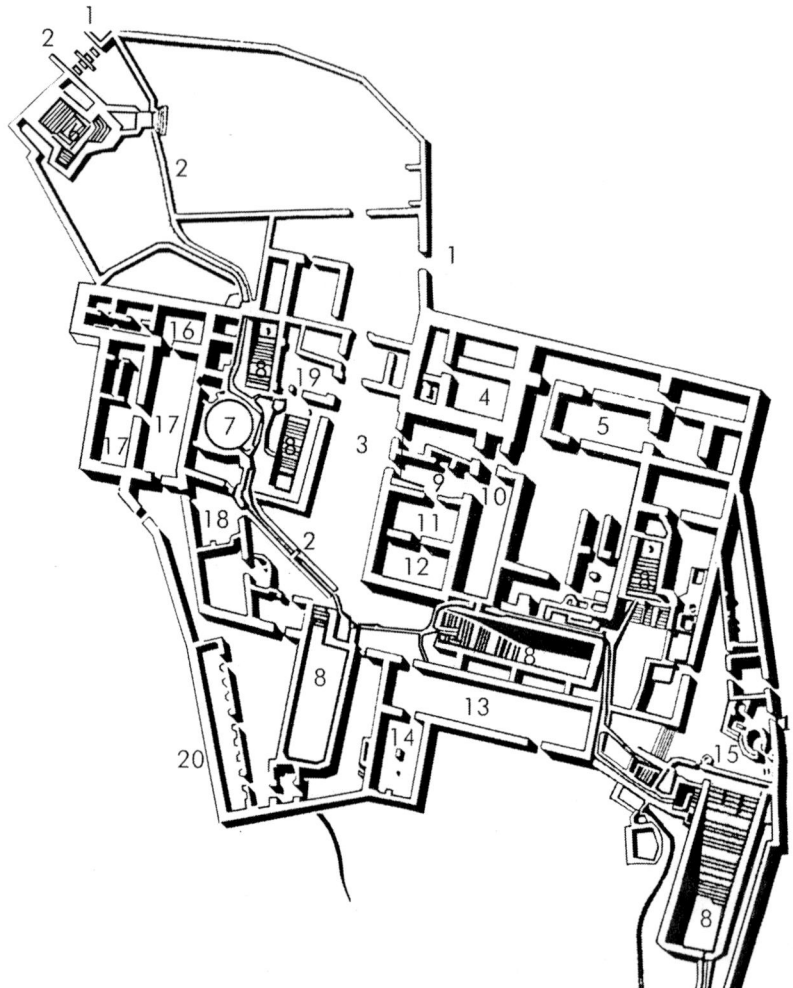

Figure 3.15
Layout of the Qumran complex: (1) gates (2) water channel (3) courtyard (4) tower (5) kitchen (6) baptistry (7) big round water cistern (8) water cisterns or *mikvehs* (9) foyer (10) *scriptorium* (11) council chamber and reading room (12) library (13) assembly and dining hall (refectory) (14) potter workshop (16) trading room (17) storerooms (18) washing room or tannery (19) workshop and (20) stable

benches, two shorter tables with concave surfaces and two inkwells. Some archaeologists dubbed this room, quite inappropriately, the *scriptorium*, or *scribal space*.

This second period of occupation is of interest as it is often assumed that the occupants can be identified with the Essenes mentioned in Josephus and in other ancient sources. The assumption is that this was a mainly celibate sect of Jewish men who attempted to live ritually pure (hence the many supposed ritual baths) and pious lives apart from other Jews (hence a building in the desert).

It is not conclusively known who lived at this site, nor what their religious convictions were.

The cemetery (about 50 m to the east) contains 1 100 graves, all orientated north to south. A small number of graves were opened and the remains (including at least one woman) were studied. The average age of death was about 30 years, typical of the lifespan in antiquity. If about a thousand people died during a century and a half it means that Qumran was occupied by a group of, generally speaking, 48 people (about 6 persons a year were buried there assuming a person stayed there for at least 8 years). The statistic of about 48 occupants is confirmed by the physical size of the buildings.

A small settlement exactly parallel to Qumran was found at Ein Feshkah, a few kilometres south of Qumran. This ruin had been occupied in exactly the same periods as Qumran and presumably by the same people.

Qumran phase 2 was destroyed in June of 68 CE by the Roman army under Vespasian. The Romans occupied Jericho at this time, two years into the First Revolt against Rome.

The final phase of Qumran is the period during which a small Roman garrison occupied the site. During this occupation, the soldiers built rooms here and there from the actual debris of the site, on top of the rubble of the destruction they had wreaked. The soldiers used only one cistern, filling the others with rubble. The garrison was withdrawn after the fall of Masada in 73 CE. A few rebels involved in the Bar Kokhba revolt of 135 CE camped at the site but did not construct any permanent structures.

The Dead Sea Caves refer specifically to 11 caves near Qumran. Qumran Cave 1 (designated *1Q* in the standard terminology) was a simple cleft or crevice in the cliff high above the plateau of the ruins of Qumran, about one kilometre north of Qumran. This cave contained a large quantity of scrolls which were removed by their Bedouin discoverers. Other finds included many scraps of linen cloth, fragments of a wooden comb, olive and date stones, palm fibre, phylacteries and quantities of pottery sherds. The pottery turned out to be jars made at Qumran, bowls, pots and lamps corresponding with the occupation of Qumran.

Ten other caves yielded finds. Today there are only traces of some of them (7Q, 8Q, 9Q, 10Q) due to erosion and earth slides. Cave 4 yielded the largest collection of manuscripts – literally thousands of fragments. About five hundred titles have been identified from among this recovery.

It was common practice for Jewish people of antiquity to hide precious possessions in caves during times of duress. In a large, three-chambered cave in wadi Nahal Hever, about four-and-a-half kilometres south of En Gedi, skeletons and artefacts were found. Among them were letters sent by Bar Kokhba (the leader of the rebelling Jews, 132–135 CE) and the Babatha papyri. During the rebellion, Babatha left her cache of documents in a 'safe' hiding place to be retrieved at a later, happier time. She obviously did not live to see that time.

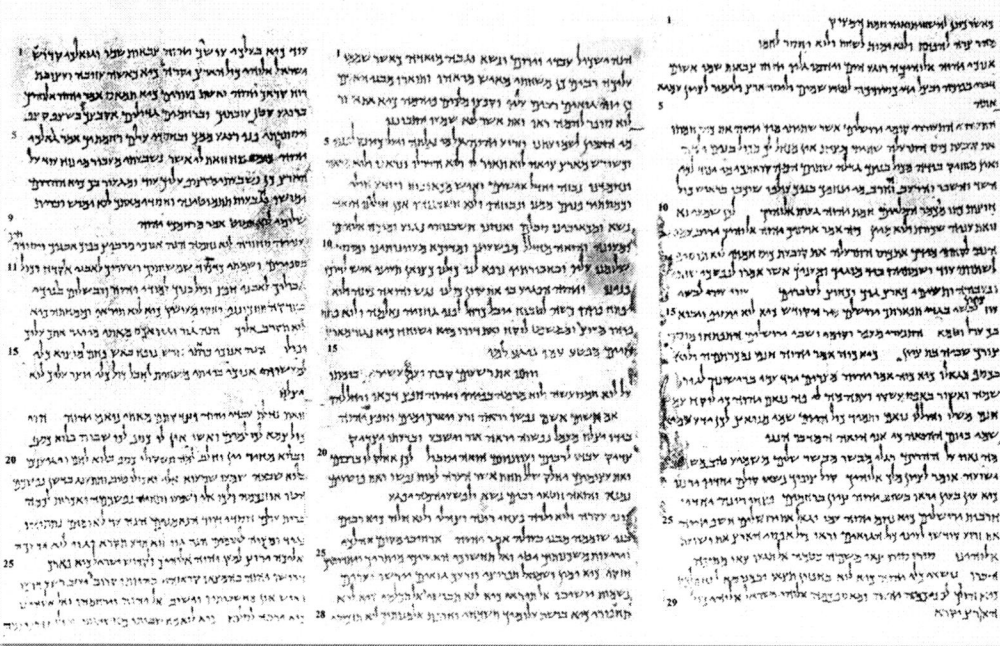

Figure 3.16
The Isaiah Scroll from Qumran. This is the most complete of the biblical manuscripts found among the Qumran scrolls. The scroll is open at Isaiah 53. Copies of all the biblical books (of the Old Testament) were found at Qumran except for the book of Esther. The Qumran finds also included many other non-biblical literature, such as apocalypses and pseud-epigrapha, commentaries on Old Testament books, hymns and other sectarian literature

There were 35 documents that belonged to Babatha dating from 93/94 to 132 CE. She and her family lived in the village of Maoza on the southern shore of the Dead Sea.

In a cave in another section of the Judaean desert, namely Wadi Marabbaat, documents from both the period before the First Revolt and the time of Bar Kokhba have been found.

The Dead Sea Scrolls is thus the name given to the deposits of ancient texts found in the Dead Sea caves along the western shore of the Dead Sea. These texts were written in Hebrew, Aramaic and Greek. The Dead Sea Scrolls are, without doubt, the most famous archaeological discovery of the twentieth century and are also one of the most important finds relating to biblical studies in the modern period.

The discovery of the scrolls began in 1947, when a Taamireh bedouin shepherd, tending his flock near the shores of the Dead Sea near the Wadi Qumran, discovered several old leather scrolls wrapped in linen and stored in jars in a cave (1Q). The largest cache of manuscripts, in 4Q, was discovered in 1952. The final cave, 11Q, was discovered in 1956.

The Dead Sea Scrolls are considered by many scholars to be the library of a Jewish community; the same one that inhabited the settlement at Qumran from the mid-second century BCE, until its destruction by the Romans in 68 CE. The scrolls can be dated palaeographically (i e, according to the characteristics of the handwriting) from the middle of the third century BCE to the middle of the first century CE, overlapping with the dates of the Qumran settlement.

For modern readers these scrolls can be divided into three categories: (1) biblical texts, (2) previously known non-biblical texts and (3) not previously known non-biblical texts (these categories were *not* used by the ancients themselves). Fragments of every book of the Hebrew Bible were found, with the exception of the book of Esther. From the manuscripts found in the caves one can deduce that the five books of the Pentateuch were considered authoritative. The Prophets must also have been considered authoritative; several commentaries on their books were found (Isaiah, Nahum, Habakkuk, Micah and Zephaniah) as well as one on the Psalms. Many of the biblical books are cited in the Qumran documents with the formulas 'it is written' or 'it is said', indicating authority. However, other books, such as *Jubilees*, are cited as authoritative in the Qumran documents, indicating a larger canon. Some texts, such as Enoch, appear in multiple copies, indicating at least a great deal of interest in, and study of, this strange book. Books such as Chronicles and Song of Solomon do not seem to have played much of a role in the sect's ideology at all.

In a subcategory of the biblical material are those texts that rewrite, comment on, or otherwise use, the canonical Bible. The genre 'rewritten Bible' occurs most frequently in the Pentateuch, in compositions such as the *Genesis Apocryphon*, an Aramaic expansion of the Abraham story in the Book of Genesis; the *Book of Jubilees*, a retelling of Genesis 1 to Exodus 15:22; the *Temple Scroll*, a representation of the Torah purportedly given by God speaking in the first person, and 4Q *Reworked Pentateuch*, a complete pentateuchal text with additions and rearrangements of material. It is difficult to ascertain when and by whom these texts were composed; there is nothing overtly sectarian about them, but many of their ideas reappear in compositions labelled *sectarian*.

A particular form of biblical interpretation, the pesher, is found among these scrolls. A pesher takes the following form: citation of a biblical verse, followed by some form of the word *pesher* (= its interpretation is), finishing with an interpretation involving characters or events associated with the community supposed to be the audience of the interpretation. A pesher can be a whole commentary on a biblical book (continuous pesher), for example, the *Habakkuk Commentary* or the *Nahum Commentary*; or a collection of biblical texts gathered around a common theme (thematic pesher), for example, the *Florilegium* or the

Pesher on Melchizedek; or an isolated interpretation of a biblical verse within a larger composition (isolated pesharim), for example, the pesher on Amos 5:26 to 27 in the *Damascus Document*. These texts are replete with sectarian ideas and language.

A final group of texts closely related to the biblical texts might be labelled *biblical paraphrases*, since they are related to a particular biblical book: examples are the *Prayer of Nabonidus*, related to the *Book of Daniel*; *4Q Pseudo Ezekiel*, related to the Book of Ezekiel; and *4Q Proto Esther*, which may be an Aramaic precursor to the canonical Book of Esther.

Rulebooks grew out of the Qumran community's interest in the biblical text and its interpretation were found among the scrolls. These include rulings relating to the calendar, ritual purity and laws on marital status, which are all stated as the reasons for the sect's separation from the rest of Judaism. The *Damascus Document* and the *Community Rule* are the two major rulebooks found among the scrolls.

The *Damascus Document* was known before the discovery of the scrolls, having been found in the Cairo Geniza (a *geniza* is a buried, used Jewish library) in the late nineteenth century. The *Damascus Document* is aimed at a sectarian group of Jews, probably the Essenes, who lived in camps in the towns and villages of Judaea. It has two parts: an 'admonition', which outlines the history of the sect in figurative language and discusses the nature of membership in the group; and the 'laws', which give the specific sectarian rules. These rules are severe, involving a strict interpretation of Jewish customs, designed to enforce a drastic separation from 'the sons of the Pit' (= all other Jews and Gentiles).

The *Community Rule*, however, is a rulebook for the life of the community. It presupposes a fairly large, isolated community, sharing meals, pooling their property, and governing themselves under the leadership of priests and certain lay officials.

Many liturgical works exist among the Dead Sea Scrolls, some sectarian. The *Psalms Scroll* from 11Q contains most of the last third of the biblical Psalter, but in a different order, plus several non-canonical Psalms, all of which are attributed to David. Some liturgical works are a collection of non-canonical Psalms (4Q380–381) and the *Words of the Heavenly Lights*, a prayer for deliverance based on the covenant relationship. Other liturgical compositions are very sectarian in nature, using language of community and separation, dualism and covenant, in addition to embracing a strict lifestyle of purity. The best known of these is the *Hodayot* (copies were found in 1 and 4Q). The majority of these hymns begin with the formula 'I give thanks to thee, O Lord', and continue with thanks for deliverance from sin and for knowledge of the way of the sect.

Many of the works from the Qumran library have strong eschatological overtones. It is clear that the sect believed itself to be living at the end of days and, further, believed itself to be at the centre of events leading up to the end. This eschatological orientation is most strikingly illustrated by the *War Scroll*, a composition that relates the events to take place in the final battle between the armies of God, which include members of the sect who called themselves the 'Sons of Light', and the armies of Belial, including the 'Sons of Darkness' (i e all those outside the sect). The *War Scroll* envisions a conflict in which the forces of Light and Darkness alternately prevail, with the final victory being wrought by God.

The Qumran 'library' is not merely a collection of miscellaneous religious texts; it is a fairly coherent collection of documents with common themes: a devotion to the biblical text supported by interpretations and readings of related texts, a strict interpretation of the law leading to a separation from the rest of Judaism (bolstered by a strong dualism and sense of predestination), and a strong eschatological hope in which their cause would be vindicated by God.

Community Rule [1QS III.18 IV,20]
These are the spirits of Truth and Deceit [or: the Lie]. Truth originates from the Light and Deceit wells up from the fountain of Darkness. The rule over all Sons of Justice lies in the hand of the Prince of Light, and they walk in the ways of the Light. The rule over the Sons of Deceit lies, however, in the hand of the Angel of Darkness, and they walk in the ways of Darkness. The Sons of Justice are deceived by the Angel of Darkness and all their sins, transgressions and guilt as well as the ... of their deeds are caused by his rule in accordance with the mysteries of God until his moment; and all their punishments and set periods of grief come through the rule of his enmity. All the spirits of his lot seek to bring the ons of the Light to a fall. But the God of Israel and the Angel of his Truth help all Sons of the Light ... and these are their ways in the world: to enlighten the human heart and to level the paths of true justice before him and to establish in him respect for the precepts of God, as well as a spirit of humility and patience, generous compassion, eternal goodness, understanding and insight, and mighty wisdom that puts its trust in all the works of God and that depends on his abundant grace, and a spirit of knowledge of all the plans of his works, an enthusiasm for the just precepts and a holy commitment to strive earnestly and to love all Sons of the Truth and to a magnificent purity that abhors all impure idols, and walks humbly in understanding all things and stays silent on the truth of the mysteries of knowledge. These are the councils of the spirit for the Sons of the Truth in the world ... But to the Spirit of Deceit belongs greed and slowness to act in the service of justice, evil and lie, pride and haughtiness of heart, deception and trickery, cruelty and gross impiety, impatience and utter foolishness, proud envy, outrageous deeds performed in a whoring spirit, filthy acts in service of impurity, a libellous tongue, blindness of eyes and deafness of ears, stiffness of neck and hardness of heart, to walk in all the paths of Darkness and evil cunning ... In both these spirits lie the origins of all humankind.

Qumran documents provide insight into a mindset/belief system shared by many of Jesus's contemporaries

Jesus's views of temple life (spiritual offerings and sacrifices) corresponds closely with the following (Mark 12.2834; Matt 12.67):

> 1QS 8.18 [= *Community Rule*]
> [T]he Council of the Community [the representatives of the 'true' faithful among Israel] shall be versed in all that is revealed of the Law, and their works shall be truth, righteousness, justice, loving kindness and humility. . .
> When these are among Israel, the Council of the Community shall be established in truth as an everlasting planting, a house of holiness for Israel, a company of supreme holiness for Aaron. The Council shall be that tried wall, that precious cornerstone, whose foundations shall neither rock nor sway in their place.
> . . . [The Council] . . . shall be a most holy dwelling for Aaron, with everlasting knowledge of the covenant of justice, and shall offer up sweet fragrance. It shall be a house of perfection and truth in Israel that they may establish a covenant according to the everlasting precepts. And they shall be an acceptable offering, atoning for the land.
>
> [and Mark 14:58]:
> 4QFlor 1.27 [= *Florilegium*, 4Q174]
> This is the House which [will be built at the. . .] in the last days, as it is written in the book of [Moses]: A temple of the Lord will you establish with your works.
> It is the House into which will enter [neither the ungodly nor the defiled], ever . . . but they that are called the holy ones.
> Yahweh will reign there forever; He will appear above it constantly, and strangers will lay it waste no more as they formerly laid waste the temple of Israel because of their sin. And He has instructed a temple made by human hands, that there they may send up, like the smoke of incense, the works of the Law.

3.11 Radicals

The 'movement' founded by Judas the Galilean (Josephus's *Fourth Philosophy*) may not have been a movement as such but a sort of family tradition. If it were a movement, it seems not to have been particularly active for the first half-century CE. In about 50 CE, however, a terrorist organisation (or, more likely, a number of 'organisations') sprang to life to fight against Roman rule by targeting 'collaborator' Jews of the ruling class, who were seen as the most compromised in doing the Romans' bidding. These Sicarii (as they came to be called after the name of a type of dagger) originated with Judas the Galilean, according to Josephus, but he is clearly guessing on this account. In any case, the Sicarii continued their activities until the actual revolt was under way but then withdrew from the fighting after the assassination of their leader in Jerusalem. Although Josephus gives little direct information, he hints that they were inspired by messianic and perhaps even eschatological beliefs. The Jerusalem leader Menahem, who played an important role during the war, seems to have declared himself king or was building up to the point of doing so when he and many followers were killed by the Zealots.

The name *Zealots* is often used to denote any anti-Roman group from the time of the Maccabees. From a historical point of view, however, the Zealots were a group that originated around 68 CE from the coalescense of several 'bandit' groups into a popular revolt in the path of the invading Roman army. Social banditry was a frequent response to the socio-economic stresses and oppressions of the time, as it is in many societies of various periods.

Evidence exists of the appearance of bandit groups in the early Roman period and in the two decades before the First Revolt. Social banditry is usually just an attempt to survive in difficult circumstances and does not necessarily imply any intent to start a widespread revolt. Serious revolt does occasionally develop when conditions become oppressive enough and large numbers support the leaders. Social banditry reached such proportions that the Roman invasion acted as the catalyst for a popular revolt which, in turn, served to bring the Zealots into being. They were evidently inspired by popular eschatological views, which kept them going in the face of the imminent Roman victory. Even as the Roman armies were breaking down the last defences, six thousand people poured into the temple court to await God's deliverance (Josephus, *Jewish War* 6.5.2).

3.12   Eschatology

Eschatological (end-time) expectations played an important role in the lives of many Jews, as much as it did not in the lives of many other Jews. Beliefs in this area were as complex and diverse as in any other aspect of Judaism at this time. Not all Jews expected a messiah, not all Jews looked forward to an eschatological event and not all those Jews who entertained both ideas allowed them to affect their lives in any way.

The messianic idea probably owes its origins to the monarchy of ancient Israel. As particular Israelites despaired of the current king or, after 587/586 BCE, the lack of a king, hope began to be placed in a future, idealised figure modelled on David (whose picture in Samuel and Kings is also idealised). However, the form these expectations and speculations took was by no means uniform. Many looked forward to a human king, certainly a larger-than-life king, but a human figure, nevertheless (*Pss Sol* 2, 17–18). The majority of those who expected a messiah probably thought along these lines. There were others who seemed to have thought of a heavenly figure (*1 Enoch*; perhaps *4 Ezra* 13). Alongside this diversity within messianic speculation was a similar assortment of views on eschatology. Some Jews, in line with much of the Old Testament, saw death as the end of the individual. Others believed in a resurrection of the body, the spirit, or perhaps both. This could be combined with a cosmic eschatology, in which the world came to a catastrophic end or gradually slipped over into the 'Messianic Age' with a minimum of trauma.

At the time, there was no consistent idea of eschatology or messianism. Both concepts could be powerful ideological forces at times, as has already been noted in several of the groups surveyed. Each case, however, must be critically examined on its own merits. There was no 'Jewish view' on any of these subjects, although there were plenty of Jews with views.

What is of real importance is not so much the different individual beliefs about eschatology, but the consequences of such beliefs. To what kinds of actions do these beliefs lead? Here, as in other things human, there is not an easy one-to-one relation between ideology and action. One's actions are not always motivated by religious ideology. Through simplification one can identify three potential outcomes of eschatological beliefs.

(1) *Quietism*. If one believed in an eschatology in which everything was done by God, one might well do nothing overtly – and this may hold true even if one had no belief in eschatology. Such individuals did see themselves as being very busy in the service of the Lord: prayer, temple worship, service to others and good deeds of all sorts. In some cases this might even lead to submission to torture; the individual being convinced that the shedding of innocent blood was another way of acknowledging God's almighty decisions. Those who entertained this perspective, saw such innocent suffering as possibly the catalyst for God to take a direct hand in human affairs. The outward activity for such people was basically no different from that of people with no belief in eschatology. The majority of Jews generally fell into this grouping.

Others felt much more passionately, but saw the human role as being more passive: prayer, obedience and patient waiting for God to fulfil his will – even the shedding of one's own blood in martyrdom. God would do what needed to be done; it was not up to humans to take matters into their own hands. They had a part to play, but their part was waiting on the Lord. They could also calculate and speculate, and these calculations and speculations fill many extant apocalypses.

(2) *Peaceful political activity*. Although the ruling class participated in the 66 to 70 CE revolt, it seems clear from Josephus that many of them did so

reluctantly. They were more at home with co-operation and compromise with their ultimate rulers. Armed revolt was not conducive to advantageous relationships with the Romans, since with skilful diplomacy much could be gained by combining willingness to help and to defuse troublesome situations with heavily veiled demands for concessions. On other occasions, passive resistance proved quite useful. In the face of growing fanaticism and moral failure on the part of the leading classes, this resistance eventually broke down, but there were times it proved effective. Religious convictions and good common sense need not be – and often are not – in opposition.

(3) *Armed resistance and revolt.* Sources reveal that in some cases, refusal to accept Roman rule was tied up specifically with beliefs about God's rule. Some Jews could only think about Judaea as subject nation with extreme bitterness. Some admired the Hasmoneans, exaggerating the traditions painting the Jews as part of a proud, independent country and even a great 'empire' – by the grace of God, they would hastily add. They believed that the correct action, either by God alone or by human agents with God's help, might put the current (first-century) situation 'right'. Some even espoused a violent revolution as the appropriate means of rectifying the situation. There were plenty of Old Testament precedents, and in the post-Hasmonean period, the Maccabees served as heroic exemplars. 'By God and my right hand (holding a sword)' might be their motto.

3.13   Rabbinic Judaism

From Judaisms to rabbinic Judaism

The religious world of the Jews of the century or so preceding the First Revolt was a pluralistic one. In fact, so diverse was the various traditions making up what is called first-century Judaism, that it is actually more appropriate to speak of first-century Judaisms

Josephus claims that among the Jews there were only four different 'schools' (i e four forms of Judaism), namely the Pharisees, the Sadducees, the Essenes and the Zealots. His own narrative, however, shows a much more complex society. Philo, a first-century contemporary, recounts somewhat about the Essenes (*Quod omnis probus liber sit* 12.75–87; *Hypothetica* 11.1–18), but does not mention Pharisees or Sadducees. Rabbinic literature mentions 24 different groups, at the time of the overthrow of the temple, claiming to be authentic Jews (all 'heretics', according to the rabbis), but does not refer to the Essenes, so dear to Josephus, at all; nor does it seem very aware of the Christians. The New Testament knows about Pharisees and Sadducees, but is completely ignorant of the Essenes. The early church of the second and third centuries refers to the 'seven' Jewish heresies during the time of Jesus. Sources clearly establish an awareness of the wide range of diversity in early Judaism.

From a historian's point of view, a great number of different groups that maintained a distinct tradition of being Jewish can be identified. It is important that the seriousness and commitment of these various groups are recognised. Radical, fierce apocalypticists; mystical apocalypticists; various groups following a prophet or messiah; traditional priests and priests committed to reform; the Therapeutae; the Sicarii; the baptismal sects; various revolutionaries and popular movements; Jewish Gnostics; charismatics, preachers and miracle-workers; the Pharisees; the Sadducees; the Essenes, and other not-yet-identifiable groups are known.

The wars with the Romans had a profound effect on the Jewish world. The Judaism created by the rabbis after the wars gradually became the dominant form of Judaism and it remained the dominant form until the nineteenth century. The rabbis were the 'winners' of ancient Jewish history. At the time they were not as dominant as their literature presented them. In fact, the 'rabbinic period' slights the opponents of the rabbis (the 'losers' of ancient Jewish history). It falsely implies that after 70 CE all Jews accepted the rabbis as their leaders, followed the way of rabbinic Judaism and believed the rabbinic version of Jewish history which, when one considers the period before 70 CE, was impossible.

Nevertheless, despite this element of pro-rabbinic bias, the 'rabbinic period' remains a useful and justifiable concept. Historians of antiquity have to rely on the literary evidence, and the major literary evidence for the Judaism of the second to sixth centuries is exclusively rabbinic.

The rabbis claim that they are the bearers of a sacred tradition revealed by God to Moses. They are the direct heirs of the communal leaders of the Jews throughout all the generations since. According to this perspective (this 'myth'), the rabbinic period actually begins with 'Moses our rabbi'. This perspective has a long history and a strong influence. Many people still view the Second Temple period through rabbinic spectacles, assuming that all the central institutions of Jewish society were under rabbinic control, and they ascribe enormous influence and power to various proto-rabbinic figures. None of these beliefs can be substantiated by historical evidence. For the believer, rabbinic Judaism is normative Judaism, and the rabbis will always be at the centre of Jewish history. For the historian, however, 'the rabbis' became meaningful entities only after 70 CE.

Yavneh

According to legend, a rabbi named Yohanan ben Zakkai was given permission to establish an academy in the city of Yavneh (sometimes called *Jamnia*) by the emperor Vespasian. Whatever the origins of the academy, the episode is extremely important in Jewish history, despite the fact that very little of the detail is known. This academy was destined to become the nerve centre of the rabbinic 'modification' of Judaism.

As an originally Jewish area which had come into Roman possession, the acknowledgement of such a Jewish institution at Yavneh represents an important concession to Judaism by the Romans. The reconstruction of Jewish life which began under Yohanan had, if not Roman sanction, at least Roman tolerance.

Yavneh is often misrepresented as a 'synod', as if it were analogous to a church council. It was actually more like a school for advanced study or specialised training centre, and the number of participants was quite small at first. Nor were its members necessarily recognised as representatives of Jews in the country. However, this group became influential in Jewish society; their work culminated in the Mishnah. It took well over a century for their work to become fully successful.

The interests of the scholars teaching at Yavneh were purity, agriculture, festivals and the lifestyle of women. They could be described as a table fellowship sect which had control of its internal affairs but not of society as a whole. Yavneh presents only a transitional phase on the way toward the dominance of Jewish life by the rabbis.

Though developing Judaism at Yavneh owes a debt to the pre-70 CE Pharisaic tradition, it was very much a synthesis of a variety of elements. Critical study of the earliest traditions reveal that Yohanan was probably not a Pharisee, but a scribe whose religion centred on Scripture.

The rabbinic period

Roman rule over the Jews continued until the Parthian and Arab conquests of the sixth and seventh centuries CE – by this time the Roman Empire had become Christian and Byzantine.

The history of the Jews after the destruction of the temple is usually called *the rabbinic period*, hence rabbinic Judaism. The word *rabbi* means 'my master' and was originally a respectful form of address (like 'sir'). During the first century CE the title was normally used by students when addressing their teacher (John 1:38). During the second century, however, the meaning of the word began to change. It remained a generic title for 'teacher' or anyone in a position of authority, but it also acquired a technical meaning: designating a member of a specific group of Jews who, from the second century to the sixth, working in both Israel and Babylonia, created a voluminous and distinctive collection of literature.

At the core of this collection is the Mishnah, the earliest of these works. The Mishnah was completed around the year 200 CE. It became the subject of two gigantic commentaries: the Talmud of the land of Israel (the Palestinian Talmud), completed around the year 400 CE and the Talmud of Babylonia (the Babylonian Talmud), completed around 500 CE. The rabbis also produced a series of commentaries on Scripture called midrash and some other works (the so-called extra-canonical tractates, such as *Sayings of Rabbi Nathan,* and the other midrash compilations).

It is best to use the term *the rabbis* to refer to the managers of this literature, in other words, relating to the society and religion of the second to sixth centuries CE of the Jews (= the rabbinic period). The term *rabbi,* when referring to a first-century (or earlier) person, is best translated, either as 'teacher' or 'master'.

A description of Judaism in the first century must take account of all these trends and teachers, and of the kaleidoscopic nature of the overall religious scene. It must also assess the extent to which the average Jew was affected by them, and the state of religious practice in the population as a whole.

Most Jews were not Gnostics, mystics, magicians, nor revolutionaries. Neither were they Pharisees. Later rabbinic literature – written at a time when Judaism was becoming monolithic – makes it clear that the average Jew was an *am ha-aretz,* one who could not be trusted to practise the strict laws of agriculture and purity laid down by rabbinic law. So much the more before 70 CE. Average Jewish men and women had such important things on their minds as keeping body and soul together (assuming they believed in a soul). For the peasant farmer, life was generally hard, and good years were offset by years of droughts and famine, as well as heavy taxation. Tithing spices and mother's purity were not the most important concerns.

They prayed the biblical psalms as well as a rich variety of other psalms and blessings concerned with crops, family and health. It is likely that many Jews prayed some form of the blessings that later became known as the *Eighteen Benedictions.* The first of these blessings as now prayed by Jews, reveal their sense of God:

Blessed are you, Lord our God and God of our Fathers, God of Abraham, God of Isaac, God of Jacob, the greatest, mighty and revered God, the most high God, who bestows loving kindnesses and possesses all things; who remembers the pious deeds of the patriarchs and in love will bring a redeemer to their children's children for your name's sake.

3.14 Diaspora Judaism

Large Jewish communities existed outside Palestine as early as the seventh century BCE. These groups originated as a result of the fall and decline of the Judaean and Israelite kingdoms during the eighth to the seventh centuries, when many people were carried into captivity in Assyria and Babylon. These Mesopotamian Jews would constitute an important centre of Jewish culture and religion which would exercise an enormous influence on Jewish history. The largest expansion of the Jewish Diaspora, or scattering, occurred in the Hellenistic era as a consequence of the extensive changes brought about by Alexander the Great.

The causes of this Diaspora are manifold. Some were led away into captivity, not only to Assyria and Babylon, but also to Egypt (by order of Ptolemy Soter, king of Egypt 323–285 BCE) and to Rome (by order of Pompey). The intention of this kind of policy was to prevent any future military threat in Palestine; all possible rebels were sent elsewhere. Many left Palestine as slaves; enslaved either by force, as punishment for transgressions, or as war reparations, or as the result of debt, in which case one could sell oneself to cover the debt. Most emigrated voluntarily, for throughout the Hellenistic and Roman eras, Palestine was the arena for conflict and war. The deserts of Judaea and even large parts of the mountains and hills of Galilee were not all that fertile and could thus not sustain large groups or extended families. As a means of existence then, agriculture and the armed forces offered ways out of poor conditions caused by population growth. As soldiers, some Jews were successful: the Jewish mercenaries who served the Ptolemies under their priest Onias were allowed to build a temple at Leontopolis in Egypt. A particularly large proportion of the Jews who settled in the cities of the Graeco-Roman world started to practise different trades and many became merchants.

Philo writes that at one stage a million Jews lived in Egypt. As far as the entire Graeco-Roman world is concerned, it may well be that the Diaspora Jewry comprised four to five million people, or five times the entire Jewish population of Palestine.

There were some interesting distinctions between the natives of Judaea and those living in the Diaspora. The differences between the Jews of Israel and the Diaspora Jews fall largely into two areas: (1) the great distance between the temple as centre of worship and the Diaspora Jews' actual home (think of Babylon's distance from Jerusalem) and (2) the fact that Diaspora Jews were a minority community in a largely pagan setting. In the Diaspora, Jerusalem and its temple were also an object of concern, interest and identity. Members of the community paid the half-shekel temple tax – a not-inconsiderable sum which represented about two days' wages for the ordinary worker. For many, the temple represented an ideal and they dreamt of a pilgrimage to worship there. They also desired ultimate burial in the land of Judaea, hopefully close to Jerusalem. Nevertheless, the realities of daily religious practice tended to be the community (mostly by means of the synagogue) and the home (the household).

Diaspora Jews largely participated in, and adapted to, the environments and communities in which they found themselves. The vast majority of them spoke and wrote (if they could write at all) in Greek. Mesopotamian Jews spoke Aramaic. In the large cities, Jews participated in the activities of the theatres and councils. In a few cities Jews served as magistrates (a magistrate in a Roman city was roughly equal to what would be called a mayor, but he also acted as the local judge) and city councillors.

4 CONCLUSION

Communities in the Graeco-Roman world cherished certain expectations of their members. Whether free or slave, male or female, citizen or disenfranchised, all had to pay their respects to the ruler (emperor and governor or client king), perform certain public duties (military service, maintenance of public buildings, local taxes) and participate in the cultic activities of the community.

The Jews' lifestyle, however, often prevented them from fulfilling all of these expectations. Jews did pray for the emperor, but not to him. The offering of incense to statues of the emperor was one of the ways in which people celebrated their participation in the empire religiously, but the Jews often refused to allow any statuettes into their houses. Sabbath customs often prevented them from participating in processions and other community activities. Jewish dietary laws sometimes forced them to turn down invitations to banquets.

Jewish groups were 'outsiders' in the eyes of other people. To forestall problems, they often requested official permission from the emperor or from local authorities to be exempted from public activities. Jewish leaders, therefore, often referred to a special kind of citizenship possessed by their people. This view caused strong reactions: many people felt that the Jews benefited from the welfare and opportunities that the cities had to offer, but were not prepared to fulfil any of the obligations or the bothersome public services, and various Greek cities suspended Jewish privileges during the first century BCE and the first century CE.

The attitudes of the Roman emperors to the Jews varied. In 38 CE, when tension in Alexandria ended in a bloodbath, the emperor Gaius had little sympathy for the Jews. However, in 41 CE, the emperor Claudius restored Jewish rights in all the cities of the Roman Empire.

This protection was to last until 70 CE. After the destruction of Jerusalem, the right to gather temple tax was cancelled; from that point, all such funds would go to the imperial coffers. From that moment too, the history of the Jews would continue to be one based on their contextual setting and the inevitable factors that accompany such contexts.

Suggested reading

Boshoff, Willem, Scheffler, Eben & Spangenberg, Izak
2000   *Ancient Israelite Literature in Context.* Pretoria: Protea Book House.

Charlesworth, James H (ed)
1983   *Old Testament Pseudepigrapha.* Vol I. *Apocalyptic Literature and Testaments.* London: Darton, Longman & Todd.
1985   *Old Testament Pseudepigrapha.* Vol II. *Expansions of the 'Old Testament,' Legends, Wisdom and Philosophical Literature, Prayers, Psalms and Odes, Fragments of Lost Judeo-Hellenistic Works.* London: Darton, Longman & Todd.

Craffert, Pieter F
1999   *Illness and Healing in the Biblical World.* Pretoria: Biblia.

Ferguson, Everett
1987   *Backgrounds of Early Christianity.* Grand Rapids: Eerdmans.

Finegan, Jack
1988   *Myth and Mystery: An Introduction to the Pagan Religions of the Biblical World.* Grand Rapids: Baker Book House.

Garcia Martinez, F
1996 *The Dead Sea Scrolls Translated*. Leiden: Brill.

Garnsey, Peter & Saller, Richard
1987 *The Roman Empire. Economy, Society and Culture*. Berkeley/Los Angeles: University of California Press.

Grabbe, Lester L
1994 *Judaism from Cyrus to Hadrian*. London: SCM Press.
1996 *An Introduction to First Century Judaism. Jewish Religion and History in the Second Temple Period*. Edinburgh: T&T Clark.

Grant, Michael
1995 *The Roman Emperors. A Biographical Guide to the Rulers of Imperial Rome 31 BC–AD 476*. London: Phoenix.

Green, Peter
1990 *Alexander to Actium. The Hellenistic Age*. London: Thames and Hudson.

Klauck, Hans-Josef
2000 *The Religious Context of Early Christianity. A Guide to Graeco-Roman Religions*. London: T&T Clark. (Studies in the New Testament and its World).

Macmullen, Ramsey & Lane, Eugene N (eds)
1992 *Paganism and Christianity 100–425 CE. A Sourcebook*. Minneapolis: Fortress Press.

Magie, David
1950 *Roman Rule in Asia Minor to the End of the Third Century After Christ*. Volumes 1 and 2. Princeton: Princeton University Press.

Malina, Bruce J
2001 *The New Testament World. Insights from Cultural Anthropology* (3rd ed rev and exp). Louisville, Ky: Westminster John Knox Press.

Martin, Luther
1987 *Hellenistic Religions. An Introduction*. Oxford: Oxford University Press.

Robinson, James M (ed)
1998 *The Nag Hammadi Library in English*. Leiden: Brill.

Sharples, R W
1996 *Stoics, Epicureans and Sceptics. An Introduction to Hellenistic Philosophy*. London: Routledge.

Stone, Michael E
1982 *Scripture, Sects and Visions. A Profile of Judaism from Ezra to the Jewish Revolts*. Oxford: Oxford University Press.

Stone, Michael E (ed)
1984 *Jewish Writings of the Second Temple Period: Apocrypha, Pseudepigrapha, Qumran Sectarian Writings, Philo, Josephus*. Assen: Van Gorcum.

Turcan, Robert

1996 *The Cults of the Roman Empire.* Oxford: Blackwell.

Versnel, Henk S
1988 'Religieuze Stromingen in het Hellenisme.' *Lampas* 21/2:111–136.

Walbank, Frank W
1992 *The Hellenistic World.* Hammersmith: Fontana.

Wells, Colin
1992 *The Roman Empire.* Glasgow: Fontana.

Part two

The teaching of the historical Jesus (27–30 CE)

5 HISTORICAL CONTEXT (63 BCE–30 CE)

Since most of the history of this period has been discussed in Part One, this section is devoted to those facets of the history of this period that are relevant to one's understanding of Jesus and his ministry; the period after Herod's death.

After Herod's death in 4 BCE, his kingdom was divided among three of his sons, Archelaus, Herod Antipas and Philip. Archelaus became ruler of Judaea, Samaria and Idumaea; Herod Antipas of Galilee and Perea, and Philip of the regions north and east of the Sea of Galilee.

In Judaea the transition was all but peaceful. The Jerusalemites demanded a reduction in taxes and the release of prisoners. Peasant revolts broke out in different parts of the country, a phenomenon that occurred sporadically until the outbreak of the Roman–Jewish war in 66–70 CE.

Archelaus's reign lasted only ten years before he was removed from his position in 6 CE. From then onwards, Roman governors ruled Judaea and Samaria. Tax was to be paid directly to Rome. This led to revolts, one of which was led by Judas the Galilean in different parts of Palestine in 6 CE.

Jesus was born shortly before the death of Herod the Great, in other words, before 4 CE. His ministry, however, took place between 28 and 30 CE while Herod Antipas was ruler of Galilee (where most of Jesus's ministry took place). Pilate was governor in Judaea and Samaria (26–36 CE) and Tiberius was emperor of Rome. Pilate was a typical Roman governor who often acted insensitively towards Jewish laws and customs. This caused tension between him and the Jews. Though, as part of Judaea, Jerusalem was formally under Roman control, and the high priest and his advisors were mostly responsible for its governance. During the Jewish festivals, the procurator or prefect came to Jerusalem with

Figure 5.1
Bust of Tiberius, Roman emperor 14 to 37 CE. It was during his reign that Jesus was crucified in Jerusalem

extra troops in case of trouble. This would also have been the case when Jesus and his disciples went to Jerusalem for the Passover in about 30 CE.

As a result of the long reign of Herod Antipas in Galilee (4 BCE–39 CE), Galilee was probably more peaceful than Judaea. This does not necessarily mean that the Jews were satisfied with their situation. No part of Palestine was totally exempt from the consequences of Roman rule such as heavy taxation, and social and economic tensions between rich and poor. The potential for insurrection was present most of the time. In such a situation of dissatisfaction, the hope for divine intervention, which in some cases manifested itself in the outbreak of violence, arose from time to time.

Within this context of dissatisfaction and poverty, Jesus emphasised care for the poor and the needy, and reliance on God. He acted as healer of the sick and demon-possessed and preached about the kingdom of God and the characteristics of a life in this kingdom. Jesus and his movement fit into a group of renewal movements within Judaism which had occurred in Palestine since the twenties of the first century. John the Baptist also led such a group.

6 JESUS AS A HISTORICAL FIGURE

6.1 Sources on Jesus

For information on Jesus as historical figure, one is, to a large extent, dependent on the four Gospels of the New Testament. Since the Gospel of John is even further removed from the historical figure of Jesus than the other three, the last-mentioned are in reality the main sources. Although Paul's letters predate the Gospels, he has already largely left the historical figure of Jesus, and the details of his life and ministry behind. The only aspects of Jesus's life that function prominently in Paul's writings are Jesus's crucifixion and resurrection.

In addition to the Gospels in the New Testament, there are a number of extra-canonical writings which are currently regarded as valuable sources for Jesus. This applies especially to the *Gospel of Thomas*, which should, according to a number of scholars, be dated among the earliest writings of the New

Testament. Attention will be paid to this when discussing the earliest Christian literature (cf Part 3).

Apart from the Gospels, in which Jesus is the main figure, a few historians of the time referred to him in passing. In his *Jewish Antiquities* (approximately 93–94 CE), the Jewish historian Flavius Josephus wrote as follows about him (later insertions excluded):

> At this time there appeared Jesus, a wise man. For he was someone who did startling deeds, a teacher of people who receive the truth with pleasure. And he gained a following among many Jews and also among many Greeks. And when Pilate condemned him to the cross on account of the accusation of the leaders among us, those who previously loved him did not cease to do so. And up to this day the Christians, who are named after him, did not die out.
>
> (Josephus, *Jewish Antiquities* 18.3.)

In his *Annals*, the Roman historian Tacitus (56–118 CE) also refers to Jesus when he says that the designation *Christians* 'comes from Christ, who had been executed by Pontius Pilate during the reign of Tiberius' (*Annals* 15.44).

These sources do not provide new information about Jesus. They merely confirm the historical existence of Jesus and a number of facts that are known about him from the Gospels. It is, nevertheless, significant that the portrayal of an outsider such as Josephus shows clear similarities with the image of Jesus encountered in the Gospels.

It will become clear in the course of dealing with the Gospels how Jesus, and what he did and said, were taken up by each evangelist in a narrative about him and was interpreted for a specific situation. Since one can only use a source sensibly when its nature is grasped, it is necessary at this stage to say something about the nature of the Gospels. As the Gospels had a long evolution, one also has to visualise how this process took place.

As regards the nature of the Gospels, it is important to realise that these writings are not historical narratives which merely report what Jesus said and did. If this were the case, there would be one Gospel only and not four (canonical) versions of the Jesus event. In some respects they differ quite substantially (cf especially the differences between the Synoptic Gospels and the Gospel of John – cf Parts 3 and 4). However, if the authors of the Gospels were not at all interested in history and therefore in the events of Jesus's life, there would not necessarily be writings which focus on Jesus's words and deeds (cf, e g the Pauline letters where Jesus's words and deeds play almost no role). Although incorporating historical material into their Gospels, some of which goes back to Jesus, the evangelists had a different aim with their writings. They were people who, themselves convinced that God was at work in Jesus and his ministry, wanted to convince others of the same. Forty years or more after Jesus's ministry, they endeavoured to spell out for different groups of people the significance of what Jesus had said and done, also with regard to himself. This implies that not everything that forms part of the Gospels goes back to Jesus as historical figure, and that information about the historical Jesus cannot simply be read from the Gospels.

Against the Gospels, as mere historical reports of what Jesus had said and done, speak the context in which they originated and the time that elapsed between Jesus's ministry and the actual writing of the Gospels. The first-century culture in which Jesus's ministry took place and in which the writings about him originated, was primarily oral. Only a small part of the population could read and write. This implies that different versions of, for example, a parable had existed from the start, since it was probably told more than once to different audiences and in different contexts. It also implies that, during the approximately four decades between Jesus's ministry and the writing of the first complete Gospel (Mark), traditions about Jesus circulated orally and, in the process, underwent changes. Sections of the Gospels which deal with the same matter or which take the same form were probably composed into smaller written sources before the Gospels were written (cf the grouping together of the same kind of material such as parables and miracle-stories). In a predominantly oral culture, traditions would still have circulated orally even after they had been written down.

From the above it is clear why it is not a simple task to reach Jesus as a historical figure. To this can be added the complexity of constructing a specific first-century Palestine context for the ministry of Jesus. It is no wonder that scholars come up with divergent views of the historical Jesus.

6.2 Quests for the historical Jesus

Intensive research on Jesus as a historical figure started when, influenced by rationalism, scholars of the eighteenth and nineteenth centuries realised that discrepancies existed between Jesus of Nazareth, the figure who lived in Palestine during the first century, and the portrayal(s) of him in the New Testament. The first to write about this was Samuel Reimarus. His work was published after his death by Gotthold Ephraim Lessing (1778). During the nineteenth century many attempts were made, especially in Germany, to recover the historical Jesus by means of historical criticism (the so-called Old Quest). While the emphasis was on historical construction, more than historical interest was at stake. In its first stages it was an anti-dogmatic movement in which the differences between Jesus as historical figure and the Christ of faith were emphasised. Only later scholars thought that by turning to the historical Jesus, could Christian faith be renewed.

During the first decades of the twentieth century optimism about the possibility of recovering the historical Jesus suffered a blow from various directions. Albert Schweitzer, in his famous book *Quest for the Historical Jesus*, convincingly demonstrated that the proposals made by scholars regarding Jesus as historical figure largely reflected their own views and ideals. Research on the nature of the Gospels underlined the problems associated with this endeavour even further. Scholars increasingly realised that the incidents reported in the Gospels were not mere historical reminiscences, and that the chronology of the Gospels did not reflect the historical life of Jesus, but had been created by the Gospel authors.

For nearly half a century the problem was put aside by stressing that the historical Jesus was not important for faith and for the church. This view was especially held and propagated by Martin Kähler and Rudolph Bultmann, the latter being one of the most influential New Testament scholars of the twentieth century. In the 1950s the problem was readdressed. While in the 'Old Quest' scholars played 'Jesus as historical figure' and the portrayals of him in the New Testament off against one another, an attempt was now made to bring the two together by pointing to the close relationship between the Jesus of history and the Christ of faith prevalent in the Synoptic Gospels. Although the evangelists were more interested in Jesus's significance than in his identity, these scholars pointed out that for them the significance of Jesus was closely related to his identity. The meaning of Jesus can therefore not be detached from the historical figure he was.

Since the middle of the 1980s, Jesus research has been resumed zealously and is ongoing (the so-called Third Quest). Characteristics of the current phase of research are especially the following: a serious attempt is made to understand Jesus within the first-century Jewish context. The construction of a more specific Galilean context for Jesus plays a crucial role in current research. In addition to the canonical Gospels, extra-canonical sources are used in the construction of the historical Jesus. Much attention is paid to method, especially social-scientific method.

The current phase of historical Jesus research is still characterised by sharp difference of opinion with regard to Jesus as a historical figure. These differences are related to a number of factors. We have pointed out that the Gospels, our main sources for Jesus, are not historical accounts in the modern sense. Since they deal with a restricted number of incidents from a short period of Jesus's life, we do not have all the pieces of the Jesus puzzle. This implies that connections between the available pieces have to be made by the scholar. Another contributing factor to the diversity in historical Jesus images is the complexity of first-century Judaism as part of the Mediterranean world, the world in which Jesus lived. The Judaism of the time, which was influenced by Hellenism, contained different facets to which scholars relate in search of the historical Jesus. Some emphasise the apocalyptic or eschatological strand in first-century Judaism and come up with Jesus as apocalyptic or eschatological prophet. Others place Jesus within the charismatic stream of first-century Judaism and regard him as a charismatic Galilean holy man.

Closely related to the specific strand of Judaism in which Jesus is situated is the facet of his ministry perceived to be the main access route to him. If a scholar, for example, chooses Jesus's words as the main access route to him as historical figure, he or she will end up with a Jesus who differs from the one reached by mainly focusing on his deeds. The method used is also a crucial factor in determining the outcome of 'historical Jesus' research. The obvious challenge of Jesus research is to sketch an image of him which accounts for both his words and deeds.

6.3 Examples of historical images of Jesus

The portrayals of Jesus as a historical figure with which scholars have come up since the end of the nineteenth century can roughly be typified as eschatological and non-eschatological.

(1) Albert Schweitzer, although criticising the historical constructions of Jesus by scholars of his time, came up with his own construction of Jesus, which was influential especially during the first half of the twentieth century. Like Johannes Weiss before him, Schweitzer emphasised that Jesus and his ministry should be understood within the world of Second Temple Judaism. For him this implied the framework of Jewish apocalypticism, the expectation of the imminent end of the world – in his view an important strand in the Judaism of Jesus's time. Jesus's ministry and proclamation had to do with the coming of the kingdom of God in the near future – an insight Schweitzer gained from his reading of Matthew 10. The kingdom at stake here is not a human moral community to be brought about in this world, but a supernatural kingdom bringing with it the end of the world.

Schweitzer mostly relied on Mark, whose basic outline he regarded as historical, and Matthew, sometimes conflating material from them. According to Schweitzer, Jesus's view of the kingdom, and his awareness and view of his messiahship were closely related. At his baptism, Jesus became aware of the fact that he was the one destined by God to be the messiah. When the disciples whom he had sent out returned and reported their success to him, he was convinced that the kingdom was about to dawn. When this did not happen, Jesus went to Jerusalem to force the issue of the kingdom by taking upon himself the suffering associated with the period before the end of the world and offering his life as an atonement for the people. In line with his view of an eschatological kingdom preached by Jesus, Schweitzer regarded Jesus's teaching as, among other things, embodied in the Sermon on the Mount, as interim ethic. As opposed to scholars who had intended to make Jesus relevant for their time, Schweitzer emphasised that the historical Jesus was a stranger to our time.

(2) Schweitzer's line of thought is, in modified form, currently pursued by E P Sanders. Sanders also emphasises first-century Judaism, particularly Jewish eschatology, as context for understanding Jesus and his ministry. In support of this view, he emphasises that the line from John the Baptist to Paul and to the other apostles is that of Jewish eschatology.

In constructing his Jesus, Sanders relies primarily on eight indisputable 'facts' about Jesus, and not so much on Jesus's words, since, in his view, they do not sufficiently explain Jesus's crucifixion and the forming of a messianic sect by his followers. The facts are the following:

- Jesus was *baptised* by John the Baptist.
- He was a Galilean who *preached* and *healed*.
- He called *disciples* and spoke of 12 of them.
- He confined his activity to *Israel*.
- He engaged in a controversy about the *temple*.
- He was *crucified* by the Roman authorities.
- After his death, his followers existed as an identifiable *movement*.
- At least some Jews *persecuted* some parts of the new movement, and apparently this continued to a time near the end of Paul's career.

Starting with Jesus's action in the temple, Sanders argues that this event, together with other important aspects of his ministry – such as the relation between Jesus and John the Baptist – and the call of the disciples, fits into what Sanders calls restoration eschatology, that is, the view that God would vindicate and restore Israel. According to Sanders, Jesus was a restorationist prophet: he regarded himself as God's last messenger before the establishment of the kingdom, which would entail God's dramatic intervention in history.

(3) Another scholar who at present propagates an understanding of Jesus and his ministry within an eschatological Jewish context is Thomas Wright. Although in theory opting for Schweitzer's route and typifying Jesus as an eschatological prophet, Wright redefines apocalyptic language by saying that it did not, as Schweitzer thought, refer to the end of the world in time and in space. Wright regards apocalypticism as the symbolic language of protest and revolution. As eschatological prophet, Jesus used this kind of language to give expression to the belief that Israel's God was acting through him and his movement was to do for Israel what the prophets had promised: the real return from exile in the spiritual sense is the real forgiveness of sin. Jesus reinterpreted traditional Jewish symbols such as loyalty to family and key elements of the Torah, in this way, redefining for his contemporaries the important aspects of their faith. Wright maintains that Jesus was conscious of his vocation: he believed that he was Israel's messiah; the one through whom God was acting to restore the fortunes of his people.

Although Wright calls Jesus an eschatological prophet, his redefinition of 'apocalyptic' in a sense makes his Jesus more of a non-eschatological figure. Apart from the way he visualises first-century Judaism as context for the historical Jesus, his portrayal of Jesus is determined by the way he views and understands the Gospels as historically reliable accounts of Jesus's ministry.

During the last few decades of the twentieth century, a number of proposals regarding the historical Jesus have been made which can be called *non-eschatological*. According to these scholars, who take the first-century context of Jesus seriously but define it differently, Jesus was mainly concerned with this world and not so much with the coming of God's kingdom in future. The kingdom is regarded by them as mainly being something of the *present*.

(4) A scholar who, since the 1970s has made a ground-breaking contribution to Jesus research, is Geza Vermes. Himself a Jew, he brought a number of important insights into the historical study of Jesus as Jew. Vermes situates Jesus within the charismatic tradition of Judaism represented by miracle-workers, such as Honi the Circle-Drawer and Hanina ben Dosa, thus typifying him as a Galilean Hasid. Vermes encountered these figures, whom he used as models for understanding Jesus, in the Rabbinic writings, which he regards as important aids in the search for Jesus as historical figure. According to Vermes, Jesus as a Hasid, or holy man, was a healer, exorcist, preacher and teacher.

Vermes is somewhat ambiguous when dealing with the kingdom of God, which is central to the view of Jesus as eschatological or apocalyptic prophet. On the one hand he points out that, in Jesus's view, the kingdom was imminent, even present in his ministry. This is an assertion which hints at some kind of temporal understanding of the kingdom. On the other hand, Vermes dismisses a temporal understanding of the kingdom as a misunderstanding of Jesus's eschatological outlook and regards debate on the time aspect of the kingdom as irrelevant. According to Vermes, Jesus the existential teacher was mainly concerned in his teaching of the kingdom with people's attitude and behaviour towards the kingdom.

Although Jesus was, according to Vermes, an observant Jew, the observance of the law was not the centre of his religion. Jesus's religion was about following God, as expressed in Luke 6:36: 'Be merciful, as your father is merciful.'

(5) Richard Horsley, in his portrayal of first-century Galilee as setting for Jesus and his ministry, focuses on factors such as the political and socio-economic circumstances at the time: the reality of foreign rule and the conflict which it caused, economic pressure on the peasantry, and the big gap between rich and poor. An important emphasis in Horsley's work, which deeply influences it, is that in first-century Palestine religion was not regarded as a part of life, separate from social, political and economic matters. In line with this insight, he regards Jesus as someone actively engaged in his world; a prophetic figure, even a social revolutionary. Jesus had a specific purpose in mind in the service of which he acted, namely the renewal of the people of Israel. The kingdom of God does not refer to something abstract which lies in the future, but to the continuing action of God, who is concerned with the liberation and welfare of his people.

(6) Various factors contribute to Marcus Borg's portrayal of Jesus. Characteristic of Borg's work is that in his construction of Jesus he makes use of most of the kinds of material about Jesus contained in the Synoptic Gospels, that is, his words as well as his deeds. Borg's Jesus is therefore multi-faceted: a charismatic who was a healer, sage, prophet and the founder of a revitalisation movement. Apart from the Gospel material Borg uses, his portrait of Jesus is also related to the fact that he utilises insights from cross-cultural anthropology, in this case a cross-cultural typology of religious personality types. At the root of the other facets of Borg's Jesus is the fact that Jesus was, according to Borg, a spirit-filled person in the charismatic stream of Judaism. What Jesus was, taught and did flowed from his experience of the 'world of spirit'. Different incidents from Jesus's life and ministry fit in with the view of Jesus as a spirit person: the voice at his baptism, his experience in the wilderness, his prayers, and the way Luke portrays him at the beginning of his ministry. This also applies to important facets of Jesus's work, such as his healings, exorcisms and his teaching of unconventional wisdom.

In reconstructing the context in which Jesus taught and acted, Borg, like Horsley, emphasises the economic pressure and conflict in first-century Palestine brought about by Roman rule. Borg believes that in reaction to this situation, the Jewish social world was increasingly structured round holiness and the polarities characteristic of it, such as being clean or unclean, pure or defiled, righteous or sinful. The politics of holiness led to greater divisions among the Jews themselves and to intensified conflict with Rome. Jesus was actively engaged withing this social world, teaching his unconventional wisdom. In a prophet-like way he called his people to change and founded a revitalisation movement, that is, a renewal movement within Israel. This movement was characterised by the presence of the spirit, itinerancy, inclusivity and compassion. Borg emphasises that, while spiritualising elements of the Jewish tradition, Jesus remained deeply Jewish and the movement he had initiated was concerned with what it meant to be Jewish.

(7) As context for his Jesus, John Dominic Crossan focuses on the broader Mediterranean context, of which Palestine formed part. Crossan paints the socio-political-religious context of Jewish Palestine as part of its wider context in dark colours. This context was one of social discrimination, cultural domination and imperial oppression – a situation in which especially the peasantry, who made up the vast majority of the population, suffered. It is in this context that Crossan's Jesus and his programme took form.

Crossan reaches his Jesus by means of a sophisticated methodology which comprises three facets: (i) he uses cross-cultural and cross-temporal social anthropology, (ii) he pays attention to Graeco-Roman history and (iii) he focuses on the literature which contains Jesus's words and deeds, identifying in these sources the layers which most probably go back to Jesus.

Characteristic of Crossan's work on Jesus is that he includes extra-canonical writings such as the *Gospel of Thomas* and the *Gospel of Peter* in the source material for Jesus, sometimes even according them a privileged position. The Gospel material – which he regards as being the earliest and therefore, in his view, the closest to Jesus – in conjunction with the context he constructs for Jesus's ministry, leads him to the view of Jesus as a Jewish peasant who resembles a Cynic sage. Jesus differed from the Cynics in that he focused on the farm rather than the marketplace, which causes Crossan to typify him as a peasant Jewish Cynic.

Another factor which, according to Crossan, differentiates Jesus from the Cynics is that he did not merely have a Cynic-like lifestyle: he had a social programme and inaugurated a social movement. That Jesus had a programme in mind which entailed the rebuilding of society on principles of religious and economic egalitarianism, comes to expression in two aspects of Jesus's ministry: (i) the practice of open commensality, that is, eating together with people of all classes, and (ii) free healing for everybody. In line with Jesus's preaching of a radical egalitarianism in society, the kingdom of God which Jesus proclaimed, was, according to Crossan, a brokerless kingdom. No broker or mediator was necessary to ensure entry into it. It was, moreover, not something of the future, but was immediately available to everybody.

7 THE LIFE OF JESUS

Since only the significant years of Jesus's life, involving his public ministry, are covered by the Gospels, not much information is available about his life prior to this.

Jesus was probably born in 5 or 6 BCE, shortly before the death of Herod the Great in 4 BCE. He grew up in Nazareth, a small town in Lower Galilee. He was a member of the lower class of society, to which at least 90 per cent of the people belonged. His parents were Joseph and Mary. The Synoptic Gospels refer to four brothers by name: James, Joseph, Jude and Simon. He also had sisters, who are not named in the Gospels.

After having been baptised by John the Baptist, Jesus began his ministry in approximately 28 CE. He called a number of disciples who participated in his ministry and carried on with it after his death. The duration of his ministry cannot be established with certainty. In the Synoptic Gospels reference is made to only one Passover attended by Jesus in Jerusalem, while John refers to three such occasions. This could, but does not necessarily, point to a ministry of three years. On his visit to Jerusalem during Passover, Jesus was arrested and crucified by the Roman authorities, probably in 30 CE. Although the divergent Gospel reports about the resurrection of Jesus make it difficult to say something historically sensible about this event, one can infer from these reports that after Jesus's death his followers had resurrection experiences which convinced them that he was alive.

We are, of course, interested in more than this bare outline of Jesus's life. We want to know what it was that caused people to flock to him in great numbers;

Figure 7.1
The barren mountains of the Judaean wilderness. It was in environs such as these that Jesus sought solitude after his baptism. The desert wilderness was also home to other religious extremists such as John the Baptist and the Essenes of Qumran

Figure 7.2
The Jordan River in northern Galilee near the Bridge of the Daughters of Jacob

what it was about him that made such a great impact on people. Before arriving at an overview, a few preliminary remarks need to be made.

In trying to know something about Jesus as historical figure, one has to keep in mind that he was a first-century Jew who shared the basic convictions of Judaism. His ministry was therefore in some sense related to the Judaism of his day, and to the hopes and expectations of his people.

Figure 7.3
View of the mountains of northern Galilee to the west across the Hyle Valley

Figure 7.4
View of the north-eastern corner of the Sea of Galilee

One has, moreover, to remind oneself of the more specific context of his life and ministry outlined earlier, that is, first-century Palestine and especially Galilee. A region which was under foreign rule would not have been without tension, with poverty and unrest ever-present realities. Yet the period during which Jesus lived and acted in Galilee was probably, as a result of the peaceful reign of Herod Antipas, not characterised by overt revolution like the time before and after him. People responded to this in different ways. From 4 BCE onwards, different military revolts, which can be called messianic movements, occurred in Palestine. They ultimately culminated in the Jewish wars. Since the second decade of the first century CE, there had also been a number of prophetic movements, such as that of John the Baptist, renewal movements which were concerned with the preservation and redefinition of Jewish identity. The group which originated with Jesus was probably related to these movements.

To understand Jesus and his ministry, it is also essential to bear in mind that in first-century Palestine important aspects of life, such as religion, politics and economics, were not, as in modern times, separated from one another. This explains why Jesus's teaching and actions could have had political consequences, which eventually led to his death. It should also caution one not to think of him in too esoteric and restricted terms, for example, as someone mainly concerned with the salvation of people's souls, as he came to be viewed in some church traditions.

Since Jesus's public ministry started with John the Baptist, this is the appropriate place to start a short sketch of Jesus. From the sparse information about John in the Gospels it becomes evident that he was a prophet concerned with judgement and renewal, who preached forgiveness of sins through baptism. Jesus linked himself closely with John and may initially even have belonged to the group of disciples around John.

As a result of the diverse material on Jesus in the Gospels, the fact that he was interpreted anew for new situations and that he evidently had more sides to him than John the Baptist, it is more difficult to form a precise idea of Jesus as historical figure. The impression of Jesus one gets from the Gospels is that of a figure who cannot comfortably be slotted into one role. He fulfilled different functions, some of which were not normally combined in comparable contemporary figures in the history of Israel. Elijah and Elisha, were, for example, both prophets and healers, but not wisdom teachers. Hanina and Honi, also charismatic figures, were both healers and wisdom teachers, but not prophetic figures.

Figure 7.5
View of the ruins of the synagogue of Capernaum. According to the Gospel accounts, in the early stages of his ministry, Jesus was 'headquartered' in Capernaum and its environs. It is possible that Simon Peter came from Capernaum as his mother-in-law (whom Jesus healed) lived there. Later tradition identified his house here and a church was built over it, but there is no substance to these traditions. The present synagogue itself stems from a later period (fourth century) although it is built on the remains of a first-century CE synagogue

Figure 7.6
Aerial view of the ruins of Capernaum. The structure in the bottom corner is the synagogue and the octagonal structure to the top left is the traditionally identified house of Peter. Archaeological evidence suggests that the house of Peter (essentially a warren of small rooms around a courtyard) was used as an ordinary dwelling until the middle of the first century CE. Thereafter, a room in the house was put to public use. This is confirmed by graffiti, some of which mention Jesus as Lord and Christ. In the middle of the fifth century an octagonal church was built on top, enshrining the venerated room. Early Byzantine pilgrims identified this as the house of Peter where Jesus stayed (Matthew 5:20)

Jesus was a prophet-like figure who gathered around him a group of disciples and went from village to village, and from town to town, healing, preaching and exorcising demons. Apart from the healings and exorcisms reported in the Gospels, and the Gospel summaries (e g Luke 4:40–41) which refer to this aspect of his ministry, the historian Josephus, as mentioned before, also referred to Jesus as 'a doer of mighty deeds'. More healing stories are told about him than about any other healer of whom one reads in the

Figure 7.7
The remains of the pool of Siloam where, according to John 9, Jesus healed the blind man. The pool was fed through Hezekiah's tunnel from the Gihon spring outside the old City of David. The picture shows the end of the tunnel from Gihon where it feeds into the Siloam pool

Figure 7.8
Remains of the bath of Bethesda in Jerusalem. In ancient Israel a series of pools was constructed here in the shallow valley to catch rainwater runoff, but in Herodian times this was a pagan healing shrine. According to John 5:1 to 13, Jesus healed a man here who had been ill for 38 years

Jewish tradition. From the crowds who followed him, it is evident that people, including his followers, attached great significance to what they had perceived to be his miracles. That he was a prophet-like figure is, for example, apparent from his conduct towards the poor and the marginalised, and his overturning of the tables of the money-changers in the temple. He was, furthermore, a teacher, as will be discussed later when his teaching is addressed. In addition, he was a Jewish leader who initiated a movement which continued to exist after his death.

At the root of his person, the different roles he fulfilled and the way in which he fulfilled them, was his charisma. *Charisma* refers to the power to attract other people and to influence them directly without using existing authorities

Figure 7.9
Near Tabgha on the shore of the Sea of Galilee. The ancient name for the site was *Heptapegon* or 'seven springs'. Early church tradition located three events from the Gospel narratives here: it is the traditional site where Jesus sat in the boat to deliver the parable discourse to the crowd on the shore; the traditional site of the multiplication of the loaves and fish, and the conferral upon Peter of the leadership in the church after Jesus's resurrection

and institutions. In Jesus's case this charisma was related to his close relationship with, and his experience of, God whom he regarded as his father. It was the source of the authority with which he spoke and acted, and of his healings and exorcisms as well as his advocating of unconventional values and modes of behaviour.

The different roles Jesus played resulted from, and cohere with, his charisma. They are also closely related to his vision and preaching of the 'kingdom of God'.

8 THE TEACHINGS OF JESUS

8.1 Jesus's teaching about the kingdom of God

Prior to Jesus, the phrase *kingdom of God* was relatively rare. The precise term that was translated as *basileia theou* in Greek does not occur in the books of the Hebrew canon and only once in the Old Testament Apocrypha (Wisdom of Solomon 10:10). The notion of God ruling as king in the present and in future is, however, prominent in some parts of the Old Testament, especially in the Psalms and the book of Isaiah (cf e g Ps 103:19; 145:13; Isa 52:7). During the Second Temple period, the idea of God's kingship was used particularly in

Figure 8.1
The Mount of Temptation in the Judaean wilderness where, according to tradition, the first and third temptation of Jesus took place. The twelfth-century monastery (Jebel Quruntal) is visible two thirds up the mountain face in the middle and to the left. Forty metres below the monastery is the Cave of Elijah, traditionally identified as the cave where Elijah fled after Jezebel had plotted against his life (1 Kings 19). The monastery looks out over Jericho to the south-east

Figure 8.2
The 'pinnacle' or the south-eastern corner of the temple esplanade, viewed from the Kidron Valley below. According to tradition, this was the site of the third temptation of Jesus (Luke 4:9)

eschatological and apocalyptic contexts, referring to Israel's salvation in the future. When Jesus uses the term *kingdom of God* and makes it central to his vision and action, he would be aware of the references to God's kingly rule.

THE CONTENTS OF JESUS'S TEACHING

Scholars differ considerably on which sayings of Jesus are genuine (cf par 8.4). References to the 93 sayings distinguished by Crossan (1989) are listed here. The texts do not necessarily reflect the sayings in the exact original form. Checking these sayings against their parallels in other Gospels and reflecting on them, promise to be a rewarding experience.

Into the desert (Matt 11:7-10); Greater than John (Matt 11:11); Kingdom and violence (Matt 11:12-13); Who has ears (Matt 11:15); The sower (Matt13:3b-8); Ask, seek, knock (Matt 7:7-8//Thom 2; 21,22, 37); Mission and message (Matt 10:7-10); Prophet's own country (Matt 13:53-58); The world's light (Matt 5:14a); Receiving the sender (Matt 10:40); The tenants (Matt 21:33-41); When and where (Matt 24:23-26); Blessed the womb (Luke 11:27-28); Against divorce (Luke 16:18); What goes in (Matt 15:10-11); Kingdom and children (Matt 18:3//Thom 22); Mission and message (Matt 10:11-14); Forgiveness for forgiveness (Matt 6:12); First and last (Matt 19:30); Hidden made manifest (Matt 10:26); The mustard seed (Matt 13:31-32); Lamp and bushel (Matt 5:15); Serpents and doves (Matt 10:16b); The planted weeds (Matt 13:24-30); Have and receive (Matt 13:12); Blessed are the poor (Luke 6:20b); Knowing the times (Matt 16:2-3); The feast (Matt 22:1-13); Caesar and God (Matt 22:15-22); Blessed are the hungry (Luke 6:21); Saving one's life (Matt 10:39); For and against (Mark 9:40); The fishnet (Matt 13:47-48); Fire on earth (Luke 12:49); Peace or sword (Matt 10:34-36); The harvest time (Mark 4:26-29); The entrusted money (Matt 25:14-28); Speck and log (Matt 7:35); The mountain city (Matt 5:14b); Open proclamation (Matt 10:27); The blind guide (Matt 15:14b); The unmerciful servant (Matt 18:32-34); The strong one's house (Matt 12:29); Against anxieties (Matt 6:25-33); Serving two masters (Thom 47); Drinking old wine (Luke 5:39); Patches and wineskins (Matt 9:16-17); Hating one's family (Matt 10:37); The Good Samaritan (Luke 10:29-37); The rich farmer (Luke 12:16-21); Blessed are the sad (Matt 5:4); The disputed inheritance (Luke 12:13-15); The pearl (Matt 13:45-46); Foxes have holes (Matt 8:19-20); Inside and outside (Matt 23:25-26); Give without return (Matt 5:42); The leaven (Matt 13:33); Jesus's true family (Matt 12:46-50); Friend at midnight (Luke 11:5-7); Fasting and wedding (Matt 9:14-15); The lost sheep (Matt 18:12-14); The prodigal son (Luke 15:11-32); The treasure (Matt 13:44); Love your enemies (Matt 5:43-44); Beelzebul controversy (Matt 9:32-34); Honours and salutations (Matt 23:5-7); Salting the salt (Matt 5:13); The other cheek (Matt 5:38-41); Leave the dead (Matt 8:21-22); Good gifts (Matt 7:9-11); God and sparrows (Matt 10:29-31); Heart and treasurer (Matt 6:21); The tower builder and warring king (Luke 14:28-32); The lost coin (Luke 15:8-10);

Looking backward (Luke 9:61-62); Blessed are the persecuted (Matt 5:10-12); Unlimited forgiveness (Matt 18:21-22); Leader as servant (Matt 18:1,4); Kingdom and riches (Matt 19:23-26); The barren tree (Luke 13:6-9); Stone and wood (Thom 77); Exaltation and humiliation (Matt 23:12); The empty jar (Thom 97); The assassin (Thom 98); Prayer and forgiveness (Matt 5:23-24); Against oaths (Matt 5:33-37); The vineyard labourers (Matt 20:1-15); Kingdom and eunuch (Matt 19:10-12a); The two sons (Matt 21:28-32); The unjust steward (Luke 16:1-7); Rich man and Lazarus (Luke 16:19-31); The unjust judge (Luke 18:2-8); Carrying one's cross (Matt 10:38).

POSSIBLE 'ORIGINAL' SAYINGS FROM THE *GOSPEL OF THOMAS*

2. He who seeks must not stop seeking until he finds,
   and when he finds he will be bewildered,
   and when he is bewildered, he will marvel,
   and will be king over everything.

3. When you know yourselves, then you will be known,
   and you will know that you are the sons of the living Father.
   But if you do not know yourselves,
   then you are in poverty, and you are poverty.

21. Mary said to Jesus: What are your disciples like? He said:
    They are like little children who dwell in a field that does not belong to them. When the owners of the field come, they will say: 'Leave our field to us!' They are naked in their presence,
    as they leave it to them and give back their field to them.

22. Jesus saw children being suckled. He said to his disciples:
    These children being suckled are like those who enter the kingdom.

37. His disciples said: On what day will you be revealed to us and on what day will we see you? Jesus said: When you undress without being ashamed, and when you take your clothing and lay them under your feet as little children and tread on them, then you will behold the son of the living one and you will have no fear.

47. It is not possible for a man to ride two horses and to stretch two bows, and it is impossible for a servant to serve two masters, either he will honour the one and despise the other.

58. Blessed is the man who has laboured (suffered), he has found life.

67. He who knows the All, but not himself has missed everything.

70. When you produce something within yourself
    that which you have produced will save you.
    When you don't have what you have produced,
    that which you don't have will kill you.

77. I am the light which is over everything
    I am the All, the All came forth from me and it has reached to me. Split the wood, I am there. Lift up the stone and you will find me there.

> 97 The kingdom is like a woman carrying a jar full of meal. While she was walking a long way, the handle of the jar broke and the meal spilled out behind her on the road. She did not know it, she did not perceive the accident. After she had come into her house, she put the jar down and found it empty.
>
> 98 The kingdom is like a man who wanted to kill a powerful man. He drew the sword within his house and ran it through the wall, that he might know whether his hand would be strong enough. Then he killed the powerful man.

Jesus did not, however, merely stick to the previous use and connotations of God's kingly rule. He frequently spoke about the kingdom of God and in diverse ways: as a place to be entered (Mark 9:47; 14:25), as something to be sought (Luke 12:31), as something of the present and of the future. The petition for the coming of the kingdom in the Lord's Prayer (Luke 11:2//Matt 6:10), for example, focuses on a future kingdom. In fact, quite a number of sayings of Jesus fall in this category (cf e g Mark 14:25; Luke 13:28//Matt 8:11).

Yet to Jesus the kingdom was not confined to the future: what was expected in future, was in a sense already something of the present (Luke 17:21). It was, moreover, related to, and present in, his most typical teaching and actions. It was there when, by means of his parables and other wisdom sayings, he challenged people to think and live differently. It was present in his meals with tax collectors and sinners, by which he anticipated a coming messianic banquet. It was especially present when he healed people and exorcised demons, thereby breaking the power of Satan and inaugurating the expected time of salvation. This is clear from Matthew 12:28, where the kingdom is specifically linked to Jesus's exorcisms: 'But if I drive out demons by the Spirit of God, then the kingdom of God has come upon you,' and, when the disciples

Figure 8.3
The caves of the god of the forest, Pan, at the ancient Paneas or Caesarea Philippi, the source of the Jordan River. It was in this area that Peter declared that Jesus was the Christ upon being asked by Jesus whom he thought he was. Jesus also named Peter as the rock upon which the church would be built

of John the Baptist came to ask him whether he was the one to come, he answered:

> Go back and report to John what you hear and see:
> the blind receive sight, the lame walk,
> those who have leprosy are cured,
> the deaf hear, the dead are raised,
> and the good news is preached to the poor'
> (Matt 11:4–5).

In the extra-canonical *Gospel of Thomas* (saying 113) the present dimension of the kingdom also comes out clearly: 'the kingdom of the Father is spread over the earth and men do not see it'. Compare also the striking expression of the same notion in saying 3:

> If those who lead you say to you: 'The kingdom is in heaven',
> then the birds of heaven will precede you,
> if they say to you: 'It is in the sea',
> then the fish will precede you.
> But the kingdom is within you and outside you.

Jesus's radical demands on his followers and his willingness to leave existing conventions behind may be related to the new era which, in a sense, he was already inaugurating and which implied the leaving behind of the old era. By relating the kingdom to his teaching and actions, Jesus showed what the kingdom of God and living within it are about. The kingdom was, at least partly, about everyday needs and about compassion towards the marginalised in society.

8.2 Jesus's subversive wisdom teaching or reversal of values

In detecting the nature, style and main themes of Jesus's teaching, the obvious access route is the various forms or genres he employed.

(1) There are the parables, of which approximately 30 are contained in the Synoptic Gospels and three 'new' ones in the *Gospel of Thomas*. Most of these probably date back to Jesus himself.

Parables refer to the short stories Jesus told, in which he utilised nature or contemporary society familiar to his listeners. The image of a sower (Mark 4) would, for example, not be foreign to people in an agrarian society, nor would that of a farmer who sent out workers to work in his land (Matt 20:1–16). By injecting an element of surprise into his stories, Jesus led his hearers out of old

Figure 8.4
Farming scene in present-day Israel. Many of the narrative details of the parables of Jesus (e g the parable of the sower) were derived from traditional methods of farming. Note the terraced hillside in the background. It was customary to terrace sloping ground and build low walls to aid water catchment

ways of looking at the world to new ways of seeing and acting. The Jews of Jesus's time who did not have good relations with the Samaritans would, for example, not easily have made a Samaritan the hero of a story. In Jesus's narrative (Luke 10:25–37) this is precisely what happens. The same applies to the parable of the Pharisee and the tax-collector (Luke 18:9–14). In the real life of Jesus's time, as would be the case today, the owner of a vineyard would have paid the workers according to the hours they worked. In Jesus's parable (Matt 20:1–16), however, those who worked fewer hours were paid the same amount of money as everyone else.

(2) Another typical form used by Jesus are the short proverb-like sayings called *aphorisms*. Aphorisms are usually described as sayings which do not reflect the conventional wisdom of a society, but the unconventional views of an individual. Some of Jesus's sayings give expression to obvious truths (e g Luke 6:44//Matt 7:16; Luke 6:13//Matt 6:24). In others, as in some of his parables, he comes up with surprising insights, in which the ordinary ways of understanding things are reversed: those who are first, will be last (Mark 10:31), those who want to preserve their lives, will lose them (Mark 8:35), and those who are willing to give, will receive (Mark 10:21–30).

In Jesus's parables and other sayings a distinct view of reality and of God comes to the fore. According to Jesus, God acts in unpredictable and surprising ways. The wages he hands out are disproportional to the work done (Matt 20:1-16). When the guests he invites to a feast do not turn up, he replaces them with people from the streets. He is compassionate (Luke 15); the one who causes his sun to rise on the evil and the good (Matt 5:45; Luke 6:35).

One should be careful not to romanticise and 'esotericise' Jesus's teaching and to detach it from the hard realities of his world and time. His teaching was, as was the rest of his ministry, related to the context of first-century Galilee. It had social implications, as is evident from his conduct towards sinners and tax collectors. Aspects of his teaching may even have referred to a reordering of society (cf e g Matt 20:1-16).

Figure 8.5
View across the Sea of Galilee from the Mount of Beatitudes

8.3 Jesus's ethical teaching

Since Jesus did not merely adhere to conventional wisdom, the questions arise as to what he thought of the law of Moses – so important to Jews – and about purity laws. Did his teaching imply the rejection of the Torah?

There are no indications in the Gospels that Jesus did away with the Torah. While sometimes showing a great amount of freedom towards it, he in some respects intensified it. This applies especially to the love commandment, which he extended from love of one's neighbour to love of one's enemy (Matt 5:23), the stranger (Luke 10:25–37) and sinners (Luke 7:36–50; cf also Mark 10:11ff and Matt 5:3ff for examples of Jesus's radicalisation or intensification of the law).

The ritual norms prescribed by the law, such as commandments about cleanliness, were not done away with by Jesus. According to Mark 1:40–45 (the healing of the leper), Jesus approved of sacrifice. He, however, considered it to be less important than the needs and interests of people. It is more important to save a life than to keep to the sabbath commandment (Mark 3:4). Reconciliation with one's brother should precede the sacrificial cult (Matt 5:23ff).

8.4 Criteria for authenticating sayings and deeds of Jesus

When New Testament scholars started to realise that, as a result of the nature of the Gospels and the complexity of their origin, it is not possible to ascribe all the sayings and deeds of Jesus in the Gospels to Jesus himself, a number of criteria were established to determine his authentic sayings and deeds. The following are most commonly used to help determine what could be attributed to Jesus.

(1) *Discontinuity with existing traditions.* According to this criterion, to qualify as authentic, a Jesus saying must differ from convictions within Palestinian Judaism and early Christianity.

(2) The *criterion of multiple attestation.* This criterion implies that sayings which appear in more than one independent source have a greater claim to authenticity than sayings which appear in only one source or in sources dependent on one another.

(3) The *criterion of coherence* implies that a saying which coheres with what has been established as typical of Jesus's teaching or action probably does belong to him.

These criteria are not without problems. As regards the first one, it can be pointed out that Jesus's teaching not only differed from, but would have shown similarities with, his Jewish milieu. He was, after all, a Jew. Between Jesus and early Christianity there would also have been continuity as well as discontinuity. If the second criterion is applied consistently, sayings which could have originated with Jesus but which are not extant in more than one independent source could be excluded.

9 THE DEATH OF JESUS

Figure 9.1

The skull-like hill popularised by General Gordon in 1883 as the site of the historical Golgotha. The Garden Tomb, touted as the tomb of Jesus, is nearby. However, the most probable site of the historical Golgotha and the tomb of Jesus is located in the Church of the Holy Sepulchre. The Holy Sepulchre is built on the site of an ancient stone quarry which was outside the city walls in the first century CE. The rocky outcrop, the tombs left in the quarry walls and the possibility of plant growth in the disused quarry make the Holy Sepulchre the likely site of Jesus's crucifixion and burial. The earliest Christian community in Jerusalem held liturgical celebrations at the site of the Holy Sepulchre until 66 CE

Figure 9.2
View of the Temple Mount in Jerusalem from the Mount of Olives across the Kidron Valley and the Garden of Gethshemane (in the foreground). The large dome on the left is the golden roof of the Dome of the Rock, which stands on the place where, according to tradition, Abraham had come to sacrific Isaac. A Muslim tradition also has it that Muhammad ascended to heaven from here

The question can be posed why Jesus – a wandering prophet, healer and teacher – was arrested by the high priest Caiaphas and crucified by the Romans. During his ministry in Galilee there appears to have been some conflict with the Pharisees and scribes about aspects of the law. This would, however, not have been enough reason to execute him. The Pharisees, in fact, play no part in the stories of Jesus's arrest and trial.

Jesus's talk about the kingdom of God and related activities may provide a clue in this regard. These utterances certainly had social and political implications, and could have created suspicion in a region which formed part of the Roman Empire (kingdom) and could have been regarded as a threat to political stability. It is significant that Jesus, who proclaimed the kingdom, was crucified in Jerusalem as the 'king of the Jews' (Matt 27:37; Mark 15:26; Luke 23:38; John 19:19).

The more immediate cause of Jesus's arrest and crucifixion was probably his 'cleansing' of the temple during his and his disciples' visit to

Figure 9.3
Inscription from Caesarea Maritima mentioning Pontius Pilate, the Roman procurator (governor) of Palestine at the time of Jesus's trial and crucifixion. Caesarea Maritima was the administrative capital of the Roman province of Palestine

Figure 9.4
The Garden Tomb venerated by many as the burial place of Jesus Christ. General Gordon was the first to popularise this site as Christ's tomb in 1883, but it is certainly not the historical tomb of Christ. The tomb itself, especially in its interior layout, conforms to other tombs from the ninth to seventh centuries BCE and was certainly not a new tomb in the first century CE as demanded by the passion narrative

Jerusalem at Passover. This action was a symbolic act through which he prophesied the destruction of the temple. Apart from the fact that Jews would regard such action against the temple as a serious offence, it probably confirmed the Jewish and Roman authorities' impression of Jesus as a troublemaker and therefore a threat to peace and order. That this happened during the Passover, when many people were together in Jerusalem, made an uprising among the people an even greater possibility. Jesus's actions as well as the context in which they took place in the end led to his crucifixion.

Jesus's crucifixion came to have immense theological significance for his followers. They believed that his embarrassing death on the cross was not in vain; that he died as a martyr 'for others'.

10 CONCLUSION

Through the ages, people have followed Jesus of Nazareth in various ways and have cherished various images of him. For some he is the saviour of their souls and the mediator which makes eternal salvation possible. For others he provides a window on God and even functions as God himself. Then there are those for whom he is the liberator from social and political injustice.

The historical search for Jesus endeavours to portray an image of him which accounts for the complexity of his person and which is not at the outset dominated by subjective beliefs. It stands to reason that this historical research cannot be entirely objective, but should for this very reason be done within the context of scholarly debate.

The recent historical Jesus research have opened new perspectives on who Jesus was, what he said and did, and what his significance was and is. The famous Irish-born author, George Bernard Shaw, for example, in actual fact anticipated the results of present-day scholarship on Jesus's view of the kingdom when he remarked: 'Jesus said: "The kingdom of God is among you." Ever since the church has looked for it somewhere else.'

The historical Jesus research presents a challenge to the churches and believers to rethink conventional dogmas and beliefs, and today many people within the church are responding to this challenge. Even if people leave the church and give up conventional Christianity, they are still fascinated by the figure of Jesus of Nazareth.

JESUS AND CHRISTIANITY

Christianity takes its name from the figure of Jesus Christ. According to early Christian tradition (Acts 11:26), it was in Antioch in Syria that the 'believers were first called Christians' (Greek: *Christianoi*). As the form of the name would imply, they were constituted (at least in the eyes of outsiders) as a Jewish faction or 'party' much like the Herodians. Historically, Christianity emerged in the Graeco-Roman world as a social, an ideological and a political phenomenon. It is exactly this fact that should lead one to consider the nature of Christianity as a religious movement in late antiquity, and in the light of this, to consider the link between Jesus Christ and Christianity. According to traditional conceptions of the history of Christianity, there is a direct line of development between the historical figure of Jesus of Nazareth and what later developed into 'mainstream', orthodox Christianity. However, as the many 'historical Jesuses' and scholarly Jesus images mentioned earlier already suggested, it is not so simple to construct a 'historical Jesus' for the very reason that a multitude of contemporary ideologies, moral philosophies, mythical imagery and acts of social experimentation exerted their influence on the formulation of the various early Christian Jesus images, as will be clear from the discussion of the early Christian literature.

Religious orientation is conditioned by many factors, from physical, psychological, social and economical, to historical. Concrete, historical religions are not static, homogeneous entities – they are multiform and ever-changing organisms, each taken up in interreligious nodal points of extensive historical dimensions. New religions emerge from their predecessors: come into existence, adapt to changing circumstances and become extinct. Even their 'extinction' is relative. Older European pagan religions lived on in the popular religion of Christian Europe. The old religions of the Graeco-Roman world exerted an indelible influence on the Christianity of late antiquity. Zoroastrianism is a good example of this. Rooted in the ancient Indo-European past, it exerted a tremendous influence on emerging Judaism, Christianity and Islam, even on Mahayana Buddhism. Another good example of this is Manichaeism, a hybrid of apocalyptic Jewish Christianity, Gnosticism, elements of Zoroastrianism and later also Confucianism and Buddhism. Every religion is taken up in this process of give and take; development and change; adaptation and integration; disintegration and reintegration, and demise and rebirth.

On a less grand scale, the same intricate process can be indicated for the emergence of Christianity in the period of late antiquity. To start with, Christianity was not a unitary movement from the beginning. There was no such coherent and singular movement called Christianity in the period of the early Principate onwards. Instead, what is becoming increasingly obvious is that 'Christianity' consisted of sometimes loosely connected, but more often unconnected, communities, groups, various popular movements of a less settled character and mendicant religious entrepreneurs who espoused sometimes vastly different ideologies, creating different epics, cutting new traditions and foundational narratives from the cloth of the past according to the demands of their present contexts, and finally, displaying an astonishing variety of relations to the cultural traditions of the Graeco-Roman world of which they were all part.

In the course of the past century and a half, it became possible through historical-critical investigation of early Christian literature (in their final editions but also the pre-final layers of tradition) to read off the diversity of social locations, social interests but especially the diversity of early Christianities from these sources. So in Q, the *Gospel of Thomas* and in the pre-Markan Jesus anecdotes, conflict narratives and miracle-stories one encounters a Jesus who is not the messiah/Christ; no critique of Second Temple Judaism; no reference to a crucifixion and no hint of a resurrection; or a Jesus who is no more and no less than an old-style traditional prophet, endowed with special enthusiasm and inspiration, and definitely not a god, if one is to go by later accounts of Jewish–Christian gospel traditions. It is surmised that these different Jesus portrayals are rooted in various early Christian 'schools'' production of their own self-images: as a school in opposition to Pharisaic Judaism, as a school for whom the change of lifestyle is the litmus test of belonging, as a school whose teachings should lead to meditation and true insight into one's true nature as child of the universe.

In the Pauline school, one finds a Christ almost divorced from historical factual existence (with very few 'historical' teachings of Jesus preserved and no memories of a historical life), whose almost sole contribution to the foundation of a Pauline discourse was the mytheme of being killed and raised from the dead, and transformed into the Ruler of the cosmos. However, it is in the department of social engineering and social experimentation that the Pauline legacy is strongest. Justified on the grounds of the mytheme of dying and rising, and drinking deeply from the wells of Graeco-Roman (especially Stoic) philosophy and ethics, issues of ethnic extraction, table fellowship and communion, obligations, honour and shame, and who determines who has their say in what Christians should do, are neatly solved, packaged and offered for the communities' consumption. While on the topic of social engineering, one need only pay attention to the abundance of literary exhortation spanning the whole period from the Apostolic Fathers to the Nicene and Post-Nicene Fathers (often without taking recourse to the example of Christ at all, as is the case, for example, with *1 Clement* whose argument is solely based on the imperial ideal of peace and concord) to understand how Christianity was literally exhorted into existence according to the needs and dictates of communities situated in different geographical settings. These communities would interact and contend with one another while holding opposing viewpoints – in the heat of a rhetorical contest, to define self, other and truth – establishing Christianities not yet standardised into an orthodox mainstream. For the earliest layers of the Christian tradition including Jewish Christianities (later defined as wayward traditions),

Jesus was not (yet) a god, nor risen from the dead, nor the substance of a grand plan to found a new, world-wide religion. In the words of Burton Mack: 'For the first forty years, ideas such as these are found only in the letters of Paul.'

Riding the first wave of the emerging new Graeco-Roman literary genre, namely the novel, came the earliest Christian fictions: the Gospels. Leading the pack was 'Mark', the first to combine the anecdotes and stories of the public ministry with an account of the crucifixion, and to affix the title 'Messiah' to the figure of the crucified hero in a type of apocalyptic vindication of the cause of the Jesus movement in the aftermath of the Roman–Jewish war. This was no Hellenistic cult of Christ, but a celebration of the destruction of the temple as ordained by God as punishment for the execution of Jesus by the Jews. In their re-editions of this work of fiction, Matthew and Luke respectively transformed the newly 'Messiah-ed' Jesus into a Christian rabbi for the benefit of a Christian synagogue in Antioch, Syria, and into a Cynic-type philosopher tamed to the tastes of an upper middle-class Jewish audience in some urban environment in Achaea or Asia Minor (as the first installment, in its combination with Acts, of the later prevalent genre of *diadochai* – or succession narratives – in heresiologies and church histories) John left the general ways of the world and turned Jesus into an anti-emperor at the head of a utopian world-turned-upside-down as the imaginary *habitus* for small collegium-like urban communities in what must have been a close relationship to Samaritan and proto-gnostic conventicles.

In the light of the army of scholars chipping away at the possibility of regarding Jesus as 'a very special person' (Mack) it is becoming impossible to continue believing in a direct and causal relationship between the genius, uniqueness and specialness of Jesus, his message and his actions, and the religion about him. To put it differently, the various early Christianities could not all have been triggered by the same historical personage, no matter how imaginably exceptional. If one surveys the range of mediator typologies for early Christianity alone, one encounters types or roles as diverse as teacher, prophet, scribe, sage, divine man, inspired poet, apocalyptic seer, preacher of judgement, messiah, son of man, son of God, divine revealer, gnostic Urmensch, cosmic lord, eschatological judge, heavenly guide and saviour. To put it even more succinctly, Christianity did not arise from one man alone.

As Burton Mack put it:

> Scholars have followed every lead and focused on every possible impulse that might have launched the Christian phenomenon: the person of the historical Jesus; what it was he taught or preached; the reasons for a recognition of Jesus as the Messiah; the reasons for a crucifixion and its trauma; the reports of a resurrection; visions of the resurrected Lord, and the experience of a new spiritual presence; the transformation of the disciples into apostles; the gathering of the first Christian community; the commission to spread the word; the conversion of Gentiles; and so forth. *None of these events are moments that all of the documents recognize as having happened, much less invested with importance as those that called their movements into existence* [own emphasis]. (1999:5)

Apart from the obvious legacy of Hellenistic Judaism, various strands of Graeco-Roman culture are woven into the fabric that became Christianity. The first is Platonic, especially Middle-Platonic, thinking, which as a school of philosophy provided nascent Christianity with the terminology for dialectics and cosmology in Alexandria and made Christian self-definition possible as opposed to paganism in the formation of the Greek–Christian tradition of education. The second is Cynic–Stoic popular philosophy, already providing for Paul the form of expression (the diatribe), but also the contents of moral–ethical exhortation. In its negative attitude to the world, this philosophy has been touted as the inspiration behind the formation of Christian asceticism. Roman conceptions of divinity, in the third place, formed the matrix for Roman–Latin Christian doctrines of God in such church fathers as Tertullian and Lactantius. The fourth strand is the widespread phenomenon of late antique mystery religions. The Christian–Jewish cult employed the language and ritual of the mystery cults and was itself transformed to such an extent that the Christian church became a mystery religion and was regarded as such by Graeco-Roman writers. As one scholar put it: 'The mysteries created the outer form in which Christianity conquered a good deal of the world.' Another strand is Christian Gnosticism which, although only part of a wider phenomenon of pre- and extra-Christian Gnosticism, nevertheless exerted a mighty pull on early Christian mentality through such widely disseminated movements as Manichaeism and late medieval sectarian movements (such as the Paulicians, Bogomils, Cathars and Albigensians) Finally, in the sixth place, Mediterranean popular beliefs and practices were sucked up as it were by the sponge of Christian tradition, determining to a large extent the character of popular Christianity throughout Europe.

The result of these developments was that Christianity became the heir to Greek *paideia*, or education, to such an extent that it was nearly impossible to distinguish between what was uniquely Christian and what not, if ever such a distinction was at all possible in the first place. Tertullian, in his famous lament on the continued matrimonial relationship between Christianity and Greek philosophy, asks:

> What indeed has Athens to do with Jerusalem? What concord is there between the Academy and the Church? What between heretics and Christians? Our instruction comes from 'the porch of Solomon,' who had himself taught that 'the Lord should be sought in simplicity of heart.' Away with all attempts to produce a mottled Christianity of Stoic, Platonic, and dialectic composition! We want no curious disputation after possessing Christ Jesus, no inquisition after enjoying the gospel! With our faith, we desire no further belief.
> (*Prescription Against the Heretics*, 7.9. Refer to the many examples of Zoroastrian apocalyptic ideas in Justin Martyr and especially Lactantius. There are many scintillating examples of comparisons between Christ and Greek and Roman deities in Justin's *First Apology*.)

The context in which these words are found, is an elaborate description of what Tertullian labelled *heresies*. Heresies, he in effect argues, are the miscreants born from incursions into Christianity of Greek philosophy. 'Pure' Christian belief became corrupted through accommodation in Graeco-Roman culture and *paideia*. However, Tertullian should not be taken too seriously. If anything, these words are only indicative of how impossible it was then, as it is now, to distinguish Christian religion from its neighbouring and contemporary worldviews and ideological positions.

Almost a century before Tertullian, Justin Martyr had tried the same. Here the tenor was somewhat different. It was still possible for Justin to compare the history of Jesus Christ with those of the Roman gods (*First Apology* 21), or to argue that Jesus's divine sonship was perfectly conceivable in view of the many 'sons of gods' in the Roman pantheon (*First Apology* 22), even that the suffering-death-resurrection complex in the Christian narrative has its counterparts in the histories of Bacchus, Hercules, Perseus and the Caesars themselves. Justin was arguing the case of the reasonableness of Christianity before the imperial court. By the time of Tertullian, a second front had opened, not only did he need to circumscribe Christian identity *vis-à-vis* Roman religion and culture, but also to define Christian identity in the face of increasing disintegration and variety (one should not forget that the original meaning of *heresy* was 'option' or 'party'). It had become increasingly difficult to ignore the centrifugal lines of development or trajectories in the growth of Christianity and to retain the (mythical) illusion of a romantic past with the first flowering and effervescence of a newly revealed divinity and his cult.

Considerations such as these led the famous historian of religion, Kurt Rudolph, to conclude: 'For the history of religions, there has never been a "pure religion": this would be an ahistorical construct. Indeed, every religion is a syncretistic phenomenon.' (1991:17–18)

Suggested reading

On historical studies

Arnal, William E & Desjardins, Michel (eds)
1997   *Whose Historical Jesus?* Waterloo: Wilfrid Laurier University Press.

Borg, Marcus J
1987   *Jesus: a New Vision. Spirit, Culture, and the Life of Discipleship.* San Francisco: HarperSanFrancisco.
1999   *The Meaning of Jesus: Two Visions.* San Francisco: HarperSanFrancisco.

Crossan, John Dominic
1991   *The Historical Jesus: The life of a Mediterranean Jewish Peasant.* Edinburgh: T & T Clark.
1994   *Jesus: A Revolutionary Biography.* San Francisco: HarperSanFrancisco.

Horsley, Richard A

1987   *Jesus and the Spiral of Violence. Popular Jewish Resistance in Roman Palestine.* San Francisco: Harper & Row.
1996   *Archaeology, History and Society in Galilee. The Social Context of Jesus and the Rabbis.* Valley Forge: Trinity Press International.

Johnson, Luke Timothy
1996   *The Real Jesus.* San Francisco: HarperSanFrancisco.

Kelber, Werner
1999   'The Quest for the Historical Jesus: From the Perspectives of Medieval, Modern, and Post-Enlightenment Readings, and in View of Ancient, Oral Aesthetics.' In Crossan, John Dominic, *et al. The Jesus Controversy.* Harrisburg: Trinity Press International.

Meier, John P
1991   *A Marginal Jew: Rethinking the Historical Jesus.* Volume 1. New York: Doubleday.
1994   *A Marginal Jew: Rethinking the Historical Jesus.* Volume 2. New York: Doubleday.

Patterson, Stephen J
1998   *The God of Jesus: The Historical Jesus and the Search for Meaning.* Harrisburg: Trinity Press International.

Sanders, E P
1985   *Jesus and Judaism.* London: SCM Press.
1993   *The Historical Figure of Jesus.* London: Penguin.

Theissen, Gerd & Merz, Annette
1998   *The Historical Jesus. A Comprehensive Guide.* London: SCM Press.

Vermes, Geza
2000   *The Changing Faces of Jesus.* Allen Lane: Penguin Press.

Wright, Nicholas T
1992   *Who Was Jesus?* London: SPCK.
1996   *Jesus and the Victory of God.* London: SPCK.

On Jesus Christ and Christianity

Mack, Burton
1996   'On Redescribing Christian Origins.' *Method and Theory in the Study of Religion* 8/3:247–269.
1999   'Explaining Christian Origins. A Theory of Social Formations.' Larkin-Stuart Lectures (Trinity College, Toronto).
2001   *The Christian Myth: Origins, Logic and Legacy.* New York: Continuum.

Riley, Gregory
1997   *One Jesus, Many Christs. How Jesus Inspired Not One True Christianity, but Many: The Truth About Christian Origins.* San Francisco: HarperSanFrancisco.

Rudolph, Kurt.
1991   'Early Christianity as a Religious-Historical Phenomenon.' In *The Future of Early Christianity*, Birger A Pearson (ed), 919. Minneapolis: Fortress Press.

1987 'The History of Religions (Religionswissenschaft) and the Religious Situation in Eastern Europe.' In *Gilgul. Essays on Transformation, Revolution and Permanence in the History of Religions,* edited by S Shaked, S Shulman, and G G Stroumsa, 14. Leiden/New York/Köln: Brill.

Van den Heever, Gerhard

2001 'On How to Be or Not to Be: Theoretical Reflection on Religion and Identity in Africa.' *Religion & Theology* 8/1 and 2:1–25.

2002 *John and the Imperial Persona. Divine Redeemers and the Conflict of Utopias.* Unpublished D Litt et Phil Thesis. University of South Africa, Pretoria.

Part three

The earliest Christian literature (30–70 CE)

11 HISTORICAL CONTEXT

During the time after Jesus's death, when the movement he had initiated by means of his ministry was carried on by his followers, the situation in Palestine remained the same as it had been during the first three decades. As in the time of Jesus, there was tension with Rome over economic, political and religious matters.

In 36 CE the governorship of Pontius Pilate came to an end. In Rome, Tiberius was succeeded by Gaius Caligula as emperor (37–41 CE). Attaching great importance to emperor worship, Caligula ordered that a statue of himself be placed in the temple in Jerusalem. This step had the potential for serious revolt amongst the Jews. Fortunately, he was eventually persuaded by Agrippa I, grandson of Herod the Great, to abandon this intention.

In addition to Galilee, where he was ruler, Agrippa I was now also appointed by Claudius – the new emperor who had succeeded Caligula in 41 CE – as king of Judaea and Samaria. On the whole, his rule – cut short after three years by his death in 44 CE – was experienced positively since he respected Jewish sentiments. After his death, Palestine again came under direct Roman control in the form of Roman procurators. From then on relations between the Roman rulers and the Palestinian population deteriorated even further. Banditry, that is, social protest movements which consisted of peasants who had lost their land as a result of economic measures and who thus took food and other necessities from the rich, increased in Galilee and Judaea.

It was in this context that the Jesus movement, which Jesus had initiated, took form. During Jesus's ministry, he mainly, though not exclusively, addressed Jews. Initially, the movement in Galilee was a reform movement among Jews and not a separate movement apart from Israel. Jesus and the members of the Jesus movement were concerned with concrete matters such as poverty and debt. The Jesus movement had an inclusive character. This is evident from factors such as that women and outcasts were 'members', the ethos of compassion which came to expression in table fellowship with outcasts, and its rejection of violent resistance to Rome. Apart from the inference that can be drawn about the Jesus movement from sources such as Q, which will be discussed later, Luke sketches, in Acts 2:44–7 and 4:32–5, the picture of a group of spirit-filled followers of Jesus in Jerusalem who sold their possessions, cared for the poor and had everything in common. Though not a mere historical report, it does provide a glimpse of one part of the Jesus movement.

According to Paul's Letter to the Galatians (ch 2 and Acts 15), the Christians in Jerusalem differed among themselves about various matters, such as circumcision for Gentiles and obedience to the law of Moses.

From the New Testament writings, especially the letters of Paul, it is clear that the Christian movement quickly spread from Palestine to other parts of the Graeco-Roman world such as Syria, Asia Minor, Greece and Rome. As early as 32/33 CE, the date of Paul's conversion, there were already Christians in Damascus. According to Acts, the first community to include Gentile Christians was the church of Antioch in Syria. This spreading of the Christian movement implied two developments. Firstly, although the movement had started in the villages of Galilee, its greatest success was in urban centres such as Jerusalem, Antioch, Ephesus, Philippi, Thessalonika, Corinth and Rome. Secondly, initially it was a Jewish movement, but it was not long before it became mainly a movement among Gentiles. In the spreading of the Christian movement and gospel to the wider Roman world, Paul, whose letters will be discussed later, was the most important figure. Geographic expansion of the movement brought about a change in the cultural environment. Although Palestine formed part of the Graeco-Roman world and was therefore also exposed to Hellenistic influences, the expansion to other areas, especially the big cities of the time, implied even greater cultural and religious diversity. As is evident from the Pauline letters and other New Testament writings, the Christian movement in these areas was confronted with other kinds of problems than those in Palestine. Ethical questions and problems arose about the work of the Spirit, against the background of Hellenistic views in this regard (1 and 2 Corinthians). The way in which Jesus was viewed and interpreted, the designations used to describe him and the meaning of these designations were also influenced by this development. In a Jewish context 'Son of God' was, for example, a relational concept used for the king or the people of Israel. In a Hellenistic environment, where the partition between humans and God was more fluid, this designation came to include connotations of divinity.

The relation between the Roman empire and emperors, on the one hand, and the Christians, on the other, fluctuated from time to time. Following the fire of 64 CE which razed Rome, the emperor Nero ordered the persecution of Christians in Rome. He did this to divert the suspicion that he himself was responsible for the fire. Utterly cruel in nature, this persecution was restricted to Rome. According to the historian Eusebius, Peter was crucified during this persecution.

12 THE FORMATION OF JESUS TRADITIONS

12.1 The *Sayings Gospel Q*

Context of Q

The Gospels in the New Testament are all narrative gospels. The words and deeds of Jesus, his crucifixion and resurrection are incorporated into a narrative about him. The narrative starts with his baptism by John the Baptist (in Matthew and Luke with narratives about his birth) and ends with his crucifixion and resurrection. Mark, the earliest of these Gospels, was written in about 70 CE.

There were, however, also other kinds of gospels in early Christianity. One kind, the 'sayings gospels', probably predate the 'narrative gospels'. A sayings gospel is a collection of sayings of Jesus. Two examples of these kinds of gospels are the *Sayings Gospel Q* and the *Gospel of Thomas*. Q no longer exists as a separate document. The Gospel of Thomas, which is an extra-canonical writing, was only discovered in 1945 in its complete form. To discuss the *Sayings Gospel Q* in a meaningful way, one needs to examine the sources of the first three canonical gospels (Matthew, Mark and Luke) (see box).

Q is reconstructed from the material common to Matthew and Luke and which is not derived from Mark. Although this source is currently only available as embedded in Matthew and Luke, some scholars are of the opinion that it initially existed as a separate writing. The *Sayings Gospel Q* was tentatively reconstructed by New Testament scholars.

It is characteristic of Q that the sayings of Jesus are not assembled at random. The sayings are organised into discourses. It is, moreover, striking that Q contains no material about Jesus's suffering, crucifixion and resurrection. This also applies to the other sayings gospel, namely the *Gospel of Thomas*.

> **THE TWO-SOURCE HYPOTHESIS**
>
> When reading the four Gospels that form part of the New Testament, it becomes clear that there are substantial differences between the Gospel of John, on the one hand, and the Gospels of Matthew, Mark and Luke, on the other. These differences will receive attention when the Gospel of John is discussed. What is of concern for the moment is the relation between the first three gospels, Matthew, Mark and Luke.

A page-through of the Gospels of Matthew, Mark and Luke, reveals that Mark consists of 16 chapters, Matthew of 28 chapters and Luke of 24. A reading of the opening verses of each Gospel shows that Matthew and Luke start with birth narratives, while Mark starts with the appearance of John the Baptist.

When these Gospels are closely compared, one realises that there are also many similarities between them. Apart from a few divergences, the events are narrated more or less in the same order. There are also great verbal similarities between the three Gospels. A careful reading of them shows that most of the material in Mark is present in Matthew and Luke. In addition to this common material, Matthew and Luke contain material not present in Mark. Of the additional material, some sections appear in both Matthew and Luke, while each of the Gospels also has material unique to that particular Gospel.

In cases where the same incident is narrated in different Gospels, it is not necessarily done in exactly the same way. Matthew may, for example, shorten a miracle which also occurs in Mark (e g in Mark 5:1-20 and Matt 8:28-34) or make other changes. Luke may perhaps add something or change the main point of a narrative.

In Gospel research these differences are used as clues from which inferences can be drawn about the origin and context of the different Gospels. With regard to their origin, the data gave rise to the two-source hypothesis about the origin of the Gospels. According to this hypothesis, the Gospel of Mark was written first. When writing their Gospels, Matthew and Luke used Mark as one of their sources. This explains why the greatest part of Mark occurs in these Gospels. For the material in both Matthew and Luke, but which is not in Mark, another source, called Q (from the German *Quelle'* = 'source'), was used. Q consists mainly of sayings of Jesus. To explain the material distinctive to Matthew and Luke, a source M is postulated for Matthew and a source L for Luke. Although this hypothesis is not the last word about the origin of the Gospels, it does explain much about their origin.

The differences between the Gospels indicate that right from the beginning, Jesus's ministry, and his words and deeds were interpreted in different ways and for different audiences. In section 11 some attention was paid to the broad social context of the New Testament writings and also to developments within early Christianity. The differences between the Gospels and therefore the realisation of different emphases in them can assist in creating a more specific context and audience for each Gospel.

Q is most probably the earliest available source about Jesus. It can be dated between 30 and 60 CE. Q dates from the time before the Jewish War (66-70 CE), unlike the narrative Gospels. The apocalyptic sayings in Q (Luke 17:27,28,34,35), where nothing is said about wars and catastrophes which will precede the end (i e about the destruction of the temple) may be an indication of this. From the references to Capernaum, Chorazin and Betsaida in Q 10:12-15 (= Luke 10:12-15, cf 'Contents of Q') it can be inferred that Q probably originated and functioned in a 'community' of Jesus's early followers in Galilee who carried

> on his work after his death. This 'community' is sometimes referred to as the Jesus movement, as was pointed out earlier. The combination of rural and urban imagery in Q also makes sense in a Galilean environment. Some of the material in Q points to people who were experiencing poverty and hunger (cf e g the Lord's Prayer and the discourse about anxiety about the necessities of life, Q 12: 22–31, 33–4). Q also contains clear traces of conflict between the people and the rulers, especially the scribes and Pharisees (Q 11:47–52) and the ruling house in Jerusalem (Q 13:34–5).

Message of Q

Since Q is regarded as containing, on the one hand, a strong element of wisdom and, on the other, apocalyptic material in the form of announcements of the coming judgement and references to the coming of the Son of Man, some researchers on Q are of the opinion that this 'document' contains more than one layer. According to this theory, Q initially mainly consisted of wisdom sayings. Only at a later stage was apocalyptic material incorporated. There is, however, no unanimity on this. In fact, some scholars regard the dichotomy between 'wisdom' and 'apocalyptic' as problematic and prefer to speak of the prophetic orientation of Q. When the message of Q is formulated, the document as a whole will be taken into account.

The 'kingdom of God' is a prominent, even a unifying theme in Q. In Q 6:20–3 the kingdom of God is proclaimed to the the poor, the hungry and the persecuted, and blessings are pronounced on them. That the kingdom of God is viewed in Q as something concrete is evident from the fact that the prayer for the kingdom is also a prayer for sufficient food and forgiveness of debts (Q 11:24, 9–13).

In Q, members of the community also receive instruction, among other things, in the form of radical ethical demands, as to how they should live and deal with the problems which they face in their community with its particular circumstances (Q 6: 27–36, 27–38, 41–2). Instructions on different matters are given to the community: on prayer (Q 11:24, 9–13), for 'mission' (Q 9: 57–62, 10:1–16) and on preparedness (Q 17:23–37).

The members of the Q community are expected to continue the work which Jesus started. His followers are sent on a mission to heal the sick and proclaim the kingdom of God (Q 10:5–9), as Jesus had been doing (Q 7:18–25). Those who do not listen, are condemned (Q 10:10–15).

Apart from the instructions to, and the promise of, God's sustenance to members of the Q community, there is in Q an emphasis on judgement, especially on the scribes and Pharisees for the negative effects their activities had on the people.

CONTENTS OF Q

The (reconstructed) contents of Q indicate that it consists mainly of different kinds of sayings of Jesus. Unlike the *Gospel of Thomas*, Q is not simply a collection of sayings, but is composed of a sequence of discourses. Since Q is regarded as being preserved most truthfully by Luke, Luke's numbering is used to indicate the units of which Q consists (e g: Luke 3:7-9 = Q 3:7-9).

Q (verse numbering according to the Gospel of Luke)

3:7-9, 16-17	John's preaching of the Messiah
4:1-13	Temptation of Jesus
6:20b-49	Jesus's inaugural sermon
7: 1-10,18-28; 7:31-35	John, Jesus and this generation
9:57-62; 10:24	Discipleship and mission
11: 24,9-13	On prayer
11: 14-52	Controversies with Israel
12:2-12	On fearless preaching
12:22-31,33-34	On anxiety over material needs
12:39-59	Preparedness for the end
13:18-21	Two parables of growth
13:24-30,34-35; 14:16-24,26,27; 17:33; 14:33-34	The two ways
15:37; 16:13,17-18; 17:16	Various parables and sayings
17:23-37; 19:12-27; 22:28-30	The eschatological discourse.

Apart from sayings of Jesus, the only other kinds of material in Q are: one miracle story (Luke 7:1-10 = Matt 8:5-13), material about John the Baptist and the baptism of Jesus (parts from Luke 3:29,16-17,21-22 = Matt 3:117) and the narrative of the temptation of Jesus (Luke 4:1-13 = Matt 4:1-11). These passages are related to Jesus's words in the sense that they portray him as a figure of authority, more powerful than John the Baptist (cf Luke 3:17). It is his words which appear in the rest of the *Sayings Gospel Q*.

The message of Q contains other facets. To Jesus's followers, including the poor and the deprived, a reversal of their condition is promised. Until that happens, they must continue the work Jesus started: heal the sick and proclaim the kingdom of God (10:2–16). In carrying out their work, they should follow the path of unconventional wisdom as opposed to those who do them injustice: love those who oppose them, pray for their enemies (cf e g Luke 6:27–36 above). And they should use what they have received in a responsible way (Luke 19:12–13, 15–26).

Apart from the instructions and the promise of God's sustenance to Jesus's followers, Q emphasises judgement, especially of the religious leaders, who are more interested in ritual than in moral purity.

EXAMPLES OF JESUS SAYINGS IN Q

Unconventional wisdom: Q 6:27–36

But I tell you who hear me: Love your enemies, do good to those who hate you, bless those who curse you, pray for those who mistreat you. If someone strikes you on one cheek, turn to him the other also. If someone takes your cloak, do not stop him from taking your tunic. Give to everyone who asks you, and if anyone takes what belongs to you, do not demand it back. Do to others as you would have them do to you. If you love those who love you, what credit is that to you? Even sinners love those who love them. And if you do good to those who do good to you, what credit is that to you? Even sinners do that. And if you lend to those from whom you expect repayment, what credit is that to you? Even sinners lend to sinners, expecting to be repaid in full. But love your enemies, do good to them, and lend to them without expecting to get anything back. Then your reward will be great, and you will be sons of the Most High, because he is kind to the ungrateful and wicked. Be merciful, as your Father is merciful.

(NIV).

Traditional wisdom: Q 6:37–42

Do not judge, and you will not be judged. Do not condemn, and you will not be condemned. Forgive, and you will be forgiven. Give, and it will be given to you. A good measure, pressed down, shaken together and running over, will be poured into your lap. For with the measure you use, it will be measured to you. He also told them this parable: Can a blind man lead a blind man? Will they not both fall into a pit? A student is not above his teacher, but everyone who is fully trained will be like his teacher. Why do you look at the speck of sawdust in your brother's eye and pay no attention to the plank in your own eye? How can you say to your brother, 'Brother, let me take the speck out of your eye', when you yourself fail to see the plank in your own eye? You hypocrite, first take the plank out of your eye, and then you will see clearly to remove the speck from your brother's eye.

(NIV).

> ### Prophetic sayings: Q 6:20–22
>
> Blessed are you who are poor, for yours is the kingdom of God. Blessed are you who hunger now, for you will be satisfied. Blessed are you who weep now, for you will laugh. Blessed are you when men hate you, when they exclude you and insult you and reject your name as evil, because of the Son of Man.
>
> (NIV).
>
> ### Apocalyptic sayings: Q 17:26–28; Q 17:34–35
>
> Just as it was in the days of Noah, so will it be in the days of the Son of Man. People were eating, drinking, marrying and being given in marriage up to the day Noah entered the ark. Then the flood came and destroyed them all.
>
> I tell you on that night two people will be on one bed; one will be taken and the other left. Two women will be grinding together; one will be taken and the other left.
>
> (NIV).

With regard to the significance of Jesus, it is clear that according to Q, this significance is to be found primarily in his words and not in his crucifixion and resurrection, as in the Pauline letters. For Q, Jesus's life and its continuation by his followers is important. Apart from the importance of Jesus's words in Q, he is also portrayed from the start as the one who overcomes the evil forces (cf Luke 4:2-12; 7:18-23; 11:14-22).

The emphasis in Q on the words of Jesus is important, since it indicates that the early Christians differed about Jesus and his significance, that is, in which facet of his life and ministry his significance should primarily be located.

12.2 THE *GOSPEL OF THOMAS*

Context of the *Gospel of Thomas*

The *Gospel of Thomas* was discovered during 1945 at Nag Hammadi in Egypt as part of a great number of manuscripts, most of them Gnostic in nature. The name, *The Gospel According to Thomas*, occurs at the end of the document and was added at a later stage to the document of which the heading reads: 'These are the secret words which the living Jesus spoke, and which Didymus Judas Thomas wrote down.' The manuscript is a Coptic translation of a writing which previously existed in Greek and of which smaller fragments were known earlier in Greek.

The author of the *Gospel of Thomas* is indicated in the prologue as Didimus Thomas Judas. This form of the name also occurs in the apocryphal *Acts of Thomas* and in other writings which had their home in Syria. The Gospel probably comes from Edessa in eastern Syria, where there is evidence of the popularity of the Apostle Thomas. As mentioned before, the sayings in *Thomas* do not all come from the same period. Part of the *Gospel of Thomas* could have been composed as early as 50 CE, while other sayings were probably not added until the second century of the common era.

There are indications in Thomas that the people among whom it functioned were wandering and homeless. The itinerant lifestyle is evaluated positively when they are in *Thomas* 42 exhorted to be 'passers-by', that is, itinerants. In *Thomas* 86 ('Foxes have their dens and birds have their nests, but human beings have no place to lay down and rest') there is a reference to homelessness, which resembles the saying in Q. Except for itinerancy, the lifestyle of this group of Christians also included the loosening of family ties and their replacement with other ties, poverty and a kind of beggarly life. Unlike the Synoptic Gospels, especially Matthew and Luke, which already presuppose a situation of settled communities and community structures, Thomas contains no indications of the formation of such structures. Thomas Christianity probably consisted of a loosely structured movement of wanderers. Access to the kingdom is promised to individuals in *Thomas*.

> **CONTENTS OF THE *GOSPEL OF THOMAS***
>
> The *Gospel of Thomas* is, like Q, a collection of sayings of Jesus (proverbs, aphorisms, parables and prophetic sayings) and contains no references to Jesus's birth, death and resurrection. Except for the fact that the document provides valuable insights into the nature of, and diversity within, early Christianity, its discovery strengthened the conviction that a

genre of sayings of Jesus existed in early Christianity. It therefore contributed to the confirmation of the hypothesis of the existence of Q as a separate document.

Scholars divided the material in the *Gospel of Thomas* into 114 sayings of Jesus, some of which are complete parables. Most of the sayings start with 'Jesus said'. While the sayings of Jesus in Q are arranged according to topics, in the *Gospel of Thomas* they (or groups of them) are linked by means of catch words. There is no indication that the writing as a whole was compiled according to a specific plan.

When reading the sayings in *Thomas*, one is struck by the drastic differences between some of them. Many of them sound familiar, since they appear in the Synoptic Gospels, among others, the following parables: the parable of the sower and the seed (*Gos Thom* 9), the mustard seed (*Gos Thom* 20), the feast (*Gos Thom* 64), the pearl (*Gos Thom* 76), and the tenant farmers (*Gos Thom* 65). Next to these are sayings which breathe a different tone and which are influenced by Gnosticism. The following is an example of this: 'Jesus said: "I took my stand in the midst of the world, and in the flesh I appeared to them. I found them all drunk, and I did not find any of them thirsty. My soul ached for the children of humanity, because they are blind in their hearts and do not see, for they came into the world empty, and they also seek to depart from the world empty. But now they are drunk. When they shake off their wine, then they will repent."' (*Gos Thom* 28).

It is also clear that the sayings do not all come from the same period. A saying such as 'Blessed are the poor, for yours is the kingdom of heaven' (*Gos Thom* 54) probably goes back to Jesus. Others come from a much later period, for example: 'Jesus said: "Lucky is the lion that the human will eat, so that the lion becomes human. And foul is the human that the lion will eat, and the lion still will become human"' (*Gos Thom* 7 – cf also chapter 3, par 4).

PARABLES THAT OCCUR ONLY IN THE *GOSPEL OF THOMAS*

8 And he said: 'The human one is like a wise fisherman who cast his net into the sea and drew it up from the sea full of little fish. Among them the wise fisherman discovered a fine large fish. He threw all the little fish back into the sea, and easily chose the large fish. Anyone here with two good ears had better listen.'

97 Jesus said: 'The kingdom of the Father is like a woman who was carrying a jar full of meal. While she was walking along a distant road, the handle of the jar broke and the meal spilled behind her along the road. She didn't know it; she

> hadn't noticed a problem. When she reached her house, she put the jar down and discovered that it was empty.'
>
> 98 Jesus said: 'The kingdom of the Father is like a person who wanted to kill someone powerful. While still at home he drew his sword and thrust it into the wall to find out whether his hand would go in. Then he killed the powerful one.'

Message of the *Gospel of Thomas*

As a wisdom writing, the *Gospel of Thomas* deals with the nature of the world and man's proper relationship with it, and life and the way it should be lived. The wisdom of the practical *world*, such as the security of home, family and possessions is rejected. This comes to the fore in many sayings in the Gospel, also those with an ascetic tendency, and has its counterpart in the lifestyle of the Thomas Christians referred to earlier.

As regards his teaching about Jesus, Thomas does not refer to Jesus as the *Son of God*, *Messiah* or the *Son of Man* – designations used for Jesus in the canonical Gospels. According to him, Jesus's role is that of the Revealer, whose words bring life. Faith in Jesus is for Thomas faith in his words. The kingdom, which is mainly a present reality in Thomas, is also portrayed as present in the words of Jesus.

13 PAULINE LITERATURE

13.1 Historical context of Paul and his letters

Letters ascribed to the Apostle Paul comprise about half the writings (13 out of 24) of the New Testament and a quarter of its volume. More than half of the story of early Christianity in the Acts of the Apostles deals with Paul's efforts to spread the gospel of Jesus Christ. Paul stemmed from an upper-class Jewish family living outside the Jewish land, far to the north in Tarsus in the region of Cilicia in the south-eastern corner of modern-day Turkey.

From his father he inherited Roman citizenship, which gave him certain valuable privileges as far as legal and criminal procedures were concerned.

Figure 13.1
Mosaic, from the museum of St Chora, of the Apostle Paul portrayed as a philosopher

Paul could demand to be respected as a Roman citizen when he was being treated unjustly (*see* Acts 16:37 and 21:39). Eventually, he used this right to appeal to the Roman emperor (Caesar) when he was jailed in Caesarea and was in danger of losing his life (Acts 25:10,11).

According to the narrative in Acts, Paul was a Pharisee who studied the Jewish law (Torah) and knew a trade: he was a qualified 'tent maker' who could support himself with linen and leather work, as he did, for instance, in Corinth and Thessalonica (*see* Acts 18:3,2; Thom 3:7–9). Acts 23:23 discloses that Paul had a sister living in Jerusalem, confirming the bond of his family with Jerusalem. The rabbinic master under whom he claimed to have studied, Gamaliel, was a grandson of the famous Hillel (60 BCE–20 CE), who had a freer view of the rule of Jewish law than his contemporary, Shammai. Hillel saw a place for the nations in God's purpose and was in favour of winning the pagans for Judaism. According to his self-testimony, Paul was a zealous promoter of Judaism to the point of persecuting Christians.

It is related that Paul at first persecuted his fellow Jews who believed in Christ as the long-awaited Messiah, but then had first-hand experience of the risen Christ (1 Cor 9:1, *see* 2 Cor 5:16) at Damascus and became one of the most influential figures in the Christian religion. He spent many years establishing

Christian communities and house-churches throughout (mainly) Asia Minor, Greece and eventually in Rome. It is important to note that his letters were written in response to real problems that had arisen in the early Christian communities. He was responsible for providing pastoral guidance and making his presence felt through his letters.

Many examples of ordinary, mostly private, letters still exist from about the time of Paul. They were usually written on papyrus and survived in dry climates of, for instance, Egypt and Palestine. Paul wrote according to the customs of letter writing in the Hellenistic world and his language was very nearly that which was generally used for everyday communication in the Roman Empire.

It is certain that Paul wrote more letters than those included in the Bible. He himself mentions letters that do not exist, or cannot be identified with certainty (*see* 1 Cor 5:9). Some letters in the New Testament (Phil, 2 Cor and Rom) give the impression that they might have been put together from parts of more than one original letter. Up to 14 letters of the New Testament were at some time regarded as written by Paul and 13 actually bear his name as author or co-author. In modern scholarship there are the following opinions, each of which will be explained in dealing with the letters individually:

(1) One of the letters was definitely not from Paul, namely Hebrews.

(2) Seven letters are clearly Pauline: 1 Thessalonians, 1 and 2 Corinthians, Galatians, Philippians, Philemon and Romans.

(3) Three letters are disputed, perhaps writen by followers of Paul: Ephesians, 2 Thessalonians and Colossians.

(4) Three probably originated from followers of Paul: 1 and 2 Timothy and Titus. These three are also called the Pastoral Epistles, from the word *pastor*, meaning 'shepherd' and used in a spiritual sense, since they contain instruction to leaders responsible for a local church.

One may also come across the names: *Captivity* or *Prison Letters,* which, as the names indicate, shows evidence of having been written while Paul was in prison. This would include Ephesians, Colossians, Philippians and Philemon.

A further distinction is made between the 'true' Pauline letters and the 'deuteropauline letters' (literally: 'second group of Paul's letters'). According to this distinction, the deuteropauline letters were written in Paul's name by students of Paul, or members of the Pauline school, which was most probably located in the environs of the city of Ephesus. These letters include Colossians, Ephesians, 2 Thessalonians and the Pastoral Epistles. They are characterised by a receding into the background of Paul's doctrine of justification, the dominance of realised eschatology over apocalyptic motifs, the central place of church discipline and church ethics, and a diminished expectation of the Parousia, or second coming of Christ.

In the New Testament collection, Paul's letters are arranged according to size. For the present survey the Pauline letters have been arranged according to a time framework and the relationship between letters.

PAULINE LETTER ELEMENTS

The letter heading

In those days a letter started with the name of the sender and the receiver: 'A to B' and a greeting, wishing 'joy'. Paul changed the Greek greeting to a blessing of 'grace' and added the Hebrew for 'peace'.

The 'thanksgiving' paragraph

Then the author or the addressee thanked a god for some or other deliverance. In Paul's letters a whole paragraph is devoted to reports about his thanksgiving prayer for the spiritual blessings of which the receivers are showing the signs. He also tells them about his prayers of intercession for them.

The body of the letter

The body of the letter contains the information or insights that the author wanted to communicate. If there is more than one theme, a relation between them is sought, to find the main reason for writing.

The closing

The so-called travelogue or apostolic Parousia element, containing plans to visit a church or to send his fellow-workers, may indicate that the communication draws to an end. The Greek letter often closed with a single word: 'Farewell'. Paul ends with personal news items and greetings by name from the author and/or from members of the community from where he is writing and a final blessing or prayer for the readers.

In dealing with the individual letters, the constituent parts and the way Paul uses them for his specific purpose will be borne in mind. This may add to one's understanding of the message he is conveying in a specific letter.

Chronology of Paul

The letters written by the apostle Paul cannot be dated with any certainty. However, Paul's missionary activity can be dated by correlating events mentioned in the New Testament with dates and events known from general world history as well as from archaeological sources. In this regard, the edict of Claudius and the Gallio inscription come to mind.

The edict of Claudius

According to the Roman historian Suetonius (*Life of Claudius* 25.4), the emperor Claudius (41–54 CE) expelled the Jews from Rome because they 'incited by Chrestus, were continually disturbing the peace.' This event took place in the ninth year of his reign (= 49 CE). This accords with the description of Acts 18:1 to 17 which reports the arrival of Prisca and Aquila in Corinth after having been driven from Rome, as well as Paul's hearing before proconsul Gallio.

The Gallio inscription

The term of office of the proconsul of Achaea, Lucius Gallio, mentioned in Acts 18:12, can be determined with a fair degree of accuracy by means of an inscription that records a letter from the emperor Claudius to the city of Delphi. The text of the letter dates it to the twenty-sixth acclamation of Claudius as emperor. Other sources indicate that the twenty-seventh acclamation had already occurred by 1 August 52 CE. The letter addresses Gallio's successor as proconsul and was written around the middle of the year 52 CE. Since the term of office of a proconsul of a senatorial province was usually one year, the inference that Gallio took up his post before mid 51 CE and remained until mid 52 CE can be drawn. Prisca and Aquila arrived in Corinth before Paul, probably in the year 49/50 CE, with Paul following shortly after. If one considers the information from Acts 18, namely that Paul stayed in Corinth for 18 months and that the Jews made use of the arrival of the new proconsul to press their charges against Paul, one can assume that the hearing before Gallio (Acts 18:12–16) took place in the middle of the year 51 CE.

> **GALLIO INSCRIPTION AT DELPHI**
>
> A reconstruction of the text of the famous Gallio inscription discovered at Delphi: reconstituted from four stone fragments of an imperial rescript issued by the emperor Claudius which mention Gallio as proconsul of Achaea (Greece). As the text can be dated, it helps to date the Apostle Paul's stay in Corinth. Since parts of the inscription have

> perished, the text has to be reconstructed. The conjectural supplements are shown in square brackets.
>
> Tiberius [Claudius] Caesar Augustus Germanicus, [Pontifex Maximus, in his tribunician] power [year 12, acclaimed emperor for] the twenty-sixth time, father of the country, [consul for the fifth time, censor, sends greetings to the city of Delphi.] I have for long been zealous for the city of Delphi [and favourable to it from the] beginning, and I have always observed the cult of the [Phrygian] Apollo, [but with regard to] the present stories, and those quarrels of the citizens of which [a report has been made by Lucius] Junius Gallio my friend, and [pro]consul [of Achaea]
>
> [Several lines follow which can be read with only partial certainty.]
>
> (Barrett, C K 1974. *The New Testament Background. Selected Documents.* London: SPCK, p. 48-49.)

Chronology of the ministry — timeline

From this point on one can correlate the details furnished by the narrative of Acts in conjunction with biographical and historical references in the Pauline letters with the relatively sure dating of Paul's Corinthian sojourn to the beginning of 50 CE to mid 51 CE. However, one should constantly keep in mind that there are numerous and often insurmountable inconsistencies between the narrative accounts of Paul's journeys in Acts and his own accounts of these same journeys in his letters.

According to the narrative of Acts 15:36 to 18:22, Paul's stay in Corinth was part of a larger missionary journey (the 'second'). This journey, some details of which are confirmed by the letters, took in places where Paul had earlier established churches and then went on to furrow new ground in Macedonia and Achaea. Thus, Paul and his companions went from Syria and Cilicia to Derbe and Lystra, then on to Phrygia and Galatia, and from there to Europe where he visited Philippi, Thessalonica, via Berea to Athens, ending up with the 18-month stay in Corinth. If time for the whole of the journey is allowed, it would be possible to locate the 'Apostolic Council' (Acts 15:129) and the subsequent confrontation between Paul and Peter in Antioch (Gal 2:11-5) to the first half of the year 48 CE.

According to Galatians 2:1, Paul visited Jerusalem in the company of Barnabas for the second time on the occasion of the 'Apostolic Council'; 14 years after his calling and conversion. This would mean that after his conversion he spent some time in Arabia before visiting Jerusalem for the first time (after more or less two years), returning to Damascus for a prolonged period of missionary

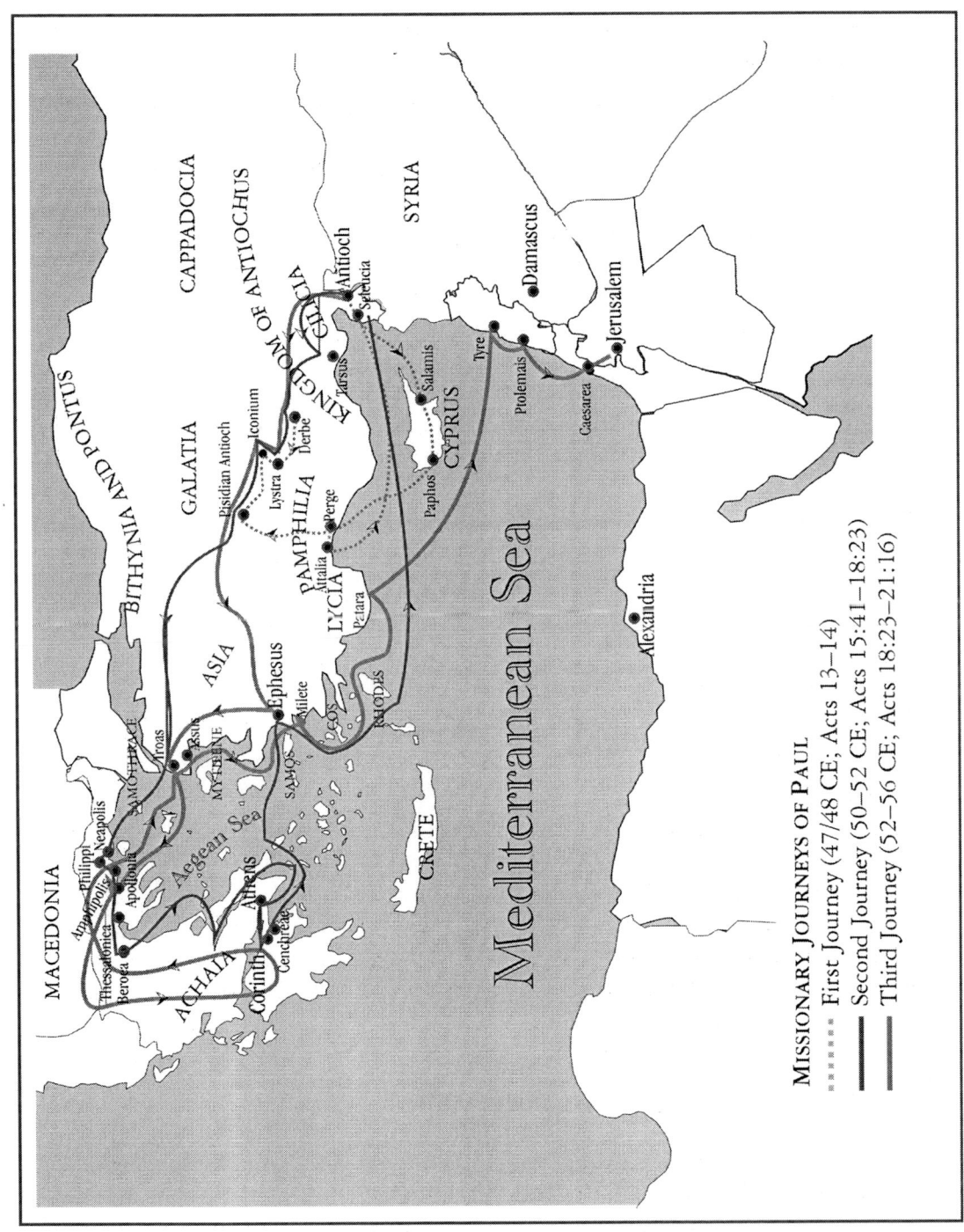

Figure 13.2
Map of Paul's missionary journeys

Figure 13.3
Close-up of the Parthenon in Athens. The Parthenon (literally: 'the sanctuary of the virgin') was the Temple of Athena

activity in Syria and Cilicia. Paul's conversion is therefore to be dated to around 33 CE, his stay in Arabia to 34 CE and his first visit to Jerusalem to 35 CE. The so-called first missionary journey is to be located near the end of this 14-year period, as the 'Apostolic Council' was convened directly as a result of the missionary work of Paul among Gentiles.

According to the summarised travel narrative of Acts 18:18 to 23, Paul left Corinth for Antioch, and while *en route* he left Prisca and Aquila in Ephesus. Although the narrative reports him landing at Caesarea and going up to Jerusalem, the difficulties involved in accommodating such a visit with other aspects of the narrative preclude one from accepting a visit to Jerusalem. From Corinth Paul journeyed via Ephesus back to Antioch. If one accepts that the return journey probably lasted from mid 51 to early 52 CE, then according to Acts 19, Paul set out in 52 CE from Antioch to

Figure 13.4
View of the *agora* ('place of assembly') in Athens. In the background is the Acropolis with the Parthenon. Athens was an important 'university city' in antiquity and it was here that Paul discoursed with Greek philosophers on the 'hill of Ares', the Areopagus, about the resurrection from the dead

Ephesus. According to Acts 19 he stayed there for two years and nine months, therefore, from the middle of 52 to early 55 CE. From Ephesus he proceeded on through Macedonia and Achaea to raise money for the collection to be taken to Jerusalem. According to Acts 20:3, Paul reached Corinth and stayed there for three months; from the beginning to middle of the year 56 CE. A Jewish plot against Paul prohibited him from returning directly to Syria, so he had to retrace his steps back through Macedonia on to Miletus in Asia Minor, and from there he travelled to Caesarea by ship. He reached Jerusalem by Pentecost of 56 CE (Acts 20:16). Not long after his arrival, he was arrested following an uproar in the temple precinct (Acts 21:27–22:30). To protect him from an assassination plot, Paul was removed to Caesarea and tried before the proconsul Felix.

According to Acts 24:27, Paul had already been in prison for two years when Porcius Festus suc-

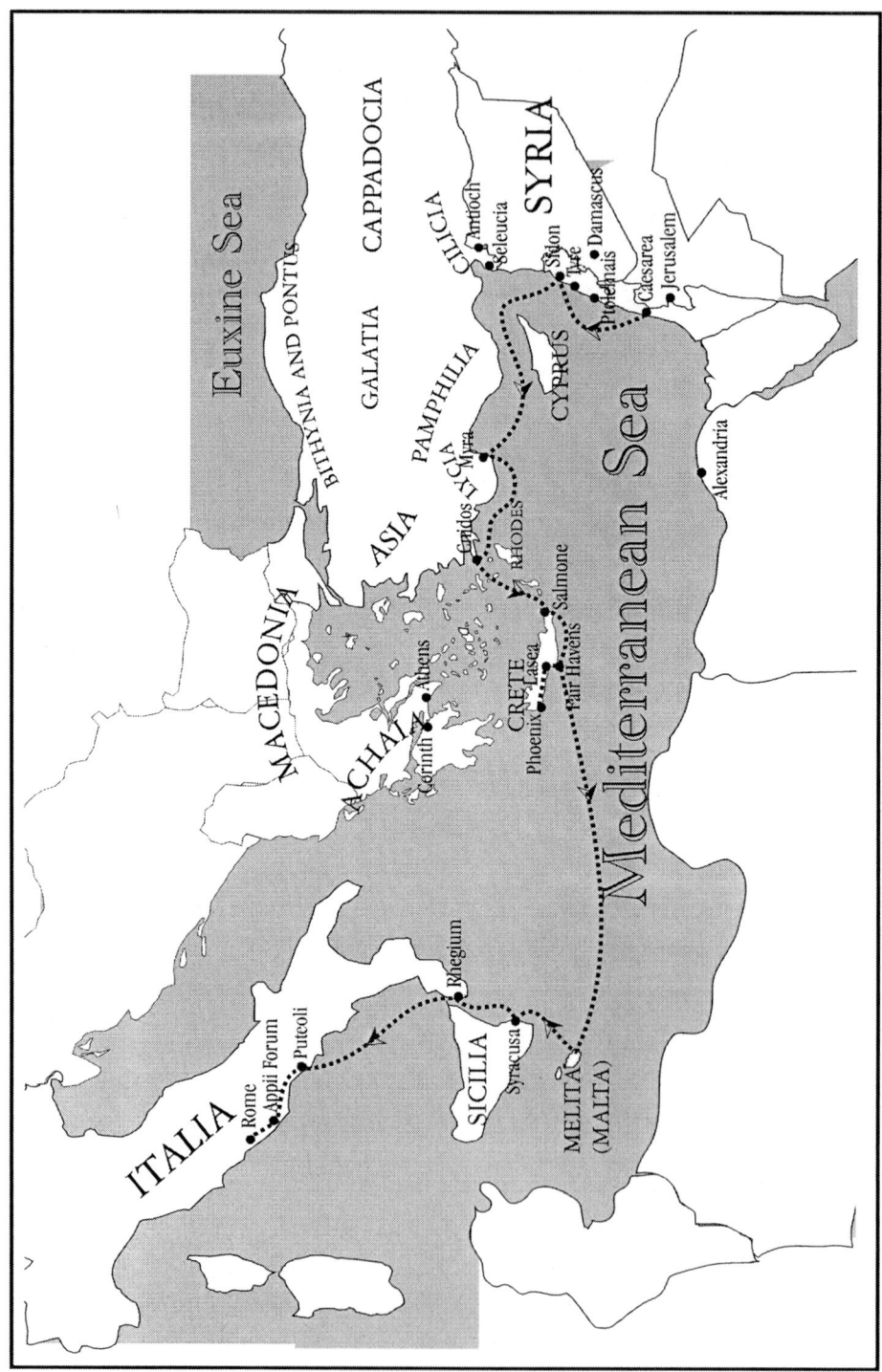

Figure 13.5
Map of Paul's journey to Rome (58/59 CE; Acts 27:1–28:15)

ceeded Felix as proconsul. Felix's term of office extended from 52/53 to 58 CE, while the high priest, Ananias, mentioned in Acts 24:1, was in office from 49 to 59 CE. So one can accept that it was in 58 CE, with the arrival of the new proconsul, that Paul appealed to the emperor (at the time, Nero) and he was sent to Rome in the same year. If the journey to Rome fell at the end of 58 or beginning of 59 CE, Paul would have arrived in Rome in the spring of 59 CE. According to the narrative of Acts, he spent two years under house arrest. That would account for his movements up to the beginning of 61 CE. Church tradition has it that Paul was martyred during the persecution of Christians under Nero following the great fire of 64 CE, although there is no corroboration of this story and the date of his death remains unknown.

13.2 Paul's Letter to the Galatians

Context of the Letter to the Galatians

It makes sense to discuss this Pauline letter first, since it deals with people and regions mentioned in the first stages of Paul's ministry. Some of these places were no longer as prominent when the scene advanced to Greece and Rome. It is accepted that Paul himself wrote the letter, but it is not certain when he did it. The reason is that there are two opinions on where these Galatian churches could have been situated. It will emerge that a reasonable case can be made for a date of 48 CE.

If the letter is seen as encompassing the cities which, according to Acts 13 and 14, Paul and Barnabas visited twice on their first journey in 48 CE, then it could have been written very early, even before the two Thessalonian letters. This is possible because these cities are situated in Lycaonia, which formed the southern part of the Roman province of Galatia. The other view is that Galatia was the original region of the Celtic people (called *Galatians* by the Romans) which was situated much further to the north in the area of Ancyra (present-day Ankara). If they are meant in this ethnic way, then certain unknown cities which Paul only visited on his second and third journey must be meant (see Acts 18:23) demanding a later date for the letter.

If one decides on the earlier date and the 'South Galatian theory', a possible date for the letter could be around 48 CE, and the place from which Paul wrote would be Antioch in Syria (Acts 14:26). The second scenario is that Paul must have written the letter from Ephesus in about 54 CE (Acts 19). Both options will be considered when other aspects of the letter are discussed. The church in Antioch in Syria sent Paul and Barnabas out and the two first sailed to the island of Cyprus, which was Barnabas's home country. There they were heard even by the Roman governor Sergius Paulus. From that point onward Paul used the Roman form of his name, 'Paulus', instead of the Hebrew 'Saul' (Acts 13:9), probably because it was more acceptable in the Greek–Roman society at which he now directed his campaign.

Certain problems occasioned the writing of the letter. News must have reached Paul and Barnabas of a severe crisis in the young Christian congregations in Galatia. There were Jews who seemingly accepted Christ, but who refused to change their Jewish way of life and worship. These Jewish Christians started demanding that people from other nations who had become Christians should be required to fulfil the demands of the Jewish religious laws. They specifically demanded the circumcision of these believers which, in Jewish practice, signified true membership of the people of God.

The Jewish–Christian 'activists' strongly opposed Paul's gospel of free grace through Christ alone and they obviously had the backing from certain Christian groups in Jerusalem. To strengthen their case, they tried to separate Paul from the well-known original followers of Jesus in Jerusalem, of whom some were regarded as the 'real' apostles of Christ. They questioned Paul's status as an apostle and tried to smear 'his gospel' as a misunderstanding of the real meaning of Christ and a 'halfway' Christianity. This situation could have arisen soon after Paul's first journey.

CONTENTS OF GALATIANS

From the structure of the letter it is clear that the three main parts in Paul's exposition should be kept in mind:

Galatians

1–2	Paul's authority and his view of the Gospel
1:1-5	An exceptional salutation
1:6-10	There is only one gospel
1:11-24	Paul's claim to be an apostle
2:1-10	Paul accepted by other apostles
2:11-14	Paul's dispute with Peter
2:15-21	Only faith saves both Jews and Gentiles.
3–4	Faith as freedom from the law
3:1-14	Only faith, not the law gives life
3:15-4:7	The place of the law
4:8-20	Paul's concern for the Galatians
4:21-31	Hagar and Sarah: an allegory.
56	Freedom to love (parenesis)
5:1-12	Freed from circumcision to love

5:16–26	Works of the flesh overcome by the fruits of the Spirit
6:1–10	Bearing one another's burdens
6:11–18	Conclusion: warning and benediction.

Message of the Letter to the Galatians

Taking into account that the Letter to the Galatians was written as early as concluded above, it is remarkable that Paul could have taken a relatively clear stand on weighty theological issues at such an early stage. Paul argued on the basis of the deepest meaning of the same Scriptures (the Old Testament) used by his Jewish opponents. It is clear that he had applied his mind to the basic insight of the Damascus vision and had formulated the meaning of Christ in his preaching. On every occasion his sermons were also aimed at the local Jews.

Paul's contribution is significant because he had not only seen the basic meaning of the Christ event. He also faced the consequences of a break with Judaism when most of his Jewish kinsfolk did not follow him into the messianic era. They opposed his missionary efforts, causing him to defend the faith of his Gentile converts.

Paul's Letter to the Galatians marks the parting of the ways of Judaism and the emerging movement of Christianity. Although the Jewish Christians were not pressurised to stop practising their revered religious customs, Pauline Christianity, in principle, no longer attached any salvational function to, for instance, circumcision or the keeping of certain holy days. This consequence of Christ's death and resurrection was perhaps easier to arrive at in the mission to the Gentiles. However, the Jewish-Christians were the people who forced the issue. They insisted that Jewish religious rites be required from Gentiles who entered into the community of God's people. Paul stood firm: either the sacrifice of Christ was sufficient, or the law of God had to be fulfilled blamelessly in every detail. Far from living a 'lawless' life, those who genuinely 'belonged to Christ', lived by the Spirit – the victor over the sinful flesh. If freedom is not abused, there is no need for the 'slavery' of formal laws and regulations: 'You are called to freedom!' (Gal 5:13).

Perhaps the most important aspect in this situation is that in chapters 5 and 6, Paul turns to the consequences of freedom. His views on redemptive freedom from law could be, and have been, misunderstood. He shows that he is quite aware of humankind's tendency to sin. He also immediately reaffirms the essence of God's law, to 'Love your neighbour as yourself' (Lev 19:18) and he warns against the devastating end towards which hatred leads. However, he indicates that the great counterbalance against lawlessness is the Spirit of God. Since the spirit is in direct opposition to the 'flesh' (here meaning human beings' inner tendency to sin) the battle between the two is inescapable in a person's spiritual life. This is a vital choice. One may either 'sow to one's own flesh' and from the flesh reap corruption, or one may 'sow to the Spirit' and reap eternal life (Gal 6:8). The evil 'works of the flesh' are named as well as the agreeable 'works of the Spirit'. Those who 'belong to Jesus Christ' have made the choice, having 'crucified the flesh with its passions and desires'. They 'live by the Spirit' and they are persuaded to 'walk by the Spirit' (Gal 5:19–26; RSV).

13.3 The First Letter to the Thessalonians

Context of 1 Thessalonians

The members of the church in Thessalonica, the capital of Macedonia in northern Greece, were mainly Greek-speaking Gentiles. This can be deduced from 1 Thessalonians 1:9 ('you turned to God from idols') and from 2:14 ('you suffered from your own countrymen.'). According to Acts 17, a small number were Jews from the local synagogue, and many of the Greek members had been 'God-fearers' already. Paul only mentions in general that the unbelieving Jews tried to prevent them from preaching to the Gentiles (1 Thess 2:16). Acts relates that the Jews at Thessalonica were actually behind the uprising of the townsfolk against Paul (Acts 17:5–9). His praise of the Thessalonians matches that with which he credited the Philippians (Phil 1:3–7). He mentions their acceptance of the gospel as 'the word of God' (2 Thess 2:13), their steadfastness in faith and their kind behaviour (2 Thess 1:3–5).

Paul first came to Macedonia when, on his second journey, he had a vision at Troas on the western coast of Asia Minor of a Macedonian begging him to come and help them (Acts 16:9). Crossing the Aegean Sea they landed in Neapolis and travelled 15 km inland to Philippi, where Paul founded his first Christian church in Europe. The church to which he writes this letter was founded by him in Thessalonica, the seaside capital of Macedonia, after his forced departure from Philippi south-westward along the Via Egnatia – the Roman main road. He soon had to flee from Thessalonica to Beroea and, being pursued, went even further to Athens (Acts 17:10). He wanted to return to Thessalonica, but this proved to be impossible (Thess 2:18), so he sent Timothy (Thess 3:2). In the meantime he proceeded to Corinth (in 49 CE), where Silas and Timothy joined him on their return from Macedonia (Acts 18:5). The good news they brought about the believers in Thessalonica may have been one of the direct reasons for writing the letter (probably around

50 CE) from Corinth. The themes in the letter indicate what information and/or correction the apostle thought necessary in the situation.

> **CONTENTS OF 1 THESSALONIANS**
>
> | | |
> |---|---|
> | 1:1 | Letter heading |
> | 1:2–3:13 | Prayer report and thanksgiving, memory of their relationship |
> | 4:1–12 | Exhortation to Christian conduct |
> | 4:13–5:12 | Letter body. On Christ's return and the resurrection |
> | 5:12–22 | Instructions and exhortation |
> | 5:23–28 | Letter ending. |

Message of 1 Thessalonians

The aim of a letter can be primarily to maintain and to renew a relationship of friendship and to share the latest news. The First Letter to the Thessalonians deals with aspects of the second coming of the Lord Jesus Christ. It may indicate that this was the main topic on which Paul felt the need to convey some additional information or teaching. He says that because Jesus had died and risen again, the 'dead in Christ' will rise first when he comes again and be joined by those still alive, so that all believers will always be with the Lord (1 Thess 4:13–18). He also responds to questions regarding the apocalyptic reckoning of 'the times and the seasons' that the 'day of the Lord' will come 'like a thief in the night', thus totally unexpectedly and precisely when people have a false sense of security. He turns the image of 'being asleep' around and applies it to people who live an immoral life. He uses the thought of the coming Lord to exhort the Thessalonians to be 'awake' and 'sober' for they are bound to obtain salvation through Christ.

There are even warnings against the vices of paganism (1 Thess 4:28). A whole catalogue of Christian virtues is listed in 1 Thessalonians 5:12 to 22, no doubt especially chosen for the circumstances of the readers. Encouragement is given in the light of severe persecution by non-believers.

13.4 The First Letter to the Corinthians

Context of 1 Corinthians

On Paul's second journey, after his rather hurried missions to Philippi, Thessalonica and Athens, he arrived in Corinth in 49 CE, and stayed for about 18 months (Acts 18:11). The city was situated on the narrow land bridge

Figure 13.6
The temple of Apollo in Corinth

between northern and southern Greece. The gulf of Corinth and the Saronic gulf are only about five kilometres apart. Much later a canal connecting the two seas was built nearby, but in Paul's time, smaller boats were actually drawn across to avoid the long voyage around the peninsula. Corinth played a strategic role between Athens and Sparta in Greek history. In 146 BCE Corinth was destroyed by the Romans and only rebuilt by Julius Caesar in 46 BCE. Although most of the remains to be seen are of Roman origin, some evidence of the magnificent Greek buildings, for instance, the Apollo temple, is still visible. As a port city (the name of the harbour on the eastern shore was Cenchrea, cf Acts 18:18) it was an important commercial and trade centre for the whole region. It contained a large number of strangers and thus had a reputation for loose morals.

The changing face of the Christian community in Corinth can be seen, even within the short time, between the two letters to the Corinthians. According to Acts 18:1 to 17, Paul stayed with Aquila and Priscilla in their house and joined them in their trade as tent makers. He started preaching in the synagogue, but met with resistance and moved to the house of Titius Justus, deciding to concentrate on converting Gentiles. It seems that the majority of believers

Figure 13.7
Street scene in ancient Corinth. Paul sojourned here from the beginning of 50 to the middle of 51 CE, teaching with his co-workers, Priscilla and Aquila.

were Gentiles from the lower economic classes of society (*see* 1 Cor 1:26). Some were wealthy, though, (1 Cor 11:21) and several of their houses were apparently used for gatherings (*see* 1 Cor 1:11, 16:19). This caused the possibility of different viewpoints being held within the ranks of the Christians. There were also Jewish converts (*see* 1 Cor 7:18), including Crispus the ruler of the synagogue. However, eventually the Jewish community brought Paul before the tribunal of Gallio, who was the Roman proconsul of Achaia. Gallio dismissed the accusations, but Paul, nevertheless, departed to Ephesus.

Paul wrote 1 Corinthians from Ephesus (*see* 1 Cor 16:8), three years after he had left Corinth (Acts 18:18), probably about 55 CE. He had heard about the problems arising in the church in the meantime and had received a number of questions from members about the Christian conduct of life.

PART THREE: THE EARLIEST CHRISTIAN LITERATURE (30–70 CE)

Figure 13.8
View of Corinth with the Acrocorinth in the background. Corinth was a harbour city on the Peloponnesian coast of Greece. It was destroyed in 146 BCE in the war with Rome and was refounded by Julius Caesar in 46 BCE as a colony for military veterans

CONTENTS OF 1 CORINTHIANS

1:1–3	Greeting and opening benediction
1:4–9	Introduction and commendation (prayer report)
1:10–4:21	Divisions in the church
5:1–6:20	Ethical problems in Corinth (sexual immorality; lawsuits)
7:1–40	Questions of sex, marriage and divorce
8:1–11:1	Eating meat sacrificed to idols
11:2–14.40	Problems of worship
15:1–58	Resurrection of the dead
16:1–18	Closing paranesis (and apostolic Parousia)
16:9–20	Greetings instructions
16:21–24	Final farewell.

Message of 1 Corinthians

Paul was set against the idea of Christian leaders, or their peculiar ideas, becoming the basis of divisions within the church. They worked towards the same goal, each one fulfilling his own function, but each one totally dependent on God for the results of his efforts. Paul's message concerning Christ is different from the 'wisdom' of mere human thought, which so fascinated the Greeks. Through his 'foolish' message, God, nevertheless, saves 'those who believe', and the 'Spirit' provided the necessary spiritual insight and discernment (1 Cor 1:18–2:15 NIV).

Those who persevere with an immoral life will not inherit the kingdom. Arguments against sexual immorality and prostitution are based on the holiness of the body, which does not belong to oneself, but the Holy Spirit.

Insight into the value and status of Christians as God's people should prevent them from filing suit against one another in a Gentile court of law.

Owing to the imminent return of the Messiah, which will be accompanied by great woes, little scope will be left for normal activities. Therefore, the unmarried state is more desirable since one is compelled to focus on God's calling. However, for those without the gift of abstention it is better to be married than to burn with desire. Believers should consider the weaknesses of their fellow believers. In deciding what is 'right' and what is 'wrong' one should not only take into consideration one's own insight, but also that of someone who may not yet have attained one's level of knowledge, reasoning or competence. This is demonstrated in respect of the eating of meat which was previously sacrificed to idols. The principle is that the freedom of Christian knowledge should always be restrained by Christian love, taking into account the perceptions of even the most 'backward' fellow Christian, for whom Christ also died.

In the light of the meaning of the celebration of the Lord's Supper as it was instituted by Christ, Christians are warned against the abuse of the remembrance meal and instructed on how to partake of it properly. The Lord's Supper should be the basis of unity and community.

The practice of the gifts of the Spirit or *charismata* (1 Cor 12–14) should lead to the building up of the community and the strengthening of Christ's body. The variety of gifts is provided by the one true God and the Spirit endows each one with gifts 'for the common good' (1 Cor 12:6,7). On the strength of first-hand witnesses to the appearances of the living Christ, one must believe in the reality of the resurrection of Christ. Without this belief, Christian faith is pointless. Christ's resurrection is the forerunner for the general resurrection of all believers. At the Lord's return, the living and the dead will be clothed in imperishable, spiritual bodies.

13.5 The Second Letter to the Corinthians

Context of 2 Corinthians

In the summary of Paul's dealings with the Corinthian Christians (cf pp 146-7) mention is made of the fact that this letter was written in Macedonia in 56 CE. (cf specifically 2 Cor 2:12; 7:6; 8:1; 9:2,4 and Acts 20:6.2). In the short space of time since the first letter there seem to have been significant changes in the situation. The main focus was now turned to the problem of people opposing Paul in Corinth. Paul had to give a broad defence of his ministry as apostle. The case of the person who had caused him personal grief (1 Cor 5:1) was taken up vigorously by the Christian community – to such an extent that Paul now had to intervene, lest the culprit be completely ousted from the fellowship (1 Cor 2:6-10). Paul also had to solve difficulties caused by a change in his plans for a visit to Corinth (2 Cor 1:17-2:3).

CONTENTS OF 2 CORINTHIANS

1:1-2	Letter heading
1:3-7	Thanksgiving and preamble
1:8-2:17	Epistolary self-commendation
3:1-4:6	Ministry of the apostle as ministry of the Spirit
4:7-5:11	Suffering with Christ and the apostle's hope
6:1-10	Glory of the apostle's suffering
6:1-17:16	Reconciliation with the Corinthians
8:1-23	Collection for Jerusalem
9:1-15	Blessing of the collection
10:1-11	Challenge to Paul's authority
10:12-18	Criteria for apostleship
11:1-15	Paul's unselfish ministry
11:16-12:13	'Fool's speech': boasting in his sufferings and weaknesses
12:14-13:10	Apostolic Parousia
13:11	Closing paranesis
13:12	Greetings
13:13	Final farewell.

Message of 2 Corinthians

Paul goes to great lengths to ensure that his relationship with the Corinthians is restored, and that they understand and appreciated his ministry among them, as well as the character of their own Christianity.

The whole letter is permeated with questions regarding the legitimacy and character of Paul's apostleship. His ministry includes both suffering and glory, just as Jesus Christ had passed through suffering to glory. Because the apostle is bound to Christ in suffering and glory, the power of Christ works in him to help him overcome all problems that befall him. His ministry is part of the reconciliation given by God, who grounds the new covenant in Christ's suffering and resurrection, and whose grace determines the life of the Church. The new covenant operates through the life-giving Spirit. God's power becomes manifest in human weakness. The measure of giving for the Lord's work is compared to 'sowing and reaping'. Reaping a good harvest depends on sowing freely. This applies to both spiritual and material abundance (2 Cor 9:6–15).

This is one of the most frank and theologically sound expositions of the religious significance of the gifts of money or goods donated to the church by believers.

13.6 Paul's Letter to the Romans

Context of the Letter to the Romans

Paul's letter to the Christian community in Rome, the capital city of the Roman Empire, is regarded as one of his most influential writings. His authorship is hardly ever denied. It is placed first among his letters in the New Testament because it is the longest. The letter is actually one of his later letters, written when he had accomplished a great deal and had matured as a theologian and author.

He writes to a church which did not come into being as a result of his own evangelising (*see* Rom 1:8–15). Christians travelling from Palestine to Rome had transmitted the faith. Yet, as the main planner of the expanding early Christianity, Paul wished to include them in his plans for further campaigns westward, even as far as Spain.

There is a tradition from the fourth century CE which claims that the church in Rome came into being when some members of the Jewish population embraced the faith in Christ. This may be confirmed by a report that the edict

Figure 13.9
View of the forum in Rome, with the remains of the Temple of Saturn in the foreground, looking out over the course of the Via Sacra. To the right is the ruin of the Basilica Julia with the three columns of the Temple of Castor behind it. Just to the left of the Temple of Castor the Arch of Titus can be seen, which celebrates Titus's victory in the Jewish War. In the middle, in the background, the Colosseum towers over the ancient ruins

of Claudius in 49 CE expelled the Jews from Rome because they caused riots 'at the instigation of Chrestus' – whatever may be meant by this phrase.

Some of Paul's statements imply a Jewish–Christian audience, for instance, in Romans 4:1, where Abraham is called 'our ancestor', 7:4–6, which speaks about being 'discharged from the law', 14:46 about the observance of certain days, and 14:14,15 about 'unclean' foods. However, there must have been a strong Gentile Christian component which is addressed in 1:5,13; 11:13 (*see* also 15:16,18). In fact, it will emerge that the letter is intensely interested in the relationship between these two component groups in the church of Rome.

It may well be that, when the Jews were allowed to return to Rome after Claudius's edict had been lifted in 54 CE, the Gentile Christians had attained a prominent position in the Church and that this caused tensions which brought about problems for the unity of the Church in Rome. In Romans 14:1 it is said

Figure 13.10
This Jewish burial memorial attests to the presence of Jews in Rome. There was a large Jewish community in Rome. The symbols are typically Jewish: the menorah or candelabra, the palm branch and the pomegranate. The inscription reads: 'Here lies Primitiva with her husband Euphrenontos. Rest in peace (or: peace in their sleep)'

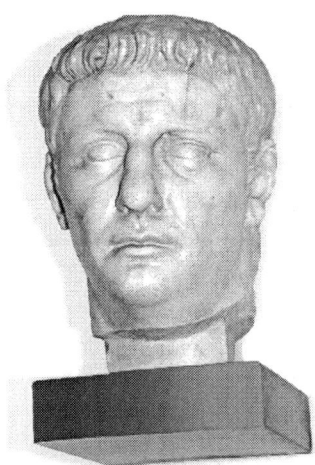

Figure 13.11
Claudius, Roman emperor from 41 to 54 CE. During his reign the Jews were expelled from Rome after disturbances involving 'a certain Chrestus' in 49 CE

that those who were 'weak' in respect of food laws should not be drawn into an argument. This may indicate that the Jewish component at that time had become a minority in the church and that Paul seems to be taking them into protection against the Gentile Christian majority. However, chapters 9 to 11 indicate that Paul's main concern lies on the theological level, with the redemptive status of Israel and of the nations.

In the Letter to the Philippians, which is regarded as having been written in Rome, Paul complains about people who proclaim Christ 'from envy and rivalry, ... to afflict me in my imprisonment.' (Phil 1:15–8 RSV). Although this reflects a somewhat later stage in the history of the church in Rome, it may be an indication that there was a variety of Christian groups (and for that matter Jewish groups) in the large city of Rome. Paul was not accepted without reservations by all the Christians when he visited the city and joined in the Christian action, even though it was from a position of 'house arrest'.

The context of Paul can be pinpointed by comparing Acts 20 to 24 with his plans in Romans 15:22 to 28 for taking the gifts from Macedonia and Achaia to the poor saints in Jerusalem and then to visit Rome. He regards his work in the eastern Mediterranean regions as being completed and turns his eyes westward to look for 'unturned soil' in which to work. From the letter of introduction to Phoebe, the deaconess of Cenchreae (the eastern harbour of Corinth), it is inferred that the letter was written in Corinth. The date, according to the occasion in Acts (20 to 24), is put at around 56 CE.

One of the main reasons for the letter was to win the support of the Christian communities in Rome for Paul's planned campaign in western Europe (Rom 15:19–24). However, he certainly also had their spiritual well-being in mind, both with his visit and with what he wrote to them in the letter (*see* Rom 1:11–15). Whilst writing a letter, Paul was partly engaged in formulating the insights which had grown on him about the consequences of salvation in Christ. Yet, all the time as he was dictating the letter he had the Christians of Rome and the Roman situation, as he saw it, in mind.

CONTENTS OF THE LETTER TO THE ROMANS

1:1–16	Introduction
1:1–7	Letter heading and greetings
1:8–12	Preamble
1:13–15	Epistolary self-commendation.
1:16–11:36	**Body of the letter: part one**
1:16,17	Letter thesis
1:18–3:20	Necessity of the righteousness of God
3:21–4:25	Possibility of God's righteousness
5:1–8:39	Reality of the righteousness of God (salvation, baptism and life in the Spirit)
9:1–11:36	Righteousness of God and Israel (the 'true' Israel and God's saving plan).
12:1–15:33	**Body of the letter: part two**
12:1–13:14	General exhortations (worship, church life, living by love, the state)
14:1–15:13	Instructions regarding the 'strong' and the 'weak'
15:14–15:29	Apostolic Parousia (presence)
15:30–15:33	Closing paranesis.
16:1–27	**Letter closing**
16:1–23	Greetings and exhortations
16:24	Final farewell
16:15–27	Benediction.

Message of the Letter to the Romans

In Romans, Paul provided Christianity with a wide theoretical basis dealing with the real significance of the gospel of Christ. Perhaps because of the 'mixed' character of the church in Rome, consisting of both Jewish and Gentile Christians, his outline of God's salvation in Christ in the Letter to the Romans provided a more balanced, comprehensive basis than, for instance, in Galatians, where he urgently had to combat a false teaching. In Romans he argues from the basic position that 'nobody is righteous' of himself, and that all are in need of 'God's righteousness'.

Paul poses a number of rhetorical questions (e g Rom 3:1,3b,5c,9,27a,31; 4:1,9; 6:1,15; 7:7,13; 8:31; 9:14,19,30; 11:1,7,11,19), where he appears to pause and then resume the argument. His main concern here seems to be: the situation of the Jews and the law since Christ's sojourn on earth. He seems to wrestle with the question: If righteousness is obtained through faith, then what is the reason for the existence of the Jews and what will happen to the Jews after Christ? This is finally cleared up in 11:11 to 32, where Paul explains the disobedience of Israel to the gospel as a temporary measure, to allow salvation to come to the Gentiles. The Jews remain God's elected people, however, and finally they too will be saved. In Romans 15:7–13 he confirms this view with a call to 'Welcome one another, therefore' and with the quotation from the Scripture: 'Rejoice, O Gentiles, with his people.' (Deut 32:43). Paul shows the same concern for Christian unity in other letters, such as Galatians and Philippians. However, in Romans it was his special concern that the sufficiency of Christ both for believers from Israel and from other nations should be acknowledged. It was vital that the Church proved capable of accommodating both.

The Letter to the Romans is a plea for Christian unity between Jewish and Gentile (mainly Roman) adherents of the faith. The situation as Paul saw it soon lost its specific relevance. The Jewish-Christians became a small minority when the Church spread rapidly among other nations in the Roman Empire. However, the basic Christian views on God's 'scheme of salvation' and the number of applications to general religious problems make it one of the most valuable witnesses to early Christian thought.

13.7 Paul's Letter to the Philippians

Context of the Letter to the Philippians

This letter is generally thought to have been authored by the Apostle Paul himself. It is classified under Paul's 'main letters' with Romans, 1 Corinthians and Galatians. The letter contains basic elements of Paul's teaching on the faith. It also qualifies as a 'prison letter' refering as it does to Paul's imprisonment at the time of writing.

The Philippian Christians belonged to the first church which Paul had founded on the European continent. He first visited Philippi on his second missionary journey in about 49 CE. Philippi could have been called 'little Rome' as it was a colony of Rome, inhabited mainly by retired Roman soldiers, amid a large number of the native people of the region. Paul had found a ready audience for the gospel. However, he had been persecuted by the local authorities and subsequently left for Thessalonica. From the outset the believers in Philippi contributed towards the apostle's work.

Later, when Paul was in prison (again), the church in Philippi sent Epaphroditus with a gift to support him. It is doubtful whether this was the same occasion of imprisonment as mentioned in the other prison letters. The situation and the mood of the apostle seem changed – he is less disturbed by the fact that he is in prison, and he even expects a favourable judgment and a possible release.

There are indications that this letter was written rather late, at about 59 to 61 CE, which would favour the traditional view of Rome as the place of origin of the letter. Ephesus is also strongly advocated as the place of origin, but that would require a date of about 52 to 55 CE.

Paul wrote the letter in order to mention the gift of the Philippians and to address certain matters about which Epaphroditus had undoubtedly informed him. Notably he had to intervene in a quarrel between two women in the church. Above all, he wanted the church to realise the meaning of the obedient self-sacrifice of Christ and of the high status to which God had then exalted him. This could enable them to take a positive view of Paul's situation, to handle their own fear of persecution and to be sure of the progress of the gospel in spite of onslaughts by opposing forces.

CONTENTS OF THE LETTER TO THE PHILIPPIANS

The most interesting aspects of the letter seem to be the 'Christ hymn' (Phil 2:5–11), the opponents (Phil 3), the 'letter of thanks' (Phil 4:10–20) and the question of the unity of the letter. Views on these problems differ greatly, however. Some scholars see the letter as a combination of more than one original letter or letter fragments. Only the letter in its present form, which contains most of the usual features of a Pauline letter, will be dealt with.

1:1–2	Letter heading
1:3–11	Preamble
1:12–30	Epistolary self-commendation
2:1–4	Admonitions to church unity
2:5–11	Christ hymn
2:12–18	Appended admonitions
2:19–24	Sending of Timothy
2:25–30	Sickness of Epaphroditus
3:1–4:1	Dispute with false teachers
4:2–9	Closing paranesis
4:10–20	Thanks to the community
4:21–3	Greetings and final farewell.

Message of the Letter to the Philippians

The repeated mention of 'joy' or 'rejoicing' in the letter is often regarded as its main theme. The overriding frame of mind can indeed be phrased as 'joy in suffering like and for Christ'. The example of Christ can be traced in every passage of the letter. The Philippians are instructed to behave in a manner worthy of the gospel of Christ, that is, they must stand firm in the struggle and not be afraid to suffer. Enjoying the wonderful love and gifts of Christ, the Philippians are encouraged to cultivate a sense of oneness in Christ by regarding others as better than themselves and by guarding the interests of others. There is a human responsibility to 'work out' the salvation which God works 'within'. This means obeying the will of God both in becoming 'blameless and pure'.

The Christ hymn (Latin = *carmen Christi*) is the centre of the letter. In the hymn itself, the cross (Phil 2:8) can be regarded as the centrepiece, marking the lowest point in Christ's path of humiliation, in between the high points of 'the form of God' (Phil 2:6) and the 'glory of the Father' (Phil 2:11). The way that Christ went is portrayed in the hymn as an example to the Christian community at Philippi. Christ left his position as Son willingly and exchanged it for that of a slave. In carrying out his mission, he discarded all privileges and finally submitted to the death reserved for a criminal. For this he was rewarded by God in three ways: he was exalted by God as Saviour, he received acknowledgement in all humanity and he achieved the glorification of God by all.

13.8 Paul's Letter to Philemon

Context of the Letter to Philemon

There is little doubt that the Apostle Paul himself penned this letter. The author was in prison, either in Caesarea (56 CE) or in Rome (58 CE).

Although several people are named in the address, it is clear that the first-mentioned, Philemon, is the real addressee of the letter. He appears to have been a wealthy person in whose house a Christian community held their meetings. He was the owner of slaves and he had a guest room in which the apostle intended to stay on visiting him. Apparently, Paul had been directly involved in bringing him to the Christian faith. On account of that he felt free to ask a favour of him.

It seems that one of Philemon's slaves, Onesimus, had run away and came to meet Paul in prison. Through Paul he converted to Christianity, and Paul sent him home to settle with his master and to stop being a fugitive from the law. Run-away slaves were usually severely punished, but fortunately Paul knew Onesimus's master, Philemon, to be a Christian, and therefore he wrote this 'letter of recommendation' for Onesimus to carry back to his master.

CONTENTS OF THE LETTER TO PHILEMON

1–3	Letter heading.
4–6	'Prayer report' (thanksgiving and request prayer)
7	Transition to the body of the letter (expression of joy, preparing for the real request)
8–22	Request of Paul concerning Onesimus
23–25	Letter ending: greetings and final benediction or blessing.

Message of the Letter to Philemon

The prime message in the body of the letter (verses 8–22) conveys the request to Philemon to accept Onesimus as he would have accepted Paul himself – as a brother in Christ and as a co-worker on behalf of the gospel. Philemon is thereby encouraged to break through the social barriers of the ancient household and accept Onesimus in his new social status even if his legal status remains unchanged. Perhaps more than anything else, the letter permits insight into the working of the household as a form of organisation in early

Christianity. The house–church shared many similarities with other household-based religious groups and institutions in the Hellenistic world. This letter shows how these social settings provided a space for the integration of individuals into a web of meaningful social relations.

14 CONCLUSION

This section deals with the earliest Christian writings which originated in the period after the crucifixion of Jesus up to the Roman war (a major event in Jewish history). As was the case with the Jews after they had lost the war, the survival of the new religion depended very much on the traditions (oral and literary) whose function it was to ensure that the contents of the religion would be handed down from generation to generation. As far as the Jews were concerned, they had lost their land and independence, making it possible for their literature to occupy a more prominent place in their religious life. As far as the first Christians were concerned, they had expected the imminent return of Jesus Christ. When this did not occur, it was also experienced as a kind of (albeit gradual) 'loss', and the production of literature filled the gap. The function of their literature was to remind the congregations of the contents of Jesus's teaching (Q and *Thomas*), but also to look for a Christian identity in the ongoing life in this world (the letters).

What emerges from a consideration of these writings is that there were, from almost the very beginning, different factions and different viewpoints within the early Christian movement. One can safely say that for the first Christians the person of Jesus was central to their faith. However, how he as person was interpreted, gave rise to different views. On the one hand, there were Christians who wanted to preserve Jesus's own religion, his attitude and teaching. In the *Sayings Gospels Q* and *Thomas* one clearly detects an attempt to preserve Jesus's views.

Paul, on the other hand, was a great intellectual thinker who developed a doctrine that would address the existential needs of Gentile Christians, especially with regard to the question of eternal life after death. Salvation for him meant salvation into eternal life, whereas for Jesus of Nazareth it meant (although he probably did believe in life after death) primarily salvation from an egocentric lifestyle to a life of altruism and love. Paul's connection with Jesus was that he took the notions of the latter's death and resurrection as the building blocks for his gospel of justification by faith which leads to salvation after death.

This powerful intellectual *tour de force* of Paul implied that he dominated Christian thought and that the simple and challenging wisdom teaching of Jesus of Nazareth became obscured. This led Rudolf Bultmann, one of the most renowned New Testament scholars of the twentieth century, to remark that Paul, with regard to Jesus, 'transformed the preacher into the preached'. Jesus and his religion mattered no longer, but the crucified and resurrected Jesus became the object of faith. Part Four attempts to show how in the later Christian literature (especially the canonical Gospels) an attempt was made to preserve something of Jesus's life and teaching, without abandoning the newly found theological significance of his crucifixion and resurrection.

Suggested reading

Arnal, William E
2001   *Jesus and the Village Scribes: Galilean Conflicts and the Setting of Q.* Minneapolis: Fortress Press.

Ashton, John
2000   *The Religion of Paul the Apostle.* New Haven/London: Yale University Press.

Crossan, John Dominic
1998   *The Birth of Christianity. Discovering what Happened in the Years Immediately After the Execution of Jesus.* San Francisco: HarperSanFrancisco.

Hengel, Martin & Schwemer, Anna Maria
1997   *Paul Between Damascus and Antioch.* London: SCM Press.

Horsley, Richard A
2000   *Paul & Politics: Ekklesia, Israel, Imperium, Interpretation.* Valley Forge: Trinity Press International.

Koester, Helmut
1990   *Ancient Christian Gospels: Their History and Development.* London: SCM.

Kloppenborg, John S (ed)
1995   *Conflict and Invention: Literary, Rhetorical, and Social Studies on the Sayings Gospel Q.* Valley Forge: Trinity Press International.

Kloppenborg, John S & Vaage, Leif E (eds)
1991   *Early Christianity, Q and Jesus.* Semeia 55. Atlanta: Scholars Press.

Mack, Burton
1993   *The Lost Gospel: The Book of Q and Christian Origins.* San Francisco: Harper.

Meeks, Wayne A
1983   *The First Urban Christians. The Social World of the Apostle Paul.* New Haven/London: Yale University Press.

Patterson, Stephen J
1993   *The Gospel of Thomas and Jesus.* Sonoma: Polebridge Press.

Riesner, Rainer
1998   *Paul's Early Period. Chronology, Mission Strategy, Theology.* Grand Rapids, Michigan: Eerdmans.

Smith, Dennis E (ed)
1990   *How Gospels Begin.* Semeia 52. Atlanta: Scholars Press.

Vaage, Leif E
1994   *Galilean Upstarts: Jesus' first Followers According to Q.* Valley Forge: Trinity Press International.

Part four

The Christian literature of the late first century (70–100 CE)

15 HISTORICAL CONTEXT

During 63 BCE Palestine came under Roman control. From then onwards military conflicts against Rome arose from time to time. Approximately at the time of Jesus's birth, Jewish revolts broke out against Rome. In 6 CE, when Judaea and Samaria came under direct Roman administration and a census was conducted for tax purposes, Judas the Galilean and his followers protested to Rome against the paying of such taxes by taking up arms. Caligula's intention to have a statue of himself erected in the temple held the potential for revolt. It would seem that during the fifties and sixties of the first century CE, under the Roman procurators Felix, Festus, Albinus and Florus, resistance to Roman government intensified as a result of unjust administration. The high priests contributed to the deteriorating situation by competing for wealth and power. The high priest Ananus even had some of his opponents executed. One of them was James, the brother of Jesus, the leader of the Christian community in Jerusalem.

A number of incidents preceded and, in the end, led to the war between the Romans and Jews. In 66 CE Florus took 17 talents of gold from the temple treasury, which caused a riot among the people. It ended in a battle, in which the people gained control of the temple mount, destroyed the bridge to the Roman fortress Antonia and besieged the Roman garrison. Attempts by the chief priests to gain control of Jerusalem were not successful. In a number of battles the city came under the control of the rebels, while the high priest Annanias and the Roman garrison were murdered. In the end, confrontation with Rome became unavoidable and real war broke out. The first phase of the war was led on the Roman side, by Gallus, legate of Syria. This task was then passed on to Vespasian, who marched against the Jews with about sixty thousand soldiers. In due course, Galilee, Perea and Judaea were occupied. The inhabitants of Jerusalem offered resistance for quite some time. The siege of Jerusalem was, moreover, delayed by the death of the emperor Nero and strife over his successor. In July to August 70 CE Titus, son of Vespasian, captured the fortress Antonia, destroyed the temple and slaughtered the defenders.

The destruction of Jerusalem and the temple – the national and religious centre – caused disruption and change in the Jewish community and had far-reaching consequences for Jews, Christians and the course of Christianity. As for the Jews, there was no longer a temple where they could worship and could go for important Jewish religious festivals. This implied that the function of the Sadducees – the party concerned with the temple – fell away. The

Figure 15.1
Titus, eldest son of Vespasian, Roman emperor from 79 to 81 CE. He was in command of the Roman forces that finally took Jerusalem and destroyed the temple (70 CE) at the end of the first Jewish War

Pharisees, who busied themselves with the interpretation of the law and its application to daily life, now became influential and initiated what would gradually become rabbinic Judaism.

It is well known that some Christians had already left Jerusalem before the war started. With the destruction of Jerusalem, the rest of the Christian community in Jerusalem was destroyed. As a result of this, the Gentile communities around the Mediterranean, more so than previously, became the main focal points of Christianity. After the destruction of the temple, relations between Judaism and Christianity deteriorated. Whereas Christians initially practised their religion within the framework of Judaism, this changed after 70 CE when the Jewish and Christian religions became, to a greater extent, competing religions. As time passed, Christians were no longer tolerated and were increasingly banned from synagogues. In this context the Gospels of Matthew and John should be understood.

The war of 66 to 70 CE was followed by two others. The first of these (115–117 CE) was an uprising of Diaspora Jews in the eastern Mediterranean. The second one was the so-called Bar Kokhba war, named after Simon Bar Kokhba, the leader of the revolutionaries. The cause of this war was probably emperor Hadrian's commission that a temple in honour of Zeus be built on the ruins of the Jerusalem temple. The war lasted three-and-a-half years and left Judaea devastated. After the defeat of Bar Kokhba, the centre of Palestinian Judaism moved from Judaea to Galilee.

In other parts of the Roman Empire Christians sporadically experienced mistreatment and persecution by the Romans. Mention was made earlier of Nero's persecution of Christians in Rome in 64 CE. The Revelation of John addresses Christian churches in Asia Minor who were being persecuted because they refused to worship the Roman emperor.

Figure 15.2
The young Nero, Roman emperor 54 to 68 CE. According to a Roman historian, he blamed the fire of 64 CE, which destroyed a large part of the city of Rome, on the city's Christian community and had many Christians put to death (the martyrdoms of Peter and Paul are attributed to these persecutions). However, persistent rumour had it that Nero started the fire himself in order to expropriate the land needed to build his extravagantly large palace, the Golden House

16 THE AFTERMATH OF THE JEWISH WAR

16.1 The Gospel of Mark as the first Jesus story

Context of the Gospel of Mark

The Gospel of Mark is, for various reasons, very important among the writings of early Christianity. Whereas before him different kinds of Jesus traditions had circulated orally, and perhaps had been compiled into small collections,

Mark was the first to write a Jesus narrative in which he incorporated different kinds of traditions about Jesus: his words, deeds, crucifixion and resurrection. Although Mark does not present Jesus's words and deeds in full and in chronological order, and comes up with his own organisation and interpretation of Jesus's life rather than with a historical account thereof, some scholars think that it resembles a kind of ancient biography, for example, that of a prophet or teacher. Others prefer to call the Gospel of Mark a foundation document for a community, which provides information about its initiator, aims and destination. Be that as it may, this genre was used by other early Christian writers (Matthew, Luke and John) and became, together with Paul's letters, the most influential instrument in the formation of the Christian consciousness.

Although the author of the oldest Gospel is called 'Mark', this author can no longer be identified with certainty. The title 'The Gospel of Mark' was only added to the writing during the second century CE. The date, aim and intended audience of this Gospel are also not obvious and have to be deduced from material in the Gospel. The Gospel of Mark translates Latin terms into Greek (Mark 5:9, *legion*; 15:16, *praetorium*; 15:39 *centurion*), and it also contains Aramaic language influences. This may point to an area where Greek was the common language, but where the underlying culture was Semitic, with some exposure to Roman culture. Syria, the region north of Galilee, may fit this description and would also be consistent with the situation during the Roman–Jewish war reflected in Mark 13.

Mark 13, which probably points to events experienced by Mark's community, may provide a clue to the more specific context addressed in the Gospel. This chapter, in which terminology from the Old Testament and from Jewish apocalypticism is used, probably refers to the situation of 66 to 70 CE when the Roman–Jewish war took place (cf Part 1) and Palestine suffered from severe unrest and resulting apocalyptic fervour (cf e g 13:68,17–23,24–31). Whilst reflecting local events (Mark 13:5–6,9–13,21–3), they are linked to events of a more cosmic nature which point to the end of the world and the frightful events preceding it. If this reading of Mark 13 is correct, the Gospel should be dated around 70 CE.

CONTENTS OF THE GOSPEL OF MARK

1:1–1:8	The appearance of John the Baptist.
1:9–3:34	Jesus starts his ministry: his baptism, temptation, calling of the first disciples, a number of healings, the calling of the twelve apostles, blasphemy against the Holy Spirit.

4:1–34	Jesus teaches by means of parables.
4:35–5:42	Various miracles: the stilling of the storm; healing of a demon-possessed; Jairus's daughter; woman with haemorrhage.
6:1–34	Jesus in Nazareth; the sending and return of the twelve apostles; the death of John the Baptist.
6:35–56	Miracles of Jesus.
7:1–23	Discussion with the Pharisees and scribes about purity.
7:24–8:10	More miracles.
8:11–21	The Pharisees ask a miracle from heaven.
8:22–9:1	Jesus heals a blind man; Peter's confession; first announcement of his death; what following Jesus entails.
9:2–32	The transfiguration; healing of a demon-possessed boy; second announcement of Jesus's death and resurrection.
9:33–50	Who is the greatest; whoever is not against us is for us; causing people to sin.
10:1–52	On divorce; the rich young man; third announcement of Jesus's death; request of James and John; healing of Bartimeus.
11:1–12:44	Jesus's entrance into Jerusalem; cleansing of the temple, controversies with the Jewish leaders in Jerusalem.
13:1–37	The apocalyptic discourse.
14–16:8	The passion and resurrection of Jesus.

Message of the Gospel of Mark

When formulating the message of Mark (and also that of the other Gospels), one has to keep in mind that not everything included in a Gospel will necessarily be directly related to its specific context. Apart from responding to specific needs or problems, Mark could also merely be retelling the story of Jesus as he understood it and found it significant. Of course, his retelling will, to some extent, be related to, and shaped by, his situation. Like every letter in the New Testament, every Gospel initially had an original address.

In searching for Mark's message to his community, it can be helpful to determine where the focus of his Gospel lies. In Mark's case the material is not only arranged around Jesus, his words and deeds. The material specifically focuses on his suffering and death. Since Mark's portrayal of Jesus is presented in the form of a narrative, one has to determine how the narrative evolved in order to gain some insight into his message. While paying attention to Mark's narrative, references will also be made to various important motifs which are related to his portrayal of Jesus: the secrecy with regard to Jesus's identity, the nature of discipleship and the Gospel interest in persecution, suffering and martyrdom.

In the first half of Mark's story about Jesus, which takes place in Galilee (Mark 1–8:26), the predominant impression one gets of Jesus is that of a powerful exorcist and miracle-worker. He exorcises demons and heals different kinds of diseases. Intertwined with this aspect of his ministry is that of Jesus the teacher, whose teaching is described as authoritative (Mark 1:27). There is also something mysterious about his teaching and about his person, as portrayed by Mark. The parables are not meant to be understood. In Mark they seem to be aimed at non-understanding (Mark 4:10–12, cf also 3:23). His mighty deeds result in misunderstanding by his disciples (Mark 6:52; 8:14–21).

Although there are indications early in the Gospel that Jesus would suffer and die (Mark 3:6), the narrative is, especially in its second part, directed at Jesus's suffering and death. When Peter ultimately identifies Jesus as Messiah, Jesus fills the concept with a content up to now not associated with the Messiah. In the eyes of Peter, the course of the narrative implies that Jesus was probably a miracle-worker Messiah. In the Gospel of Mark, Jesus, however, renounces this view by indicating that the Messiah is the Son of Man who will be delivered, killed and rise again (Mark 8:31). Jesus's prediction is repeated twice in the Gospel (Mark 9:12,31; 10:31–33) and ends in the passion narrative which takes up such a large part of the Gospel of Mark (Mark 14:1–16:8) that the Gospel has been typified as a passion narrative with a long introduction. Only after Jesus's suffering and death does his true identity as Son of God become known (Mark 15:39). According to Mark, the real key to understanding Jesus and his mission is his suffering, not his powerful deeds or even his teaching.

Why Mark's strong emphasis on the passion of Jesus? Is this emphasis intended to state something about the significance of Jesus's death, that is, his way of reconciling people to God? Although the Gospel contains two references to this (Mark 10:45; 14:24), it is not clear whether Mark emphasises or merely presupposes this. Does he, by means of his emphasis, perhaps want to stress that God reveals himself specifically in the suffering Jesus, and not in another aspect of his life, such as his miracles. Such is the view of some New Testament scholars. Is Mark's focus on Jesus's suffering presented against an incorrect assumption about Jesus or about the nature of the disciples' authority? While these possibilities cannot be excluded, this prominent aspect of the Gospel of Mark probably relates to his context. Mark 13 suggests that Mark's community found itself in a state of suffering and persecution. While encouraging his readers in this situation, he emphasises Jesus's passion in order to show that, just as Jesus had to suffer, they, his disciples, had to be prepared for discipleship which involved suffering. Mark's portrayal of the disciples in his Gospel as people who do not understand Jesus, his mission and the true nature of discipleship (Mark 8:22–26; 10:46–62) may be part of his way of emphasising what discipleship of Jesus entails and a warning against misunderstanding its nature.

17 ECHOES OF PAUL: THE DEUTEROPAULINE LITERATURE

17.1 The Letter to the Colossians

Context of the Letter to the Colossians

As a deuteropauline letter, Colossians was most probably not written by Paul himself. The letter contains no information about its place of composition and reflects, in the style of pseudepigraphical fiction, information about Paul: he is in prison (cf Col 1:24, 4:3,10,18), but in the company of a number of co-workers in the Gospel, of whom Tychicus will probably carry the letter, whilst Onesimus and Mark will also depart for Colossae (cf Col 1:1–8, 4:7–14). The letter thus predisposes knowledge of Paul's co-workers as well as knowledge of the same type of false teachings as opposed in Galatians. This leads one to conclude that the author is portraying Paul as continuing the struggle against, for him, the falsifications of his gospel. It is closest to the life of Paul, probably having been written around 70 CE.

The Colossian Christians lived in the Lycus valley, some 170 km inland from the sea at Ephesus, with two other New Testament towns, Laodicea and Hierapolis, close by. The author of the letter did not personally visit Colossae, but Epaphras informed him of its inhabitants' situation. Epaphras was 'one of them' and seemed to have played a major role in planting the church in all three neighbouring towns (*see* Col 1:7,8; 4:13). From the letter one can gather that he must also have brought disturbing news about 'heretical' teachings being propagated in Colossae. The problem seems to have been caused by a 'mistaken' piety that had been propagated among the people, leading to an 'improper' way of life. It may have been caused by an outside group of Jewish mystics who opposed the preaching of the gospel. They could have claimed that by mystical ascension they could take part directly in heavenly worship with the angels around the throne of God. The author warns the Colossians against people who might lead them astray with 'beguiling speech' (Col 2:4) and by 'philosophy and empty deceit' (2:8 RSV), 'which depends on human tradition and the basic principles of this world rather than on Christ.' (2:8 NIV). They were being lured by an 'appearance of wisdom' into a 'self-imposed worship' with a faked humility and a harsh discipline of the body, which demanded that they avoid handling, tasting or touching things of this world and strictly observe festivals and holy days (Col 2:20–23). The Colossians had to bear in mind that they had 'died with Christ' in all these forms of bygone piety and had been raised with him to his coming glory.

CONTENTS OF THE LETTER TO THE COLOSSIANS

1:1–2	Letter opening
1:3–12	The prayer passage with a thanksgiving and petition
1:13–20	A credal (faith) statement with a Christ hymn in 1:15–20
1:21–23	The meaning of this credal statement for the readers
1:24–2:5	An 'apostolic apology', with a hint at the 'apostolic Parousia'
2:6–4:6	Body of the letter, containing teaching and exhortation
4:7–9	The 'travel plans'
4:15	The letter closing with a long list of personal greetings, followed by the final blessing.

Message of the Letter to the Colossians

The letter emphasises the full presence of salvation in Jesus Christ. Christ is the complete revelation of God, and being united with Christ, the believers share fully in God's presence. Through baptism, the Colossians already live in the all-encompassing realm of Christ's lordship. No other practices, rituals or philosophy ('man-made religion') are necessary to participate fully in salvation. The cosmic lordship of Christ makes the demand for circumcision, ascetic practices, humility and worship of angels pointless. Although their resurrected life is an objective reality, it is not a public, observable reality for it is hidden with Christ in God. Although they are already saved, the Colossians must orientate their lives to the future revelation of salvation and live by that hope. The ethical instructions in this context demonstrate what it means to be the image of God (Col 3:10).

17.2 The Letter to the Ephesians

Context of the Letter to the Ephesians

Although most manuscript copies contain 'Ephesus' as the address of the letter, there are a number of early witnesses who know the letter without this designation. In some copies it reads abruptly 'to the saints and believers who are ...' This leads to the view that it may have been a circular letter, intended for more than one church, while leaving a space for each name to be inserted, or erasing one name to give it a general character. Indeed, the letter does not have a particular situation in mind and does not convey greetings to specific people. Only Tychicus is mentioned in Ephesians 6:21 as carrier of the letter. The fact that according to 2 Timothy 4:12, Tychicus is sent to Ephesus may have given rise to the idea that the letter was originally meant for the Ephesians. Although the context of composition can no longer be determined with certainty, the extensive familiarity with Colossians (almost the whole of Colossians is found in some way or another in Ephesians) would argue for a location in Asia Minor.

When the letter was drafted is limited by the date of Colossians, on the one hand (around 70 CE), and the mention made of it in the letters of Ignatius (around 110 CE), on the other. The most probable time frame for the writing of Ephesians is around 80 to 90 CE.

The apostle's status is that of imprisonment, since he calls himself a 'prisoner' in Ephesians 3:1 and 4:1 and that of 'an ambassador in chains' in 6:20. It is obviously the same imprisonment as that from which Colossians was written at about the same time, in view of the similarities between them and the fact that Tychicus was entrusted with the delivery of both. More can therefore be learnt about Paul's situation from Colossians. Less than usual is known about the situation addressed in Ephesians and the reason for writing. The teaching is of a general nature containing instruction of young Christian communities who had to deal with paganism. They are also urged to forge harmonious relations with Jewish believers.

Figure 17.1
The single column that remains of the magnificent Temple of Artemis in Ephesus. It was known as one of the seven wonders of the ancient world and was the largest Greek temple in antiquity (measuring 70 × 130 m with 127 columns, 20 m in height). It was destroyed by the Goths in the third century as well as by Christian looting

Figure 17.2
Statue of Artemis, the patron goddess of Ephesus. During festivals in Ephesus, in honour of this many-breasted fertility goddess, her statue was carried through the streets of the city. She was the personification of life itself and provided the powers of nature with her life-giving energy, hence she was called 'the mother feeding all of creation'. Paul (cf Acts 19) met with opposition from businessmen selling small gifts depicting the goddess and her temple

CONTENTS OF THE LETTER TO THE EPHESIANS

1:1–23	Introduction
1:1–2	Letter heading and greeting
1:3–14	First thanksgiving
1:15–23	Second thanksgiving.
2:1–3:21	**Body of the letter: part one**
2:1–10	The believers 'once' and 'now'
2:11–22	The church of Jews and Gentiles
3:1–13	The apostle as minister of the mystery of revelation
3:14–21	Intercession and doxology.
4:1–16	**Body of the letter: part two**
4:1–16	Admonition to realise the unity of the body of Christ
4:17–24	The old and new humanity
4:25–5:20	Individual admonitions
5:21–6:9	Household code.
6:10–24	**Closing of the letter**
6:10–20	Concluding paranesis
6:21–22	Recommendation of Tychicus
6:23–24	Final farewell.

Figure 17.3
The theatre at Ephesus where, according to Acts 19:21 to 40, a tumultuous crowd instigated by the silversmiths of the city, shouted 'Great is Artemis of the Ephesians!' This was in response to Paul's missionary work there. He spent three years of his life in this important harbour city

Message of the Letter to the Ephesians

Jesus Christ is exalted and enthroned together with God in the heavenly realm, from where he rules over heaven and earth, and over the rulers, powers and aeons who are subject to Christ. He fills the universe with the fullness of his life. His church is thus elevated to a cosmic status, permeated by Christ, and is the realm of salvation. Through his death on the cross, Christ reconciled Jews and Gentiles into his one body, the unity of which is created and guaranteed by the one God, one Lord, one Spirit, one faith, one baptism and one future hope. Christ is the cornerstone on which this church is built. Just as Christ has already attained victory, so the elected church already finds itself in the present sphere of salvation experienced in the sacraments, especially baptism. Salvation being already present does not mean that there is no hope of a future redemption. Believers are reminded to resist the oppressive powers 'on the evil day' (Eph 6:13) and to live in accordance with God's will so that in the coming judgement they will be found worthy of the kingdom of God. Ethical instructions regulate the life of the congregation and involve a sharp critique of the pagan manner of life (e g the Artemis cult).

17.3 The Second Letter to the Thessalonians

Context of 2 Thessalonians

It makes sense to read this letter together with 1 Thessalonians, although scholars are divided about the question whether Paul wrote it himself. One of the reasons why Paul's authorship is doubted is that it is so similar to the first letter, suggesting that the first letter may have served as a 'model' for the second. The New Testament scholar, William Wrede, argues convincingly in his 1903 study of the authenticity of the letter, that 2 Thessalonians is dependent on the first letter and is therefore a pseudepigraphical letter.

Apart from differences in language and style, the main differences between the first and the second letter lie in their respective portrayals of end-time events. The immediate expectation of the imminent Parousia characteristic of the genuine Pauline letters is replaced with a different course of events in which an eschatological adversary (the 'man of lawlessness') first has to appear. The Parousia is delayed and in contrast to the first letter, a schedule of eschatological events is presented here which begs calculation of the time of the Parousia. Whereas in 1 Thessalonians the emphasis is on the appearance of the risen Christ, in this letter it is the destruction of the adversary that is in the forefront.

As to dating, the similar topics and themes it shares with texts such as 2 Peter would suggest a time of writing at the end of the first century, and consequently, as is the case with 2 Peter, a place of composition somewhere in Asia Minor or Macedonia.

CONTENTS OF 2 THESSALONIANS

1:1-2	The letter heading. The opening blessing is expanded by stating its origin as God and Christ.
1:3-10	Thanksgiving report in 1:3 to 10 and in 2:13,14.
2:1-3:15	The 'body of the letter' or main part of the letter. Christ's return and Christian conduct in the light of his second coming.
3:16-18	Letter ending and benedictions.

Message of 2 Thessalonians

The steadfastness and growth in faith and love, in spite of the suffering endured by the Thessalonians, is commended. A correction is made to the idea that the day of the Lord is no longer a future prospect, but has already come. It may be that the idleness which the author so sternly rebutted was the result of this mistaken view that there was no longer a day of the Lord ahead. Whatever the excuse, it is squarely dealt with in the plain statement: 'If anyone will not work, let him not eat.' (2 Thess 3:10).

Opposition and disobedience had become manifest since the first letter. Therefore the emphasis regarding the coming 'day of the Lord' has shifted here from the joy it promises the believers to the vengeance and punishment which the Lord will inflict on the godless and those who disobey the Gospel of the Lord Jesus. The need for judgement is underlined by the climax of evil which comes before the 'day of the Lord' through the actions of the 'man of lawlessness'. He is currently still 'restrained', but will be destroyed by the Lord at his coming (2 Thess 2:8). The question about the 'assembling' of the believers to meet the Lord (2 Thess 2:1) is not explained further. One may assume that the viewpoint of the first letter on this matter is confirmed. But the impression that it was to happen 'very soon' is softened considerably by the new perspectives.

17.4 The First Letter to Timothy

Context of 1 Timothy

The three Pastoral Epistles, 1 and 2 Timothy and Titus, are regarded by most scholars to have been compiled not by Paul himself but by some of his followers. The term 'Pastoral Epistles' is derived from the word *pastor*, meaning 'shepherd' and is used in a spiritual sense, since they contain instruction to leaders who are responsible for a local church. The three letters are very similar in form.

The Pastoral Letters reflected the context of the third Christian generation. It is clear that the church organisation was different from that of the early days of Paul. The informal house–church of Paul's day seems to have given way to a more settled organisation, with a fixed system of offices and office-bearers. The church's reflection is no longer focused on its debate with Judaism but on its position in a pagan environment. The reference to 'sound doctrine' seems to imply that the fluidity of the expressions of faith of an earlier era had become fixed in doctrinal and credal statements. The letters to Timothy address the situation in Ephesus and probably also originated there. Both letters presuppose the presence and work of Timothy in Ephesus as advocate of Pauline theology even though 2 Timothy claims to originate from Rome (2 Tim 1:17).

A possible date for these letters may therefore be late first century. They concern the call to warn those who were falling away from the true faith and, positive instructions concerning the worship, offices and Christian life of various groups in the church.

CONTENTS OF 1 TIMOTHY

1:1–20	Introduction
1:1–2	Letter heading
1:3–20	Timothy's assignment: to combat false teachings; nature of these false teachings; the significance of the law; sound doctrine as the best antidote against false beliefs.
2:1–3:16	**Letter body: part one**
2:1–3:16	Directives and regulations regarding church rule: Intercession; about men and women in church services; elders and deacons, the church as the vehicle and guardian of the revealed truth of the gospel of Jesus Christ.
4:1–6:2	**Letter body: part two**
4:1–11	Opposition to false teaching
4:12–5:2	Church leader as model
5:3–13	Status and enrolment of widows
5:17–25	Office of elders (presbyters)
6:1–2	Christian slaves.
6:3–20	**Closing of the letter**
6:3–13	Concluding paranesis
6:20–21	Concluding admonition and final benediction.

Message of 1 Timothy

It should be clear that at the time when 1 Timothy (and the other Pastoral Epistles) were written, there was no longer a need to formulate the basic elements of faith in Jesus Christ. There were, however, opposing religious views which went against the core of the Christian faith, and there was a need to reaffirm the teachings of a sound faith. The nature of the false teaching is not quite clear but it seems to have originated in Jewish circles and comprised an ascetic tendency, which rejected the value of material creation, disapproving of marriage and rejecting the future resurrection. It was another 'philosophy' with an affinity for disputes over trivial matters.

There were still no uniform offices or practices in the church. The function of the apostle was in the process of being split up into various specialised offices. The office of 'elder' was taken over from the Jewish communities, whilst the term *bishop* initially indicated the function of 'overseeing' of the 'elders'.

The letter is aimed at persuading church leaders to excel in the establishment of the Christian faith and its moral values in the local communities. In 1 Timothy, as in the other Pastorals, one of the strongest thrusts is the emphasis on moral and ethical behaviour. It is important to note that this was regarded as of prime importance for office-bearers in Christianity even more than the prescriptions for their church service.

17.5 The Second Letter to Timothy

Context of 2 Timothy

The letter was written from Rome requesting Timothy, who is seemingly still in Ephesus, to join the author before the winter (2 Tim 4:21). The letter gives the impression of a 'last will' of the author – impressing on Timothy the power and the scope of the Gospel heritage, urging him to be courageous in the struggle for the true faith, and holding himself up as the example of a triumphant campaigner for the Lord in spite of countless sufferings.

CONTENTS OF 2 TIMOTHY

1:1–2	Letter heading and benediction
1:3–5	Preamble: thanksgiving, exhortation and report
1:6–14	Epistolary self-commendation
1:15–18	Reports on Paul's imprisonment
2:1–13	Apostle as model of suffering
2:14–26	Personal ethical standards
3:1–9	Description of the false teaching in the 'last days'
3:10–17	Timothy's apostolic succession
4:1–8	Testament of Paul
4:9–18	Information about Paul's personal experiences, his situation and his expectations
4:19–22	Letter ending, greetings, final benediction.

Message of 2 Timothy

Timothy is persuaded in a number of ways to excel in the establishment of the Christian faith and its moral values in the local communities. He should not be daunted by hardships, persecution or suffering. The gift of God is not a spirit of timidity, but a spirit of power, love and self-discipline (2 Tim 1:7). Positively, the worthy example of Paul himself in this regard can be followed. There must be single-mindedness like that of a soldier or an athlete in pursuit of the gospel cause. There is an immense reward! Against the corruption and deceit in the 'last days' the equipment with 'God-breathed' Scripture should be put into effect.

17.6 The Letter to Titus

Context of the Letter to Titus

Titus was of Greek origin and he first comes into the picture accompanying Paul on his journey from Antioch in Syria to Jerusalem (Gal 2:1–3, *see* Acts 11:25–30). He was sent with the 'tearful letter' to the Corinthians, whereupon he could convey the good news to Paul in Macedonia that the Corinthians had repented (2 Cor 7:6,13,14). In 2 Cor 8:6 Paul instructs that Titus should complete the collection for the poor in Corinth before he (Paul) arrives there. Corinth therefore seems to be the special charge of Titus at that stage.

According to this letter, the author plans to spend the winter in Nicopolis (Titus 3:12), on the west coast of the Greek region of Epirus, and he requests that Titus join him there. At the time of writing, he may still have been in Macedonia, where 1 Timothy was written with a very similar message. Paul had worked jointly with Titus on the island of Crete and left him there to continue establishing the church on Crete, having instructed him personally (Titus 1:5). The letter urges the appointment of 'elders' in every town and sets the moral standards expected from them as 'bishops'. Just as in 1 Timothy, Titus lays great emphasis on the quality of Christian morals.

CONTENTS OF THE LETTER TO TITUS

1:1–4	Letter heading
1:5–16	Directives concerning church order: elders must be appointed; requirements for the office of elder; command to act against false teachers
2:1–15	Instructions regarding various groups in the church: elderly men and women, young men and women; slaves

3:1–11	Submission to government and authority and the behaviour towards those with whom the faith is shared.
3:12–14	Concluding instructions and travel plans.
3:15	Letter ending, greetings and final benediction.

Message of the Letter to Titus

Titus is persuaded to excel in establishing the Christian faith and its moral values in the local communities. He is especially charged with finding the right persons to be appointed as 'elders' from a society that showed many signs of corruption, brutality, immorality and plain laziness (Titus 1:12). The criterion set for the office of elder is no less than 'blamelessness', which is further defined as: 'not overbearing, not quick-tempered, not given to much wine, not violent, not pursuing dishonest gain. Rather he must be hospitable, one who loves what is good, who is self-controlled, upright, holy and disciplined' (1:7,8 NIV). Then he must hold firmly to the 'trustworthy message' and refute false teaching. Titus himself is urged to instruct the various categories of believers according to their responsibilities: the 'older men' and 'older women', the 'younger men' and the 'slaves'. Jesus Christ gave himself to redeem the believers from all wickedness 'and to purify for himself a people that are his very own, eager to do what is good'. His glorious appearing is to be awaited. (1:13 NIV).

18 GENERAL LETTERS

18.1 The First Letter of Peter

Context of 1 Peter

Martin Luther rated the First Letter of Peter as a book which, together with the Gospel of John and the Pauline letters, belongs to the core of the books of the Bible. It is indeed, 'one of the noblest books in the New Testament'. The letter seems to have been held in high regard in the early church as it is presupposed by such authors as Polycarp (Pol *Phil* 8:1; 1:3; 10:2) and Papias

Figure 18.1
Mosaic, from the museum of St Chora, of the Apostle Peter portrayed with the keys to the church

(Eusebius *Eccl Hist* 3.39.17). The letter goes under the name of Peter, but was most probably not written by the Apostle Peter. Among the reasons for this is the fact that the letter lacks eyewitness testimony to the passion of Jesus; the number of similarities between this letter and the letters of Paul (it seems to take up the tradition prevailing among the churches of Asia Minor); the spread of Christianity presupposed in Asia Minor, and the ecumenical perspective that points to a later phase in the history of early Christianity.

The author presents the letter as having been sent from Rome (1 Pet 5:13 'your sister [church] in Babylon sends you greetings'). After 70 CE, *Babylon* was used as a code word for *Rome* (cf *Sib Or* 5.143; 5.159; *2 Bar* 11.1; 67.7; *4 Ezra* 3.1,28,31). But although the Petrine–Pauline tradition was located in Rome according to church tradition, and although there are similarities between this letter and

Figure 18.2
The young Domitian, second son of Vespasian, Roman emperor 81 to 96 CE

1 Clement which *was* sent from Rome, the most probable setting for its composition is Asia Minor. This letter was first known and mentioned in the east where the description of Babylon for Rome also originated. Furthermore, the specific admonitions of the author presuppose knowledge of the situation in Asia Minor such as obtained in the late first century. The persecution mentioned in the letter does not refer to local acts of discrimination but to a more systematic and widespread persecution. In this state of conflict, Christians were arrested by local authorities (who sought to promote the cult of the emperor) because they were Christians ('for the sake of the name alone'). Such acts of persecution are documented as being at the time of Domitian and not earlier under Nero, Vespasian or Titus. Thus the letter and the situation it addresses are most probably to be situated near the end of the reign of Domitian (±93–96 CE). The mention of believers in the various Roman provinces listed in 1 Peter 1:1 presupposes the spread of Christianity to the northern provinces of Pontus and Bithynia, a situation confirmed for the period 90 CE by the letters of Pliny the Younger (10.96.6–7).

At the time of writing, the problem of the relationship between Gentile and Jewish–Christians so acute in the letters of Paul seems to have been replaced with the problem of the relationship between Christians and pagans. This implies a later phase of the early Christian mission and, as such, situates the letter as part of the effect of the Pauline tradition in Asia Minor. The Christians addressed in this letter lived in small communities in the areas listed in the address. The Christians formed what could be called 'an alternative community', strangers in the world (1 Pet 1:1), and they were mostly from the labour class; some possibly slaves among the rich landowners and merchants (1 Pet 2:11–17).

CONTENTS OF 1 PETER

The first letter written under Peter's name is a typical Hellenistic (popular Greek) letter. It has a heading mentioning the author and his addressees, and conveys greetings to them and blessings at the end. The body of the letter is in the form of a theological treaty, which breathes the spirit of consolation and exhortation for Christians. The theme is that Christians must preserve their faith and live amid suffering and persecution.

1:1–2	Salutation.
1:3–2:10	Praise for God's mercy; a pure, Christian life; the new spiritual temple.
2:11–4:6	Relationships in everyday life: conduct amid Gentile criticisms and *vis-à-vis* the state; mutual relations regarding slaves and spouses; importance of a blameless life; radically breaking away from every form of evil.
4:7–5:11	Suffering and the coming judgement: the end is near, office-bearers and members of the church must observe their duties with diligence.
5:12–14	Silvanus's assistance to Peter. Final greetings and salutation.

Message of 1 Peter

The First Letter of Peter is a Pastoral Letter, which supports and strengthens Christians who are under severe attack and are suffering intensely.

The Christians who are addressed are urged to maintain their true and dignified lifestyle. They must play their role as an alternative society within the world by courageously coping with their situation amid hostile people around them, abiding by the great expectation of the future with Christ their Lord.

Their religious convictions and theological credos need to be put into operation every day.

The First Letter of Peter states that suffering does not come upon believers as blind fate, as the Hellenists believed. This fallacy had to be discarded, because suffering was part of God's plan of salvation.

Peter addresses the suffering to give them a new perspective of hope. They are encouraged to maintain a strong Christian lifestyle, to be steadfast and to excel in their obedience to faith. He deals with three major aspects of Christian life, namely (1) suffering, (2) expectations of the future (hope) and (3) the joy of faith amid suffering.

Furthermore, through suffering their faith is tested, refined and strengthened (1 Pet 1:16f, 4:12). Christ's suffering serves as an example of God's works of salvation. This message is confirmed by the titles given to Christ as the main figure in Peter's exposition, titles which describe his role and actions, namely Jesus is the Lord (*Kyrios*), he is the Christ (12 times), and he is the Shepherd of his flock (1 Pet 2:25; 5:1–4).

18.2 The Letter of Jude

Context of the Letter of Jude

Some years ago, the Letter of Jude was called: 'The most neglected book in the New Testament.' Since then, this – the almost smallest document in the New Testament – has been 'rediscovered' and more attention has been paid to it. Viewpoints on the author of the letter, who goes under the name of a certain *Jude* (Judas), vary considerably. The letter is presented as being written by Jude, the brother of Jesus. This implies that he is the brother of James, the brother of Jesus (verse 1). The Jude of the letter is most probably not the brother of Jesus, for the question remains: why does he not refer to himself directly as the brother of Jesus? The 'brother' of verse 1 can be interpreted in the sense of co-worker. Furthermore, the dispute between orthodoxy and heresy, and the topic of the advent of false teachers as a sign of the last days (cf 1 Tim 4:1–3; 2 Tim 4:3–4; 1 John 2:18, 4:1–3; Did 16:3) point to the post-apostolic period. Verses 17 to 18 in Jude look back on the time of the apostles as the time of the laying of the foundations of the church and from the perspective of a later period.

The letter can thus be classified as pseudepigraphical and given its use by the author of 2 Peter, can possibly be dated to the end of the first century (somewhere between 80 and 100 CE) and can, consequently, be located in Asia Minor.

In terms of the contents, it is often alleged that Jude breathes the undertones of the so-called early Catholicism. This means that it tends towards set forms of credal orthodoxy (*see* verse 3): there is a fading of the hope of Christ's second advent, and an increasing emphasis on church offices and the authority of bishops.

The church(es) addressed in Jude's letter are most likely a predominantly Jewish–Christian community in a Gentile society somewhere in Asia Minor. It could not have been Syria, because neither of the two Syrian churches ever accepted Jude's letter as canonical.

The occasion for writing this very brief letter is spelt out in the letter itself, namely in verses 3 to 4. This section of the letter also forms the theme of the letter. The theme consists of two parts, namely (1) an appeal in verse 3 to Jude's readers tot carry on fighting for their faith and (2) the background to this appeal in verse 4 which describes the character of the false teachers and their judgement by God. The body of the letter – verses 5 to 19 and 20 to 23 – works out this theme by way of an exposition.

The false teachers, who operated as opponents in the Christian communities concerned, were apparently a group of travelling charismatics. Their teaching consisted of proclaiming and practising a very aggressive doctrine of antinomianism. This means that although they claimed to be followers of Christ, they rejected all moral authority over their lives, including that of Moses (*see* verses 8–10) and of Jesus himself (*see* verses 4 and 8). They abused the so-called freedom in the Spirit and spoke insultingly of the angels who, in their view, were the evil beings who gave the law and administered the moral order of the world, doing humankind no good at all (verses 8–10). Consequently, these false teachers indulged in immoral behaviour, especially sexual misconduct (verses 6–10) and conformed to the permissiveness of their pagan environment. Furthermore, they claimed possession of the Spirit, and the experience of ecstatic phenomena and prophetic visions (verses 8 and 19).

Jude addresses this religious and social context with a view to warning, guiding and comforting the true Christian community or communities.

CONTENTS OF THE LETTER OF JUDE

Jude is a typical Hellenistic letter. It also shows traces of an epistolary sermon; the letter form proving to be an appropriate and effective way of communicating over a distance with the audience addressed. The letter comes from learned circles and is written in good Greek in a lively and vigorous style, using a rich and varied vocabulary.

1–2	Address and opening.
3–4	Theme: appeal to fight against opponents and false teachers.
5–19	Background of the appeal. Midrash exegesis on the prophecies in Jewish sources of the doom of the ungodly (*see* 2 Pet 2).
20–23	Exposition of verse 3: the appeal expressed in an exhortation.
24–25	Doxology and closing of the letter.

Message of the Letter of Jude

In this very short letter written by Jude, the author pastorally addresses members of the true believing community or communities and warns them against former fellow-members who have gone astray spiritually. His spiritual guidance is taken from the Jewish–Christian traditions and is expounded in the style of classical Jewish exegetes of that period. He appeals to his audience to keep on fighting against the opponents and their heretical teachings as Epicureans and against their permissive lifestyle.

The background to this appeal, as spelt out in Jude 5 to 19, is a description of who and what these apostate (a person who abandons his or her religious beliefs) members were. They were dangerous and devastating to the true members of the church. Jude gives several examples of persons and types who were objects of God's wrath and judgement. These examples come from Old Testament times and the traditions of the Old Testament, *1 Enoch* and the *Testament of Moses*. These types are, for example, people from Egypt, untruthful angels, people from Sodom and Gomorrah, Cain, the deceit of Balaam and the rebellion of Korah. God had pronounced his condemning judgement over these people and had executed it. This was announced by prophets of doom such as Enoch (*see* Jude 14–16). Even the apostles warned them that in the final time scoffers would come into the midst of the congregation, divide the church and proclaim their godless message. This would prove that these false teachers were real people who did not have the Spirit. Jude warns the believers to be on the outlook and to guard against these deviant so-called members of the church. In actual fact, they denied the authority and teaching of God through the prophets, Jesus and the apostles (*see* verse 4, *passim*; cf 2 Peter 2). Their doom is long awaited and very much overdue.

> **RELATION OF JUDE TO 2 PETER AND OTHER BOOKS**
>
> Jude has a direct relationship with 2 Peter, specifically with 2 Peter 2. Jude was written earlier than 2 Peter. The Old Testament, or Hebrew Bible, figures prominently in Jude. Two Jewish apocryphal works, *1 Enoch* (*see* verses 6,2 to 16), and *The Testament of Moses* (*see* verse 9) are referred to and cited in Jude. The author of Jude seems to be familiar with Jewish moral teaching (*see* verses 5 to 7 and 11), while the letter contains no traces of Paul's letters.

18.3 Second Letter of Peter

Context of 2 Peter

The second letter written under Peter's name differs significantly from the first one. This is in respect of the author, the contents, the structure and the addressees. There are close similarities between this letter, especially chapter two, and the letter that appears under Jude's name. It is widely accepted that the author of 2 Peter relied heavily on Jude (with the exception of verses 9 and 14 to 15, almost the whole of Jude is incorporated into 2 Peter). Of all the New Testament books, these two letters are the most neglected.

Since 2 Peter differs so fundamentally from 1 Peter, it could not have been written by the same author. The developed doctrine of inspiration (2 Peter 1:20–21) and the reception of the letter in the early church would suggest that the letter was written at a later time, that is, long after the time of the Apostle Peter (whose own death may be hinted at in 3:4). Although the letter's acceptance into the canon was long disputed (it is missing from the Muratorian Canon and Origen still lists it among the 'disputed writings'), it is part of the broad range of Petrine literature in the early church. The *Apocalypse of Peter*, written about 135 CE in Egypt, presupposes the letter. As proof that it was written earlier, one can point to the collection of the letters of Paul (3:15–16), the use of the letter of Jude, and the problem of the delay of the Parousia, which is similar to *1 Clement* 23 to 37 (and which is dated to ± 96 CE). All these sources suggest a time of composition at the very end of the first century.

The association of the letter with the *Apocalypse of Peter* might suggest Egypt as place of origin. However, the use of the pseudonym 'Simon Peter' together with the explicit association with 1 Peter (3:1) creates the impression of being addressed to the same churches in Asia Minor as 1 Peter. The number of Hellenistic religious philosophical concepts employed (terms such as *knowledge, godliness, endurance, self-control, virtue, eyewitness* and *divine power*) suggests both a Hellenistic (Jewish) author and a thoroughly hellenised audience. The churches concerned are characterised by confusion about ethics, problems regarding interpretation of Scripture, and questions regarding the timing of the Parousia.

The author's aim is to remind the believers of the tragic fact that some members of the churches had become false teachers and false prophets who operated as heretics and as scoffers in the heart of the churches. They had done an enormous amount of harm to the true apostolic tradition. These heretical members of the churches had accepted ideas of the Epicureans. This implied that they totally rejected the concept of God's judgement after death and the truth of the resurrection of the dead. According to them, there was no such thing as divine providence. God was someone far beyond their grasp, one who was totally free from trouble. He did not react in anger and punish, nor did he bless the good. The idea of a god who is present and acts in this world, destroys humans' freedom and spoils their right to pleasure. Therefore, they had doubts about God's providence and judgement, and about Christ's second coming. They also rejected Christian ethical codes of life, implying that people needed to live their lives free from prescripts.

Since the occasion for writing happened to be the last message of the author, the letter is in the form of a typical farewell address.

> **FAREWELL ADDRESSES OR TESTAMENTS**
>
> Farewell testaments were quite well known in ancient times. Examples abound: Jacob's testament to his 12 sons (Gen 49), each of Jacob's 12 sons left a testament (*Testament of the Twelve Patriarchs*), Moses's testament to Israel (Deut 33:1–29), Joshua to his followers (Josh 24), Jesus's farewell discourses as reported by the fourth Gospel writer (John 13–17), Paul's address to the elders of Miletus (Acts 20:17–35) and Peter's testament here in 2 Peter. It also displays the characteristics of a homily (sermon) an apology (defence) and a polemic (verbal attack).

Common material from early Christian layers of tradition can be identified in this letter. The material is related to sections from the Gospel of Matthew: the transfiguration scene of Matthew 17:1 to 7 (2 Pet 1:16–18); revelations about false prophets of Matthew 24:11 (2 Pet 2:1–3); the thief in the night of Matthew 24:43 (2 Pet 3:10), and cosmic regeneration of Matthew 19:28 (2 Pet 3:11–12), respectively. Similar themes are also found in Paul's letters to the Romans, 1 Thessalonians, and 1 Corinthians, as well as Jude and 1 Peter, as was shown earlier.

> **CONTENTS OF 2 PETER**
>
> | | |
> |---|---|
> | 1:1–2 | Salutation |
> | 1:3–11 | Introduction: preamble |
> | 1:12–21 | Departure of the apostle and the power of memory |
> | 2:1–22 | Advent of false teachers |
> | 3:1–13 | The certainty of the Lord's return |

| 3:14–18a | Closing paranesis |
| 3:18b | Doxology. |

Message of 2 Peter

The author provides a summary of his message in 2 Peter 1:3 to 11. It is, in essence, a theological statement which states that God has bestowed on believers everything they need for living a godly life in this world. He gave, and still gives, people adequate knowledge and insight into what life, belief and God himself are all about.

Included is a promise of escaping the corruption prevailing in this world. God even provides for the believer to be a partaker in his divine nature, that is, the believer's nature and inclination are changed and geared to a higher level of being properly God-orientated in his or her life so that he or she becomes immortal and incorruptible.

Then follows a communication on issues relating to the end-time, the promise of salvation and entering into the kingdom of heaven, and God's judgement and punishment of the ungodly ones.

Furthermore, Peter tells his audience about the Epicurean spirit among members in the church. These members scoff at the other members and lead them astray; away from Jesus Christ. They adhere to, and proclaim a scepticism by postulating the so-called fourfold remedy for real life, namely:

(1) God is not to be feared

(2) death is not frightful

(3) the good in life is easy to obtain, (i e by pursuing pleasure and freeing yourself from obeying ethical codes of conduct)

(4) evil is easy to tolerate.

Hence, these people deny any idea of God's providence, the resurrection of the dead, and that God in Christ shall come again as Final Judge. They urge people to live in lust and pleasure. The whole of the letter is occupied with an unveiling of these false prophets, and the devastating effect of their teaching and its effects on humans. Peter refutes their teachings and arguments through an appeal to the authoritative words of Jesus and the apostles, as they were transmitted in the legacy of the Christian traditions of Paul, the Gospels and Jude.

Peter continues by quoting examples from Old Testament times to support the apostolic truth. In this respect, he calls to mind the fate of the disobedient angels, the wicked ones in Noah's time, the people of Sodom and Gomorrah, Balaam (*see* 2:1-9,15-16). This reaffirms the fact that God knows how to rescue the godly from trial, and that he keeps the unrighteous under severe punishment until the day of Final Judgement – a day which shall come like a thief in the night (2 Pet 3:10).

18.4   The Letter of James

Context of the Letter of James

For a long time the Letter of James was regarded as one of the earliest documents of Christianity, dated as early as 45 CE. If the 'James' who wrote the letter was indeed a well-known and respected figure through the whole of the early Christian church, then only James the son of Zebedee and James the brother of Jesus could have been intended. James the son of Zebedee was executed in 44 CE under Agrippa I (Acts 12:2) and so could not be the author, as the letter certainly stems from a later period.

A number of features characterising the letter preclude James, the brother of Jesus, from being the author. Central themes of Jewish–Christian theology, such as circumcision, the Sabbath, Israel, purity laws and the temple play no role in the letter. Neither Israel nor the Jews are mentioned, and the problem of the relationship between Gentile and Jewish–Christians is not mentioned at all. Furthermore, it is significant that Job, and not Jesus, is held up as example of willingness to suffer. If verse 3:1 implies an attack on the teaching office, it is strange that the author does not claim special authority if he is indeed the brother of Jesus. In any case, the reception of the letter in the church speaks against James being the brother of Jesus. Prior to 200 CE there is almost no evidence of any influence or literary trace of the letter. It is not mentioned in the Muratorian Canon, or by Tertullian, and Eusebius also speaks of its authenticity being doubted. It only became accepted as canonical after 200 CE. This would be strange if the author was indeed the brother of Jesus.

The situation addressed by the letter is similar to that implied in the writings of Luke, the Pastoral Epistles and Revelation. Christian communities underwent change towards the end of the century with more and more wealthy people entering the church. This led to increasing conflict and polarisation with the communities. The rich are given preferential treatment (James 2:1), the needy are neglected (James 1:27; 2:15-16), and jealousy, quarrelling and fighting occur in the communities. This fits into the pattern of the social history of the post-Pauline churches. In this context of change in social structure the connection between faith and action was broken.

The majority of exegetes accept that James is a pseudepigraphical writing, written by an unknown Hellenistic Jewish–Christian with a thorough Greek education. As a result, Alexandria is often mentioned as place of origin, Alexandria, Egypt, being a centre of Jewish–Hellenistic wisdom literature, as well as a harbour city and business centre (which would account for the presence of the rich). In the light of its place in the development of the social history of Christianity, the time of writing is estimated to be late to the end of the first century.

The letter is addressed to people living in the 'dispersion' (Greek: *diaspora*), that is, Jewish people who were forced through circumstances to make a living outside the Jewish land. The Jewish leaders in Jerusalem used to write official letters to such Jewish communities living among other nations in the Roman Empire, to encourage and advise them on the 'correct' way of life according to Jewish beliefs.

The Letter of James exhibits the traits of a wisdom writing: teaching by showing the good or the bad outcome of a 'wise' or a 'foolish' life.

ON THE DATE AND AUTHORSHIP OF THE LETTER OF JAMES

The spirits are divided on the date and authorship of the Letter of James. Many scholars take the James of the letter to be the brother of Jesus. The many Jewish–Christian traditions contained in the letter are strikingly similar to the Jesus tradition, and the strong emphasis on the unity of faith and works may point to the strict Jewish–Christian James as author. These factors would point to an early date of composition, especially if one reads a polemic against Paul into the section on the unity of faith and works (James 2:14–26). However, the absence of such central themes of Jewish–Christian theology as circumcision, the Sabbath, Israel, purity laws and the temple, as well as the fact that not Jesus but Job is held up as example of willingness to suffer may point away from James, the brother of Jesus, to some other author. Furthermore, the presupposed church situation may indicate the social conflicts arising with the growing gulf between rich and poor (a situation also reflected in the Gospel of Luke, the Pastoral Epistles and Revelation) as well as a post-Pauline debate on faith and works (similar to the deuteropauline letters). Most telling, however, is the absence of literary use of James by authors of the early church before 200 CE. Eusebius writes in his *Church History* that the authenticity of James was in doubt, and its canonical status remained disputed for a very long time. This would have been unthinkable had the brother of Jesus been the author. That would then argue for a much later date. While advocates of the authenticity of the letter date it early, should one presume that it is a pseudepigraphical writing (as the evidence would seem to suggest), then a date of composition by the end of the first century CE would be preferable.

CONTENTS OF THE LETTER OF JAMES

Some of the examples James uses as a test of whether one's life can pass the divine measure are the following:

1:2-4	Remaining steadfast in life's trials.
1:5-8	Praying wholeheartedly for God's 'wisdom' (= Spirit)?
1:9-11	Riches are but temporary.
1:12-18	Blaming God for temptation.
1:19-27	Getting angry and speaking foolishly (*see* also 3:1-12 and 4:11-12).
2:1-13	Judging according to wealth and appearance.
2:14-6	Faith leading to action, or only religious talk.
3:13-18	Getting ahead by all means, or deeds of kindness and peace? (*See* also 4:1-10 and 5:1-6.).
4:13-17	Honouring God as the one who 'runs the world'?
5:7-11	Waiting patiently for the good that God brings about.
5:12	Speaking the truth even without taking an oath.
5:13-18	Regarding illness and health as religious concerns.
5:19-20	Willingness to help those who have gone astray.

Message of the Letter of James

The aim of James's letter is to show an unsettled early Christian community – possibly living in 'squatter camp' conditions – by practical examples that certain types of conduct are incompatible with the new life through Jesus Christ. Notably, there had been a 'problem with poverty' in the church, causing people to look down on the very poor and to pay undue homage to the obviously wealthy members of society. To persist in these and other wrongful actions meant to go astray, away from the salvation that was available through Jesus. In every case the correct conduct is given. James urges all Christians to point out such shortcomings in conduct to one another and help those going astray to find the right path again (*see* James 5:19). James reminds Christians that the true faith in the Lord Jesus must become visible in the choice between wrong and right, and in the willingness to redress wrongs in everyday life.

18.5 The First Letter of John

Context of 1 John

Although 1 John is usually regarded as a letter, it lacks the typical characteristics. The author of the writing and the addressees are not mentioned, and it contains no greetings. Some regard it as a sermon of sorts in which the author reminds his readers of aspects of their faith and exhorts them to a specific way of conduct.

There are clear similarities between the language and concepts used in the Gospel of John and 1 John. Many of the themes encountered in the Gospel of John appear here. The introduction of 1 John reminds one of the prologue of John's Gospel. Important common themes are the contrast between light and darkness (1 John 1:5; 2:8-9), truth and untruth (1 John 1:6; 2:4,21,27; 3:19; 4:6,20; 5:7), the community and the world (1 John 2:15; 3:1,13; 4:35; 5:19) and life and death (1 John 1:2; 3:14-15; 5:11-13). In the Gospel *world* is used in a positive and negative sense (e g 1 John 1:10; 3:16), but in the letters nearly always in a negative sense (cf 1 John 2:16-17). The first letter of John also contains references to the believer's sharing in the Holy Spirit (1 John 2:20,27; 3:24; 4:2,6) and there is an emphasis on love which should come to expression in deeds (1 John 3:11,14,18; 4:7,11-12,21). The First Letter of John was probably written a few years after the Gospel, at about 100 CE. By this time the situation of the Johannine community had changed. The dispute with the synagogue was no longer the issue. There is, in fact, no trace of this in the letter, which may indicate that a final schism between the community of John and the synagogue had already taken place and the community no longer had contact with the synagogue. In 1 John the persons who differed from those in the community – here called *antichrists* and *false prophets* – were not a group outside the community (the Jews), but a group that had previously been part of the community. In 1 John 2:19 they are referred to as follows: 'They went out from us, but they did not really belong to us. For if they had belonged to us, they would have remained with us; but their going showed that none of them belonged to us.'

As in the Gospel of John, the identity of Jesus is the main issue here. It seems as if the 'opponents' underemphasised Jesus's humanity, his coming in the flesh, which implies that for them only his divinity mattered. In the light of the high Christology of the Gospel, it is quite conceivable that such a view about Jesus could have developed among Johannine Christians. In addition to their view of Jesus, the false prophets or 'opponents' in John were, moreover, of the opinion that because they believed in Jesus they had no sin, so that they refused to acknowledge their sin or the need for atonement through the death of Jesus (1 John 1:8–2:6). They also seemed to have disobeyed the love command on which John put so much emphasis (1 John 2:7-11; 3:11-17,23; 4:7-12,20-21), and they claimed to teach by the authority of the Spirit (1 John 4:1).

CONTENTS OF 1 JOHN

1:1-4	Opening statement
1:5-2:11	Walking in the light as a sign of fellowship with God
2:12-17	Admonitions and warning
2:18-27	The 'last hour' and the true confession or denial of Christ
2:28-3:24	The children of God and the children of the devil
4:16	Two kinds of Spirits
4:7-21	Love: its nature and demands
5:1-12	Victory and testimony
5:13-21	Conclusion.

Message of 1 John

Although John wrote with the dissidents in mind, the focus of his letter is not on those who had left the community, but on those who still formed part of it.

In reaction to the false prophets who claim to speak by the authority of the Spirit (1 John 4:1), John not only reminds the community that they all have the Spirit (1 John 2:20,27), but emphasises tradition and the traditional commandment as control over prophetic enthusiasm (e g 1 John 2:7-8). In contrast to the content of their teaching, John emphasises that Jesus is the Son of God who came in the flesh (1 John 2:22-23; 4:2-3). As regards their claims to sinlessness, John acknowledges the reality of sin, but also points to the possibility of forgiveness (1 John 2:1,2).

The teaching in 1 John is more comprehensive than that part of it directly related to the views of the false prophets. It deals comprehensively with the theme of love – God's love for human beings and human love for God. These two are, according to John, closely related. God's love came first and was manifested in sending his son to the world, so that human beings might have life (1 John 4:9). The proper response to God's love is love for one another (1 John 2:15; 3:1; 13; 4: 3-5,11-12; 5:13,19), sometimes called love for the brother (1 John 4:21). John strongly emphasises the relationship between love and deeds: not only should love for God result in obedience to his commands

(1 John 5:2), it should also become manifest, in a very practical way, in one's conduct towards one's 'brother'. In the words of 1 John 3:17: 'If anyone has the necessities of life and sees their brother in need and shuts up their compassion from him, how does God's love abide in that person?'

Even what may be regarded as one of the most esoteric of books in the New Testament is closely related to a way of life.

18.6   The Second Letter of John

Context of 2 John

The Second Letter of John has the form of a personal letter, although it does not contain, as did personal letters of the time, the name of the sender and the addressees. It came from the elder and was directed at 'the chosen lady', which refers to a church closely related to the elder and the Johannine community.

The situation here is similar to that of 1 John. As in 1 John, dissidents and antichrists who have departed from the 'true doctrine' are described. They do not acknowledge that Jesus Christ came in the flesh (2 John 7), something which is of the utmost importance to the author of the letter.

CONTENTS OF 2 JOHN

1–3	Greetings
4–6	Exhortation to love those who walk in the truth
7–11	Do not receive those who spread deception
12–13	Fulfilment of joy.

Message of 2 John

As in 1 John, John here also warns against the teachings of those referred to earlier.

So strong does the author feel about the dissenting teaching of those who bring another doctrine, that he commands his readers not to receive these people in their homes or even greet them.

As in 1 John, there is an exhortation to the members of the community to love one another. This love entails a life according to God's commandments (cf 2 John 5b,6):

> I ask that we love one another.

> What love means is to live according to the commandments of God.
> This is the commandment that was given you from the beginning,
> to be your rule of life.

18.7 The Third Letter of John

Context of 3 John

John's third letter is the briefest writing in the New Testament. With regard to form and content, it resembles the personal letter of the time even more closely than 2 John. It is short and could easily have fitted on a sheet of papyrus. Coming from the elder it was addressed to his friend Gaius.

The Third Letter of John is not, as are his other two letters, concerned with doctrinal matters. It deals mainly with the question of hospitality towards 'the brothers', that is, wandering preachers.

CONTENTS OF 3 JOHN

Verses	
1–4	Greetings to the beloved brother Gaius
5–8	Praise for Gaius's hospitality
9–10	Criticism of Diotrephes' defiance
11–12	Commendation of Demetrius for his faithfulness
13–14	Desire for a personal visit
15	Greetings.

Message of 3 John

Gaius is commended for the hospitality he has shown towards those who proclaim Christ and he is requested to continue likewise. Demetrius is also commended for his faithfulness.

In contrast to this, the elder expresses his aversion to the conduct of Diotrephes, which reflects a lack of hospitality.

19 THE LETTER TO THE HEBREWS

Context of the Letter to the Hebrews

Apart from this letter, nothing is known about the author of the book Hebrews. His teaching is in agreement with Paul's main ideas, but his interests and style are quite different. Other figures from earliest Christianity are suggested, for instance Luke, Barnabas or Apollos. One must, however, concede that he cannot really be identified. It is only possible to draw a religious profile of both the author and the readers from the text of the letter.

The first readers are described in the title: 'To the Hebrews'. It has, however, been established that this label was added to the letter after its inception. It is clear that these people were Christians (Heb 3:1ff, 6:4–9, 10:23) of the second generation (Heb 2:3). Whether they were mainly of Jewish or Gentile extraction cannot be determined with certainty. We hold that the group must have had some special connection with the temple and its sacrificial system. As regards at least some of the readers, a priestly character may be assumed, due to references to the sacrificial system and to their teaching ability (Heb 5:12). The priestly circles were, furthermore, known for their keen interest in the history of Israel and their attempts to reinterpret it according to the needs and viewpoints of their day.

In spite of the reference to 'those from Italy' in Hebrews 13:24, one cannot assume that Rome was either the place where the Hebrews lived, or where the author had conceived the letter. If Jerusalem is surmised as being their home city, they must have belonged to a separate class, since it is recalled that they had made contributions towards the needs of the poor believers (Heb 6:10). They would then have been better off than most of the Christians in Judaea, of whose poverty Galatians 2:10 and Romans 15:26 speak.

The fact that there is no reference to the fall of the temple in Jerusalem during the Roman conquest may indicate that the letter was written before 70 CE. However, the author deliberately refers to the original tabernacle ('tent of worship') in the desert and not to the temple in Jerusalem. The First Letter of Clement (96 CE) first mentions the letter to the Hebrews which points to the fact that it had made its appearance by then. The reference to suffering in Hebrews may date it to the reign of the emperor Domitian (81–96 CE) for it is known that he persecuted Christians. That would fit in with the deduction from Hebrews 2:3 that the readers were second-generation Christians.

Figure 19.1
Model of the Ark of the Covenant carved in stone. It is housed in the synagogue at Capernaum

In Hebrews there are many expressions indicating that this group had lost the zeal they had once shown, and that they were starting to get critical of the high demands Christianity was making on them. They no longer seemed to be convinced of the unique value of the coming of Jesus Christ. As a minority group they were tempted to return to a Judaism based on the Old Testament only, the established religion, practising its century-old sacrificial system and enjoying a privileged status with the Roman authorities.

In the Letter to the Hebrews the sections on religious truths and on practical consequences for one's everyday life are not separate. The letter contains several passages on Christian doctrine (teaching), with several passages of exhortation (encouragement, instruction) in between.

CONTENTS OF THE LETTER TO THE HEBREWS

1:1–4:13	Part one
1:1–4	Eschatological speaking by the Father through the Son
1:5–14	Testimony of the Scriptures about the Son
2:1–4	Admonition: hearing and obeying the word
2:5–18	Son and the sons
3:1–6	Admonition: look up to Jesus the High Priest
3:7–4:11	Entrance into God's rest through faith
4:12–13	Admonition: God's word judges.

4:14–10–3	**Part two**
4:14–16	Introductory admonition
5:1–10	Jesus, the High Priest who shares human experiences
5:11–6:20	Admonition: challenge to grow in knowledge and faith
7:1–28	A High Priest according to the order of Melchizedek
8:1–13	New covenant
9:1–28	New heavenly cultic worship
10:1–18	Sacrifice of Jesus made once for all
10:19–31	Admonition: challenge to confidence in the faith.
10:32–13:25	**Part three**
10:32–39	Holding on to faith in sufferin
11:1–40	Earlier faith witnesses.
12:1–29	Holding on to faith
13:1–19	Concluding parenesis
13:20–21	Benediction
13:22–25	Admonition: apostolic Parousia; greetings and farewell.

Message of the Letter to the Hebrews

The author takes his audience's thoughts back to the time of the formation of the religion and nationhood of Israel. He works with the image of the journey of the forefathers from the bondage of Egypt through the desert of Sinai into their own land in Palestine. Two legendary figures fulfilled crucial roles on that journey: Moses was the prophetic civil leader, whereas Aaron the high priest conducted the sacrificial system in the tent of worship. However, the author argues, as Son of God, Jesus is ranked infinitely higher than Moses. He has brought the final word of God and he has done what Moses and Joshua failed to do. He leads the people of God to the real state of 'rest' with God, which he has already reached. With such a leader, nobody should get discouraged along the difficult road of this life. Jesus has also done what Aaron and the priests of Israel only symbolically did: he brought the effective and final sacrifice for sin, which opens the way to God in worship. Sacrifices and priests are no longer needed and every believer may advance freely to worship God anywhere through Christ Jesus.

The overarching theme of Hebrews has recently been defined as follows: 'Christ's revelatory work is so excellent and perfect that the first Christian readers, who are lagging behind in the religious struggle, are summoned once more, as God's people *en route* to the consummation, to persevere in faith.' This places the emphasis on Jesus as the 'final Moses' who proclaimed God's will and leads God's people from all nations along life's dangerous way to the destination of 'rest', if only they hold on to him in faith, hope and love. There is still another main theme in the letter: on the road through the wilderness there is a tabernacle in which the priests step in for God's people in worship. This is the image behind the work of Jesus as High Priest, who brought the final sacrifice on the cross. According to Hebrews, this actually took place in the heavenly sanctuary. So now the people of Christ, whoever and wherever they are, can freely draw near to God, without guilt and without anybody else having to mediate.

20 MANIFOLD JESUSES: GOSPEL IMAGES OF JESUS

20.1 The Gospel of Matthew

Context of the Gospel of Matthew

In imagining the context for the Gospel of Matthew, one is dependent on clues in the Gospel itself as well as on knowledge about the broader developments during the time referred to earlier. Clues in the Gospel are, firstly, the way in which Jesus's opponents are portrayed. In this Gospel, the Pharisees are not only portrayed as the main opponents of Jesus (cf Matt 5:20, 15:12-14 and especially ch 23); it is clear that they find themselves in a position of authority (cf the fact that they are mentioned together with the chief priests), which they held after the destruction of the temple in 70 CE. To this can be added that the Gospel contains clear signs of separation between Matthew's community and Israel, such as references to 'their synagogues' (Matt 4:23; 9:35; 10:17; 12:9; 13:54) and announcements that the kingdom is taken away from the Pharisees and chief priests (Matt 21:43; 22:1-14). There are, moreover, indications in the Gospel that Matthew was writing for a church (or a number of Christian communities) which had already developed into an institution with rules and a formal organisation. Of all the Gospels, the word *church* is used only in Matthew (16:18 and 18:17). The liturgical trend (cf its version of the Lord's Prayer with that of Luke) confirms the view that the Gospel of Matthew functioned in a formal, organised context.

From the survey made of developments within Judaism and early Christianity, it is obvious that, after the destruction of the temple in 70 CE, the Jewish community and religion had undergone substantial changes. These changes resulted in the Pharisees becoming the most influential party. During this period the Christian and Jewish religions gradually became more separated. The data in the Gospel referred to above indicate that such a situation is presupposed by Matthew. In a situation of estrangement between Jews and Christians, the church's position in respect of, and in relation to, the Jewish religion had to be spelt out. An explanation was needed for the fact that Christians no longer worshipped in the synagogue despite the fact that their religion had its roots in Judaism and that Jewish symbols, such as the law, were still important to them. The Gospel of Matthew has clear indications of continuity with, and a movement away from, the Jewish religion and its main emphases.

As regards Matthew's position in the developments that took place within early Christianity, one can detect a movement away from the earliest phase of early Christianity encountered in Q; that of a loosely structured movement with wandering figures who exercised influence over small groups of people in rural villages and towns. The Gospel of Matthew deals with urban Christian communities.

Many scholars infer from the Jewish nature of the Gospel and its relation to Q that Matthew was from Syria, possibly Antioch. The scope of Matthew's writing is so comphrensive that he probably had a number of congregations in Antioch or even in Syria as a whole, in mind.

On the one hand, the Gospel contains pronouncements according to which Jesus's mission was intended only for Israel (Matt 2:6; 9:36; 10:23; 19:28). This is supported by utterances in the Gospel which show signs of hostility against Gentiles (Matt 6:32). On the other hand, one encounters in the Gospel the realisation that Jesus was rejected by the Jewish leaders and the inhabitants of Jerusalem (Matt 27:25), while Gentiles were commended for their faith (Matt 8:10; 15:21–28). In fact, from the birth narrative onwards (Matt 2:2) until the end when the disciples were commanded to go to all the nations and make disciples (Matt 28:19), the Gospel reflects a distinct universal tendency. It seems, therefore, that both Jews and Gentiles belonged to Matthew's community.

With regard to the structure and composition of the Gospel of Matthew, a number of significant features can be pointed out. Although Matthew more or less follows the same story-line as Mark, he does not start with Jesus's public ministry, but with his genealogy and birth (Matt 1; 2). What is especially significant in determining Matthew's own emphasis, is that from chapter 5 onwards, he includes a large amount of teaching material, most of it compiled in five discourses reminiscent of the five books of the law. The best known of these discourses is the Sermon on the Mount which, in the course of history, exercised vast influence, not only inside the church, but, as a moral code, also outside it. Matthew alternates the discourses with narrative material. The miracle-stories come later in the Gospel, mainly in Matthew 8 to 9, and are usually revised and shortened. In Matthew the emphasis is clearly on Jesus's teaching, which constitutes, according to him, the focus of Jesus's ministry. The emphasis on teaching continues until the end of the Gospel (Matt 28:19), when Jesus commands his disciples to teach.

CONTENTS OF THE GOSPEL OF MATTHEW

1–2	Genealogy and infancy narrative
3–4	John the Baptist and the beginning of Jesus's ministry
5–7	First discourse: the Sermon on the Mount
8–9	Miracles of Jesus
10	Second discourse: the commission of the 70
11–12	John the Baptist and controversies over Jesus's miracles
13	Third discourse: Jesus's parables
14	Death of John the Baptist and various miracles
15	Discussion of purity, various miracles
16:1–12	Jesus and the Pharisees and Sadducees
16:13–28	Peter's confession and teaching on discipleship
17	Transfiguration; healing; the question about temple tax
18	Fourth discourse: the community rule
19	Teaching on divorce, possessions and eternal life
20	Parable of the labourers in the vineyard; John and James's request; a healing miracle
21:12–2	Entry into Jerusalem; cleansing of the temple and the cursing of the fig tree
21:23–22: 46	Source of Jesus's authority; his teaching in Jerusalem
23	Woes on the Pharisees
24–25	Fifth discourse: apocalyptic discourse
26–28	Passion and resurrection of Jesus.

Message of the Gospel of Matthew

Matthew repeatedly emphasises to a community – of which many members had a strong Jewish background, but who had by this time formed a separate community – that Jesus and his ministry should not be viewed separate from the Old Testament. On the contrary, Jesus is, according to Matthew, the one in whom the prophesies of the Old Testament were fulfilled (cf Matt 1:22,23; 2:15,17–18,23; 4:14–16; 8:17; 12:17–21; 13:35; 21:45; 27:9–10). Matthew anchors Jesus and his ministry by means of the fulfilment quotations in the traditions of Israel and confirms his community's continuity with the past, despite discontinuity.

The law – the central religious symbol of Israel – is, according to Matthew, not made invalid by Jesus, but is fulfilled by him (Matt 5:17). The law thus remains valid, also for the Christians he addresses in his Gospel. However, Matthew emphasises, especially in the Sermon on the Mount, some differences between the traditional teaching of Israel and the teaching of Jesus (Matt 5:21–22,27–28,31–32,33–34,38–39,43–44). Since Jesus, according to him, transcends the law, what is at stake for Christians is the law as interpreted by Jesus. According to Matthew's Jesus, not only the deed, but one's disposition is important (Matt 5:21–30). Christians should do more than the law literally expects from them. They should love even their enemies (Matt 5:38–47). Matthew positively links the concept of 'righteousness', which occurs frequently in his Gospel, with deeds. In the Gospel of Matthew no contrast is made, as in Paul's letters, between righteousness through faith and righteousness through works.

Matthew gave specific advice to his community regarding their conduct towards one another and towards apostates. In Matthew 18 he emphasises things such as humility, compassion and forgiveness.

It was pointed out in the discussion on the Gospel of Mark that the aim of the Evangelists was, among other things, to spell out the significance of Jesus for their own situations: to portray him in a way relevant to their own audiences. For Matthew, Jesus is the one in whom the Old Testament prophecies are fulfilled, he is the teacher, greater than Moses, on whose teaching the church is founded. He is, according to Matthew, the Son of God obedient to his Father and to whom all authority in heaven and on earth is given (Matt 28:19). Most importantly, Jesus is, according to Matthew, not only the one through whom God works, but the one in whom God himself is present among people (Matt 1:23, cf 28:20).

20.2 The Gospel of Luke and the Acts of the Apostles

Context of the Gospel of Luke

The Gospel of Luke was, unlike the other Gospels, not intended as a single writing. It formed part of a work in two volumes, with the Acts of the Apostles as its second part. This is clear from the introductions of the two writings (Luke 1:1-4; Acts 1:1-2). According to these writings, they are both dedicated to the same person, while the prologue to Acts refers to the 'first book'. Apart from the prologues, other elements in the writings (e g style and themes) support the view that they were intended as two parts of the same work. One reason why these writings appeared as two separate writings right from the start may be their length. Luke and Acts are the lengthiest two books in the New Testament and it would not be possible to fit them into one codex. In studying the Gospel of Luke one has to remember: this evangelist did not, like the others, stop with Jesus's death and resurrection. He narrates how the church continued that which Jesus had initiated. He tells this as one story. For this reason the two writings will be discussed together.

The aim of this Gospel is clearer than in the case of Matthew and Mark. In the prologue of his Gospel, Luke states the purpose of his Gospel as follows:

> Therefore, since I myself have carefully investigated everything from the beginning, it seemed good also to me to write an orderly account for you, most excellent Theophilus, so that you may know the certainty of the things you have been taught.
>
> (Luke 1:34, NIV)

The terminology Luke uses here was also used by historians of his time. In line with his consciousness of, and attention to, history, Luke links the story of Jesus and the church a few times with the broader historical context (cf Luke 1:5; 2:1-2; 3:1-2; Acts 18:12). Luke, however, does not give a complete account of the origin and developments within early Christianity. He selects and omits information as he thinks proper. In Acts, for example, there is no information about the Jesus movement in Galilee, while Jesus's ministry mainly took place in this region. The focal points in the Acts are not the rural areas, but the cities. Apart from selection and omission, it is clear that not everything in Acts can be regarded as a factual account of events. This can be inferred from the substantial differences between Luke's account of Paul's speeches and Paul's views as reflected in his own letters. Acts can therefore only, in a restricted sense, be of help in constructing the history of the early church.

In the brief survey of developments within early Christianity (cf above) it is apparent that the Jesus movement probably started in the thirties of the first century CE as an unstructured movement among Jews in Palestine. When Luke wrote his books by the end of the first century, the situation had already changed drastically. At this stage the church was already a well-organised entity (see the discussion on the Gospel of Matthew). From Paul's letters and from Acts it is known that by this time, house-churches existed where believers gathered to worship. Instead of a rural setting, such as that in which the Jesus movement originated, Luke's writings reflect an interest in the cities. In line with this interest the book of Acts reaches its climax in Rome, the capital of the then-known world. To situate Luke's writings, it is important to remember that by this time Paul and the other apostles had taken the message about Jesus to other areas. This implies that the composition of the church changed to include great numbers of Gentiles. By this time the church no longer consisted solely of the poor, as in the Q community.

That Luke's writings belong to a context in which the gospel was preached outside the national boundaries of Judaism can already be detected in his own Gospel (e g Luke 4:16–32). In Acts this becomes even more evident. Right at the beginning of Acts one reads: 'and you will be my witnesses in Jerusalem, and in all Judaea and Samaria, and to the ends of the earth' (Acts 1:8, NIV). The fact that Luke was positively disposed towards Gentiles in general, and more specifically to the Roman authorities is in keeping with the scenario of Gentile Christians (cf Luke 7:5; 23:4,14–15,22).

Luke's writings were probably dedicated to a sponsor (Theophilus). This fact is illuminating. Writing dedicated to a sponsor was usually read at meals at which the rich and the educated were gathered. In most cases the sponsor paid to have the writing copied. Luke's erudite language and style are an indication that the Gospel was written with such a context in mind. Theophilus here probably represents a group of wealthy and influential people in the church. That quite a number of these Christians were wealthy, coheres with the fact that many parts of Luke are addressed to wealthy people or at least presuppose a wealthy household (cf e g Luke 15:11–32; also Luke 16:1–9; 14:7–14; 17:7–10; Acts 16:11–15). Some of Luke's teaching is, however, addressed to the *poor*, which implies that Luke's community included the less fortunate.

Luke's interest in, and emphasis on, Gentile Christians do not imply that he did not care for Jews or that Jews did not form part of his audience. The book of Acts contains a number of references to Jews' conversion to Christianity (Acts 14:1; 21:20). The discussion of table fellowship in Acts 2 supports the view that Luke had an audience of both Jewish and Gentile Christians in mind. The Jew/Gentile problem is thus one of the matters he addresses.

THE CONTENTS OF LUKE-ACTS

Luke

1:1–4:13	**Introduction and birth narratives**
1:1–4	Introduction.
1–2	Birth of John the Baptist and Jesus.
3:1–20	Activity and imprisonment of John the Baptist.
3:21–4:13	Baptism, genealogy and temptation of Jesus.
4:14–9:50	**Jesus's ministry in Galilee**
4:14–15	Jesus preaches in Galilee
4:16–30	Jesus in the synagogue at Nazareth.
4:31–44	Jesus heals a demon-possessed and Peter's mother-in-law.
5:16:19	Callings and more miracles.
6:20–49	The Sermon on the Plain.
7:1–8:3	More healings; John the Baptist's question about Jesus.
8:4–21	The parables of the sower and the lamp.
8:22–56	Various miracles: the stilling of the storm; the Gadarene demoniac; Jairus's daughter; the woman with a haemorrhage.
9:1–17	The mission of the twelve; Herod thinks Jesus is John, risen from death; the feeding of the five thousand.
9:18–27	Peter's confession; what following Jesus entails.
9: 28–43	Transfiguration of Jesus, healing of a boy.
9:44–50	Jesus speaks about his death and resurrection; talk about who is the most important.
9:51–19:27	**The travel narrative**
9: 51–62	The Samaritans reject Jesus; on following Jesus.
10:1–42	Sending and return of the 72 disciples, parable of the Good Samaritan and Jesus's visit to Martha and Mary.
11:1–32	On prayer; Jesus and Beelzebul; the sign of Jonah.
11:33–12:3	The light of the body; Jesus rebukes the Pharisees, warning against hypocrisy.
12:4–59	Confessing Jesus; anxieties of life, various parables.
13:1–35	Various forms of healing and parables, lament over Jerusalem.
15	The parables of the lost sheep; lost coin and the lost son.
16	Parables on riches and poverty: the dishonest manager; the rich man and Lazarus.
17	Sayings of Jesus; the healing of ten lepers.

18:1–14	The widow and the judge, and the Pharisee and the tax collector.
18:15–43	Jesus and the children; on possessions and eternal life; healing of a blind man.
19:1–27	Jesus and Zacchaeus; parable of the golden coins.
19:28–24:53	**Jesus's ministry, death and resurrection in Jerusalem**
19:28–48	Jesus's entrance into Jerusalem; the cleansing of the temple.
20:1–47	Jesus's teaching in Jerusalem.
21	Apocalyptic discourse.
22–24	Passion, resurrection and ascension of Jesus.
Acts	
1:1–2:47	The beginning of the church: the promise and outpouring of the Holy Spirit and Peter's sermon on the day of Pentecost.
3:1–5:42	The church and the Jewish authorities.
6:1–9:31	The church begins to expand: Stephen's speech and stoning; Paul's persecution of the church; his conversion.
9:32–11:18	The beginning of the Gentile mission; two miracles; Peter and Cornelius; Peter reports back to the Jerusalem church.
11:19–14:28	The mission from Antioch to Asia Minor: the congregation in Antioch; Peter is imprisoned and released; Paul and Barnabas preach on Cyprus, Antioch, Ikonium and Lystra.
15:1–35	The meeting in Jerusalem; discussion about the Gentiles.
15:3–18:17	Paul's missionary work in Macedonia and Achaia: Timothy joins Paul; the conversion of Lydia; Paul and Silas in prison in Philippi; riot in Thessalonica; Paul and Silas in Berea; Paul in Athens and in Corinth.
18:18–20:38	Paul's mission in Asia Minor: Paul in Antioch; in Ephesus; to Macedonia and Greece, talk with the elders in Ephesus.
21:1–28:31	Paul's arrest and imprisonment; ending with the preaching of the Gospel in Rome.

As is the case with Matthew, the contents and structure of the Gospel of Luke in many respects resemble that of Mark. Luke differs from Mark in that, like Matthew, he starts his Gospel with the story of Jesus's birth (and that of John the Baptist). The most prominent difference is that he omits Mark 6:45 to 8:26 and from Luke 9:51 to 18:14 inserts a lengthy section which takes the form of a journey Jesus undertakes to Jerusalem. This section contains much of the material unique to Luke. Of Luke's 17 distinctive parables, 16 are in this section, including the well-known ones of the Good Samaritan (Luke 10:30–37) and the Prodigal Son (Luke 15:11–32).

It should also be noted that the structure of Luke's Gospel revolves around Jerusalem and is directed towards it. In Luke, Jesus is repeatedly portrayed as being on his way to Jerusalem

> (cf 9:51,52; 17:11). In Acts, Jerusalem serves as the starting point from which the Gospel spreads to other areas.

Message of Luke-Acts

One of the matters Luke deals with in his writings is the relationship between Jewish and Gentile Christians. It is mentioned earlier that Luke's audience probably consisted mainly of Gentile Christians. For a community of this kind, which was perhaps inclined to loosen its ties with Judaism, Luke, time and again, emphasises the continuity between Judaism and Christianity. The motif of prophecy and its fulfilment in the life, words and deeds of Jesus, which is so prominent in his inaugural sermon (Luke 4:16–30), should be understood in this context. By stressing the continuity between the church and Israel, Luke could, of course, have been encouraging Jewish–Christians who felt that they were cut off from their past.

In a church characterised by diversity in composition and outlook, Luke shows that solutions can be reached by means of compromise. In Acts 21:21 to 26 one reads about a compromise reached on the law as it pertained to Jews and Gentiles. According to Acts 6:1 to 6, Hellenistic and Palestinian Jewish–Christians had indeed come to a satisfactory agreement on financial support for widowed women.

Luke also emphasises the universalistic nature of the Gospel. According to him, the Christian message should result in the breaking down of social, economic and ethnic boundaries. The salvation to which he attests, is meant for everybody, especially those who were traditionally not in high esteem, such as the poor, sinners and women. In Acts, Luke shows how this view was put into practice by the spreading of the gospel from Judaea and Samaria to the capital of the Roman Empire.

Although Luke's writings were to a great extent addressed to the wealthy in society, his sympathy clearly is with the poor. In his Gospel the literally poor are called 'blessed' (Luke 6:20), not the poor in spirit, as in the Gospel of Matthew (Matt 5:3).

A number of places in the Gospel contain harsh criticism of the rich (Luke 6:24; 12:16–21; 16:19–31). He exhorts the rich to share their riches with the poor; to use their riches in the correct way. He even says that discipleship involves a radical break with one's possessions (Luke 14:33).

In Acts the picture is somewhat different. Whereas in the Gospel of Luke giving is meant to be for the benefit of the poor in general, in Acts it is mainly the Christian poor who receive goods from more wealthy Christians. The stringent measures on possessions in Acts last only for the first five chapters. Thereafter one reads about a number of wealthy people, none of whom are criticised for the possession of goods (cf Acts 13:1; 16:14; 17:12).

Luke is, furthermore, deeply concerned with the lost and with sinners, as emerges from his most famous parables (Luke 18:9–14; Luke 15).

Luke assigns an important role to women. Not only Joseph and Zechariah, but Mary and Elizabeth are the focus in the birth narratives of Jesus and John the Baptist, respectively, as narrated in the Gospel of Luke. In addition to the twelve disciples, a number of women sometimes accompanied Jesus on his journeys (Luke 8:13). Incidents and parables about women are frequently placed next and parallel to those about men (cf e g Luke 7:1–10,11–17; 13:10–17,14:1–6; 15:1–7, 15:8–10).

In Luke-Acts a number of names and titles are used to interpret Jesus, thereby giving expression to his significance (e g Lord, Messiah, Prophet, Son of God and Son of Man). In the important scene near the beginning of Luke's Gospel (Luke 4:16–30) Jesus is portrayed as fulfilling Isaiah's prophecies about one who will proclaim good news to the poor (Isa 61:1, 2). According to Luke, Jesus is the one who cares for the poor and the lost, and who speaks of a God who does the same. Although Luke portrays Jesus as the one who brings salvation for the whole world, he does not interpret the death of Jesus as an atoning death, that is, death for the sins of humanity. For Luke, salvation lies in insight into the fact that the righteous one died unjustly, as a martyr. Luke also portrays Jesus as obedient to God, even unto the death. In Luke, Jesus's life is, moreover, presented as an example for his followers. They are expected to live as he lived; to do what he did.

20.3 The Gospel of John

Context of the Gospel of John

Although church tradition of the second century ascribes the Gospel to John, the Gospel is, in fact, anonymous. As is the case with the other Gospels, the title 'according to John' was only added during the second century when apostolic authorship had become essential for the acceptance of a document. Careful study of the Gospel led scholars to the conclusion that the Gospel in its present form is the product of a long process in which different phases can be distinguished and different individuals played a part. It is, for example, clear that John 21 is an addition to the original composition.

> ### THE JOHANNINE WRITINGS
>
> Five New Testament writings are ascribed to 'John': the Gospel of John, three letters and the book of Revelation. The Gospel and letters of John show great similarities with regard to style and ideas. In all of them there is an emphasis on unity, love and life. A distinction is made between 'insider' and 'outsider', and dualisms such as light and darkness, truth and falsehood, and life and death are used. These terms relate to a Gnostic view of the world. They also contain signs of conflict, with the figure of Jesus in the centre.
>
> On account of these similarities most scholars regard the Gospel and letters of John as having their origins in the same circle. Revelation differs from the other Johannine writings in that it reflects the style and thought world of apocalyptic Christianity. The different conceptual worlds, namely that of Gnosticism and apocalypticism, do not necessarily imply that the origin of the Apocalypse is totally unrelated to that of the Gospel and letters.

The Gospel had initially concluded with John 20:31. It is also possible that the prologue had been added at a later stage. However, the oldest manuscripts of John contain both the prologue and chapter 21. The Gospel in its final form is to be dated about 90 CE. It was probably composed in Ephesus.

It is well known that Christianity had started as a movement within Judaism. According to Acts and the letters of Paul, the early Christians initially still had access to the Jewish synagogues. This also applied to the Johannine Christians. For them, Jesus was the fulfilment of expectations in the Hebrew Scriptures, to which there are many references in John (cf e g 1:35–49). As time passed by, as noted earlier, the relations between church and synagogue deteriorated.

The Gospel of John reflects a context after 70 CE in which a schism of even more serious proportions than was the case in Matthew's Gospel is at stake. The Greek term *aposunagogos* ('to be banned from the synagogue') is used three times in the Gospel (John 9:22, 12:42, 16:2) and points to a state of conflict with, separation from, and persecution by, the Jewish synagogue, which was a reality at the time when the Gospel was written. This conflict also explains the hostile references to 'the Jews'. This expression occurs 70 times in the Gospel and refers mostly, though not always, to the religious authorities hostile to Jesus. In the first part of the Gospel – especially in chapters 5 to 9 – there are numerous references to disputes between Jews and Christians. The Johannine Christians and the Jews had different opinions about Jesus, which was the

Figure 20.1
Entrance to the Market in Ephesus

cause of the dispute and the hostility between the two groups (John 5:18; 10:33).

In both the first and the second parts of the Gospel all attention is focused on Jesus. As a result of this, interest in the law and its execution – of crucial importance to Jews in the time after the destruction of the temple and which played an important role in the letters of Paul and the Gospel of Matthew – faded away. Jewish institutions such as ritual purification, the temple and worship in Jerusalem (John 2–4), and Jewish feasts such as the Sabbath and Passover (John 5–10) were regarded as being replaced with Jesus.

Although the Gospel of John reflects a state of conflict with the 'Jews', he wrote primarily with his own community in mind. This community formed a close unity with a tradition of its own, exhibiting a sense of exclusiveness (e g John 17:9–14). The members were loyal to one another but isolated

Figure 20.2
The Celsus library in Ephesus, an example of the magnificence characterising this important city as 'first and foremost metropolis of Asia'

from the world 'outside'. John's community was at odds not only with the Jewish synagogue, but also with the world in general. This is evident from various sayings in Jesus's farewell discourses (e g John 15:18ff), which provide a glimpse of the context of, and problems within, John's community.

THE GOSPEL OF JOHN AND THE SYNOPTIC GOSPELS

In the discussion of the Gospels of Matthew, Mark and Luke, we indicated in passing that they differ in many respects from the Gospel of John. Before paying attention to the message of John's Gospel, it could be illuminating to point out some of these differences.

These differences are evident right from the start. The Gospel according to John starts with a prologue in which Jesus is designated as the *Logos*. Nowhere else in the New Testament is such an attribute to Jesus recorded. John's chronology and geography differ from that of the Synoptics. Whereas in the Synoptics his ministry mainly took place in Galilee, in John Jesus's ministry is mainly located in Judaea, with a movement to and fro between the two regions. Unlike the Synoptics, John refers to Jesus's attendance of three feasts (John 2:13; 5:1). In John the cleansing of the temple appears at the beginning of the Gospel (John 2:13–22), and not at the end as in the Synoptic Gospels.

The long farewell discourses and Jesus's prayer for his disciples (John 14–17) may be regarded as distinctive of John. Other sections which do not occur in the Synoptics are Jesus's conversations with Nicodemus (John 3) and with the Samaritan woman (John 4). John also contains a number of miracle-stories which do not appear elsewhere, of which the changing of the water into wine (John 3:1–21) and Lazarus's raising (John 11:1–44) are best known.

> There is a striking difference between John's rendering of Jesus's teaching, and the rendering of the Synoptics. In the Synoptics he teaches by means of parables and short sayings. However, in John he speaks in long discourses about symbolic themes such as light, truth and life (John 11, 14–17). The discourses in John centre around Jesus himself rather than around the kingdom, as in the Synoptics. As to the deeds of Jesus, John contains no exorcisms.

Also relevant with regard to the context of the Gospel of John is the milieu into which the Gospel with its characteristic view of the world fits. This Gospel presents a dualistic view of the world according to which the world consists of two levels, namely one above and one below. The level above is the abode of God and that of light, life and truth. In contrast to this is the level or dimension below, characterised by darkness and death. This view of the world underlies the contradictions such as light–darkness, truth–untruth, spirit–flesh and life–death. For a long time a Greek background was presupposed for this worldview and terminology in the Gospel of John. This perception has changed since the discovery of the Qumran Scrolls. In these documents, similar kinds of opposites are encountered which reflect a form of Judaism. It has been realised that John could have been drawing from both the Hellenistic and the Jewish thought worlds, which partly overlapped during the time when John wrote his Gospel.

Emphasis on the role of the Paraclete in the Gospel of John may point to a situation in which Spirit-filled prophets who spoke the words of Jesus as the risen Lord were active.

CONTENTS OF THE GOSPEL OF JOHN

> Apart from the prologue (John 1:1–18), the Gospel of John can be divided into two sections. Chapters 2 to 12 deal with the public ministry of Jesus, while chapters 13 to 21 are concerned with Jesus's teaching to his disciples (and on another level to the Johannine community) and his passion and resurrection.

1–12	**Part one**
1:1–18	Prologue.
1:19–5	Testimony of John the Baptist; first disciples; calling of Nathanael.
2	The wedding at Cana; cleansing of the temple.
3	Dialogue with Nicodemus; John's testimony to Jesus.
4	Dialogue with a Samaritan woman, healing of the official's son.
5	Healing at the pool of Bethesda; the authority of the Son; the witnesses to Jesus.
6	The feeding of the multitude and Jesus as the bread of life.
7	Jesus teaches in the temple at the feast of Tabernacles; attempts to arrest him; difference of opinion about him.
8	The adulterous woman; Jesus and the Jews.
9	The healing of the blind man and the aftermath of the episode.
10	Jesus as the good shepherd; Jesus at the festival of dedication.
11	Death and raising of Lazarus.
12	Anointing in Nazareth; entry into Jerusalem; his glorification.
13–21	**Part two**
13	Last meal with his disciples; the foot washing; Jesus discloses that one of the disciples will betray him; Peter will deny him.
14	Farewell discourse, the promise and coming of the Paraclete.
15	Allegory of the vine, exhortation to bear fruit through acts of love.
16	The work of the Paraclete, Jesus has conquered the world.
17	Jesus's prayer for himself, the disciples and future believers.
18–20	The passion and resurrection; appearances to the disciples.
21	The miraculous catch of fish; the future role of Peter and that of the beloved disciple.

Message of the Gospel of John

Since Jesus himself and his significance are of such crucial importance to the Johannine community, also in the dispute with the synagogue, one would expect some elaboration on Jesus's significance. This is precisely what happens in the Gospel. From the first verse of the prologue onwards the significance of Jesus is spelt out in an unprecedented way. He is called 'the Word' (Logos) through whom all things have been made (John 1:3). Other designations which are postponed until later in Mark, occur in John's first chapter: *Christ* (1:41), *Son of God* and *King of Israel* (1:49) and *Son of Man* (1:51).

Jesus is to John the Son of God sent by God to earth (3:16,17,34), the one who comes from the Father and who will return to the Father. He is the one in whom God is made fully known (John 1:18). He is also the one in whom salvation is to be found for those who believe in him (John 3:16). In John there is a strong emphasis on belief in Jesus himself, that is, an entrusting of oneself to Jesus. In this Gospel the signs (miracles), furthermore, point to Jesus's identity.

To match John's Christology, Jesus's death is not a tragic event in his Gospel. John emphasises not his humiliation, but his glorification. Whereas in Mark Jesus dies with a cry of dereliction on his lips (Mark 15:34), in John Jesus's last words are a triumphant: 'It is finished' (John 19:30).

According to John, Jesus's 'first coming' to the world is of crucial importance (John 3:16–21). The future is already here. Jesus has already overcome the world (John 16:33). People's response to Jesus in the present – belief or disobedience – determines whether they will have eternal life or be judged (John 3:36; 5:24). Salvation is therefore a present reality. Despite the strong emphasis on the present, so characteristic of John's Gospel, in a number of sayings the traditional view of a future resurrection and judgement is retained (John 5:28,29; 11:24).

In accordance with the exclusivistic nature of the Johannine community referred to earlier, the members of John's community are exhorted to love one another. The love commandment is here restricted to love for Christians who together formed part of the community (e g John 13:34; 15:12–13). Nowhere in John does one encounter the commandment to love one's neighbour or one's enemy (as is found in Matthew). Apart from the general love commandment, John does not provide guidelines for specific situations, as is the case with the Synoptic Gospels. In addition to love for one another, the Johannine Christians are called to unity with one another and with the risen Lord (John 17) and to abide in Jesus (John 15). These exhortations fit in well with the egalitarian nature of the community as a result of the fact that they all possessed the Spirit.

When reading the Gospel of John together with the confessions of fourth and fifth-century communities, it is clear that this Gospel played a crucial role in the formulation of the church's view of Jesus.

THE JEWS IN THE GOSPEL OF JOHN

In the Gospel of Matthew, and even more so in the Gospel of John, there is a strong polemic against *the Jews*. Though rooted firmly in its Jewish environment, the Gospel of John is probably the most anti-Jewish Gospel. In John 8:44, in response to the Jews who held that they had one father, God, the Johannine Jesus says: 'You are from your father the devil, and you choose to do your father's desires'.

The term *the Jews*, which occurs 70 times in the Gospel of John, has in this Gospel various shades of meaning. In a few cases it functions as a nationalistic or religious designation (cf John 4: 22; 18:33,35). In other cases it refers to Judaeans (John 8:31). Mostly, however, it refers to the religious authorities who are hostile to Jesus, the opponents of Jesus (e g John 1:19; 2:18,20; 5:10,15,16; 8:22). The context of this polemic is the struggle between church and synagogue in the Evangelist's time at the end of the first century. The way John characterises 'the Jews' is therefore clearly shaped by historical circumstances and by theological interests. Taking into account the first-century context of a small Christian community which became separated from the larger Jewish community and tried to establish itself, the hostility against the Jewish authorities and the strong language used in the Gospel is, in a sense, understandable.

Although not anti-Semitic in its intent in the sense that not race, but opposition to Jesus, is condemned, Johannine scholars point out that the Gospel has a potential for anti-Semitism, especially when taken at face value. In the past it was sometimes not only read as supporting anti-Semitism, but it also contributed to the development of anti-Semitism. The issue of the Jews in John's Gospel is a good example of the danger of de-historising the writings of the New Testament and of the necessity for studying them critically and historically.

21 INTIMATIONS OF THE END-TIME: THE REVELATION OF JOHN

21.1 The book of Revelation

Context of the book of Revelation

The book of Revelation was written somewhere along the western coast of Asia Minor, probably in Patmos. The author refers to himself as John, but does not identify himself as a disciple or apostle of Jesus. He was probably a prophet who went from place to place and was therefore familiar with the communities to which he wrote.

An apocalyptic writing coheres with, and answers to, a situation of crisis (cf box: Revelation as apocalypse). The book of Revelation contains indications that it was addressed to Christians being persecuted for the sake of their faith. This persecution resulted from the Christians' refusal to take part in emperor worship (Rev 13:4,12–17; 14:9–12; 16:2; 19:20). There were probably also internal religious conflicts, symbolically referred to by means of 'Nicolaitans' (Rev 2:6,15) and 'the synagogue of Satan' (Rev 2:9).

> **REVELATION AS APOCALYPSE**
>
> To be able to understand the Revelation of John it is imperative to know something about its literary genre. In the first verse the author refers to his book as the apocalypse of Jesus Christ. Books or sections of books of this nature occurred at an earlier stage among Jews. Daniel 7 to 12, for example, belong to the same literary genre. In the Synoptic Gospels the so-called little apocalypse (Mark 13 par) appears. Other well-known apocalypses are *1 Enoch* and *4 Ezra*.
>
> An apocalypse was regarded by its writer as a revelation received from God by means of an otherworldly messenger (e g an angel). In such a revelation, current, earthly circumstances are interpreted in the light of the transcendent world and of the future. It especially envisages salvation in the future.
>
> Crucial to the understanding of an apocalypse is that it coheres with, and answers to, a crisis situation. By interpreting history in a specific way, it, as it were, draws the attention away from the current depressing situation to the transcendent world and the future. By

PART FOUR: THE CHRISTIAN LITERATURE OF THE LATE FIRST CENTURY (70–100 CE)

Figure 21.1
Model of the Altar of Zeus in Pergamon. A magnificent structure, it was called the 'seat of Satan' in the letter to the church in Pergamon in Revelation 2:12 to 13

Figure 21.2
View over Pergamon from the mountain top. This magnificent city was laid out against the side of the mountain with its monumental public buildings on, or near, the crest of the mountain. The ruins in the foreground represent the original location of the famous altar of Zeus, now completely rebuilt in the Staatliche Museen zu Berlin

Figure 21.3
Reconstructed remains of the Jewish synagogue at Sardis. This was the largest Jewish synagogue in the Diaspora in antiquity

Figure 21.4
The 'hot mineral falls' of Hierapolis, modern Pamukalle, a Hellenistic city founded in the third century BCE. Later it became an important commercial centre and in the Christian era an important bishopric and later a metropolitan see. Behind the city a hot mineral spring wells up and its overflow covers the rocks below with white deposits of lime which create the appearance of a frozen cascade as seen in the picture. Hierapolis overlooked the city of Laodicea about 9 km away. The church of Laodicea was one of the seven churches of Asia addressed in Revelation 3:14 to 22. The church is rebuked for allowing its material affluence to make it spiritually 'wretched, pitiable, poor, blind and naked'. The proverbial lukewarmness has to do with the condition of the city's water supply. The water supplied by the spring at Baspinar, it is suggested, was tepid and nauseating by the time it was piped to Laodicea, unlike the therapeutic hot water of Hierapolis or the refreshing cold water of Colossae; hence the rebuke, 'Would that you were cold or hot!'

Figure 21.5
Temple of Hadrian in Ephesus. Ephesus was an important centre for emperor worship and was awarded the right to host the emperor cult (the *neokorate*) twice. This entailed the right to build a temple to the imperial cult and the staging of games in their honour. In 125 CE Hadrian was lauded as the New Dionysus upon his entry into the city

doing so, it supplies a meaningful frame of reference in which people can see their situation and act.

An apocalypse has a strong visionary character. The Revelation of John frequently refers to visions and contains many references to 'see' (Rev 1:2,12,17; 4:1; 5:1,2,6,12; 7:1,2; 9:1,17; 18:1; 20:1,4,11,12; 21:1,2,22). In order to see, John has to undertake a heavenly journey, something typical of apocalyptic literature (cf Rev 4:1). Visions are alternated with other genres such as doxology, songs of victory and blessings.

Typical of an apocalyptic writing is the use of symbols. In the Revelation of John numbers play an important part, especially the numbers 4, 7 and 12 (cf Rev 4:6; 5:1; 8:6; 15:1; 16:1). A number of animal symbols are also used, such as 'the lamb'. Reference is also made to cosmic phenomena, such as earthquakes (Rev 6:12–17), thunder and lightning (Rev 8:5). All this gives the apocalypse of John a mysterious character.

The apocalypse of John differs from other apocalypses in two respects. Firstly, John writes in his own name and not under the name of a famous person of the past. Secondly, the form of John's apocalypse differs from that of others in that the apocalypse is embedded within the framework of a letter.

In interpreting an apocalypse, two things should be avoided: its contents should not be interpreted literally and it should not be regarded as aimed directly at one's own situation.

Figure 21.6
The Artemis temple at Sardis. Sardis was famous in antiquity as the capital of the Lydian empire and for the legendary king, Croesus. It was home to a very large Jewish community in Hellenistic times. Sardis is mentioned in Revelation 3:1 to 6 as one of the churches addressed in the seven letters to the churches in Asia Minor

> These two errors were frequently made in the past when, for example, Revelation 20 verses 4 to 6 were regarded as referring to a literal period of thousand years on earth and when the number 666 was often applied to a controversial ruler of the interpreter's own time.

The question is which persecution the author had in mind. People within the Roman Empire were usually free to practise their own religion as long as they were willing to acknowledge the Roman gods and sacrifice to the Roman emperors. The Jews, who worshipped one God, were obviously not willing to take part in such practices. Their special position was acknowledged by the Romans. As Christians gradually came to exist and function as a separate group, they were no longer protected by the concession to the Jews and therefore not excused if they did not acknowledge the Roman gods. Some Roman emperors insisted on being worshipped as gods. Refusal to do this could cause

Figure 21.7
Obverse of coin with head of Domitian. The inscription names him Imp[erator] Caes[ar] Domit[ianus] Aug[ustus] Germ[anicus] Cos III (= Consul) Cens[or]. Domitian obtained the title *Germanicus* after his victorious campaign in Germany in 83 CE during which he extended Roman territory into Germany. Domitian, while professing a strong aversion to bloodshed, was nevertheless given to extreme punishments and bloody executions. His strong reverence for antique Roman religion made him intolerant of dissent, political and religious (which in Roman times amounted to the same thing). His increasingly paranoid and autocratic rule was the context of, and occasion for, sporadic localised pogroms against Christians, as witnessed by the Revelation of John.

Figure 21.8
Reverse of the same coin, showing Domitian seated on a podium in front of the portico of a temple. The inscription reads 'Domitianus Imp[erator] VIII . . . Lud[i] Saec[ulares] (= Secular Games)' and on the podium itself is inscribed *Suffimentum* (= Incense). The event portrayed is the Secular Games (or 'games commemorating the start of a new era') of 88 CE commemorating his victories in Dacia, also the occasion of a triumph in 89 to celebrate the victory. The image shows him distributing gifts to citizens standing in front of him.

trouble for Christians. From the *Annals* of Tacitus it is evident that Christians were persecuted by Nero during 64 CE. This persecution was, however, restricted to Rome and was not concerned with the emperor cult. According to early Christian tradition, a persecution of Christians took place under Domitian and it is possible that Revelation was written during this time (95–96 CE).

CONTENTS OF THE BOOK OF REVELATION

1:1–3	Prologue to the book as a whole
1:4–8	Introduction to the circular letter to the churches in Asia
1:9–20	John's vision of Jesus as the Son of Man
2–3	Seven letters to the seven churches in Asia Minor
4–5	John's vision of worship in the royal throne room in heaven; Christ as the Lamb receives the sealed book of prophecy
6	The Lamb opens six of the seven seals
7	Sealing of those who will be spared; worship of the saints
8–9	The seventh seal; six of the seven trumpets blast portending disasters
10	The mighty angel and the prophet John's reception and digestion of the scroll
11	The contents of the scroll and the sounding of the seventh trumpet
12	The woman and the monster
13	The beast from the sea; the beast from the earth
14	The Lamb and his 144 000 followers; announcement and execution of judgement
15	Seven angels and the last seven plagues
16	The seven bowls
17	The harlot and her destruction
18	The fall of Babylon
19	Joy in heaven; the marriage of the Lamb
20	Satan is bounded and conquered; the Last Judgement
21:1–22:5	The new heaven and new earth; the new Jerusalem
22:6–21	Jesus will come soon.

Message of the book of Revelation

Addressing a state of persecution and suffering, John emphasises that, although the evil powers cannot easily be restrained and the Christian community will therefore suffer, this is only part of the picture. Contrary to how it seems, they can be assured that God is in control. This is, according to the author, the real but concealed state of affairs. God, who is portrayed by the author of Revelation as intervening directly in human affairs, is not only the creator of the world, but also the one who will ultimately save it, contrary to present appearances. He will defeat the evil powers and vindicate his people, the Christian community.

John's portrayal of Jesus is meant to sustain the Christian communities in their difficulties. In the opening vision he is typified as the Son of Man who is also the First and the Last (Rev 1:17–18). He is the one who has fulfilled the divine plan for salvation and therefore deserves to be worshipped (Rev 4:11; 5:9). He is also the Lamb, who is here regarded as a sacrifice of cosmic significance.

Since God and Christ are in control, the community John is addressing is exhorted to endure, even unto the death (Rev 2:10). Those who suffer as Christ had suffered and nevertheless remain faithful, will in the end be rewarded, while the unrighteous, worldly powers will be judged.

APOCALYPTIC, APOCALYPTICISM AND APOCALYPSES

The meaning of the terms

The terms *apocalyptic* and *apocalypse* are derived from the Greek word *apokalypsis* ('revelation'). The terms describe a mind-set or worldview (*apocalypticism*) or the texts that express to a greater or lesser extent this mind-set or worldview (*apocalypses*). The mere presence of an apocalyptic passage or section does not make a specific text as a whole an apocalypse. Apocalypses are texts that are stamped throughout by the visionary language and aspects characteristic of apocalypticism. Although one speaks of apocalypticism as a cultural mind-set and worldview it needs to be borne in mind that the texts that are classified among the apocalypses are often so dissimilar and contradictory in attitudes towards the events of the end-time and description of the various heavens and Paradise as to caution against viewing apocalypticism as a unitary movement.

The genealogy of apocalypticism

The history of apocalyticism as worldview and as cultural mind-set is difficult to trace and reconstruct. However, it is safe to say that apocalypticism has a genealogy that incorporates mainly four diverse 'backgrounds'. The first is ancient oracles and oracular literature such as the *Potter's Oracle* in Egypt and the *Chaldaean Oracles* in Babylonia, or the *Sibylline Oracles* preserved in Rome, which should not be confused with the Jewish–Christian *Sibylline Oracles*. Then there are ancient prophetism and prophetic literature, especially in respect of their pronouncements of judgement and deliverance. Many scholars take apocalypticism to be an extreme offshoot of Old Testament prophecy in which a heightened sense of the end with its concomitant ideas of catastrophic end-time judgement, deliverance and restoration have come to dominate. The third strand is utopian imperial ideology such as the Darius inscriptions at Bisitun and Susa, and Roman imperial 'mythology' evidenced in Vergil's *Aeneid* and the fourth Eclogue, aspects also reflected in such Jewish texts as *1 Enoch* and the Jewish–Christian *Sibylline Oracles* (especially *Sib Or* 3). A fourth strand is wisdom literature, especially Hellenistic Jewish wisdom speculation on the correct understanding of the inner workings of the cosmos and the principles governing history.

The cultural setting of apocalypticism

With these remarks on the genealogy of apocalypticism, the cultural setting of this worldview has been hinted at. Apocalypticism was not confined to Jewish and Christian circles. Jewish and Christian apocalypticism was, arguably, derived from Persian antecedents. The many similarities between Jewish and Christian apocalypses and Persian apocalypses, sometimes to the point of almost verbal correspondences, seem to illustrate this. Persian apocalyptic texts such as the *Bundahishn*, the *Bahman Yast* and the (lost but reconstructed) first-century BCE *Oracle of Hystaspes* contain motifs, images and larger constellations of ideas that occur in almost all the classical Jewish and Christian apocalypses, in many Qumran scrolls, but also in rabbinic material, Christian apocrypha (especially the Coptic *Apocalypse of Peter*), the Apostolic Fathers and in the early Church Fathers (most notably Lactantius's *Divine Institutions Epitome Books 7 and 8*).

Many ideas forming part of the complex of end-time views, such as the fiery catastrophic end to the world, end-time judgement, resurrection of the dead to eternal life, and hell as a fiery cess pit penetrated into Jewish religion from the Persian world during the Hellenistic period. However, apart from these specific visions on end-time events, apocalypticism was very much a Graeco-Roman phenomenon, driven by the same inherent logic as other religious and philosophical views.

What was this 'logic'? According to the scholar of Jewish and Graeco-Roman religions, Martin Hengel, this 'driving logic' was the quest for 'higher wisdom through revelation'. There are many similarities between the quest for revelation and contact with the gods in apocalyptic and non-Jewish Graeco-Roman material. The period was characterised by a general trend towards attempts at breaking the code of the mystery of divine purpose and the nature of divine presence in history, with a concomitant concern for establishing the right code of ethical conduct. In a period during which the ways of the gods were by no means self-evident any more due to political-historical vicissitudes and wide-ranging changes in worldviews and the ways the gods were conceptualised, revelation of divine mysteries became an indispensable way of giving meaning and purpose to human existence. Typical mechanisms of establishing divine purpose are claims to revelations of mysteries of the future and the course of history, descriptions of mystical ascent and access to divinity, doctrines of angels as mediators of revelation, astrology and the movement of the stars as predictions of future events, and theurgy or divine contact evoked through magical practices. These mechanisms were featured across the board in oracles, apocalypses, Jewish as well Graeco-Roman philosophical works, magical practices, mystical 'theologies' and other religious works, and political ideologies. If understood in this light, it is easy to see why a close relationship always existed between apocalypticism and later mystical traditions, such as Merkabah ('throne chariot', a reference to the chariot vision in Ezekiel) and Hekhalot ('heavenly palaces') mystical traditions in Judaism, and gnostic tradition.

Dating of the phenomenon

Apocalypticism emerged around the beginning of the second century BCE, since it seems from internal evidence from some of the early apocalypses (or parts of them) that they allude to political circumstances during the rule of some of the later Hellenistic kings. Many apocalypses are composite and multi-layered texts, and have a long and complex composition history. It is clear that apocalyptic texts grew through use and continual reapplication to new circumstances and reinterpretation. They thus became expanded to include oracles of judgement not only against the Hellenistic ('Macedonian') kings, but also against the dominant political authorities in Jerusalem (the Hasmonean royal house and Jewish aristocracy) and later, of course, against Roman imperial power. The Jewish apocalypses that survived were preserved solely in Christian circles where they were copied and edited to the extent that Christian elements made their way into these texts (e g the acrostic poem referring to Christ as well as the long poem on Christ's career in *Sib Or* 8:217—336). Apocalypses continued to be written in the Christian world throughout the early Christian centuries until the later Middle Ages and even beyond. However, the heyday of apocalypticism, the time it exerted its greatest influence on the Mediterranean world, was from the second centuries BCE to the end of the second century CE.

Morphology of apocalypticism

The following features are among the most important characteristics of apocalypses. It is to be noted that they do not all feature in each apocalyptic text.

(1) They narrate visions or auditions sent by God to the visionary and typically these visions occur in the context of a dream or trance. Certain topics appear regularly in apocalyptic visions, namely the resurrection of the dead, expectations of cosmic distress and the restoration of a Golden Age sometimes accompanied by the appearance of a saviour figure, heavenly journeys and tours of hell, visits to, and descriptions of, the heavenly throne rooms, and visions of God.

(2) Heavenly intermediaries, usually angels, interpret these visions or auditions, or act as guides on these tours of heaven and hell.

(3) The use of intense, graphic and grotesque symbolism often derived from ancient mythology (the extraordinary large size of the heavenly city, grotesque human figures and numerous animals and monster, for example).

(4) Most apocalypses are pseudonymous. They are published under the names of heroes from antiquity. The two possible exceptions are the Revelation of John and the *Shepherd of Hermas*.

(5) An imminent expectation of the end of this world age and the inception of the new aeon are described. Often this is accompanied by a division of world history into periods of thousand years (or millennia).

(6) This imminent end will be inaugurated and accompanied by cosmic catastrophes such as floods, droughts, falling stars, earthquakes, conflagration, war and human discord.

(7) Dualism characterises many apocalypses, namely dualisms regarding people (the righteous versus the wicked), powers (God versus Satan) and time periods (this age versus the age to come).

(8) The dualistic worldview goes hand in hand with determinism; the view that the course of history is set and will unfold according to a predetermined plan without much scope of changing its course. Therefore, the wicked will remain wicked with little chance of repentance. What will happen, 'must happen'.

(9) The portrayal of the unfolding of history according to a predetermined plan ties in with another important feature, namely *ex eventu* prophecy, or prophecy after the fact. This is also enabled by the ascription to an ancient author. Contemporary events are described as if they were prophesied to occur in exactly this way long ago. The book of Daniel is a good example of a narrative set in the sixth century BCE, but accurately describing the events leading up to the Maccabaean revolt of *c.* 167 BCE.

(10) Cosmic or astronomical speculation marks many apocalypses. These take the form of sky journeys and tours of heaven and hell with descriptions of visions of God, his place of abode and the place of punishment. Renewed attention to this feature lends credibility to the twofold classification of apocalypses as either historical (revealing the course of history, judging current historical events) or cosmological (mystical) in nature, providing visions of God.

Most important Jewish and Christian apocalypses from the period

Most of the following apocalypses started life as Jewish apocalypses, but through reappropriation, reinterpretation and redaction they were Christianised for use by Christians. Many only survived as complete texts in much later (Christian) translations.

1 (*Ethiopic Apocalypse of*) *Enoch*
3 (*Hebrew Apocalypse of*) *Enoch*
Treatise of Shem
Apocalypse of Zephaniah
Greek *Apocalypse of Ezra*
Questions of Ezra
Apocalypse of Sedrach
3 (*Greek Apocalypse of*) *Baruch*

2 (*Slavonic Apocalypse of*) *Enoch*
Sibylline Oracles
Apocryphon of Ezekiel
4 Ezra
Vision of Ezra
Revelation of Ezra
2 (*Syriac Apocalypse of*) *Baruch*
Apocalypse of Abraham

Apocalypse of Adam   *Apocalypse of Elijah*
Apocalypse of Daniel

In the Old Testament itself the following examples occur:
Isaiah 24 to 27   Zechariah 9 to 14
Daniel 7 to 12

Among the Dead Sea Scrolls of Qumran there are the following:
Parts of the *Apocalypse of Enoch* (including the *Book of Giants* and *Astronomical Enoch*)
The War Scroll   *Messianic Apocalypse* (4Q521)
Pesher Habakkuk ('Commentary on Habakkuk')

In the New Testament one finds:
Mark 13 (= Matthew 24–25; Luke 21:5–37)   The Revelation of John

Early Christian apocalypses are:
Didache 16   *Shepherd of Hermas*
Apocalypse of Peter   *Ascension of Isaiah.*
5 and 6 Ezra

The importance of apocalypticism

The New Testament scholar Ernst Käsemann once made a famous statement about apocalypticism, namely that apocalypticism was the mother of Christian theology. While apocalypticism is certainly not the only fount of Christianity, apocalyptic thinking and ideas pervade Second Temple Jewish literature, the New Testament and other early Christian literature. Thanks to apocalypticism, ideas about the coming of a heavenly redeemer (the 'Son of Man'), end-time judgement and resurrection of the dead, the second coming of Christ, the Antichrist, and the end of this world and the rebirth of a new world became part of the core of Christian belief. These ideas persisted even though the urgent sense of an imminent end to this world gradually diminished.

At times during Christian history, but especially during the Middle Ages, in times of stress and upheaval, apocalyptic thinking flared up to stir restoration or revitalisation movements or social revolutions. In this regard, one can think of the legacy of the thirteenth-century monk, Joachim of Fiore in Florence, and the sixteenth-century leader of a peasant revolt in Germany, Thomas Müntzer. Apocalyptic imagination left its mark on religious art too. The many woodcuts of the fifteenth-century master, Albrecht Dürer, depicting scenes from the Revelation of John, for example, attest to the continuing presence and relevance of apocalyptic ideas in Christian thinking.

22 CONCLUSION

In the last quarter of the first century a long time had already elapsed since Jesus's crucifixion and death. This had the result that there was an ever-increasing need for literature that would record past events. Especially the Gospels of Matthew, Mark and Luke ensured that the words and deeds of Jesus would not sink into oblivion. However, this period also provided the opportunity for an ongoing reflection on what the Jesus movement meant. It also became the object of its own reflection in , for example, the Acts of the apostles; the first 'history of early Christianity' which exists.

From the deuteropauline letters and the general letters one can see the same kind of reflection. Guidance had to be given on how Christians should behave and act in this world before Christ's second coming. The church as such also became part of the 'salvation history' which was perceived to have occurred in the person of Jesus. Despite this concentration on earthly life, the early Christians never gave up their expectation of the coming of Christ. This is remarkable, since their earlier expectations had been dashed. It seems that the message of, and about, Jesus had a power in its own right, which was independent of subsequent (expected) history. This adaptative reflection of early Christian writers and their coming to terms with the fact that Jesus did not come immediately, provided the basis for the survival of Christianity up to today.

Suggested reading

Balch, D L
1991   *Social History of the Matthean Community*. Minneapolis: Fortress Press.

Bauer, David R & Powell, Mark A (eds)
1995   *Treasures Old and New: Recent Contributions to Matthean Studies*. Atlanta: Society of Biblical Literature. (Symposium Series 1)

Botha, Pieter J J
2000   *Daily Life in the World of Jesus*. Pretoria: Biblia.

Burridge, Richard A
1992   *What Are the Gospels? A Comparison with Greco-Roman Biography*. Cambridge: Cambridge University Press.

Horsley, Richard A
2001   *Challenging the Order: an Introduction to Mark's Gospel*. Louisville: Westminster John Knox Press.

Kingsbury, Jack Dean (ed)
1997   *Gospel Interpretation: Narrative-critical and Social-scientific Approaches.* Harrisburg: Trinity Press International.

Marsh, C & Moyise, Steve
1998   *Jesus and the Gospels: an Introduction.* London: Cassell.

Neyrey, Jerome H (ed)
1991   *The Social World of Luke-Acts: Models for Interpretation.* Peabody: Hendrickson.

Saldarini, Anthony J
1994   *Matthew's Jewish–Christian Community.* Chicago: University of Chicago Press. (Chicago Studies in the History of Judaism)

Stanton, Graham
1989   *The Gospels and Jesus.* Oxford: Oxford University Press.

On apocalypticism

Collins, Adela Yarbro
1996   *Cosmology and Eschatology in Jewish and Christian Apocalypticism.* Leiden: Brill. (Supplements to the *Journal for the Study of Judaism* 50)

Collins, John J
1982   *The Apocalyptic Imagination.* Grand Rapids: Eerdmans.
1997   *Seers, Sibyls and Sages in Hellenistic–Roman Judaism.* Leiden: Brill. (Supplements to the *Journal for the Study of Judaism* 54)

Collins, John J (ed)
1998   *The Encyclopedia of Apocalypticism.* Volume 1. *The Origins of Apocalypticism in Judaism and Christianity.* New York: Continuum.

Part five

Beyond the New Testament: the making of Christianity and its emergence into the world

23 CREATING CHRISTIANITY

This survey of ancient Israelite and early Christian writings ends with second-century Christian literature. The reason for including later Christian literature is that Christianity only became what it is today in the period leading up to the important councils of Nicaea and Chalcedon (i e between the fourth and fifth centuries CE), when the questions surrounding the collection of canonical writings had been settled, and the main outlines and formulations of Christian doctrines fixed. Having established authoritative tradition, the Christian church created its own identity as Christian religion among Jewish and other Graeco-Roman and oriental cults and philosophies.

This section aims to show how the character of Christianity was created from the multiform traditions and religious kaleidoscope of Graeco-Roman antiquity. It developed in a crucible of dialogue and ideological conflict involving very different viewpoints. The scope of the current study extends to the second century. The third century and onwards was the age of the patristic writers, and this body of literature would also take one too far outside the boundaries of an introduction to biblical literature.

What does emerge from a survey of this kind is that Christianity was 'woven together' from different strands of tradition. This is important for one's understanding of the historical (textual) sources serving as the fount from which Christianity as religion was born. All along it has been suggested, and alluded to, that the Christian epic had been created from the Hebrew (or Jewish) and New Testament epics, as well as the Jesus traditions, and Graeco-Roman philosophical and religious traditions. By 'epic' is meant the way a community 'imagines a set of stories and symbols with respect to the past and how such a community imagines them to relate to the present'. By selecting stories, figures as examples, texts, symbols and images from the textual tradition as well as oral and cultural tradition, a world or symbolic universe and ethic are created, and an identity and lifestyle formed. All this takes place in dialogue with the historical context and in answer to historical events and circumstances. This became obvious. A similar case was argued with regard to the development of the Jesus traditions that became the New Testament, as is also the case with second-century Christian literature. Second-century Christian use of Second Temple Jewish epic and of first-century Jesus traditions throws light on the way early Christians understood these traditions and indeed can serve as an important clue to the meaning of biblical texts. The

Figure 23.1
Wall painting of the good shepherd, a symbol of *humanitas*, of being part of a caring community in which one found kinship peace in times of turbulence amidst the threats and sufferings of daily life. The symbol of the *criophorus* (or 'ram/sheep carrier') was a very old Near Eastern symbol, eventually taken over by Christians from the contemporary cults of Orpheus and Hermes, who were both portrayed as good shepherds

Figure 23.2
Early Christian burial memorial. The *benemerentes* ('well deserving') in the last line is equivalent to the modern 'in fond memory'. The accompanying symbols are telling: Jonah disgorged by the sea monster, the good shepherd carrying the sheep and a lion (recalling Daniel in the lion's den?), plus an anchor at the bottom. These symbols were regularly used together. The Jonah cycle symbolises peace in an alien environment; the good shepherd: peace in a caring living community; Daniel in the lion's den: escape from a deadly situation; and the anchor: security in a hostile culture. Early Christian symbols such as these evoke a sense of peace and well-being; of being saved and protected from the harsh realities of living under oppressive conditions

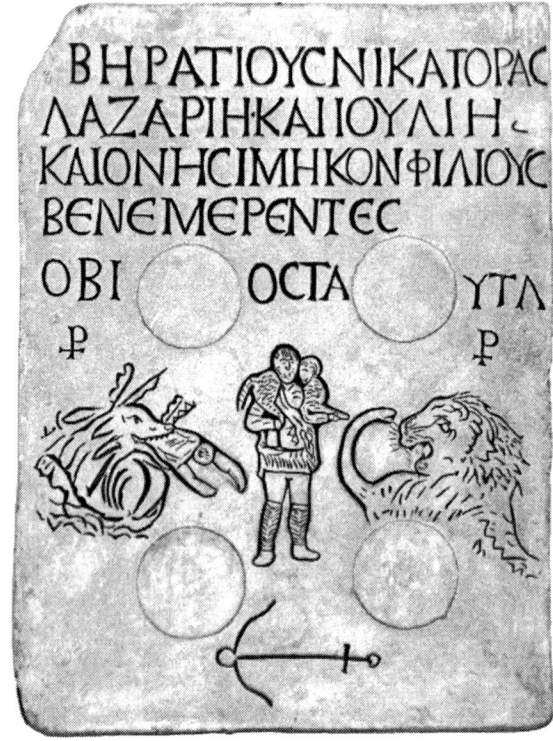

Figure 23.3
Fractio panis. Relief carving showing the believers reclining at the table breaking bread (in front and being served from the basket on the left). Early Christian depictions of meals are not to be understood as referring to the eucharist or Lord's Supper (the Passover meal of the Gospels), but to early Christian communal meals

Figure 23.4
Fresco of bread and fish from the catacomb of St Callixtus in Rome. It symbolises the early Christian cult meal in its various incarnations of *koinonia* meal, *agape* and *refrigerium* (or: meal with the dead). From epigraphical evidence it is known that bread and fish were the staple fare at cult group meals. By employing these symbols, early Christians implied that Christian communities functioned along the same lines and had the same social significance as Graeco-Roman burial societies, cult groups or schools

recent constructions of the historical Jesus, for example, rely strongly on later versions and attestations of such Jesus traditions.

The early Christian epic was constructed from multiple 'ways of speaking' or discourses, which are, in essence, different sets of selections of images, authoritative stories and figures as examples. Six such discourses have been identified, namely wisdom discourse, miracle discourse, apocalyptic discourse, prophetic discourse, suffering–death discourse and pre-creation discourse.

(1) *Wisdom discourse* focuses on the transmission of wisdom from Jesus to his followers and then by Christian believers to others. The wisdom sayings of Jesus in Q and of the Gospel writers as well as fixed proverbs of philosophical and ethical nature (such as found in later church writers) would count as examples. The point of wisdom sayings is change or strengthening of behavioural patterns. As was characteristic of Hellenistic philosophy (as 'life science') in general, wisdom presupposes that 'proper insight into life can equip people to live satisfactorily in the world'.

(2) *Miracle discourse* is based on the assumption that God can miraculously intervene to the benefit of the believer. The believer is expected to fulfil

Figure 23.5
Symbols of deliverance: Jesus the healer. On this sarcophagus in l'Eglise Sainte Quitterie du Mas, Aire-sur-l'Adour in France, one can see the healing of the paralytic (top on the left of the inscription plate), the raising of Lazarus (bottom left), and the healing of a possessed boy (bottom right). In the bottom middle is the good shepherd with, to his left, a young man and Daniel in the lion's den. To his right are Adam and Eve. In the top right-hand corner is the depiction of the sea monster disgorging Jonah. In combination this is a powerful expression of the meaning of salvation for early Christians, namely delivery from danger and illness

certain conditions for the attainment of divine benefits. These values are displayed in the ancient healing cults but are also reflected in the gospel traditions, as well as in narratives of a more folkloric nature such as the apocryphal acts of the apostles and some of the martyrologies.

(3) *Apocalyptic discourse* is an ensemble of expectations of a catastrophic end-time action of God to bring salvation and judgement as well as renewal of the world. Retribution for the unjust and reward as well as a utopian existence for the just are awaited. Apart from the Jewish apocalypses, this is found in sections of the New Testament (e g 'Little Apocalypse' of Mark 13), the Revelation of John and such second-century material as the *Sibylline Oracles* and the *Pastor of Hermas* and the *Apocalypse of Peter*.

(4) Underlying *prophetic discourse* is the assumption that the people to whom God has given a tradition of salvation have gone astray and need to be attacked or brought back. This is what polemics between Christians and Jews, and between Gentile Christians and Jewish–Christians are all about. It is significantly present in Pauline literature but also in the sizeable body of writings of the apologists.

Figure 23.6
Detail of Mas d'Aire sarcophagus showing the sea monster disgorging Jonah. This was an important early Christian symbol. As with other symbols, it represents salvation from the dangers that threaten life in the ancient world

(5) *Suffering–death discourse* presents an interpretation of Jesus as having died vicariously for sinners as a martyr for God's cause, and that he was raised from the dead. It does not only function as interpretative matrix for an understanding of the figure of Jesus, it also serves as interpretative tool for understanding Christian life in contexts of persecution.

(6) *Pre-creation discourse* places the figure, work and significance of Jesus in a cosmic framework. Jesus is related to the world of God through many images such as incarnated Wisdom, Word or divine revealer. This is especially developed to great heights in gnostic literature.

All these discourses or modes of speaking can be discerned in second-century Christian literature. Some discourses are more prevalent than others in certain geographical areas and among certain Christian groupings, though never exclusively. Examining early Christian tradition in this way helps to describe the diversity and the various trajectories or streams of tradition that flow through early Christianity. Christianity was never a monolithic entity, and this is certainly the case with the first three centuries of the Christian era.

24 CHRISTIANITY IN THE SECOND CENTURY

The history of Christianity in the second century is determined by three main factors, namely its relationship with its parent, Judaism, relations with pagan neighbours and the internal multiform developments.

Figure 24.1
Obverse of coin with head of Hadrian, Roman emperor 117 to 138 CE, who rebuilt Jerusalem as the pagan city of Colonia Aelia Capitolina. The inscription on the coin reads 'Hadrianus Augustus P[ater] P[atria] (= Father of the Fatherland)'

As shown earlier (*see* Part 1, especially paragraphs 3.3, 3.4, 3.9 and 3.11–12), the history of Judaism was a tumultuous history in the period between the two Jewish wars of 66 to 73 CE and 132 to 135 CE, including the Jewish insurrections in between (such as the riot in Cyrenaica and Alexandria in 117 CE). Both wars proved disastrous for the Jews. The first left the temple in ruins and in the second, the city of Jerusalem was razed. After 135 CE, in spite of an earlier promise to rebuild the city, emperor Hadrian decided rather to refound the city as a pagan city, Aelia Capitolina, and banish Jews from it. The position of Judaism as a legal or permitted religion, however, remained unchanged.

As Judaism reorganised itself after 70 CE it developed a new identity from which early Christianity started to diverge to an ever greater extent (*see* part one). Christian communities existed in close proximity to Jewish communities with the result that tensions and riots between the two groups flared up regularly. After the Jewish war of 66 to 73 CE, the Jewish temple tax was converted by the Flavian emperors into a punitive tax on Jews for the war, the *fiscus judaicus*. This forced the issue of who was a Jew and, in a way, contributed to the formation of a distinct Christian consciousness. Church writers report that much mob violence against Christians was instigated or flamed up by Jews. This hostility contributed to the difficulties Christian communities experienced in the Roman world, since they gained a reputation as being troublemakers. The early apologetic works set out to demonstrate the difference between the Christian faith and Judaism, and answered the charges from Jewish and pagan side.

Christian communities gradually developed new forms of organisation, parallel with the new evolving social organisation of Judaism. Whereas earlier the Jesus movement had predominantly been (at least in rural Galilee) a movement of itinerant charismatics, and had remained so in the eastern provinces for a long time, Christianity spread through missionary activity and immigration to the big urban centres of the empire where it gradually transformed into a settled movement requiring new organisational forms. Earliest Christianity can be labelled an *egalitarian movement*. However, in this period classes of leaders began to emerge in hierarchical authoritarian structures. The bishop formed the pinnacle of authority in a tripartite structure of bishop-presbyter-deacon which would later become so dominant that it emulated the organisational structures of other associations and cult groups. As a social phenomenon, Christian communities appeared to the outsider to be a typical philosophical school-cum-voluntary society. So the earliest Christian apologists advertised Christianity as a 'philosophy'. Peregrinus, the Cynic philosopher, who briefly flirted with Christian belief, described himself as a *thiasarches* ('leader of an association').

It was perhaps the regular nocturnal meetings of Christian groups which evoked the same suspicion against them as was directed against other cult groups in the Roman world. In 186 BCE the Dionysiac Bacchanalia had been suppressed in Rome for its supposed immoral character, taking place at night out of the public eye. The same hostility greeted other oriental mystery and ecstatic cult groups. Exclusive groups always created the suspicion of being seedbeds of political subversion. The exclusive nature of Christian religion naturally also provoked the ire of Roman writers, leading to the accusation of Christian religion being misanthropic, socially subversive, atheistic and a *superstitio* ('a foreign and strange cult'). It offended Roman religious sensibilities.

Christian communities, when not embroiled in disturbances with Jewish groups, were rather left alone and kept out of the public eye. Whatever instances of 'persecution' there were, were the results of local pogroms and conflicts. It is in this light that one should understand the correspondence between Pliny and Trajan on the matter of the 'punishability' of the Christians. Trajan's

Figure 24.2
Bust of Trajan, Roman emperor 98 to 117 CE. In 116 CE he had to contend with massive and violent insurrections of Jews in various Diaspora centres, Cyrenaica (mainly), but also Egypt, Judaea, and Cyprus. Some of these uprisings were inspired by messianic fervour

successor, Hadrian, reissued directives concerning the Christians and denounced the activities of informers eager to settle other personal scores. Hostile popular opinion against the Christians reached a climax during the reign of Marcus Aurelius. It not only led to various incidents of persecution but was also characterised by a period of intellectual attacks on Christianity which led to the first extensive apologies on the part of the Christians.

The pagan philosopher, Celsus, described the Christian church as a movement still Jewish in character, but divided among a number of warring sects. Internally, Christianity was very much divided into different 'streams' along a continuum. It ranged from the more ascetic, encratite Christianity endemic in Egypt and Syria (characterised, among other things, by movements of itinerant charismatics and ascetic conventicles), through Jewish–Christian, Pauline-type, Johannine mystic, culturally mainstream (influenced by Stoic philosophical ideas) to heterodox groupings such as the various types of Gnosticism and the radical Paulinism of Marcion.

The main contender for the heart and soul of 'mainstream' Christianity was Christian Gnosticism. It was a confluence of Middle-Platonic philosophical ideas, Jewish (including Jewish mysticism) and Christian (especially Johannine) thought as well as popular oriental traditions. It rose to prominence in the second century through the activities of such illustrious theologians as Heracleon, Basilides and Valentinus. They all originally came from Egypt, but established themselves in Rome as prominent Christian teachers. The first continuous commentaries on New Testament writings were produced in these circles. The challenge they presented to 'catholic' and 'orthodox' Christianity lay in the status of Scripture, and the true nature of the church. Gnostics were accused of proliferating all sorts of scriptures without due recognition of the emerging Christian canon. They also tended to see the church in spiritual terms and not as a visible organisational network, with the result that they were accused of undermining the authority of the office of the bishop and of allowing women to lead in worship.

> ### EARLY CHRISTIANITY AS CULTIC SOCIETY
>
> The earliest Christians met in what must have looked to outsiders very much like a philosophical school; a burial society or a mystery cult group. The earliest house-churches exibited characteristic features of all of these: they met regularly, sang hymns 'as to a god' (Pliny), performed rituals (baptism and eucharist) and expounded the teachings of the school founder, Jesus of Nazareth. Just as was the case with other burial societies or guilds, they formed tightly knit social organisations, created the social context for imagining themselves as taking part in the heavenly banquet, through the opportunities provided for

feasting. The earliest depictions of Christianity as social phenomenon (the paintings on the catacomb or burial chamber walls in Rome) show them feasting at the table in scenes reminiscent of the narrative of the multiplication of the loaves. They are shown reclining at the table with loaves of bread, fish and goblets of wine. Bread, fish and wine were the typical fare (so one reads in inscriptions) of these school, society or cult group get-togethers. They must have been joyous occasions (hence the regularity with which the term *joy* is used in connection with the early Christian eucharist). Through occasions like these the early Christians experienced relief from the stresses and burdens of the harsh conditions of life under a paranoid military rule. This is illustrated in figure 24.3, a wall painting from the catacomb of Priscilla in Rome. Fractio panis – the 'breaking of the bread' depicted in a wall painting from the catacomb of Priscilla in Rome. The painting shows the diners reclining at the table, with loaves of bread, fish and a goblet of wine on the table. Through scenes like this early Christians portrayed themselves as cult groups meeting regularly for a common meal. The specific location of such paintings, namely in burial chambers, suggests that the social setting of these meals is the 'meal for the dead', a celebration of communion with the living dead

Figure 24.3

Note the characteristic pose: diners reclining at the table (A), so typical of banquets in antiquity. In front of the diners are a goblet of wine (B) and two plates of fish (C). On both sides of the diners are baskets filled with loaves of bread (D). If one were to compare this painting of an early Christian 'love meal' (a forerunner of the eucharist) with the painting of a mystery cult group in figure 24.4, one would understand how similar the activities of Christians must have looked to other cult groups in the Graeco-Roman world. This painting comes from the underground chamber of Vibia in Rome.

Figure 24.4

The scene is called the *Induction of Vibia* (probably the owner of the property (A)). She is met at the door or gate by the good angel (*angelus bonus* (B)) who leads her into a banquet. The naming of the banquet scene 'Judgement of the Good' (*bonorum iudicio*), (C) and the diners as the 'justified' (*iudicati*) (D) indicate that this is to be understood as a depiction of afterlife as a heavenly banquet. Note again the round loaves of bread in front of the diners (E), the servants serving the fish (F) and the large amphora of wine standing to the right (G). Scenes like these employed themes from the mystery cults which portrayed the induction of individuals into the cult and hence into (eternal) bliss. It is also related to the way philosophical groups understood themselves. A long tradition existed of philosophical groups' meetings taking the form of a *symposion* or banquet, but it was especially characteristic of the late Hellenistic and Roman periods that philosophical schools began to take on the characteristics of religious cult groups, in particular mystery cults. Neo-Orphic and neoplatonic philosophy, which arose more or less simultaneously with Christianity, resembled mystery religions in practices and teachings. The neoplatonic philosopher, Apollonius of Tyana, a contemporary of the Apostle Paul, was portrayed in the five-volume *Life of Apollonius* by Philostratus as a philosopher-cum-magician-cum-miracle-worker-cum-healer, very much in the same manner as the Gospels portrayed Jesus Christ.

Other relations existed as well between Christianity and the philosophies of the day, especially the philosophy dominant in the first century of the Christian era, namely Stoicism. The spiritualising theology of Paul (the view that God does not dwell in temples nor needs sacrifices), the 'natural theology' of Paul (the view that God can be discerned in the harmonious functioning of the cosmos, e g Romans 1:19–20; the life according to the law of nature as moral aim, e g Romans 2:14–15), the catalogues of vices, the catalogues of virtues and the duties of the various members of the households, all exhibit typical Stoic thought and themes.

Figure 24.5

Thus the early Christians understood themselves in terms of a mystery cult group-cum-philosophical school. The symbols they employed to portray their narrative or cult story were derived from these contexts. In Figure 24.5, a marble plaque in the Museo Nazionale delle Terme in Rome, Jesus is portrayed as a philosopher wearing the philosopher's garb of cloak and staff in hand (A), with his disciples (B) and a society of believers partaking in a banquet of bread (note the baskets of loaves of bread in front of the seated diners (C). To the right (D) is a scene depicting the raising of the son of the widow of Nain (Luke 7:11ff). This combination of scenes portrays Jesus as philosopher, as miracle-worker-cum-healer and the believers as a cult group feasting together.

25 JEWISH–CHRISTIAN GOSPELS

The Jesus movement, as the New Testament presents it, was firmly rooted in Jewish society, culture and religion. However, the Christianity of the fourth and fifth centuries – the time of the great and definitive church councils of Nicaea (325 CE) and Chalcedon (451 CE) – was a religious tradition very much at odds with Judaism and Jewish-Christianity. The paths had diverged to such an extent that Jewish-Christianity had become marginalised. Jewish-Christian traditions were at the time almost consistently branded as heterodox or heretical.

Jewish-Christianity, however, did not simply disappear or shrink away into oblivion. Various Jewish-Christian groups displayed a vitality and ongoing existence into the late Roman period and beyond. Jewish and Jewish-Christian traditions and theology made a substantial contribution to the development of such heterodox movements as Manichaeism and Gnosticism. The importance of Jewish-Christianity lies in the evidence it provides for diversity in Judaism in the first few centuries of the Christian era.

Strictly speaking, the whole of the New Testament should count among the writings of Jewish-Christianity, although the term is usually (and in this context) reserved for that section of early Christianity that continued to display typical Jewish features in theology and way of biblical interpretation, as well as continued adherence to, and identification with, the Jewish social and cultural heritage.

It is difficult to reconstruct with any certainty the history of any Jewish-Christian group of the second century from the many references in the Church Fathers to Jewish-Christian groups. Some Church Fathers tended to associate all Jewish-Christian groups with the Ebionites. Among the proliferation of names of Jewish-Christian sects in the Church Fathers one can at least point to two groups that can be taken to be the direct heirs to the earliest Jesus movement in Palestine and Syria. They are the Nazarenes and the Ebionites. The Nazarenes, as far as can be established from the references in the Church Fathers, were Jews who believed in Jesus as Messiah. According to tradition, they fled the destruction of Jerusalem to Pella in the Decapolis. After that, they maintained mostly a presence in the area east of the Jordan, but were also found in Jerusalem (i e before all Jews were expelled from the city in 135 CE), Galilee and later to the north in the area of Beroea in Syria. The Nazoraeans were characterised by 'orthodox' Christian beliefs. They were trinitarian, accepted the Gentile mission, and continued to observe aspects of Mosaic law such as circumcision and the Sabbath. What is known about the Ebionites is that they had a 'low Christology' according to which Jesus was adopted as God's Chosen One at his baptism. The Ebionites were concentrated mainly to the east of the Jordan River. These Jewish–Christian groups attest to the continuing presence of an ascetic type of Christian spirituality more or less directly related to the original Jesus movement of itinerant disciples.

The three Jewish–Christian gospels discussed here are preserved solely in quotations in the writings of the Church Fathers and hence exist only in fragments. It is therefore difficult to say much about the content or theological viewpoints. One has to rely on conjecture and guesswork.

25.1 The *Gospel of the Hebrews*

The fragments that exist of this Gospel deal with the baptism of Christ, the Last Supper and his appearance to James, the brother of Jesus, after the resurrection. Jewish wisdom theology is present in the Gospel in the presentation of the Holy Spirit as Mother of Jesus. The Mother–Spirit is understood as a mighty power which gives insight and inspires prophecy. Jesus is the special recipient of the Mother–Spirit who, in a mythological account, whisks him away by the hair to Mount Tabor. At Jesus's baptism the Spirit descends and rests on him – an event that describes the filial union between Jesus and God. Jesus is adopted as God's Son in baptism. The way of salvation is described in mystic-gnostic terms in a chain of steps as 'seek ... find ... marvel ... reign ... rest'. 'Rest' is an indication of union with God. The similarities with similar ideas found in texts of a gnostic nature and with links to an Egyptian context, lead one to situate this Gospel in Egypt in the early second century. It was probably the gospel text of a small group of charismatics.

> ### GOSPEL OF THE HEBREWS
>
> The *Gospel of the Hebrews* is known only from citations in the Church Fathers.
>
> > And if any accept the *Gospel of the Hebrews* here the Saviour says: 'Even so did my mother, the Holy Spirit, take me by one of my hairs and carry me away on to the great mountain Tabor.'
> >
> > (Origen: *Commentary on John* 11:12; *Homily on Jeremiah* XV.4; Jerome: *Commentary on Micah* 7:6; *Commentary on Isaiah* 40:9; *Commentary on Ezekiel* 16:13)

> To those words this is equivalent:
>> He that seeks will not rest until he finds; and he that has found shall marvel; and he that has marvelled shall reign; and he that has reigned shall rest.
>>
>> (Clement of Alexandria: *Stromateis* V 14.96)
>
> Both citations from Schneemelcher, W (ed) 1991. *New Testament Apocrypha. Volume I. Gospels and Related Writings*. Louisville: Westminster John Knox Press, 177.

25.2 The *Gospel of the Nazarenes*

From the way the *Gospel of the Nazarenes* is cited by the Church Fathers, it can be argued that it was probably roughly identical to the Gospel of Matthew in content. It is thus a gospel of the synoptic type, although the narratives show signs of fictional embellishments. The gospel is preoccupied with Jewish law and the Jewish people, and breathes the spirit of Judaism even though it rails against Jewish leaders and institutions such as, for instance, it polemicises against the rich and those living extravagantly. The narrative must have included scenes of Jesus's baptism, death and resurrection, and the account of his nativity is implied.

The gospel presupposes Matthew and is cited by the church writer Hegesippus (±180 CE). It must therefore have been written in the first half of the second century. It was probably at home in a smallish community of most likely Syrian Jewish–Christian Nazarenes, where poverty was prevalent. The *Gospel of the Nazarenes* may have originated in the area around Beroea in Syria.

25.3 The *Gospel of the Ebionites*

The *Gospel of the Ebionites* features only in a small number of fragments. This is a synoptic-type gospel, which presupposes knowledge of, and contact with, Synoptic Gospel traditions and is mentioned by the heresiologist Irenaeus (±180 CE). The inference can be made that the gospel originated in the first half of the second century.

According to the Church Fathers, the Ebionites were found in the area east of the Jordan River, where the gospel was written. However, it conspicuously begins only with the appearance of John the Baptist, and the baptism of Jesus, contains an account of the last supper, and a narration of the passion and Easter. It presupposes the Gospel of Matthew but in the presentation of the baptism of Jesus harmonises all three canonical Synoptic Gospels into a single account. The absence of the nativity story is due to theological interests. The

Ebionites denied the virgin birth of Jesus. In their Christology, Jesus became the divine Son of God at the union with the Holy Spirit at the time of his baptism. His baptism serves to present him to John the Baptist to be acclaimed Son of God. Jesus came to do away with sacrifices. That points to the Ebionite audience's hostility towards the temple cult. The depiction of John's food as only honey without the locusts, probably points to vegetarianism.

The aforementioned features demarcated the Ebionites as a heretical group *vis-à-vis* the Catholic Church, as distinct from the Nazarenes who were in essence orthodox.

26 APOCALYPTIC LITERATURE

26.1 The *Sibylline Oracles*

The term *Sibylline Oracles* refers to a collection of 12 apocalyptic books in verse format originally produced in Jewish circles but edited, expanded and eventually transmitted, and later used extensively solely in Christian circles. They do not constitute a coherent collection, being dated variously from the second century BCE to the seventh century CE, and originating in diverse contexts. Books 3, 5, and 11 to 14 are ascribed to Egypt as context of origin, while books 4, 6 and 7 are usually identified with Syria, books 1 and 2 with Asia Minor and book 8 vaguely with the larger area of the Near East.

The title *Sibylline Oracles* refers to an ancient tradition in the classical world of prophecies purportedly uttered by a prophetess called the Sibyl. The origins of this name are obscure. Such traditions of prophetic utterances circulated widely in the classical world.

These oracles were characterised by graphic and picturesque depictions of a cataclysmic end to the world through conflagration ('fire') or water flood. They functioned as pronouncements of judgement aimed mainly at the Greek ('Macedonian') and Roman political leaderships and empires. The view of the *Sibylline Oracles* on eschatology, especially the original Jewish texts underlying the present Christian forms, is chiefly political in nature. They imagine the resurgence of a glorious kingdom and a transformation of the earth into an ideal kingdom under the rule of an ideal king. In the Christian redactions of these oracles one finds evidence of a belief and interest in the fate of individuals after death and eschatological judgement, as well as descriptions of the sufferings of the damned and the resurrection of the saints in an earthly paradise.

Although a number of historical allusions and references are made in these texts, they provide evidence not so much of historical events as of popular attitudes and beliefs in the Graeco-Roman world, of the fears and struggles and world outlook of peoples in the Near Eastern world. They show how pervasive the general ideology of resistance to the imperial ideologies was, first of the Hellenistic empires and then that of Rome.

The *Sibylline Oracles*, in particular, and the apocalyptic tradition, in general, had a long and enduring influence on the development of the Christian worldview. They were often quoted by Church Fathers and their vision of the Last Judgement had an important impact on the development of millenarian thinking in the Middle Ages as well as on liturgy, literature (e g Dante's *Inferno*) and art.

26.2 The *Apocalypse of Peter*

The *Apocalypse of Peter* was one of the important texts of apocalyptic character in the early church. It is cited by Clement of Alexandria (who regards it as Holy Scripture), by Theophilus of Antioch and Methodius of Olympus (who likewise regarded the apocalypse as inspired). Although the original version no longer exists, certain references in the text can help one guess the time of origin. The early Church Fathers' citations, especially those of Clement of Alexandria, set an upper limit to the date of origin (end of the second century CE). The apocalypse must have had its origins well before that. The mention made in the *Apocalypse of Peter* of *4 Ezra* helps to set the lower limit to the dating, *4 Ezra* having been written at around 100 CE. If one interprets the parable of the fig tree in chapter 2 as referring to the Jewish antichrist who persecutes the Christians, namely Simeon Bar Kokhba (the Jewish messianic revolutionary leader during the war named after him), then one arrives at a date of probably 135 CE.

The *Apocalypse of Peter* is an important witness to the way in which oriental traditions about the end of the world (especially Iranian end-time lore) and folkloric motifs from the mystery religions as well as Egyptian eschatological ideas were mixed in the great melting pot from which Jewish apocalypticism emerged. This is the background from which Christian apocalypticism eventually sprang. These ideas lived on into the Christian Middle Ages.

> **APOCALYPSE OF PETER**
>
> 5   And it will happen on the day of judgement of those who fell from faith in God and sinned: cataracts of fire will be let loose, and pitch-black darkness will set in and cover and veil the whole world; the water will be changed and appear as burning coals and everything in her will burn, and the sea will become a fire; under the heaven there will be a fierce fire that will not become extinct and [this fire] will flow for the judgement of wrath. And the stars will melt in the fire as if they have not been created . . . as soon as the whole creation is dissolved, the people in the east will flee to the west . . . and everywhere they will run into the wrath of the fearful fire. And while an unquenchable fire drives them, and brings them to the wrathful judgement in the stream of unquenchable fire that flows with fire burning in it, and because its waves separate them from another in its seething maelstroms, there will be much gnashing of teeth among the children of humankind.

26.3 Other apocalyptic works

The dialogue between early Christianity and Judaism, and the remains of Jewish–Christian thought remained visible in the way early Christian writers took up Jewish works of an apocalyptic character and remoulded them into Christian visionary texts which, through their after-the-fact prophecies, attempted to justify Christian supercession of Judaism. After the disastrous end of the Bar Kokhba revolt of 132 to 135 CE, Jewish apocalyptic fervour died down and synagogal Judaism developed in directions which had no place for apocalypticism. Christians, however, took over the apocalyptic tradition because they found in this genre of literature reflections of their own concerns, namely a fixation on the end and end-time, God's judgement and the coming of the Christ–Messiah. They found in their own belief in Christ as Messiah and end-time Saviour a fulfilment of these apocalyptic traditions.

The *Testament of the Twelve Patriarchs* represents a Christian adaptation of an older Jewish genre, namely testaments as fictional legacies designed to lay the foundations for the future existence of the addressees. It is centred on ethical exhortations calling on the addressees to live under the guidance of the spirit of truth and to spurn the spirit of the lie.

The Jewish–Christian text known as *5 Ezra* is actually a Christian addition added to the Jewish apocalypse of *4 Ezra* as its first two chapters (there is a *6 Ezra* which is a two-chapter addition to the end of *4 Ezra*. It is not included in this discussion, since it stems from the third century). The text *5 Ezra* is an indictment against Judaism for failing to be obedient to the commandments of God. They are replaced as people of God with the church of the Gentiles.

The *Ascension of Isaiah* is another visionary text of which the Jewish original was a description, based on legend and folklore, of the martyrdom of Isaiah. A section on the death of Christ, the mission of the apostles, the persecution of the church and the destruction of the antichrist is inserted into this frame narrative. One can see in this juxtaposition how, for early Christians, the folktales of the martyr death of Isaiah became the interpretative matrix for an understanding of Christ and their own existence.

Apocryphal revelatory literature such as the *Letter of the Apostles* dating to between 120 and 150 CE is related to the apocalypses. The letter is a dialogue between the risen Christ and his apostles. It originated in Jewish–Christian circles of probably Rome or Alexandria where the danger of early gnostic thought posed a threat. The text is a warning against the gnostic devaluation of the body, since Christ had come in the body, performed miracles and had risen from the dead. He would therefore appear at the end of time to judge, and all would be resurrected to be judged in the body.

Papias, the bishop of Hierapolis in Asia Minor, was a contemporary of Polycarp (according to Eusebius in his *Church History* 3.36.1–2). His large, five-volume work called *The Exposition of the Words of the Lord* exist only in cited fragments in Eusebius's *Church History*. Papias's writings may be situated at around 125 CE. The work is noteworthy for its evidence of a still lively oral tradition in early Christianity, of which Papias says that he finds the 'living word of the Lord' preferable to dead letters. Another important feature is the millenarianism and end-time expectations which he shares with Justin and Irenaeus, and which were characteristic of Jewish thinking of the time (e g the canonical Revelation of John, and the Jewish work *4 Ezra* and the Syrian *Apocalypse of Baruch*). According to these end-time views, an earthly utopian kingdom is expected, followed by the resurrection of the dead, the judgement and then a heavenly kingdom.

The close similarity of Papias's millenarianism to Jewish apocalypticism was the reason for the strong reaction levelled against him.

27   THE APOSTOLIC FATHERS

The title *Apostolic Fathers* is given to a very diverse collection of early Christian writings. These writings are traditionally regarded as having been written by authors who had been in contact with the living apostles or had been their disciples or disciples of their disciples, in other words, authors directly or indirectly associated with the apostles. The Apostolic Fathers are dated variously from the end of the first century (± 96 CE in the case of *1 Clement*) to the middle of the second century (± 145 CE in the case of the *Shepherd of Hermas*).

This collection consists of the following texts: the letters *1 Clement* (to the church in Corinth), *2 Clement* (a homily or sermon in the form of a letter), the *Letter of Barnabas*, the letters of Ignatius (to the Philadelphians, the Magnesians, the Trallians, the Ephesians, the Romans, the Smyrnaeans and to Polycarp), the *Letter of Polycarp* (to the church in Philippi), the *Didache* (an early church order), the fragments of Papias (from his *Expositions of the Words of Our Lord Jesus Christ*), the *Shepherd of Hermas* (a visionary book on the state of church life in the church of Rome), the *Martyrdom of Polycarp*, the *Letter of Diognetus* and the fragment of Quadratus (the last two being apologies).

The interest generated by this collection of texts derived from the view that these texts represent, together with the New Testament, the oldest and most primitive stage of the history of the Christian movement, roughly representing the first 150 years of Christian history. They are therefore indispensable as sources for an understanding of the fate and history of Jesus traditions; their growth and development into Christianity as a world-wide religious movement; the earliest interpretations of the Jesus traditions, and into the historical circumstances which shaped the emerging Christian tradition. Furthermore, they represent a stage in the history of Christianity in which the Christian canon of Scripture had not yet been fixed. Some of these texts (evidenced from testimonies of the early Church Fathers) enjoyed a popularity, wide acceptance and almost canonical status in the early church even to the extent of regularly being read in the liturgy (in the case of *1 Clement*). That they were important texts for the early Church may be deduced from documentary evidence: in the hand-written manuscripts of the Bible, most of them were included as appendices to codices containing the New Testament or parts thereof.

Finally, the Apostolic Fathers exhibit between them as wide a variety of forms of religious experience as can be found throughout the rest of the literature of early Christianity. The outlook of *1 Clement* is related to the thought world of Paul as represented by his letters. The *Letter of Polycarp* is related to the thinking found in the *Pastoral Epistles*. The letters of Ignatius combine Pauline thought with a type of Johannine mysticism. Both *1 Clement* and *Ignatius* contributed to the growth of the authority of church offices in the direction of the monepiscopate (the individual church under the leadership, direction and rule of a single bishop who had authority). *Clement* and *Ignatius* show an openness towards the use of Graeco-Roman popular culture. In contrast, the *Didache* and *Letter of Barnabas* make use of, and show, an intimate familiarity with Jewish and Jewish–Christian material and folklore. This is also represented by the *Shepherd of Hermas*, which uses Jewish angelology and apocalyptic thinking. The *Fragments of Papias* show an author very much at home in millennialist and apocalyptic thinking. Again, *2 Clement* represents an example of Synoptic Gospel-type of Christianity adapted in the light of contemporary Jewish thought. The *Martyrdom of Polycarp* evidences the confluence of Jewish martyrology, Christian narratives and Graeco-Roman holy man or divine man ideas in the creation of the phenomenon of the Christian holy man or saint. Finally, the apologies of *Quadratus* and *Diognetus* show how early Christians had striven to engage in dialogue with the upper echelons of Roman society, employing terms familiar to the Roman elite.

27.1 The *Didache*

The *Didache* (Greek for 'teaching') or, to call it by its full title, *The Teaching of the Twelve Apostles*, was written under a pseudonym. The work was certainly not written by the twelve apostles, and it creates the impression of being a compilation of various sources, most notably a version of the *Two Ways Tractate*, chapters 1 to 6, (forms of which are found in the *Letter of Barnabas* and in Jewish texts such as the *Manual of Discipline* from Qumran, 1 QS III.18–IV.20), a short baptismal and eucharistic liturgy (ch 7, 9–10), a church order (ch 11–15), and an apocalyptic portrayal of end-time events (ch 16).

The author created a church order by transmitting Jewish–Christian tradition. The *Didache* is not a 'theological work', but a rule for church praxis, a handbook of Christian morals, of church ritual and church discipline.

It seems that the *Didache* was written in a time of change characterised by the increased urbanisation of the Jesus movement and the gradual settling down of wandering prophets in static communities, with a resulting change in church organisation. Because of this, it is valuable as a window on the earliest post-New Testament history of the emerging Christian movement. It provides

Figure 27.1
Fresco of Jesus teaching, from the catacomb of St Callixtus in Rome. By appropriating such symbols, early Christians conveyed their sense of Christianity as a 'philosophy' and Jesus as first and foremost a teacher of the correct lifestyle to be followed. Hence his portrayal as a bearded philosopher in the style of Moses or the wandering philosopher of the Roman world. It stresses Jesus's function as mediator of revelation and authoritative teaching. The absence of crucifixion scenes in early Christian art seems to suggest that, for Christians in the first three centuries, the crucifixion was not nearly as central an idea as was conceived later

insight into the history, life and organisation of early Christian communities in a specific region in the eastern Roman provinces.

Although Egypt was earlier also touted as place of origin of the *Didache*, it is at present accepted that it originated in Syria or in the Syro-Palestinian border areas. Certain references seem to recall the phenomenon of the Jesus discipleship movement – of wandering charismatic prophets and wandering Jesus followers – which was characteristic of the ministry of Jesus in his lifetime and the crowds gathered around him. This is something characteristic that can still be 'read off' from the way the words of Jesus are preserved in, for example the Q source, which seems to presuppose such a loose and unsettled organisation. The *Didache* addresses a situation in which travelling prophets and disciples still happen to sojourn temporarily amongst settled Christians. Guidelines are laid down to evaluate whether the prophets are true apostles (measured against the 'behaviour of the Lord', and their exploitation of goodwill). The *Didache* counteracts the underlying esteem urging the church to honour their bishops and deacons more. It would seem that the danger of the settled leaders, bishops and deacons, being supplanted and overshadowed by the awe-inspiring figures of itinerant prophets existed.

Since the sources used by the author of the *Didache* stem from a period in the late first century, it is to be accepted that the *Didache* was written early in the second century, around 110 to 120 CE.

DIDACHE

1. There are two ways, the way of life and the way of death, and there is a great difference between the two ways. The way of life, then, is this: First, you shall love God who made you; second, love your neighbor as yourself, and do not do to another what you would not want done to you. And of these sayings the teaching is this: Bless those who curse you, and pray for your enemies, and fast for those who persecute you.

5. And the way of death is this: First of all it is wicked and accursed: murders, adultery, lust, fornication, thefts, idolatries, magic arts, witchcrafts, rape, false witness, hypocrisy, double-heartedness, deceit, haughtiness, depravity, self-will, greediness, filthy talking, jealousy, over-confidence, loftiness, boastfulness; persecutors of the good, hating truth,

7. And concerning baptism, baptize this way: Having first rehearsed all these things, baptize in the name of the Father, the Son, and the Holy Spirit, in running water. But if you have no running water, baptise in other water; and if you cannot do so in cold water, then baptise in warm water. But if you have neither, pour out water three times upon the head into the name of Father and the Son and the Holy Spirit. But before the baptism let the baptiser fast, and the baptised, and whoever else can; but you shall order the baptised to fast one or two days before.

9. Now concerning the Eucharist, give thanks this way. First, concerning the cup:

We thank you, our Father, for the holy vine of David your servant, which you made known to us through Jesus your Servant; to you be the glory for ever.

And concerning the broken bread:

We thank you, our Father, for the life and knowledge which you made known to us through Jesus your Servant; to you be the glory for ever. Even as this broken bread was scattered over the hills, and was gathered together and became one, so let your Church be gathered together from the ends of the earth into your kingdom; for yours is the glory and the power through Jesus Christ for ever.

But let no one eat or drink of your Eucharist, unless they have been baptised into the name of the Lord; for concerning this also the Lord has said, 'Give not that which is holy to the dogs.'

27.2 The *Letter of Barnabas*

This 'letter' is actually a theological tractate set in a letter framework. It is characterised by its use of Jewish traditions to promote a spiritual and non-literal understanding of Jewish rituals and scripture. The 'Barnabas' of the title was therefore certainly not the travel companion and co-worker of Paul, since the Barnabas mentioned in Acts and the Letter to the Galatians participated in a literal observance of Jewish cultic rituals.

Although it is not known who the Barnabas of the title is, one can surmise from the reference in 16:3 to the destruction of the temple that the letter–tractate can be dated after 70 CE. The other limit to the date of its composition is set by the reference to the possible rebuilding of the temple in 16:4 ('For owing to the war it was destroyed by the enemy; at present even the servants of the enemy will build it up again'). It seems possible that this refers to the planned rebuilding of the temple by the Roman emperor Hadrian as a pagan temple in *circa* 135 CE. If *Barnabas* 16:4 refers to this event, then the letter was written before 135 CE.

Even if this dating is broadly acceptable, one still cannot conclude on the strength of the contents what the occasion of the polemic of *Barnabas* was. Perhaps the most one can say is that the type of polemic implies a community in close contact with Jewish communities at a stage when the Christian tradition was still being defined in contrast and opposition to the emergent rabbinic Judaism. Barnabas employs halakhic traditions characteristic of early Judaism as is later known from the Mishnah.

Barnabas creates the impression of being part of the oral tradition out of which the canonical gospels grew. In this way, the letter–tractate of *Barnabas* opens a window onto the development and growth of the oral Jesus tradition together with the early Christian appropriation of the Jewish epic (use of themes and symbols in order to define the religious and world outlook) and provides a close-up look at how a small section of the Jewish people started to redefine themselves by reinterpreting their Jewish heritage in the light of the Jesus tradition. One can then safely say that most probably this letter–tractate is evidence of the thinking in process in Jewish–Christianity.

27.3 The *First Letter of Clement*

The *First Letter of Clement* is, to a certain extent, an extraordinary text. While on the one hand deeply indebted to Jewish–Christian tradition (with its use of the Old Testament and Christian credal and liturgical elements), it is also clearly modelled on the example of political rhetorical speeches of a genre well known in the Roman Empire.

The letter was sent in the name of the Apostolic Father Clement from Rome to the church in Corinth purportedly at the end of the first century. It quickly attained almost canonical status, and for a time at least, was part of the canon of the churches of Egypt and Syria.

The overarching value system binding the work together and forming the basis for the whole argument, is the principle of order, harmony (or concord) and peace. The exhortations of the text were, in the end, derived from its Graeco-Roman context, especially from political philosophical conceptions. The phrase 'peace and concord' occurs throughout *1 Clement*, and the author describes his letter at the end as 'an appeal for peace and concord' (*1 Clement* 63:2). By the end of the first century CE 'peace and concord' had become a description of the well-being of the state, describing the cessation or absence of strife and civil war. This situation is thereby endowed with positive value. It recurs regularly in writings of philosophers and orators, in histories, inscriptions and coins. People wishing to find their right place in the cosmos (the ordered whole of the universe) and endeavouring to be found worthy of God in the judgement, should do 'virtuous deeds before him in concord' (*1 Clement* 21:1).

While it is not certain what situation necessitated this letter, *1 Clement* employs the ideology of the empire in order to create a culture of harmony, peace and concord in the Christian church following the example and analogy of the Roman imperial ideology. By embracing this imperial ideology, Clement and his church endorsed the Roman imperial power as God-given, 'established by God on earth as earthly counterpart to the heavenly kingdom'. The *First Letter of Clement* is thus characterised by a positive attitude towards the Roman state.

For this reason *1 Clement* is an important witness to the growth of the Christian movement in the Graeco-Roman world. It bears witness to the process begun earlier in some of the Gospel portrayals of Jesus in imperial–messianic terms in order to create an anti-empire, a counter-society to the Roman political system. However, by now the church had begun to move in the direction of establishing itself as an empire. The realisation of such an empire finally came about with the conversion of the Roman emperor Constantine, and the proclamation of Christianity as official state religion in the early fourth century.

27.4 The *Second Letter of Clement*

The *Second Letter of Clement* is transmitted in the manuscripts together with the *First Letter of Clement*, but this letter was authored by somebody other than the person responsible for the first letter, judging by the difference in style and message. The *Second Letter of Clement* is really a sermon in letter form.

The document dwells at length on repentance and self-control as the characteristics of a holy life, interpreted as an ascetic lifestyle, including righteousness, fasting and one of the most important forms of virtue and penitence, almsgiving. Holiness means abandoning worldly concerns ('hating the indulgences of the soul', *2 Clement* 17:7; 'giving up wicked lusts', *2 Clement* 16:2). The insistence on penitence and the specific interpretation this is given by *2 Clement*, namely that

> Almsgiving is therefore good even as penitence for sin; fasting is better than prayer, but the giving of alms better than both; and love "covers a multitude of sins", but prayer from a good conscience rescues from death. Blessed is every man who is found full of these things; for almsgiving lightens sin.
>
> (2 Clement 16:4).

This perhaps indicates a situation where Christian spirituality is interpreted in terms of a life of renunciation of worldly pleasures and goods. The emphasis on salvation from the flesh (because Jesus Christ worked salvation through his sufferings in the flesh) and rewards in the flesh, motivates the audience to strive to attain the kingdom of God, which will come when all good works are accompanied by ascetic practices (ch 12). The exhortations of *2 Clement* are undergirded by references to the coming judgement, in which sinners will be burned in everlasting fire.

The *Second Letter of Clement* frequently refers to 'the books' (= Old Testament) and 'the apostles' (= New Testament) as authorities. Numerous references to the Old Testament and to the Synoptic Gospels, Matthew, Mark and Luke, as well as isolated citations from Pauline and the Catholic Epistles (such as Romans, 1 Corinthians, Philippians, Ephesians, 1 Timothy, Hebrews and 1 Peter) and from its namesake, *1 Clement*, probably presuppose a familiarity with the written New Testament, and thus indicate a stage of growing recognition of the authority of written testimony. Its use of *1 Clement* and the inclusion of a number of Jesus sayings from the apocryphal *Gospel of the Egyptians* also illustrates the openness of the early Christian tradition as not yet fixed in a delimited canon at this relatively early stage of its development. The *Second Letter of Clement* is conventionally dated as between 140 and 160 CE.

27.5 The *Letters of Ignatius*

The seven *Letters of Ignatius* were written *en route* to Rome where Ignatius was taken prisoner by a company of ten Roman soldiers to be thrown to the wild beasts. According to church tradition (preserved in Eusebius's *Church History* 3.22), Ignatius was the third bishop of Antioch in Syria following the Apostle Peter and Euodius. The exact historical circumstances that caused Ignatius to be arrested and sent to Rome for execution cannot be reconstructed (apart perhaps from the general remark that it seems to have been a short and localised persecution in Antioch; the result of a disturbance between Christians and Jews, perhaps. The general situation implied by his letters seems to fit the reign of the emperor Hadrian (98–117 CE). Eusebius's placing of his martyrdom during the latter half of Hadrian's reign (*Church History* 3.36) would thus date the writing of these letters around 110 CE.

From Antioch in Syria, Ignatius and his company of soldiers travelled across Asia Minor via Philadelphia to Smyrna. From Smyrna, where he was visited by representatives of the various churches, he wrote letters to the churches in Ephesus, Magnesia, Tralles and Rome, and from the next stopover in Troas on the coast of Asia Minor, Ignatius dispatched a letter to the church in Philadelphia which he had visited before stopping in Smyrna. From Troas he also sent two letters to Smyrna, one to the church there and the other to its bishop, Polycarp.

Ignatius's *Letter to the Ephesians* is characterised by an insistence on unity under guidance of the bishop, the rejection of false doctrines spread by false teachers and an emphasis on the fleshly nature of Christ's coming into the world and his sufferings. His *Letter to the Magnesians* likewise stresses the importance of harmony and obedience to the bishop and presbyters. This document also contains a lengthy rejection of Judaism ('It is monstrous to talk of Jesus Christ and practise Judaism' Ign *Magn* 10:3). In the *Letter to the Trallians* too the theme of submission to the authority of the bishop and the presbyters is very prominent. The exhortation to submission is motivated by a comparison of the deacons to Jesus Christ, 'even as the bishop is also a type of the Father, and the presbyters as the council of God and the college of Apostles' (Ign *Trall* 3:1). The injunctions to submission to the authority of the bishop and presbyters are interspersed with warnings against heresy (docetism) and references to the real, fleshly death and resurrection of Jesus Christ. Ignatius provides a colourful description of his journey towards Rome through Asia Minor in his Letter to the Romans. He bids them not to attempt to save him from martyrdom since his wish is to 'attain Christ' (Ign *Rom* 3:3). He will fully become a disciple of Christ through the glory of martyrdom. In this way he will share in the 'Passion of my God' (Ign *Rom* 6:3). Warnings against heresy and schism are again at the forefront of the *Letter to the Philadelphians*. Those who 'belong to God and Christ, are with the bishop' (Ign *Phil* 3:2). The Philadelphians should practise unity, which should become visible in the unity of their celebration of the eucharist. Strong warnings against Judaism are given: Christianity superseded the old dispensation of Judaism. The *Letter to the Smyrnaeans* impresses upon its audience the reality of Jesus Christ's coming in the flesh, his sufferings and resurrection in the flesh. Again, there are warnings against heretics, docetists, and the letter ends with a strong call to submission to the bishop and presbyters, without whom nothing may be done in the congregation. In Ignatius's *Letter to Polycarp*, the latter is enjoined to perform the duties of his office diligently, to care for the weaker members of the congregation as well as the widows, and to resist heresy. The church should be exhorted to labour in unity.

The *Letters of Ignatius* had a significant impact on the development of early Christianity; their usefulness lay in their portrayal of the reality of the incarnation, suffering and resurrection of Jesus Christ.

Closely connected to this was Ignatius's polemic against heresy and Judaism. The heresy opposed by Ignatius was a type of docetism, the denial of the real or fleshly incarnation, suffering and resurrection of Jesus Christ (especially concentrated in the letters to the Trallians and the Smyrnaeans). This is treated as a type of Judaism or, at least, a type of Judaising Christianity (*see* especially the letters to the Magnesians and the Philadelphians).

Furthermore, emphasis on submission to the bishop and presbyters pictures a conception of ministry and church organisation that goes beyond what is found in the New Testament. In the light of Ignatius's equation of the bishop with God or Christ, and the overseers with the apostles, these letters went a long way in contributing to the creation of the hierarchical structure later so characteristic of the Catholic Church.

Ignatius's 'theology' of martyrdom portrayed martyrdom as the desired goal of discipleship and as the ultimate expression of union with God and Christ.

All in all, Ignatius's thought world is drenched with, and steeped in, the multifarious oral tradition of the emerging early Christianity. As such, his letters form an important witness to the creation of a mainstream Christianity with an identity distinct from that of its parent religion, Judaism.

27.6 The *Letter of Polycarp*

The *Letter of Polycarp* should be considered in conjunction with the letters of Ignatius. It was written in response to an invitation by the church in Philippi. Polycarp, the bishop of Smyrna, mentions that he wrote this letter as a covering letter for a collection of Ignatius's letters requested by the church in Philippi. Apart from that, it contains lengthy admonitions addressed to the church at Philippi. They are exhorted to live virtuous lives, to care for one another through good works and philanthropy, to forgive, and to persevere in the hope and righteousness. Perseverance can demand the ultimate measure of endurance in faith, namely martyrdom, which bears witness to the reality of the cross of Christ. The hope of a fleshly resurrection motivates towards doing God's will and following his commandments, a life characterised by sober living. Furthermore, false teachings are to be eschewed. The heresy against which they are warned entailed a denial that Jesus Christ had come in the flesh, as well as a denial of the resurrection and judgement.

The importance of this otherwise unremarkable letter lies in the use early Church Fathers made of it to establish the line of succession or continuity with the apostles from the New Testament era. The growing importance of this tradition indicates how the Church Fathers were beginning to trace the contours of orthodox tradition by means of these 'lines of succession' much in the same vein as the various lives of the philosophers in antiquity determined the authoritative and orthodox version of each respective philosophy.

27.7 The *Shepherd of Hermas*

From the beginning, the establishment of Christianity in Rome took the form of founding a number of household churches under the guidance of wealthy patron–overseers, the hosts who provided the houses for the community meetings. After the analogy and example of Jewish synagogues, a number of such house–churches existed in the different districts of the city, without a central unified organisation and authority structure. As a result of the cultural importance of patronage and the emphasis on honour and esteem, a situation arose where schisms often occurred due to competition for authority and honour, especially when there was conflict between charismatic-inspired leadership and the leadership positions going hand in hand with patronage. It is this situation of 'schismatic competition' and abuse of wealth that is addressed by *1 Clement* and the long apocalypse called The *Shepherd* (or *Pastor*) *of Hermas*.

According to the second-century *Canon of Muratori*, the author, Hermas, wrote *The Shepherd* while his brother, Pius, 'was sitting on the throne of the church of the city of Rome.' Pius was bishop of Rome around 140 to 154 CE, which means *The Shepherd* must have been written around then. It creates the impression, however, of having grown over a long period of time.

The Shepherd of Hermas is a long composite work consisting of five visions, twelve commandments (or 'mandates') and ten parables or similitudes. The five visions are cast in the form of a Jewish apocalypse. These visions describe the trials and tribulations that will befall the Church as well as its salvation. The 'mandates' evoke the genre of Jewish–Hellenistic homilies, but even so, the 'mandates' employ the literary figure of the revealer giving the commandments, a technique not unfamiliar to apocalypses (especially dialogues of the revealer, much like other early Christian material such as the *Letter of the Apostles* or the *Dialogue of the Saviour*). The commandments have to do with faith and the Christian lifestyle. The similitudes or parables, concerned with abstention from wealth, evil desires and steadfastness of faith, display similarities to the type of imagery occurring in other apocalyptic books such as *1 Enoch*, where a parable is followed by a request for explanation and interpretation. This aspect displays a side of apocalypse that is very near to mysticism, namely the revelation of heavenly secrets. Finally, although the visions, mandates and similitudes have much in common with similar Jewish material, there is no evidence of direct use of the Hebrew Old Testament or the New Testament.

28 CHRISTIAN APOLOGETICS

Already early in the history of Christianity it was necessary to defend the reasonableness of Christian belief. The purpose of apologies was the defence and justification of the existence of the Christian faith. This was especially true when addressing the emperor or other political official. In this way, an attempt was made to 'win a place in the sun' for Christianity. Moreover, in a cultural context of a highly agonistic competition for adherents between religious movements, apologies served as important advertising space and recruiting activities.

Aristides of Athens wrote an apology addressed to the emperor Hadrian, which therefore has to be dated to between 117 and 138 CE. Aristides starts with a discussion on God, who is portrayed as Mover and Creator in terms of Stoic philosophical ideas. That is followed by an exposition of the religious views of various peoples, including the Jews. The Christians have found the truth, that is why they love God, keep his commandments and help the oppressed and poor. Therefore the emperor should not heed the slander of the Greeks. Aristo of Pella wrote a dialogue that purportedly took place between Jason, a Christian from Jewish descent, and Papiscus, a pagan. Using texts from the Old Testament interpreted allegorically, Jason proved that Jesus was the Son of God. The result was that Papiscus converted and became a Christian. The allegorical method used by Jason and the note in Origen (who mentions this work) that Papiscus came from Alexandria make it very probable that the dialogue was written in Alexandria.

28.1   Justin Martyr

Justin Martyr was one of the most important of the early apologists for the Christian faith. The reason for this was his unique combination of Christian and pagan ideas in his presentation of the Christian religion to his pagan audience.

Justin was born from pagan parents in Sichem in Samaria. He studied philosophy and drifted from philosophical school to philosophical school (from Stoic, Aristotelian or Peripatetic, to Neopythagorean to Platonic philosophy), none of which, according to his later testimony, satisfied him. Then he encountered Christianity during a stay in Ephesus, and it was the fearlessness of Christians in the face of death which made a big impression on him, so much so that he became a Christian, for to him 'Christianity was the real philosophy'. He ended up in Rome where he founded a philosophical school during the reign of Antoninus Pius (138–161 CE). He was eventually beheaded, together with six companions in 165 CE.

Justin produced three works: *A Dialogue Against Trypho*, and two apologies, the first was addressed to the emperor Antoninus Pius and the second to the prefect of Rome, Urbicus.

Justin met Trypho the Jew while staying in Ephesus. Later in Rome he wrote his *Dialogue Against Trypho* based on his recollection of the debate between them which had stretched over two days. The *Dialogue*, understandably, treats a number of issues dealing with the relationship between Christianity and Judaism. The first part contains a discussion on the law and issues such as circumcision, dietary regulations, the Sabbath and sacrifices. According to Justin, Jewish–Christians are saved as long as they do not require others to live according to the law.

The second part deals with the incarnation of Jesus Christ and the virgin birth. The underlying issue is the reality of salvation. Consequently, Justin argues in favour of the view that the kingdom of Christ will come at the end of time and that it will last a thousand years (an idea found in many apocalypses).

In the third part of the *Dialogue*, Justin presents the church as the New Israel which has replaced the nation of Israel. Numerous citations from the Old Testament provide evidence of the fact that Christians had by then developed a distinctive way in which the Old Testament had to be interpreted.

Figure 28.1
Bust of Antoninus Pius, Roman emperor 138 to 161 CE

Justin addresses the *First Apology* to the emperor Antoninus Pius. In it he states that the Christians should not be persecuted solely because of the 'name' (= Christ). They are not atheists but support the emperor as well as Roman government. Justin then proceeds with a discussion of worship of the gods and sacrifices, and describes Christian worship, baptism, the eucharist and the weekly assembly of the church.

With the *Second Apology*, Justin addresses the prefect of Rome, Urbicus, who had recently executed three Christians. Justin asserts that it has always been the case that the just have been persecuted by the unjust. However, the just, enter heaven, while the unjust will be judged and punished.

28.2 Apologies and writings addressed to a pagan or Gentile readership

In the *Letters of Paul and Seneca* dating from ± 200 CE, Seneca is purported to express his appreciation for the high ethical standards of Paul's ethical exhortations in his letters. Although Paul's style leaves much to be desired,

Seneca concedes that God speaks through the mouths of innocents. The *Letter of Pilate*, also dating from ±200 CE, has Pilate reporting to the emperor that he only very reluctantly handed Jesus over to the Jews. The Romans are thus exonerated from the death of Jesus. Through these writings Christians attempted to communicate with the highest levels of Roman society.

The Apology of Quadratus

According to the church historian Eusebius, Quadratus was a 'hearer of the apostles', meaning he had had direct contact with the living apostles. We know his apology only from a quotation in Eusebius's *Church History* (4.3.2). Quadratus is the earliest Christian apologist of which there is any existing evidence. The apology was addressed to the emperor Hadrian, presumably on one of his visits to Athens in Greece (124–125 CE). From the one single quotation extant, one gets a picture of Jesus Christ as Saviour who heals and raises people from the dead.

The *Letter to Diognetus*

This is an anonymous work addressed to a certain Diognetus, otherwise unknown. Diognetus is portrayed as a Gentile eager to learn about the Christian religion. The letter is an exposition of the Christian faith and its difference from both Graeco-Roman religions and Judaism. It touches on the way Christians view God and the gods, the Christian lifestyle and their relationship with the world, the origin of the Christian religion in the revelation of God and his plan of salvation.

An interesting feature of the *Letter to Diognetus* is the absence of biblical quotations and the many names given for Jesus Christ, child (8), Logos, maker (7:2), king, God, man (7:3), nurse, father, teacher, counsellor, physician, mind, light, glory, strength and life (9:6).

28.3 Other apologetic works

In the *Easter Homily* (written about 170 CE) Melito of Sardis presented the contents and meaning of the paschal celebrations in very Jewish terms and thought. Melito of Sardis wrote in Asia Minor in a context where Easter celebrations took place on the same day (Friday) as the Jewish paschal celebrations. This proximity of Jewish and Christian communities naturally contributed to a much greater approximation of Christian and Jewish paschal theology.

Figure 28.2
Equestrian statue of Marcus Aurelius, Roman emperor 161 to 180 CE, the 'philosopher-emperor' who meditated on Stoic philosophy, the nature of order and humankind's relation to it

Another text taking issue with Jews and pagans is the *Kerygmata Petrou*, or the 'Preaching of Peter'. It now exists only in fragments cited in Clement of Alexandria's *Stromateis*. The author emphasises faith in the one God through which everything exists, and polemicises against pagan religion (idolatry) and the way Jews hold fast to the law. The Christians represent the third way. People come to faith when they see how all the prophecies of the prophets are fulfilled by Christ.

The homily *Adversus Judaeos*, or 'Against the Jews' was written under the name of Pseudo-Cyprian. It was written in Rome at around the end of the second century. According to *Against the Jews*, the Christians are the heirs of Christ. The Jews killed the prophets and that is why they deserved to suffer and forfeit their inheritance. The Jews 'among us' come to the baptismal bath as convicted people. It seems to be directed not so much at Jews outside the Christian community as at those Jewish–Christians inside the Christian church who continued to value their Jewish heritage. This probably reflects the situation in Rome where it had always been problematic for Gentile Christians and Jewish-Christians to coexist peacefully in religious communities.

Of the *Apology of Miltiades* only the reference in Eusebius's *Church History* that he addressed it 'to the rulers of the world' (meaning the emperors Marcus Aurelius, 161-180 CE, and Lucius Verus, 161-169 CE) exists. According to tradition, Miltiades gained a reputation as refuter of Montanists, Greeks and Jews. Only the titles of the apologies of Apollinaris, bishop of Hierapolis, have been preserved. He is reported to have addressed an apology to Marcus Aurelius, five against the Greeks and two against the Jews. He also wrote refutations against the Montanists. The *Apology of Athenagoras* pleads the case of Christians before the emperors Marcus Aurelius and Commodus in highly literate Greek and accomplished rhetorical style. He refutes the three main charges against Christians, namely that they are atheists, cannibals and that they are guilty of incest. To the charge of being atheists, Athenagoras answers that although Christians do not worship the gods, they do worship the One God. They cannot be cannibals since they have such a high regard for life that they do not practise abortions. To the charge of incest, Athenagoras argues that Christians have a high regard for marriage and virginity.

29 ON THE WAY TO DEFINING 'MAINSTREAM' AND POPULAR CHRISTIANITY

29.1 The *Protevangelium of James*

The depiction of the life and ministry of Jesus Christ in the earliest gospel tradition started with the baptism of Jesus by John the Baptist in the Jordan River (Mark 1:9-11par). In the earliest Christian community this 'beginning of the Gospel' (as in the Gospel of Mark) was supplemented by material portraying the birth of Christ. Thus the two canonical birth narratives (in Matthew and Luke) are affixed to the life story of Jesus. Legendary traits are present in these infancy narratives, and this trend was continued and expanded in later Christian material. The motive for the development of many later infancy narratives was an interest in filling in the missing details of Jesus's life (often through use of highly legendary traditions, fantasies and fables) as well as a theological interest (e g among gnostics and docetists who found the idea of the perpetual virginity of Mary and the 'unrealistic' portrayal of the child Jesus as a 'small adult' of particular value in denigrating the humanity of Christ). Perhaps the most well known of these early expansions of the nativity story was the second-century *Protevangelium of James*.

The *Protevangelium of James* was probably written in the early second half of the second century (not long after 150 CE), since early church writers such as Justin Martyr, Clement of Alexandria and Origen show familiarity with some of the important themes from this narrative (the birth of Jesus in a cave and the descent of Mary also from the lineage of David). The ignorance about Palestinian geography and Jewish customs may point to a non-Jewish author.

The *Protevangelium* is in reality a narrative about the miraculous birth of Mary, Jesus's mother. It recounts the annunciation of her birth (very much in analogy to the annunciation of John's and Jesus's birth in the canonical Gospel), how she is born to the rich Joachim and his wife Anna. It tells of her upbringing in the temple until the age of 12 years and how she is 'given' to Joseph, an elderly widower, through a divine sign. While weaving part of the temple curtain, she receives the annunciation of the birth of Jesus and while *en route* to Bethlehem with Joseph, she gives birth to Jesus in a cave. Nature miracles such as the arresting of nature accompany his birth. The narrative ends with the murder of Zacharias, the father of John the Baptist.

The *Protevangelium of James* is culturally important for several reasons. Its depiction of Mary's miraculous birth and implied perpetual virginity (Joseph is portrayed as an elderly widower who already had other sons and daughters, thereby explaining why Jesus had brothers and sisters) had a powerful influence on the imagination of the early church and inspired the development of Mariology, the devotion of Mary. In spite of attempts by Church Fathers (such as Jerome) and later popes (e g Damasus, Innocent I and Pius V) to negate the influence of these legendary portrayals of Mary, they remained an important feature of popular religion right through late Antiquity and into the Middle Ages. This later led to the formulation of the doctrines of the Immaculate Conception of Mary as well as the Assumption of Mary. The emphasis on the perpetual virginity of Mary was highly valued in eastern Christianity, the Jewish–Christian Ebionites, the Coptic, Syrian and Armenian churches as well as among the Greek Church Fathers, because of their affinity for its promotion of the ideal of virginity. These legendary narratives, furthermore, had an enormously important influence on the development of religious art throughout the Middle Ages and into modern times.

29.2 The *Gospel of Thomas*

The *Gospel of Thomas* was discussed earlier in the context of the development of the Jesus tradition, especially in connection with the Q source (consisting of Jesus sayings) and of the Gospels of Matthew and Luke. It is therefore sufficient to point out here that the final version of the sayings gospel, called the *Gospel of Thomas*, probably originated around the middle of the second century in the environs of eastern Syria in the vicinity of the city of Edessa. It is now accepted by many scholars that although only about half of the sayings contained in it have parallels in the Synoptic Gospels while the other half represents completely unknown sayings of Jesus, these sayings betoken a type of religiosity that could very well historically have been characteristic of the message of the historical Jesus. Hence the usefulness of the Gospel in reconstructing the historical Jesus.

From the early third century onwards, heresiologists and Church Fathers consistently mention the *Gospel of Thomas* in connection with heterodox Christian groups such as the Manichaeans and count it among the 'rejected writings'. Earlier, a full text of the gospel known only from these references, was discovered in 1945 among the Coptic gnostic texts from the library at Nag Hammadi. This raises the interesting question of its historical value as religious text. The anti-institutional, anti-ritual and ascetic character of the sayings was probably very much at home in the type of movement around a 'Jewish Cynic peasant type of figure' (John Dominic Crossan in his *The Historical Jesus. The Life of a Mediterranean Jewish Peasant.*). If this characterisation of the earliest Jesus movement and Jewish–Christianity in rural Syria as a movement of displaced, dispossessed itinerant followers of Jesus is correct, then it is clear that what later became 'orthodox Christianity' was created by the early Church Fathers contextualising Christian belief for a Graeco-Roman urban environment and consistently marginalising Jewish–Christian traditions.

29.3 Apocryphal Acts of the Apostles

What did the Christian beliefs of 'the people on the ground' look like? Most likely not what one would expect; not as sober and doctrinally (recognisably) correct as accepted mainstream texts (such as the Apostolic Fathers) would lead one to believe. To answer this question, one should not turn to the doctrinal and formal theological treatises of theologians and Church Fathers, especially those figures who came to represent authoritative tradition. One needs to turn to those texts that preserved the 'voice of popular religion'. Few classes of early Christian literature ('class' rather than 'group', since the acts discussed here do not form a coherent group) display the features of popular piety of a fairly wide spectrum of early Christians as do the apocryphal Acts of the Apostles. In the *Acts of John*, the *Acts of Andrew*, the *Acts of Peter*, the *Acts of Paul* (which include the *Acts of Paul and Thecla*) and the *Acts of Peter and the Twelve Apostles* (to name only those which certainly stem from the second century) one encounters a unique opportunity to experience a close-up view of Christian popular religion. Owing to their nature as popular narratives, they give a glimpse of the world of their audiences, their beliefs and values, social contexts, cultural contexts, manners and customs, legends and folklore, development of early Christian culture as well as early Christian traditions about 'legendary' exemplary saints, the apostles. Thus, for an understanding of the development of early Christianity into a 'global' religious movement in the second and third centuries and into the Middle Ages, these texts are indispensable and most valuable resources.

These works stand out among the other early Christian theological works for the character they exhibit. For one thing, the apocryphal acts of the apostles certainly look like Christianised versions of Graeco-Roman novels; a literary genre that started to emerge and flourish simultaneously with the appearance of the apocryphal Acts. The novels and the apocryphal Acts have several features in common: long sections of travel narratives and adventure tales, a fixation on the marvellous feats of the main character and an erotic element.

Furthermore, the apocryphal Acts extol the virtues of the apostles concerned, thereby contributing to the rise of veneration of the apostles as holy men after the fashion of similar stories about pagan philosophers and holy men (such as the long narrative of Philostratus on the life of Apollonius of Tyana, a neoplatonist philosopher and contemporary of Jesus Christ and Paul). Hand in hand with this feature go an interest in, and depiction of, various miracles performed by the apostle saint. John raises the priest of Artemis from the dead, Paul converses in the circus with a lion he had baptised, Peter conducts conversations with a dog, and makes a smoked fish come to life and swim after being thrown into a pond. Culturally, these apocryphal Acts of the Apostle were important as they stood at the beginning of the emerging cults of the saints, a feature of Christian popular religion that would remain present even past the Middle Ages into the modern period.

In outlook on the world and society, and in theology these apocryphal Acts display an independence and divergence from 'official theology and churchmanship' (Schneemelcher). Their high regard for chastity and sexual abstinence, and support for what is called 'encratite Christianity' (*encratite* means 'ascetic'), the prominent role of women who are sometimes even portrayed as authorised to administer the sacraments (e g Paul who gives Thecla the right to administer baptism), and the absence of any sense of the authority of ecclesial bodies, structures or officials, as well as a piety informed by life-giving insight and the embodiment of divinity (hallmarks of late Antique neoplatonic and gnostic thought), all of these features contributed to localising the apocryphal acts of the apostles on the boundaries between orthodoxy and heterodoxy and heresy. Their popularity and use of Christian tradition and legend indicate that the church as a whole had by the end of the second century not yet come to a fixed definition of what was orthodox and what heterodox. The boundaries were still fluid.

If one can characterise the aim of the apocryphal Acts at all, it can probably be said to be the entertainment, instruction and edification of educated audiences making use of popular traditions and legends. We have reason to believe that the audiences of these acts were educated (and perhaps quite wealthy) Christians who were open to novelistic fiction and other forms of Graeco-Roman literary communication and rhetoric. Even so, they originated in a context of increased interest arising in the course of the second century in the figure of the apostle as guarantor of authoritative tradition and as *theios aner* (divine man) who points the way to salvation in similar fashion as others from the surrounding world. In this, the acts are important witnesses to the piety of Christians and particular Christian groups in the second century and further, a piety centred on holy men and miracles.

The *Acts of John*

The *Acts of John* was probably written in the second half of the second century and its most likely area of origin was eastern Syria. In the narrative John is pictured as an itinerant, charismatic preacher accompanied by a changing band of male and female disciples, making it probable that the audience was a community without developed organisational forms, in the manner of gnostic conventicles. This impression is strengthened by the portrayal of Jesus as intangible and unreal.

The storyline has John travelling Asia Minor performing miracles – healings, resurrections and the destruction of the temple of Artemis – and delivering a lengthy sermon on Jesus's appearance on earth (which includes a dance hymn 'The Hymn of Christ') and the mystery of the cross.

The *Acts of Peter*

The *Acts of Peter* must have been written before 190 CE as it is known that Tertullian, the Latin church father and apologist, cited from this text in his *On Baptism*, which made its appearance around the end of the second century. The place of origin is broadly conceived to be the area of Asia Minor (with Rome an outside possibility).

Much of the *Acts of Peter* is devoted to accounts of miraculous feats by the apostle, various marvels, resurrections and apparitions. Most of the action takes place in Rome where Peter battles with, and overcomes, Simon Magus (i e 'the magician' from Acts 8).

The most famous scene from the *Acts of Peter* concerns Peter's flight from Rome to flee a plot against him. However, he meets the Lord outside the gate entering Rome. Then follows the scene where Peter asks the Lord '*Quo vadis?*' ('Where are you going?') Christ answers that he is going to Rome to be crucified again. Peter understands that this would be his fate. The narrative ends with his martyrdom. Peter is crucified upside down.

The following excerpt is part of a scene set in Rome in which the Apostle Peter does battle with Simon the magician (of Acts 8).

ACTS OF PETER

12. But Simon said to the dog inside the house: "Tell Peter that I am not inside." The dog said to him in front of Marcellus: "You most godless and shameless man, you enemy of all living beings and of those who believe in Christ Jesus, a dumb animal is sent to you taking a human voice to prove and convict you a crafty swindler. So many hours had you to think only to say: 'Say I am not here?' You were not ashamed to raise your powerless and useless voice against Peter, the servant and apostle of Christ, as if you could hide from him who commanded me to speak to your face. And this not for your sake but for the sake of those whom you deceived and sent to destruction. Therefore, you shall be cursed, you enemy and corrupter of the way to the truth of Christ". The dog came to Peter who sat with the crowd who had come together to see the face of Peter; and the dog reported what had happened between him and Simon. The dog then said: "Messenger and apostle of the true God, Peter, a difficult contest with Simon, the enemy of Christ, and his followers awaits you, but you will bring back to the faith many of those who have been deceived by him. Therefore you will receive a reward from God for your work." After these words the dog fell down at the feet of the Apostle Peter and died. When the crowd, in complete amazement, saw the talking dog, some of them threw themselves at the feet of Peter, but others said: "Show us another miracle so that we can believe in you as the servant of the living God".

The *Acts of Andrew*

The *Acts of Andrew* was probably written somewhere between 150 and 200 CE, possibly towards the lower end of this timeframe. It moves very close to gnostic thinking in its dualism between flesh and spirit.

The *Acts of Andrew* recounts the travels of the apostle Andrew to Greece and from there through Asia Minor to the coast of the Black Sea (the city of Sinope) and back via Nicaea and Byzantium to Thrace and Macedonia to end up in the city of Corinth. Along the way he performs exorcisms, resurrections, miracles (among them stilling a storm while on sea) and healings and baptises new converts. The story ends with his martyrdom on the cross.

The *Acts of Paul* (including the *Acts of Paul and Thecla*)

The *Acts of Paul* was written in Asia Minor sometime before 200 CE. Women play an important role in the narrative (the portrayal of Thecla's baptism of herself on the authority of Paul) and continence (self-restraint especially of passions and desires), resurrection and sexual abstinence are emphasised. The text plays down the value of this world.

The *Acts of Paul* is based on popular traditions about Paul and his travels. The long episode of his sojourn in Antioch is called the *Acts of Paul and Thecla* due to the centrality of the figure of Thecla. Thecla's refusal to get married after being converted by Paul leads to her condemnation. She miraculously escapes death more than once, as does Paul in the course of the narrative. Paul is eventually martyred in Rome.

The *Acts of Peter and the Twelve Apostles*

The second century narrative of the *Acts of Peter and the Twelve Apostles* deals with a call for the church to return to the original commission of the apostles and apostolic lifestyle. It promotes the idea of apostolic poverty and polemicises against the rich. An encratite or ascetic emphasis is present in the injunction not to eat meat (although nothing is said about sexual abstinence or marriage). Christ is depicted as a healer in the garb of Lithargoel, a (Jewish) healing deity in the mould of Asclepius.

Even though no clear and unambiguous indications exist in the narrative itself, certain clues may help to situate the text. It seems to have originated within a relatively small and closed group of Christians and from the way poverty is presented one may think of groups such as the Jewish–Christian Ebionites. The name and figure of Lithargoel itself suggests a Jewish background. The way asceticism is presented and propagated brings to mind the phenomenon of Syrian itinerant ascetics reminiscent of the earlier Jesus movement. This would make the area of Syria a candidate for the context of origin.

The story recounts the strange experiences of Peter and the other apostles sometime after the crucifixion in a mysterious island city called Habitation where they meet Jesus as a healing deity in the guise of a doctor who commissions them to minister to the poor.

29.4 Tatian and his harmony of the four Gospels

The Syrian church writer Tatian is known for two works, an apology entitled *Oration to the Greeks* and the *Diatessaron*, a harmony of the four Gospels. According to the biographical self-description in the *Oration*, Tatian was originally from the 'land of the Assyrians' where he adhered to pagan philosophy. He went to Rome, converted to Christianity there and became a disciple of Justin. The *Oration* was written there. He left Rome at around 172 CE to return to his native Syria and he probably settled in the important eastern Syrian city of Edessa. He wrote the *Diatessaron* in Edessa and it was in these environs that it established itself as the dominant gospel text for almost three centuries.

Tatian put forward an extreme type of Christianity that earned him the reputation of being the father of the Encratite movement, a tradition that rejected marriage as well as the partaking of meat and wine. This type of Christianity was especially prevalent in Egypt and Syria, and for a long time, it was characteristic of Christian traditions in the eastern provinces of the Roman Empire. According to the *Oration*, Adam (and through him all humanity) was created with a free will and in possession of the Spirit. Through abuse of the free will, humanity came under the dominion of demons. Only through radical renunciation of all worldly things can the relationship with the Spirit be re-established. Greek civilisation and thought are radically rejected in favour of the Christian lifestyle, which is extolled. There is nothing of value for Christians in the theatre, or in philosophy. For him there is no possibility of a synthesis between Christianity and classical culture as there was in Justin's thinking.

Of most enduring and profound influence was his harmony of the four Gospels, the *Diatessaron*. The mere fact that this harmony could become so popular and remain so for so long in Eastern Christianity suggests that the four Gospels had not yet received canonical status as fixed and established texts at the time. The *Diatessaron* is not a simple harmony of the present four canonical Gospels. It originated in a context where various oral gospel traditions of a more legendary nature circulated and which could be characterised as religious folklore. The *Diatessaron* incorporates some of this extra-biblical material. An example of this is the portrayal of Jesus's baptism where, after the event, it is said that a light shone on the water of the Jordan River.

Occasionally, Tatian's own input is discernible. At the place where Jesus teaches on marriage (corresponding with Matthew 19:5), instead of 'And He [God] said: "Therefore the man will leave father and mother"' it reads 'And Adam said' thereby making marriage a human institution. This fits in with his encratite and ascetic leanings according to which marriage was not necessarily divinely ordained law for humankind.

The *Diatessaron* was such a popular text that it was translated into many languages and survived into the Middle Ages, translated and in use in various western European dialects.

29.5 Theophilus of Antioch

According to Eusebius, Theophilus was the sixth bishop of Antioch. One should thus place his activities at around 180 CE. He was the author of a three-volumed work *To Autolycus,* and a *Commentary on the Gospels and Proverbs* as well as refutations of the heterodox writers Hermogenes and Marcion. According to his own testimony, he had earlier been an unbeliever who had converted to Christianity after discovering how the prophecies had been fulfilled in Christ.

In the first volume of *To Autolycus* he argues that God is the creator of heaven and earth, and should alone be worshipped. The emperor is no god and should not be accorded any divine honours but at most be revered and honoured. The second volume is a comparison between biblical prophets and Greek writers and philosophers Homer and Hesiod, the Stoics and the Platonists. Only the biblical prophets were inspired with divine insight. The last volume presents an overview of history in which the primacy and superiority of Christian writings over Greek literature is demonstrated. Theophilus made use of anthologies of citations from Greek literature as well as Jewish apologetic works. He was the first person to use the term *trinity* and meant by that the trinity of God, Word and Wisdom. Under the influence of Jewish wisdom speculations, Jesus and the Spirit are presented as appearances of the one Wisdom. God contained the Word, the medium through which God came into contact with, and entered, the world. It is the Word which was present in Paradise and consorted with Adam.

29.6 The *Sentences of Sextus*

The *Sentences of Sextus* is a collection of Greek proverbs to which a number of Christian pronouncements have been added. Since Origen mentions the work, it must have originated in Egypt late in the second century. *The Sentences* is evidence of how Christians appropriated Greek and Roman morals, and thus adapted themselves to the thought worlds of the people among whom they lived. The work was very popular among the monks in Egypt in the growing monastic movement as a result of its ascetic outlook. The body, the flesh, money and possessions were to be avoided, as was joy. The wide diffusion of these *Sentences* indicates to what extent early Christians saw a model of ethics and Christian lifestyle in this work. This is a clear example of how Christians were starting to appropriate Graeco-Roman morality to make it their own.

29.7 The *Odes of Solomon*

The *Odes of Solomon* is a collection of early Christian hymns of a very Jewish character. They are hymns of thanksgiving for the coming of the Messiah and the experience of eternal life. Different kinds of connections have been identified between the *Odes* and other literature, Jewish and Christian. Close similarities in thought and tone between the *Odes* and the *Hymns of Thanksgiving* (1Q Hodayot) from Qumran, the Gospel of John as well as some letters of Ignatius of Antioch have been recognised. If the connection between Ignatius and the *Odes* can be maintained, then one should date the Odes to the end of the first century or the beginning of the second century. Such a dating would make this one of the earliest post-biblical Christian texts. The similarities with the thought world of John's Gospel and the *Letters of Ignatius* cause one to think of Syria, the region between Edessa and Antioch, an area in which many Jewish–Christian communities were found, as context of origin.

The *Odes* are joyous celebrations of the advent of the Messiah whose coming had inaugurated a Paradise here and now on earth. The implied communal context of the hymns would suggest liturgical use and therefore they provide a view of early Christian worship with its apparent emphasis on baptism, joy over experience of the resurrected and living Messiah, and exhortations to high morals and righteousness. God does not work through intermediaries but is close and present even though the *Odes* emphasise the appearance of the Messiah, the incarnation, crucifixion, resurrection and descent into Hades. Immortal life is experienced as being here and now. The world is divided between a world 'below' and a vastly superior world 'above' under the control of two spirits respectively, the Evil One and the Holy Spirit. This is a dualism similar to that in the Qumran *Community Rule*, the *Shepherd of Hermas, Barnabas* and the *Didache*. The ethical exhortations centre on love as the concretisation of virtue.

30 NARRATIVES ABOUT THE CHRISTIAN MARTYRS

The emerging genre of Christian martyrologies owed part of its existence to the Jewish martyrologies in *2 Maccabees* and *4 Maccabees*, where the death of the faithful is portrayed in Greek philosophical terms (such as non-suffering and immovability), which serve to heroise the deaths of the martyrs. The Christian martyr narratives interpret the deaths of the believers as rooted in the death of Christ which they exemplify. Those martyr narratives that embellish the accounts of the deaths with legend and fantasy move in the direction of laying a foundation for the development of a cult of the saints.

Justin Martyr's *Second Apology*, to the prefect Urbicus of ±150 CE, contains the *Martyrdom of Ptolemaeus*, an account of the death of a Christian wife of a pagan husband and Lucius. The *Martyrdom of Justin*, from 165 CE, recounts the execution by decapitation of Justin and six co-believers. The *Martyrdom of Carpus, Papylus and Agathonice*, from ±165 CE, is a narrative about the three being sentenced to death for refusing to sacrifice to the emperor. Eusebius cites the narrative of the martyrs of Lyon in his *Church History* telling of the persecution of churches in the Rhone Valley in Gaul in 177 CE where Christians had been decapitated or thrown to wild beasts. Eusebius's *Church History* also contains the narrative of the martyrdom of Apollonius during the reign of Commodus (180 to 192 CE). In the account of the martyrs of Scilli in North Africa (180 CE), we have the oldest report of the details of an interrogation in Latin. The *Martyrdom of Perpetua and Felicitas* dating from the end of the second century or the beginning of the third century, from Carthage in North Africa, commends the steadfastness of the women who had been comforted by visions.

Figure 30.1
Three young men in the fiery furnace (Daniel 3): one of the more popular themes from the Old Testament in early Christian art. The friends of Daniel portrayed amidst overpowering flames represent survival and peace in a very hostile environment, and the social setting is perhaps one of political harrassment

30.1 The *Martyrdom of Polycarp*

The *Martyrdom of Polycarp* is the first martyr narrative in early Christianity. It was composed at around 155 CE by the church of Smyrna and addressed to the church of Philomelium. Although placed within the framework of a letter, it is essentially a narrative. It starts with a description of the deaths of some martyrs who had preceded Polycarp. The bulk of the text, however, is devoted to a recounting of the martyrdom of Polycarp himself, how he had been sought out by the police, betrayed by a young slave, arrested and brought before the crowd in the theatre. A lengthy altercation with the Roman proconsul followed, during which the proconsul tried to persuade the venerable old Polycarp to recant and sacrifice to the emperor, upon which the famous pronouncement followed: 'For eighty and six years have I been his servant, and he has done me no wrong, and how

Figure 30.2

Interior of the Colosseum in Rome. Begun by Vespasian, construction lasted from 70 to 80 CE when it was finished and inaugurated in the reign of Titus. This large and splendid amphitheatre (unrivalled in antiquity) was used to stage wild animal hunts, public executions and gladiatorial fights

can I blaspheme my King who saved me?' (*MPol* 9:3). Polycarp was then burnt at the stake.

The Christians purportedly gathered Polycarp's ashes and bones. and interred them in a place dedicated to the 'relic'. That was the start of a cult of the martyr, according to the narrative, as the date of his martyrdom was remembered every year. The events recounted and the text itself mark an important change in Christian popular religion, for they furnish evidence for the emergence of a Christian cult of the hero or holy man.

The veneration of the martyr Polycarp is very similar to the values espoused by Jewish martyrologies such as *2 Maccabees* (chapters 6 to 7) and *4 Maccabees*. A way of life of total commitment and obedience to the will of God, even to the point of death, is emphasised. They have in common too an expectation of a reward for endurance. In the words of *2 Maccabees*, it is an expectation of life after death, while the *Martyrdom of Polycarp* speaks of 'the crown of immortality' (*MPol* 17:1). Characteristic of both traditions is the use of the philosophical concept (drawn from contemporary hellenistic thought) of the martyr as 'spiritual athlete' who embodies the traditional (Stoic) Greek virtues of unflinching endurance and impertubability (*MPol* 18:3). Apart from this, the miraculous events of the fiery death (the flames bowing out so as not to consume Polycarp and the extraordinary amount of blood flowing from the martyr's body dousing the fire) lend an air of the fantasy to what is becoming the folk religion of veneration of saints.

Finally, another important and interesting feature of the *Martyrdom of Polycarp* is the comparison drawn between the passion of Christ and the death of the martyr. The martyr's death is labelled more than once as 'imitation of Christ'. It is a way of showing his 'unsurpassable affection for Christ' (*MPol* 17:3). The sacrifice of martyrdom is a sharing 'in the cup of Christ, for the resurrection to everlasting life, both of soul and body in the immortality of the Holy Spirit' (*MPol* 14:2).

31   HETERODOX CHRISTIAN WRITINGS

Historically speaking, 'heterodox Christianity' should be understood to refer to all those forms and traditions that had been part of emerging Christianity, but which were eventually marginalised or suppressed in the process of 'making' mainstream Christianity. Although this category would, strictly speaking, include Jewish–Christianity, in this context we refer to those traditions that were identified to be sectarian or gnostic.

Most of the knowledge of Christian Gnosticism derives from texts from the Nag Hammadi library of the fourth century CE. By comparing these texts with citations and references in early Church Fathers such as Irenaeus, Hippolytus or Ephiphanius, one can connect these texts loosely with some or other trajectory or tradition in the emerging gnostic movement. Gnosticism itself was not a monolithic movement. Although most gnostic texts show evidence of some significant connection with Jewish thinking (in worldview, cosmology, demonology or mythology) some streams are more Jewish than others. Sethian Gnosticism (so called because of the prevalence of traditions relating to the mythological figure of Seth) was more Jewish in character, while Valentinian

Gnosticism (named after the great gnostic teacher Valentinus) was more neoplatonic, thus more philosophical, in orientation. The discussion here will focus on two second-century CE Valentinian gnostic works.

GNOSTICISM

The term *Gnosticism* is derived from the Greek word for knowledge (*gnosis*). Someone who has this knowledge is called a *gnostikos*. The term *Gnosticism* refers to a fairly diverse cultural and religious phenomenon of late antiquity, from the late first to early second century onwards, but in continuity with significant cultural, philosophical and religious antecedents predating the second century. In short, one can characterise it as the mentality and mind-set of a large part of the later Graeco-Roman period. Gnosticism is not a single or monolithic religious tradition. Rather, the term describes (1) a broad cultural tradition or mind-set; (2) a characteristic syncretic mixture of Graeco-Roman philosophies; (3) a type of religious outlook or worldview with a concomitant set of defining doctrinal positions and (4) collections of writings that to a greater or lesser extent display the features characteristic of this worldview or cultural tradition.

Gnosticism as a broad cultural tradition

For a long time opinions have been divided about the dating of the origins of Gnosticism, and whether one can, in fact, speak of a pre-Christian Gnosticism. What is at stake in the debate is the relationship between early Christianity and Gnosticism. While there were voices in past scholarship advocating the existence of a pre-Christian Gnosticism, and who found in the New Testament traces of it (e g in the Gospel of John, Ephesians and Colossians the 'Christianising of Gnosticism'), or a polemic against it (e g in the *Pastoral Epistles*), it is now accepted that Gnosticism as a distinct phenomenon is a product of the late first century, but especially the second century and later. However, even this viewpoint needs to be made relative. Judging from the existing collections of Coptic Christian gnostic literature (as, e g the so-called Nag Hammadi Library) it is clear that many fourth-century texts preserved in Coptic are translations from earlier Greek or Syriac versions, which are dated to the second and third centuries, the underlying literary sources of which may even date to the first century CE. The different types of materials preserved in Coptic Christian gnostic literature, such as fragments of Plato, other Greek philosophical treatises, (Egyptian) Hermetic literature, and then in particular the heavy presence of Jewish material (such as Adamic or Sethian traditions) would suggest an origin for Gnosticism independent of early Christianity, but probably 'on the margins of early Judaism' (Kurt Rudolph).

Several cultural strands are woven into the making of Gnosticism. The first is the sense of alienation experienced by Jews and other members of Graeco-Roman urban societies alike from the dominant political and economic culture of the early empire. Gnosticism as worldview and as ideology expresses the resistance of oriental cultures to perceived Greek and Roman domination and exploitation of oriental societies. (This explains the many references to foreignness or being a foreigner in the texts.) The prevalence of Jewish traditions in gnostic literature indicates the special role played by Jews in the reformulation of their place in society *vis-à-vis* their alienation from it. Jewish cosmogonic speculations, that is, mythological interpretations of the Genesis narrative of the origin of creation and humankind, as well as the history of fall and redemption, provide the framework for gnostic mythology. However, they also reinterpret and invert earlier traditions to such an extent that they arrive at meanings that are the opposite of what was originally intended. In this sense they can be said to exhibit an 'exegetical protest' against the dominant worldview at the time. The 'democratisation of connection with divinity' by emphasising the presence of the divine in the *gnostikos*, is perhaps a way of enhancing the social status of members of the lower social, political and economic echelons of Graeco-Roman society.

The second strand (and connected with the first) is Jewish apocalyptic and wisdom traditions. Apocalypticism and later Jewish wisdom are characterised by a pessimistic attitude towards the world. The world and the powers ruling it are so depraved and evil that salvation can only come about through a destruction of the world and the inauguration of a new world. Jewish wisdom in the period is characterised by speculation on the inner workings of the cosmos and its pessimistic stance towards finding any logical order to the universe. In such a worldview, humankind is seen as exposed to the incomprehensible machinations of fate.

The third strand is Iranian or Zoroastrian apocalyptic lore with its periodisation of world history into thousand-year periods (thus making calculation of the end-time as well as the appearance of the end-time saviour possible). Inherent in this is also a strong dualism between good and evil, and history as the site of the struggle between the two. Iranian apocalypticism left its indelible mark on Jewish and Jewish–Christian apocalypticism as well as on the dualism of the Dead Sea Scrolls of the Qumran community. The ethical and historical dualism of Jewish and Iranian apocalypticism (good versus evil; this world versus the world to come) is replaced in Gnosticism with the dualistic contrast between body (matter) and soul.

A fourth strand is magic and theurgy. Magical texts abound with a plethora of spirit beings controlling human fate or (parts of) the human body. Many of these 'spirit characters' also appear in gnostic texts in similar roles, either as spirit agents of the evil creator god or as mediators of saving revelation. The same proliferation of scrambled-vowel god names and other magical names that is found in magical texts is found in gnostic literature too. Theurgy (the conjuring up of the presence of the deity through magical practice), is also in evidence among the gnostic writings witness the similarity of the magical evocations in, for example, the *Gospel of Truth* to those of the *Mithras Liturgy*.

Gnosticism as a characteristic syncretic mixture of Graeco-Roman philosophies

Apart from Iranian and Jewish apocalyptic and wisdom traditions, Gnosticism also fed on contemporary philosophies. In this regard, one has to think specifically of Middle-Platonism as well as the intellectualising interpretation of the mysteries. The platonic philosophical tradition had always known the duality of God and world, body and soul, spirit and matter, and these dualities formed the basis of the gnostic worldview. Middle-Platonism, the form of Platonism prevalent at the time, and in vogue in Alexandria at the time of the great Jewish philosopher, Philo, as well as the famous gnostic schools of the early second century, concerned itself with the transition from the single divine unity (or abstract God as the ultimate 'unknown' god) to the infinite diversity of the world. This process was conceived as a series of emanations of aspects of divinity from spirit to matter. The capturing of spirit in matter meant the exile or alienation of spirit from its origin.

Certain intellectualising interpretations of the mysteries contributed to the sense of distance between the world of humans and that of the One God. Here one can point to Apuleius's novel *The Golden Ass* with its description of the initiation of the main character, Lucius, into the cults of Isis and Osiris. Osiris is called the 'great god, the father of all the gods.' The initiation into his cult meant the attainment of knowledge and insight into the true nature of divinity as well as humankind's relation to it. Another Middle-Platonist philosopher, Plutarch, wrote his thesis, *On Isis and Osiris*, on their cult and mythology. Plutarch interprets the role of Isis to be that of giving *gnosis* of the one who is the highest god, the First and the Lord. According to his etymology, the name *Isis* means 'knowledge'. Works such as these contributed to the idea that there is a 'god beyond god.' Apart from this, they also suggested that *real* reality is to be sought beyond superficial appearances. The work of the famous Jewish philosopher, Philo of Alexandria, roughly a contemporary of Jesus of Nazareth and also a Middle-Platonist philosopher, contributed vastly to the popularity of allegorical interpretation of scripture in his emphasis on the 'deeper meaning' of biblical texts, arrived at through a philosophical reinterpretation of the text beyond the literal meaning. According to his interpretation of the first three chapters of Genesis, *The Creation of the World*, the creation of the world spoken of in Genesis, is not the physical or material world but the idea or image of it. Similarly, (in the first creation narrative in Genesis 1) the first human being created is not the real Adam but the androgyne 'model' of humankind, as human mind. God creates with the help of 'fellow workers' who are later responsible for evil in humankind. According to Philo, the creation narrative of Genesis 2 recounts the creation of the physical man who is composed of the dust of the earth as well as immortal soul, or divine breath. The trouble arises when the female is created and the original unity of the human being is broken and sexual desires arise the beginning of injustice and transgressions of the law.

Gnosticism as worldview and set of defining doctrinal positions

Gnosticism was not a unitary movement. There were several gnostic systems or schools in existence alongside one another. It is, however, safe to say that they were all characterised to a greater or lesser extent by a world-rejecting ascetic ethos and a de-appreciation of sacramental ritual in favour of salvation through insight. This does not mean that gnostic groups had no liturgies or rituals. Evidence from the Church Fathers suggests that gnostic groups were organised like voluntary associations, religious clubs or cult groups and that rituals were part of their meetings.

There was no single gnostic myth, only variations of it. The fullest version of a gnostic myth is the one presented in the *Apocryphon of John*. According to the gnostic vision, a number of emanations (= external aspects that function as independent beings) appeared from the unknown god, among them *Sophia* (or 'Wisdom'), who brings forth the monster creator god, Yaldabaoth. He, in turn, creates the angels to rule over the world and to assist him in creating the first man. The first man is created in the image of the father, the most-high god, and is brought to life by Yaldabaoth who breathes light particles into him. The angel rulers then create a material body and existence for man, and trap him in an existence dominated by evil influences, among which sexual desire. Christ appears to enlighten humans as to their heavenly origins. Those who possess this knowledge and lead ascetic lives are saved.

Another important feature of gnostic literature is the presentation of the figure of Jesus. In many texts Jesus is portrayed as a luminous (i e divine) figure even in his appearance among men. Especially with regard to his crucifixion he is shown as a 'laughing Messiah', that is, he laughs at the ignorance of people who think they have crucified the Son of God, while they touched only a material body. The heavenly Jesus is completely untouched by the suffering on the cross of the earthly man Jesus of Nazareth. Underlying these conceptions is a sense of the incompatibility of human and divine, and they represent an attempt to solve the problem of the relationship between the two, something finally formulated by the orthodox church in the period between Nicaea and Chalcedon. So the emphasis is less on Jesus as crucified Son of God, than on Jesus as divine revealer or mediator of divinity in which the gnostics can partake as well.

Since no single text stemming from gnostic groups has been found giving a description of their history, one has to rely on the writings of heresiologists (e g Irenaeus, Hippolytus and Epiphanius) and other Church Fathers to reconstruct the history of Gnosticism and the various gnostic groups. Most trace the origins of Gnosticism back to the world of Samaria and Syria (the world of 'heretical Judaism'), and more specifically to Simon the magician from Acts 8. Second-century writers such as Justin Martyr, Irenaeus and Hippolytus (from the third century) portrayed Simon as a gnostic redeemer and revealer, who was accompanied by a female partner called *Helena*, also named *First Thought*. The later system of Simonians which they described, focused on the liberation of the First Thought (imaged by Helena) from her imprisonment in the human material body.

Later 'founders' of gnostic schools were Satornilos (Saturninus) and Cerinthus who appropriated the figure of Jesus in the gnostic scheme of redemption and developed docetic Christologies. According to tradition, Simon's disciple Menander transmitted the gnostic teachings to Satornilos of Antioch and to Basilides of Alexandria. Marcion who came from Sinope in Pontus but settled at Rome around the middle of the second century as Christian teacher can be counted among the gnostic teachers although he was not strictly speaking a gnostic himself. He was a student of the gnostic teacher Cerdo and his system does portray traits of gnostic dualism.

Where the epicentre of Gnosticism in the first century CE was Syria and Asia Minor, the centre for Gnosticism shifted to Alexandria in the second century. Basilides was active here during the reigns of emperors Hadrian and Antoninus Pius (117–161 CE). The most important of the gnostic teachers and school founders was Valentinus who also came from Egypt and went to Rome in 140 CE and taught there for almost 30 years. Other writers from the Valentinian school include Ptolemy and Heracleon (who produced the first commentary on the *Gospel of John*).

In the third century CE the prophet Mani fashioned a syncretic gnostic theology from Jewish, Jewish–Christian, Zoroastrian and other gnostic traditions. This became known as Manichaeism, and it rapidly spread through the ancient world from Spain to China. It was for a time at least more widespread and with more adherents than 'orthodox' Christianity. Its characteristic dualism lived on in various ascetic groups with dualistic worldviews such as the Bogomils and the Paulicians in the Balkan, and later in the Middle Ages, the Albigensians and Cathars in northern Italy and southern France.

A collection of literature

Gnosticism was known for most of history only from highly tendentious portrayals in the anti-gnostic writings of church fathers as well as from citations of their gnostic works. The fortunes of Gnosticism changed in the twentieth century with the discovery in 1945 in the desert of Egypt of the so-called Nag Hammadi Library. The 'library' was a set of codices containing manuscripts of gnostic texts in Coptic translation. This was essentially a Christian collection presumably 'manufactured' by Coptic monks from nearby monasteries and hidden in clay pots at the base of a cliff during a time of persecution by orthodox Christians. Apart from the texts from Nag Hammadi, some papyrus manuscripts now housed in London and Berlin also contain well-known gnostic texts.

31.1 Apocryphon of John

The *Apocryphon of John* is one of the most important works of gnostic literature. Originally written in Greek but now extant only in Coptic translations, it contains the fullest exposition of the 'gnostic myth' of all the various gnostic texts. This alone makes it an invaluable resource for studying Gnosticism as religious movement as well as for understanding later Graeco-Roman religious mentality and worldview in general. That it was regarded by gnostics themselves as foundational myth is shown by the pride of place occupied by this text – in three of the Nag Hammadi codices it is placed first, serving as a sort of introduction to the collection. Since the summary of gnostic teachings given by Irenaeus in his *Against Heresies* accords almost completely with the cosmological visions given in the *Apocryphon of John*, it is accepted that Irenaeus knew some version of this text (if not the final version). This would place the date of composition of the original version of the *Apocryphon of John* around 180 to185 CE, the time of writing of *Against Heresies*.

According to the frame narrative, John, the son of Zebedee, visits the temple in Jerusalem only to be confronted by a Pharisee on the absence of Jesus. In his anguish to understand the origins of the Christ and the heavenly realm, the pre-existent Christ appears to him. The rest of the text is a narration by 'John' of the revelations dictated by the pre-existent Christ. In an account coloured by highly complex cosmological speculation (various emanations of light-beings emerge from the highest divinity, conceived in Greek philosophical terms as an abstract entity) a mythological description is given of the creation, fall and salvation of humankind in terms of Genesis 1 to 4. This apocryphon attempts to provide an answer to two basic questions, namely, what is the origin of evil? How can one escape this evil world to return to humankind's heavenly home?

According to the vision of the apocryphon, the fall occurred when Sophia ('Wisdom') decided to bring forth a being without the prior approval of the great Spirit, her consort. She creates Yaldabaoth, the demiurge, or evil creator god. He, in turn, creates angels to rule the world and assist in creating the first man after the image of the perfect Father. Yaldabaoth is conned into breathing life into the image and thus begins the struggle between the forces of light and the forces of darkness for control of the divine particles in humankind. Man is imprisoned by the dark forces in a human, fleshly body, and to prevent escape from evil further, woman and sexual desire are created.

Salvation occurs when Christ is sent down to humankind to remind them of their heavenly origin. Only those who attain this knowledge and live ascetic lives return to the realm of the light.

31.2 The *Gospel of Philip*

The *Gospel of Philip* is not a gospel in the accepted sense of the word. Although it does contain some Jesus sayings (adding up to 17, out of which 9 are quotations and interpretations of sayings found in the Synoptic Gospels) as well as a few short stories about Jesus, there is no narrative framework as in the canonical Gospels. This gospel rather creates the impression of a compilation of ideas loosely connected by catchwords and phrases. In essence, it is an anthology of theological statements on the sacraments and on ethics.

In character the document displays much the same type of thinking as the gnostic teacher Valentinus, who was active in Rome from 138 to 158 CE. For example, it contains the Valentinian doctrine of the Saviour as the Bridegroom of the lower Sophia, and the angels of the Bridegroom as the seed of the lower Sophia. Other Valentinian features are the name for Wisdom, namely Achamoth, the mystery of the bridal chamber and the relative redemption of the psychic demiurge. This connection is used to date the gospel to the period of the middle of the second century CE and slightly later. As to its place of origin, the most likely context is recognised as being Syria because of the interest in Syriac words and etymologies, and its perceived knowledge of Eastern liturgical and sacramental practices, familiarity with Eastern sacramental catechism and the propagation of encratite ethics. One can imagine a situation in which the Christian gnostic *Gospel of Philip* was used as a type of sacramental catechism.

Its loose, disjointed structure makes identifying a coherent thematic line impossible. However, it does seem to centre on the question of Christian initiation and the sacraments associated with initiation. If one can dare to find a 'central perspective' in the *Gospel of Philip*, it should perhaps be seen as the reunion of Christ and the believer which takes place in a sacramental bridal chamber. The following statement summarises the gospel: 'The Lord did everything in a mystery, a baptism and a chrism and a eucharist and a redemption and a bridal chamber' (*Gos Phil* 67, 27–30). This probably describes five stages or aspects of one process of initiation, since in places the eucharist, baptism and chrism are connected to the bridal chamber in the benefits they effect. The sacrament of redemption is not described and onecan only guess at what exactly is envisaged concretely with the sacrament of the bridal chamber. What one can deduce, however, is that it refers to the climax of union with God.

THE GOSPEL OF PHILIP

59.9 [T]ruth did not come into the world nakedly, rather it came in prototypes and images: the world will not accept it in any other form. Rebirth exists along with an image of rebirth: by means of this image one must be truly reborn. Which image? Resurrection. And image must arise by means of image. By means of this image, the bridal chamber . . . 60 The Lord [did] all things by means of a mystery: baptism, chrism, eucharist, ransom, and bridal chamber . . . 68 There were three offering places in Jerusalem: one opening to the west and called the holy; another open to the south and called the holy of the holy; the third open to the east and called the holy of holies, into which the high priest alone could enter. The holy building is baptism, the holy of the holy is ransom, the holy of holies is the bridal chamber. [Baptism] possesses resurrection [and] ransom; ransom is in the bridal chamber . . . thus, its veil was torn from top to bottom, because certain people from below had to ascend . . . 83 Chrism has more authority than baptism. For because of chrism we are called Christians, not because of baptism. And the anointed [Christ] was named for chrism, for the father anointed the son; and the son anointed the apostles, and the apostles anointed us. Whoever has been anointed has everything: resurrection, light, cross, holy spirit; the father has given it to that person in the bridal chamber, and the person has received [it]. The father existed in the son, and the son existed in the father. This [is the] kingdom of heavens.

31.3 The *Gospel of Truth*

As with the *Gospel of Philip*, the *Gospel of Truth* is not a gospel in the accepted sense of a long narrative about Jesus Christ, his deeds, teachings, passion and resurrection. It derives its name from the opening words of the text, 'the gospel of truth is joy'. The term *gospel* is used here in its original meaning of 'good news'. If indeed it is this same *Gospel of Truth* that is also mentioned by Irenaeus in his *Against Heresies* (3.11.9) in connection with Valentinus, then one can set the date of composition of the *Gospel of Truth* between 140 (near to the acme of Valentinus's career) and 180 CE (the time of writing of Irenaeus's *Against Heresies*). Written in good literary Greek style, it is sometimes held to emanate from the pen of Valentinus himself. This gospel too displays ideas and themes in common with other fragments of Valentinus's works.

The *Gospel of Truth* resembles works such as the canonical Letter to the Hebrews, where doctrinal exposition is alternated with ethical injunctions. It too appears like a homily or long sermon, as is the case with the Letter to the Hebrews.

In short, the *Gospel of Truth* deals with the falling into error of humans and their consequent estrangement from God, the Father. Jesus is the name of the ineffable and incomprehensible Father, he is the revealer of the Father and the teacher of the way back to him. His death on the cross is the revelation of the essence of the Father and shows the way back. This revelation produces unity with the Father which results in authentic existence, which is depicted as wakefulness, joy and delight. In the final section, the process of being drawn to the Father and the reintegration with the primordial source is described. The Father attracts as an alluring perfume. The final goal of return is rest in the Father.

31.4 Marcion and his theology

In the history of early Christianity Marcion deserves special mention for the influence he and his movement exerted on the history of the church from the second century into the fifth century CE. Marcion, a contemporary of Valentinus, hailed from the important commercial port of Sinope on the Black Sea. He came from a Christian family and was part of the intellectual elite of the city where his father was a bishop. Marcion was a shipowner and merchant by profession and probably travelled widely. After spending time in the coastal cities of Asia Minor, Ephesus and Smyrna, where, according to church writers, he had fallen foul of the Christian churches (Polycarp of Smyrna called him 'the first-born of Satan'), Marcion arrived in Rome at around 140 CE, at the time when Valentinus was teaching there and during the papacy of Hyginus (136–140 CE).

In Rome Marcion became a disciple of Cerdo the Syrian from whom he acquired some of his outlook on the two gods, 'the God proclaimed by the Law and the prophets is the Father of our Lord Jesus Christ, for the one is known and the other is unknown, one is just and the other is good.' From what can be reconstructed from his theology, Marcion must have had an intense personality and sharp intellect, and did not tolerate contradictions or compromise. He joined a Christian community in Rome and tried to expound his teachings at a synod, but was rejected and excommunicated from the Christian church in 144 CE. Another view has it that he tried to become bishop of Rome but was beaten to it by Hippolytus, as a result of which he broke away to found his own church, complete with a hierarchy of bishops, priests and deacons.

The Marcionite church differed from the Great Church, however, in one important aspect: women were allowed to the priesthood. The Marcionite church was successful, since it is known from the testimony of early Church Fathers (Justin Martyr and Tertullian) that the church had spread throughout the world: through Italy, Egypt, Mesopotamia and Armenia and was still flourishing in the fourth and fifth centuries CE.

Marcion expounded his doctrines in a (now lost) work called *Antitheses*. In this work he set out to show the opposition between two gods, one the creator, the artisan or demiurge, the God of creation and ruler of this world, and the other the unknown and incomprehensible, hidden God. The demiurge, or Yahweh of the Old Testament, is the god of law and justice, while the hidden God revealed through the act of pure and total grace in the Son of God, is the good God who represents love and grace. There is a qualitative distinction and distance between God, on the one hand, and humankind and the world, on the other. The demiurge thus has nothing in common with the good God. This is demonstrated by comparing the Old Testament ethics with the ethics of Jesus in the New Testament and the thought of Paul. Jesus suffered a real death on the cross in order to free humankind from the claims of the demiurge. These doctrines led to an emphasis on purity and perfectionism which included rejection of marriage ('not wanting to help populate the world made by the demiurge').

Marcion's lasting contribution to his own church, but also to the Christian church in that it provided an important impetus for the formation of the Christian canon, was the production of two texts for use in the church. They were the *Evangelicon* and the *Apostolicon*. Marcion found support for his views in the Gospel of Luke (*Evangelicon*) and the true letters of Paul (*Apostolicon*). He therefore excised from his canon all documents containing Jewish ideas and theology, that i, the whole of the Old Testament, the Gospels of Matthew, Mark and John, Acts, Revelation and the general letters and some other letters of Paul. Even the Gospel of Luke and the ten accepted Pauline letters were expunged of Jewish elements.

It has been said that Marcion correctly saw that the Old Testament was about the historical faith of Israel, and had nothing to do with Christianity. No amount of metaphorical understanding, typology or allegory could turn it into a sufficient source of faith for Christians, for God's highest gift to humankind was the revelation and teaching of Christ. Christian believers needed their own canon of scripture independent of the Septuagint and Jewish–Christian texts.

32   THE EMERGENCE OF THE CHRISTIAN

CANON

When one keeps in mind the varied and chequered history of the writing of the various books of the early Christian movement; how the individual books were addressed each to a different community at different stages, one needs to ask how it happened that the 27 books that came to comprise the New Testament were collected into an authoritative collection of Scripture: what is meant by calling them the 'canon' of the New Testament?

32.1   The term *canon*

The word *canon* is derived from the Greek word *kanoon* which, in turn, is derived from the Hebrew word *kaneh* meaning 'reed, corn-stalk' but also in the further sense of 'measuring reed', 'measuring rod', 'measuring stick'. It is from this basic meaning that the Church developed the meaning of 'rule' and 'list' for the word *canon*. Thus one finds in the early Church that the word *canon* is also used for 'rule/canon of truth', 'rule/canon of faith' and 'rule/canon of the church'. With these terms the early Church gave expression to, and summarised, the doctrinal truth and faith that were taught by the Church. Later the same term *canon* was also transferred to the writings accepted as authoritative and normative by the Church in which it believed this normative faith to be contained and propounded. From this point, the term was also transferred to the authoritative list of accepted writings in the meaning of 'list', hence 'canon of Scriptures' or 'canonical writings'.

32.2   Early Christian apocrypha

Although the process of canonisation of Scripture was far advanced by the end of the third century to the middle of the fourth century CE, it was by no means a straightforward and simple process. Some of the writings currently incorporated into the New Testament remained questionable as to their canonical status up to the fourth century and beyond (e g the general epistles and the Letter to the Hebrews as well as the *Apocalypse of John*). In some circles those that were excluded from the canon were at times considered authoritative (e g the *Gospel of Peter*, the *Apocalypse of Peter* and the *Shepherd of Hermas*). Apart from the writings that comprise the New Testament at present, a great many others were also produced in the course of the first few centuries which imitated the New Testament writings and which also claimed the status of Scripture. Many of them are essentially expansions and retellings of early

Christian traditions. They are called *Apocrypha* ('of hidden origin'). This means that they were held not to have been written by the apostles or their disciples and thus that there is no direct link between them and the living voice of Jesus himself. Furthermore, they are 'hidden' in the sense that they were not permitted for use in Christian worship, since their teachings were not deemed to conform to the rule of faith of the Church.

Some of the best-known Apocrypha are:

Gospels:
Gospel of the Nazarenes   *Gospel of the Ebionites*
Gospel of the Hebrews   *Gospel of the Egyptians*
Gospel of Truth   *Gospel of Thomas*
Gospel of Philip   *Gospel of Peter*
Protevangelium of James   *Infancy Story of Thomas*
Dialogue of the Saviour   *Book of Thomas the Contender*

Writings related to the apostles:
Epistle to the Laodiceans
Correspondence between Paul and Seneca
Acts of Andrew   *Acts of John*
Acts of Paul   *Acts of Peter*
Acts of Thomas
Ascension of Isaiah   *Apocalypse of Peter*
5 and 6 Esra   *Christian Sibylline Oracles*

32.3 The emerging authority of Scripture

The letters of Paul were perhaps the first writings of the New Testament to be collected as 'Scripture'. This is possibly the collection of letters that the author of 2 Peter (3:15-16) refers to and implicitly regards as 'Scripture'. With the passing of time, the Pastoral Letters (1 and 2 Timothy and Titus) as well as Hebrews were added, somewhere in the second century CE. Hebrews was initially not accepted as authoritative scripture, especially in Rome, because of the belief that the Apostle Paul was not the author of the letter.

The *Canon of Muratori*, a list of the books of the New Testament, written in Rome towards the end of the second century CE, omits Hebrews from the canon. Origen, the famous theologian and head of the Christian school in Alexandria in the early third century CE, reports, however, that Hebrews was accepted everywhere and although he doubted Pauline authorship for Hebrews, he nevertheless accepted it for inclusion in the canon on the grounds that the thought expressed in it was Pauline. With the acceptance of

Hebrews, the collection known as the 'Pauline corpus' was essentially complete. Other letters under the name of Paul circulated in the early Christian world, but were not accepted like the Third Letter to the Corinthians and the Letter to Laodicea.

With the composition of the canonical Gospels as they are known, the oral traditions about Jesus had not been exhausted. Oral tradition continued alongside the textual tradition. It is from the world of oral Jesus tradition that further retellings of the Jesus story emerged with a view to reinterpreting and reapplying the Jesus tradition to new situations and contexts, and to serve various theological ends, for example in Jewish–Christian and gnostic groups. In the course of the first four centuries or so, a comparatively large number of gospels emerged. Some covered much the same ground as the four that had become canonical (e g, the *Gospel of Thomas* and the *Gospel of Peter*), others developed the theme of the infancy of Jesus (as did the *Protevangelium of James* and the *Infancy Story of Thomas*) and some purported to contain the post-resurrection instruction of Jesus to his disciples (e g the *Dialogue of the Saviour* or the *Book of Thomas the Contender*).

The canonical Gospels, Matthew, Mark, Luke and John, quickly gained popularity, importance and ascendancy never to be lost, although until the end of the second century the Gospel of John had in some areas been in disrepute, mainly as a result of its popularity and use among gnostic groups. The earliest testimony to the Gospels as 'Scripture' comes from the middle of the second century, in a written sermon (homily) falsely ascribed to Clement, bishop of Rome, designated *2 Clement*. Chapter 2 reads: 'And again another scripture says, "I came not to call the righteous, but sinners"' in this way giving evidence that the Gospel of Matthew (9:13) was by then regarded as Scripture. At about the same time, Justin Martyr, speaks of 'the memoirs of the apostles or the writings of the prophets [which] are read as long as time permits' (*Apology* 1.67). Elsewhere he mentions 'the memoirs made by the apostles, which are called gospels' (*Apology* 2.33.66). It is clear from references like these that the Gospels were gaining status as Scripture. Although they had initially been anonymous, they now circulated under the names of the apostles.

32.4 Witnesses to the formation of an authoritative collection of Christian writings

The *Canon of Muratori* lists canonically recognised works: the four Gospels: Matthew, Mark, Luke and John; the *Acts of the Apostles*; thirteen letters of Paul (including the Pastoral Epistles, but omitting Hebrews); Jude, 1 and 2 John;

Wisdom of Solomon; and two apocalypses (the *Revelation of John* and the *Apocalypse of Peter*). It explicitly rejects the letters to the Laodiceans and the Alexandrians which it regards as forgeries under Paul's name. The author also concedes that the *Apocalypse of Peter* is disputed 'which some of our people do not want to have read in the Church'. The most interesting part of the *Canon* relates to its dealing with the *Shepherd of Hermas*. As Hermas was almost a contemporary of the author of the *Canon*, *The Shepherd* could not, in his view, be counted among the canonical and authoritative Scriptures. This, despite the fact that it obviously was a very popular work, since the *Canon* allowed it to be read but not be used publicly in the church (for worship or in the liturgy). According to the *Canon*, the *Shepherd* was not to be counted among the prophets (i e, the Old Testament) 'since their number is settled' or among the apostles, that is, the New Testament. These words are significant as they bear evidence of how consensus had been created in the early church about the books accepted as authoritative and canonical. The list was viewed as being closed, although what exactly constituted the 'closed list' might differ from place to place and from time to time. The *Canon of Muratori*, furthermore, rejects writings by the gnostic teachers Arsinous, Valentinus, Miltiades and Basilides. This again is significant, for it indicates one of the important reasons for motives behind the closure of the canon of Scriptures, namely to distinguish between true teaching, the rule of faith of the Church, and the false teachings of heretics. More on this later.

From the end of the second century CE onwards, the church maintained the four Gospels as canonical and resisted including other gospels. Acts was accepted, as were the thirteen letters attributed to Paul. The other letters remained in dispute for some time. In some circles some were dropped and others added, but there was a growing tendency towards more consensus on what constituted the canon of the New Testament.

With regard to third century witnesses to the canon of the New Testament, two theologians stand out, namely Tertullian (160–220 CE) who wrote in Latin in North Africa in the city of Carthage, and Origen (185–254 CE) who wrote in Greek in the city of Alexandria in Egypt. Tertullian was the first writer to speak of the 'New Testament' for the Christian writings as distinct from the Old Testament. According to Tertullian, the New Testament consisted of the four Gospels, the thirteen letters attributed to Paul, Acts, Revelation of John, 1 Peter, 1 John and Jude. If this list is compared with the *Canon of Muratori* we can see that 2 John, *Apocalypse of Peter* and the Wisdom of Solomon were omitted, but that 1 Peter had been added. Origen had travelled widely and concerned himself with the question as to which books constituted the Christian Scriptures for all churches everywhere. He distinguished between the 'generally acknowledged writings', the 'false writings' (forged by false teachers, such as the *Gospel of the Egyptians, Gospel of the Twelve*) and the 'writings over whose authenticity there is doubt' (2 Peter and *Shepherd of Hermas,* for instance). Unambiguously accepted for Origen were the four Gospels, Acts, thirteen Pauline letters, 1 Peter, 1 John and the Apocalypse of John. The other general epistles were frequently cited by him, but according to his statements, were not generally recognised. Among those disputed in some places he included James, Jude, 2 Peter, and 2 and 3 John. Other writings treasured and cited by Origen but which were not regarded as Holy Scripture were the *Shepherd of Hermas,* the *Didache* or *Teaching of the Twelve Apostles,* and *Acts of Barnabas.*

The *Apocalypse of John* remained disputed up to the fourth century in the eastern part of the Church, while from the end of the second century it belonged firmly to the canon in the Western, Latin, part. Hebrews was initially accepted as a Pauline letter in the Eastern part of the Church, while the Western part rejected it up to the fourth century CE. As regards some general epistles, the uncertainty lasted a long time. Only gradually did a seven-letter canon develop out of the originally accepted group of three (James, 1 Peter, 1 John).

In the fourth century CE the drive and tendency towards unification in every sphere of the church (e g liturgy and canon of Scripture) largely came to a climax. A fourth-century writer, Eusebius of Caesarea, completed his famous *Church History* in 325 CE. In this historical work he devoted a chapter to the question of the canon. Following the example of Origin, he distinguished between three classes of documents: (1) the 'generally recognised writings' (the four Gospels, Acts, fourteen Pauline letters – thus, despite reservations, including Hebrews – 1 John and 1 Peter); (2) works 'which in some churches are recognised and in some disputed' (the remaining general epistles) and (3) the 'spurious and therefore rejected writings' (*Acts of Paul, Shepherd of Hermas, Apocalypse of Peter, Acts of Barnabas* and the *Didache*). It is clear from the descriptions of Eusebius that in the Eastern Church of the fourth century CE more than one possible make-up of the canonical collection of New Testament writings existed. The New Testament canon could vary between 21 books (i e without the four smaller general epistles and the *Apocalypse of John*) and 26 books (without the *Apocalypse of John*).

Eusebius also knew that some apocryphal writings had to be rejected (e g the *Acts of Paul* and the *Apocalypse of Peter*), which indicates that despite the stabilisation of the canon of which he gave evidence, the inauthentic writings were still read and used in various Christian communities.

In the course of the fourth century, consensus grew as to the limits of the New Testament canon. A clear acknowledgement of the canon of 27 books appeared in the *Thirty-ninth Festal Letter of Athanasius, Bishop of Alexandria*, in the year 367 CE. This letter largely confirmed what had come to be accepted as the norm for the canon of the New Testament in the Church. As 'springs of salvation' he counted only the 27 books in which 'the doctrine of piety is proclaimed'. This list of Athanasius contained the writings that have since been recognised as the New Testament. As opposed to them he mentioned the Apocrypha fabricated by the heretics. Beside a few Old Testament Apocrypha, the *Didache* and the *Shepeherd of Hermas* were permitted for reading by those newly admitted to the Church, although these books were not part of the canon (they did evidently enjoy high esteem).

THE *FESTAL LETTER OF ATHANASIUS*

The relevant section in Athanasius's *Festal Letter* reads as follows:

Without hesitation the books of the New Testament are to be named, and it concerns the following: the four Gospels of Matthew, Mark, Luke and John, then after them the Acts of the Apostles and the seven so-called catholic letters of the apostles – namely the one by James, two by Peter, furthermore, three by John and following on these, one by Jude. To them are added the fourteen letters of the Apostle Paul, written in the following order: the first to the Romans, then two addressed to the Corinthians, and after these the one to the Galatians, directly following on that the one to the Ephesians, then the letter to the Philippians and to the Colossians and two addressed to the Thessalonians as well as the Letter to the Hebrews, two also to Timothy, one to Titus and the last one to Philemon. Further also the Revelation of John.

These are the founts of salvation, from which the thirsty can drink their fill of the words contained in them. In them alone is the doctrine of piety proclaimed. No-one should add something to them, or take away from them . . .

For the sake of greater clarity I will further add, while I am pressed to write, that there are also other books apart from these, that although they are not canonised, nevertheless are recommended by the Fathers as reading matter for those who have newly joined and desire to be instructed in the doctrine of piety: the Wisdom of Solomon, the *Wisdom of Sirach*, Esther, *Judith*, Tobith, the so-called *Teaching of the Apostles* [= *Didache*], and the *Pastor* [= Pastor of Hermas]. And, beloved, although the former are canonised, and the latter are recommended reading matter, note that the Apocrypha are nowhere mentioned. They are, rather, the fabrication of heretics who wrote them down when the fancy took them and then generously ascribed an early date of origin for them in order to be able to draw on them as supposedly ancient writings and so have grounds to deceive the unsuspecting.

In the first part of the fourth century CE the Latin-speaking churches of the western Mediterranean world accepted a canon consisting of the four Gospels, the thirteen letters of Paul, 1 John, 1 Peter and Revelation of John. This concurs with Tertullian's canon minus the Letter of Jude. In the latter half of the century, the canon accepted in Alexandria and set forth by Athanasius gradually became the standard so that when Jerome translated the Greek New Testament into Latin (the so-called *Vulgate*, which became the standard Latin translation in the Western church), he followed the canon set forth by Athanasius.

The *Festal Letter of Athanasius* in the eastern part of the church and the work of Jerome in the western part of the church marked the formation of the canon of the New Testament as it is now. This canon came to be accepted everywhere, except in Syria. Until the end of the fourth century CE the canon in Syria consisted of the *Diatessaron* (Tatian's harmony of the four Gospels), Acts and fifteen letters of Paul (including a third letter to the Corinthians). At the beginning of the fifth century CE, a list substituted the *Diatessaron* with the four Gospels and omitted 3 Corinthians. In the first quarter of the fifth century, the Syrian church moved closer to the rest of the church by accepting the four Gospels, Acts, fourteen letters of Paul, James, 1 Peter and 1 John. After that, christological controversies drove a wedge between the Syrian church and the rest as a result of which there was no longer any establishment of ties with the Syrian canon and that of the rest of the church.

32.5 Factors in the formation of the New Testament canon

Although the church was already tending towards a canon of authoritative Scriptures in the course of the first centuries of the Christian era (as can be seen from the citations of New Testament writings in Christian literature as well as from allusions and references to collections of 'Scriptures'), several factors contributed to a crystallisation of the process. In this regard, one can point to the formation of the Old Testament canon, and the controversies surrounding Marcion, the Montanists and the gnostics.

By the end of the first century CE the canon of the Old Testament had largely been decided on, when finality was reached on the extent of the last part of the Old Testament, the so-called Writings. The Christians, along with Greek-speaking Hellenistic Judaism, accepted an Old Testament canon (in Greek translation, which was merely referred to as 'Scripture') encompassing a wider range of books than the present Old Testament. For example, it included *1 Esdras, 1 and 2 Maccabees, Tobit, Judith, Susanna* and *Bel and the Dragon* (both in Daniel), Wisdom of Solomon, *Wisdom of Jesus Sirach, Prayer of Manasseh, Prayer of*

Azariah and the *Song of the Three Men* (in Daniel), *Baruch*, the *Letter of Jeremiah* and the *Additions to Esther*. The basic dilemma posed by the Old Testament canon for early Christianity was the relationship conceived to exist between the Old Testament, accepted by the church as authoritative Scripture, and the revelation in Jesus Christ. Christianity displayed a new spiritual self-awareness which altered the function the Old Testament had in Judaism and so shifted the centre of gravity of faith. Early Christian writers, among them *1 Clement*, *Barnabas* and *Ignatius* were at pains to indicate that the Old Testament contained essentially types or prefigurations of salvation in Christ. Gradually, it became the case in Jewish–Christian controversies that recourse had to be taken to appeals to the Jesus tradition itself (i e to Christian, New Testament, writings). Connected to this was the fact that Christians attached the same value to the Old Testament as the Jews did. They saw it as God's perfect revelation and law. This immediately necessitated the question about the status of the

Figure 32.1
The remains of the colossal statue of Constantine. The original was 15 m high and erected in the New Basilica or Basilica of Maxentius in the Roman Forum. Constantine was instrumental in declaring Christianity a permitted religion in 311 CE. However, after his victory in the battle of the Milvian bridge in Rome, where he defeated his co-emperor Maximian, he took the initiative to Christianise the empire. It is said that he adopted the Christian symbol of the cross after seeing a vision of the cross being superimposed on the sun. Under his direction and chairmanship the Council of Nicaea met in 325 CE to finalise doctrinal matters regarding the person of Christ

Figure 32.2
Carved relief illustrating the function of the emperor as chief priest of the state religion. Pictured here is Septimius Severus (Roman emperor 193–211 CE, in the middle) and his wife, empress Julia Domna, sacrificing. Septimius Severus was the first African to be emperor of Rome, having been born in Lepcis Magna in Libya. Under the Severan family the worship of the sun god was especially promoted and solar worship started to supplant the traditional Roman pantheon. Septimius Severus's nephew, Elagabalus, was the high priest of the Syrian cult of the Unconquerable Sun deity. A century later the cult of the Invincible Sun was transformed by Constantine the Great into the cult of Chirst (described by him as 'the most lawful and most holy religion') when the sun was combined with timage of the luminous cross, thereby identifying the One Supreme Power with Jesus Christ. Parallel to this 'monotheistic' tendency was the promotion of the cult of the god-like holy man, Apollonius of Tyana. Already venerated earlier, evidence suggests that his cult received a major boost under the Severans. The empress Julia Domna commissioned the philosopher Philostratus to write the five-volumed *Life of Apollonius*, and their great-grand-nephew, Severus Alexander, had cult statues of Apollonius, Orpheus, Abraham and Christ (next to the deified emperors) in his *lararium*, or palace shrine. This evidences the growing elevation of the god-like holy man to the position previously occupied by the traditional gods, as well as the gradual 'upward mobility' of Jesus Christ into imperial circles. The process came to a head with the Christianisation of the Roman Empire under Constantine in the fourth century

writings containing the new and final revelation of God's salvific purpose in Christ. The eventual outcome of this process was the formation of a Christian canon of Scripture of equal status to the previously accepted 'Scripture', hence a division of Scripture into an 'Old' and 'New' Testament.

Controversies in the early church furthered this drift towards a unified and closed canon of Christian scriptures. The role of Marcion, the Montanists and the gnostics can be considered here specifically.

Marcion (see paragraph 31.4) rejected the Jewish writings of the Old Testament and purged his canon of the New Testament of all elements reminiscent of theology. He believed that the revelation by Jesus had been corrupted by the twelve apostles and was only preserved purely by Paul. In his canon he retained the ten letters of Paul which were in his day deemed to be the extant of the Pauline corpus (as a result of their anti-legalistic stance) and only one Gospel, that of Luke (since Luke was a companion of Paul). Marcion probably edited his collection of Pauline letters and the Gospel of Luke to bring them into line with his understanding of the revelation of God. Since the body of accepted Scriptures was at the heart of the theological controversy between Marcion and the church, this controversy added to the impetus to delineate the canon of accepted Scriptures in the church. Before Marcion, the tendency in the Church had been to add new writings to the body of accepted Scriptures to make up the Christian Scriptures. The author of 2 Peter (3:15–16) simply added the letters of Paul to the other scriptures, that is, to the Jewish Scripture (the Old Testament). Justin Martyr in the middle of the second century CE added the 'memoirs of the apostles' (the gospels) to the 'prophets' (i e, the Old Testament). With Marcion, that changed as he rejected the Jewish Scriptures and substituted his own canon for them. Although the church was eventually successful in its dispute with him, the Jewish Scriptures were henceforth separated from the Christian Scriptures in a dual canon of Old and New Testament.

The movement known as *Montanism* originated in Phrygia in Asia Minor at around 156 CE in the city of Hierapolis. It took its name from Montanus, the person who had started the movement. It soon spread very widely throughout the Roman Empire and continued to flourish up to the fifth century CE. It was basically an ecstatic, prophetic and charismatic movement claiming to continue the charismatic life and practices of churches, such as that of Corinth of the New Testament. Montanus believed that the Holy Spirit spoke through him and that he was the promised Paraclete of John 14 to 16. He was accompanied by two prophetesses, Priscilla and Maximilla. Maximilla practised prophecies of doom along the lines of the *Apocalypse of John*. These canonical works, the Gospel of John and the other Johannine writings, as well as the *Apocalypse of John*, were very popular in Montanist circles and, as a result, suspect in other parts of the church. The importance of the Montanist movement lay in the fact that its adherents believed that they had received new revelations through the Spirit. With the practices of the Montanists, the church was faced with the question of the openness of the Jesus tradition towards new revelations. What was at issue was the fundamental question of the function and significance of historical tradition (as embodied in the nascent canon of Christian Scripture), its completeness and its relation to present revelation. In this way, the church was affected by the problem of the consolidation of the normative tradition. Through Montanism the questions of the normative character of the tradition, its exclusiveness and also its correct interpretation were brought closer to a solution in the church. This strengthened the move towards the finalisation of the canon of the New Testament.

The importance of Gnosticism for the emergence of a fixed New Testament canon cannot be overlooked. Gnosticism was a widespread cultural movement in the Graeco-Roman world which propagated the saving knowledge that frees the individual from bondage to evil matter. In its Christian form, it proclaimed Jesus as the heavenly Redeemer who descended from above to illuminate and enlighten believers as to their heavenly origin from God and thus to partake of saving knowledge. In gnostic circles very many works were written – gospels, letters, acts, revelations or apocalypses and other types of literature – which professed to present old revelations and traditions, literature governed above all by the concern to impart true and genuine teachings of the Revealer, Jesus Christ. They were not initially produced so much in opposition to the writings of the church, as rather in analogy to the free handling of the Jesus tradition which in the first half of the second century was still a common phenomenon in the church. Old Jesus traditions were handed down, but at the same time expanded, reinterpreted, transmuted and modified, and new traditions even invented, and put under the names of writers and figures from the old tradition with a view to propagating own ideas as genuine, old and reliable statements of revelation. The debate with Gnosticism compelled the church to reflect upon the true and genuine tradition. This does not mean that the formation of the canon is to be understood solely as a defence by the church against the gnostic threat, but in this conflict the safeguarding of the tradition was regarded as tantamount. Whereas with Marcion the church insisted on an expanded canon, with the gnostics the church eventually had to delimit the number of accepted writings.

In the light of the foregoing, it is interesting to note how the *Canon of Muratori* polemicises in its delimitation of the canon against the Marcionites (by rejecting the *Letters to the Laodiceans and the Alexandrians*), against the gnostics (by rejecting the works of the gnostic teachers Arsinous or Valentinus, Miltiades and Basilides) and against groups such as the Montanists in its insistence upon the closure of the canon ('among the prophets whose number is settled, or among the apostles to the end of time'). These controversies certainly contributed to the crystallisation of the Christian canon of the New Testament.

33 CONCLUSION

In the second century CE a considerable growth in the amount of Christian literature can be detected. These writings addressed the problems of their day and are not, in the first place, aimed at preserving the pure words of Jesus, or even the history of past events. Since they are religious writings with clear 'theological intentions', their historical value should be critically assessed before being used in any historical investigation.

The increase in literature also had the result that a 'canon' developed. Because Christian literature was no longer a novelty, the question arose as to which collection of writings would have authority and which could be used as a yardstick for evaluating the many ideas that were now expressed within the framework of Christianity. Eventually, the canon was established and the belief in the authority of the New Testament writings became part and parcel of Christian faith itself.

Suggested reading

Benko, Stephen & O'Rourke, John J (eds.)
1971 *The Catacombs and the Colosseum. The Roman Empire as the Setting of Primitive Christianity*. Valley Forge: Judson Press.

Cameron, Averil
1991 *Christianity and the Rhetoric of Empire: the Development of Christian Discourse*. Berkeley: University of California Press.

Filoramo, Giovanni
1990 *A History of Gnosticism*. Oxford: Blackwell.

Grant, Robert M
1988 *Greek Apologists of the Second Century*. London: SCM Press.
1990 *Jesus in the Second Century*. London: SCM Press.

Hofmann, Heinz (ed)
1999 *Latin Fiction: The Latin Novel in Context*. New York: Routledge.

Jefford, Clayton N, Harder, Kenneth J & Amezaga, Louis D
1996 *Reading the Apostolic Fathers: An Introduction*. Peabody: Hendrickson.

Klijn, A F J
1991 *Jewish Christian Gospel Tradition*. Leiden: Brill. (Supplements to *Vigiliae Christianae* 17)

Lake, Kirsopp (trans.)
1970   *The Apostolic Fathers.* Volumes 1 and 2. London: Heinemann. (Loeb Classical Library)

Macdonald, Lee Martin
1995   *The Formation of the Christian Biblical Canon.* Peabody: Hendrickson.

Metzger, Bruce M
1987   *The Canon of the New Testament: Its Origin, Development and Significance.* Oxford: Clarendon Press.

Morgan, John Robert & Stoneman, Richard (eds)
1992   *Greek Fiction: The Greek Novel in Context.* New York: Routledge.

Pagels, Elaine
1979   *The Gnostic Gospels.* Harmondsworth: Penguin.

Pritz, Ray A
1988   *Nazarene Jewish Christianity from the End of the New Testament Period Until Its Disappearance in the Fourth Century.* Leiden: Brill. (Studia Post Biblica 37).

Roberts, Alexander & Donaldson, James (eds)
1994   *Early Church Fathers: the Ante-Nicene Fathers.* London: T&T Clark.

Robbins, Vernon K
1996   'The Dialectical Nature of Early Christian Discourse'. *Scriptura* 59: 353–362

Rudolph, Kurt
1983   *Gnosis: The Nature and History of an Ancient Religion.* Edinburgh: T&T Clark.

Schneemelcher, Wilhelm (ed)
1991   *New Testament Apocrypha.* Volume I. *Gospels and Related Writings.* Louisville: Westminster John Knox Press.
1992   *New Testament Apocrypha.* Volume II. *Writings Related to the Apostles; Apocalypses and Related Writings.* Louisville: Westminster John Knox Press.

Snyder, Graydon F.
1985   *Ante Pacem: Archaeological Evidence of Church Life before Constantine.* Macon, GA: Mercer University Press.
1999   *Inculturation of the Jesus Tradition: the Impact of Jesus on Jewish and Roman Cultures.* Harrisburg, Pa.: Trinity Press International.

Staniforth, Maxwell (trans.)
1968   *Early Christian Writings: the Apostolic Fathers.* Harmondsworth: Penguin.

Torjesen, Karin-Jo
1996   '"You are the Christ": Five Portraits of Jesus from the Early Church.' In Borg, Marcus J (ed). *Jesus at 2000,* 73–88. Boulder, Co: Westview Press.

Trebolle Barrera, Julio C
1998   *The Jewish Bible and the Christian Bible. An Introduction to the History of the Bible.* Leiden: Brill.

Wilken, Robert L
1984   *The Christians as the Romans Saw Them*. New Haven: Yale University Press.

General reference works

(These works constitute only a very limited selection of the literature that is available.)

Duling, Dennis C & Perrin, Norman
1994   *The New Testament: Proclamation and Parenesis, Myth and History*. Fort Worth: Harcourt Brace College.

Ehrman, Bart D
1997   *The New Testament: a Historical Introduction to the Early Christian Writings*. New York: Oxford University Press.
1998   *The New Testament and Other Early Christian Writings: a Reader*. New York: Oxford University Press.
1999   *After the New Testament: a Reader in Early Christianity*. New York: Oxford University Press.

Freedman, David N (ed)
1992   *The Anchor Bible Dictionary*. New York: Doubleday. (Also available on CD-ROM.)

Koester, Helmut
1982   *Introduction to the New Testament*. Volumes 1 and 2. Berlin/New York: De Gruyter.

Schnelle, Udo
1998   *The History and Theology of the New Testament Writings*. Minneapolis, MN: Fortress Press.

Index

Actium, battle of 11, 34
Agrippa I, grandson of Herod, king of
    Judaea 47–48, 49, 129, 200
Agrippa II, tetrach of Batanea, Trachonitis
    and Auranitis 47, 49
Albinus, procurator of Palestine 173
Alexander the Great 11, 24, 83
am ha-aretz 83
Ananias, high priest 149
Ananus, high priest 173
Annanias, high priest 173
Antipas, son of Herod 46–47, 91–92, 104
Antipater 43
Antoninus Pius, Roman emperor 272, 273, 294
aphorisms, *see* Sayings of Jesus
apocalypticism, apocalyptic, apocalypses,
    eschatology (including worldview) 57,
        66–67, 78–80, 122, 220, 234–239,
        246, 291;
    beliefs held by revolutionaries 77, 79, 80;
    Jesus and 96, 97–98;
    Q/Jesus sayings and 133;
    New Testament writings and 142, 153,
        167, 176, 185, 194, 197, 199, 227–231;
    second-century literature and 257ff,
        260, 262, 271, 273
Apollonius of Tyana 30, 252, 279
Archelaus, son of Herod 46, 49, 68, 91
Aretas IV, Nabataean king 47
Aristobulus I, Hasmonean king 66
Aristobulus II, Hasmonean king 42–43
Aristotelian, Peripatetic philosophy 272
astrology 27, 29
Athanasius, Church Father 305–307
Augustus 25, 34–35, 44, 46

Babatha Papyri 72
banditry, and brigandage 49, 51, 77, 129
Bar Kokhba, leader of revolt against Rome,
    see Revolts against Rome
Basilides, Christian gnostic teacher 250,
    294, 303, 311

Ben Zakkai, Yohanan 81
Borg, Marcus 99
Bultmann, Rudolph 95, 168
burial societies, *see* voluntary associations

Caiaphas, high priest 117
Celsus, pagan philosopher 250
Cerinthus, Christian Gnostic teacher 294
Cerdo, Gnostic teacher 294, 299
Claudius, Roman emperor 85, 129, 143;
    edict of 143, 160
Cleopatra VII 11
Commodus, Roman emperor 276, 288
Constantine 266
Crassus 34
Crossan, John Dominic 100–101, 278
cult groups, *see* voluntary associations
Cynicism, Cynics 30;
    Jesus as 100–101;
    Christianity and 123

Dead Sea Scrolls 73–77, 223
Diaspora Judaism 83–85, 201
divine (holy) men 30–32, 262;
    Jewish 66, 80, 104;
    Jesus as 96, 98, 99–100, 122;
    Christian saints as 279, 286, 288
Domitian, Roman emperor 37, 192, 207, 232

Egyptian Jew 66
Eighteen Benedictions 83
Ein Feshka, near Qumran, Essene site 71
Eleazar the Pharisee 64
epic, Christian 2
epic, Second Temple Jewish 243
Epicurean, Epicureanism 30, 196, 197–198
epiphanies 30
epiphanius, heresiologist 289, 294
eranoi, *see* voluntary associations
Essenes 62, 65, 66–67, 80
Eusebius, Christian historian 130, 200, 202,
    268, 274, 284, 286, 305

Felix, procurator of Palestine 147, 149, 173
Florus, procurator of Palestine 173

Gaius Caligula, Roman emperor 47–49, 85, 129, 173
Gallio, Roman proconsul of Achaea, and Gallio inscription 143–144, 155
Gallus, legate of Syria 173
Gamaliel, grandson of Hillel 140
Gentile Christianity 130, 160, 163, 167, 192, 207, 211, 215–216, 218, 276
Gnosticism 67, 138, 220, 236, 280, 290–295, (gnostic myth) 295;
   Christian 123, 137, 247, 250, 254, 277, 289–290, 302, 308, 309, 310
Graeco-Macedonian empires, *see* successor kingdoms

Hadrian, Roman emperor 175, 248, 250, 265, 268, 272, 274, 294
Hanina ben Dosa 30, 98, 104
Hasmonean dynasty, Hasmoneans 42–43, 79, 236
healers, healing, healing shrines 27–29, 30, 56
Hegesippus, Christian historian 256
Hellenism, hellenistic, Graeco-Roman period 11–13, 223, 235, 251;
   Judaism of 83, 96, 123, 201
Hellenistic economy, 16–17
Hellenistic society 14ff 16
Heracleon, Christian gnostic teacher 250, 294
Herod, the Great 43–46, 48, 57, 91, 101
Herodians 48
Hesiod, classical Greek writer 284
Hillel, and house of 65, 140
Hippolytus, heresiologist 290, 294, 299
holy men, *see* divine men
Homer 284
Honi the rainmaker 30, 98, 104
Horsley, Richard 99
Hyrcanus, high priest 42, 44
Hyrcanus II, Hasmonean king 43

imperial cult, *see* ruler cults
Irenaeus, heresiologist 256, 289, 294, 295

Jerome, Church Father 306
Jerusalem, destroyed 51, 55, 173–174
Jesus movement (including Christian movement) 48, 62–63, 129, 130, 167, 215, 239, 309;
   character of in second century 249, 250, 263, 278;
   ascetic, encratite 250, 267, 278, 280, 283, 283–284, 285
Jewish-Christianity 122, 150–151, 160, 163, 191, 192, 194, 196, 200, 207, 211, 218, 250, 254ff, 265, 269, 275, 278, 285, 289, 302, 309;
   Ebionites 254, 255, 256, 277, 283;
   Nazarenes 254
Jewish education 56
Jewish Gnosticism 66–67, 80
Jewish law, Torah 55ff, 117;
   Jesus and 115;
   Paul and 140;
   New Testament writings and 212–213, 218
Jewish mysticism, Merkavah mysticism, Hekhalot mysticism 66–67, 236, 250
John Hyrcanus, Hasmonean king 64
John the Baptist 47, 66, 92, 101, 104, 131, 256, 276, 277
John the Essene, leader in revolt against Rome 67
Jonathan Maccabeus, Hasmonean king 68
Josephus, Jewish historian 67, 77, 93
Judaea 42–43, 46–47, 49, 51, 64–65, 68, 91, 129
Judas, Jewish prophet 66, 67
Judas the Galilean 49, 77, 91, 173
Julius Caesar 25, 34, 44
Justin Martyr 124, 286–287, 294, 299, 309

Kähler, Martin 95
Kingdom of God 99, 107, 109, 111, 117, 133, 137, 157, 185, 273

Lactantius 123, 124
Lessing, Gotthold Ephraim 94
Lucius Verus, Roman emperor 276

Maccabees 77, 80
magic 27–30, 292

Manaemus, Essene prophet 66
Manichaeism 123, 254, 278, 294
Marcion, heterodox Christian leader 250, 294, 298–300, 308, 309
Marcus Aurelius, Roman emperor 250, 276
Mark Antony 11
martyrdom, Jewish 79;
    Christian (including martyrologies) 246, 247, 262, 270, 286–289
Masada 71
Menahem, Jerusalem leader 77
Menander, Christian Gnostic teacher 295
messiahs, *see* popular movements in Judaism
Mishnah 82, 265
miracle-workers, *see* divine (holy) men
Montanism, Montanists 276, 309, 310, 311
Muratorian Canon 200, 271, 302, 303, 304, 311
Mystery religion(s) 23, 249;
    Christianity and 123, 250

Nag Hammadi, site and library 137, 278, 289, 290, 295
Nahal Hever, near Qumran 72
neo-Orphic, neo-Orphicism 252
neoplatonic, neoplatonism 252, 280
Neopythagorean, Neopythagoreanism 30, 272
Nero, Roman emperor 130, 149, 173, 175, 192, 232

Octavian, *see* Augustus
Onias, Jewish teacher 66
Onias, Jewish priest 84

Palestine, politics and socio-economic situation 42ff
patronage (including clientship) 15, 270–271
Peregrinus, Cynic philosopher 249
pesher, type of biblical interpretation 74
Pharisees, including Pharisaic Judaism 63–64, 65, 80, 83, 117, 121, 174;
    Jesus sayings and 133–134;
    Paul as 140;
    portrayed in New Testament writings 211, 295
Philip, son of Herod 46–47, 91

Philo, Jewish philosopher 67, 293
philosophers 30
philosophy, Graeco-Roman: 245;
    moral philosophy 285
Philostratus, philosopher 279
Platonic/Middle-Platonic philosophy 123, 250, 272, 284, 293
Pliny the Younger 192, 249
Plotinus 30
Plutarch, Greek philosopher 293
Polycarp, bishop of Smyrna 268, 270, 298
Pompey 34, 51, 84
Pontius Pilate 91, 129
popular movements in Judaism, baptismal movements, messiahs, prophets, and teachers ('schools') 64–65, 66, 80, 92, 104, 129
Porcius Festus, procurator of Palestine 149, 173
prophets, *see* popular movements in Judaism
Ptolemy, Christian gnostic teacher 294
Ptolemy Soter, Hellenistic king of Egypt 84

Qumran, as Essene community 67;
    caves and site 70–72;
    history 68–71;
    scrolls, *see* Dead Sea Scrolls
Rabbinic Judaism, rabbis 62, 80–83, 174, 265
radicals, Zealots, Sicarii 77–78, 80
Reimarus, Samuel 94
religion, as human discourse 3
religion, city or polis 11, 19
religion, Hellenistic and Graeco-Roman 17ff, 30, 295;
    New Testament writings and 197, 274
religion, Jewish 55–56
revolts against Rome, rebellions, insurrections and First and Second Jewish War (Revolt) (including Bar Kokhba) 51, 66, 67, 71–72, 77, 80, 91–92, 104, 129, 173, 175, 248, 258–259;
    Jesus as revolutionary 99;
    Q/Jesus sayings and 133;
Roman economy, and taxation 36–37, 49
Roman Empire 11, 12, 32ff, 236;
    imperial ideology 266
Roman Republic 34

Roman society, social classes, living conditions 35, 38–42
ruler cults 23, 25–27

Sadducees, priestly establishment, and high priest 62, 63–64, 80, 173;
 portrayed in New Testament writings 210
sages, *see* divine men
Sanders, E P 97
Sanhedrin 46
Sayings of Jesus 109–110; 113–114;
 authentic sayings 115–116
schools, philosophical 20, 30
Schweitzer, Albert 95–97
scribes 117;
 Jesus sayings and 133–134
Shammai, and house of 65, 140
Sicarii, *see* Radicals
Simeon Maccabeus, Hasmonean king 68
Simon, Essene prophet 66
Social clubs, *see* voluntary associations
Stoic, Stoicism 30, 121, 250, 252, 272, 284, 289
successor kingdoms, Ptolemaic, Seleucid, Ptolemies and Seleucids 13, 24, 84
Suetonius, Roman historian 143
Syncretism 19;
 Christianity as 25

Tacitus, Roman historian 93, 232
Talmud, Palestinian and Babylonian 82
temple, in Jerusalem: destroyed 52, 133, 173, 265;
 cult 55–56, 57–61, 84, 118, 122, 207, 211

temple, at Leontopolis 84
Tertullian 123, 124, 200, 281, 299, 306
Therapeutai 67, 80
Theudas 66
thiasoi, *see* voluntary associations
Tiberius, Roman emperor 25–27, 37, 91, 129
Titus, son of Vespasian, Roman emperor 51, 173, 192
Torah, *see* Jewish Law
Trajan, Roman emperor 249
triumvirate 34
Trypho, the Jew 272
two-source hypothesis 131

Urbicus, prefect of Rome 272, 273, 286

Valentinus, Christian Gnostic teacher 250, 295, 296–298, 299, 303, 311
Vermes, Geza 98–99
Vespasian, Roman emperor 37, 51, 71, 81, 173, 192
visionaries, *see* divine men
voluntary associations 16, 20–23, 30, 293;
 early Christianity as 250–253

Wadi Marabbaat, cave in Judaean desert 72
Wrede, William 185
Wright, Thomas 98

Yavneh 65, 81–82

Zadok the Pharisee 49
Zealots, *see* radicals